ERSITY OF
INCH

Communication in Investigative and Legal Contexts

Wiley Series in

The Psychology of Crime, Policing and Law

Series Editors

Graham M. Davies[1] and Ray Bull[2]

[1] *University of Leicester, UK*
[2] *University of Derby, UK*

The Wiley Series in the Psychology of Crime, Policing and Law publishes concise and integrative reviews on important emerging areas of contemporary research. The purpose of the series is not merely to present research findings in a clear and readable form but also to bring out their implications for both practice and policy. In this way, it is hoped the series will not only be useful to psychologists but also to all those concerned with crime detection and prevention, policing and the judicial process.

For other titles in this series please see www.wiley.com/go/pcpl

Communication in Investigative and Legal Contexts

Integrated Approaches from Forensic Psychology, Linguistics and Law Enforcement

Edited by

**Gavin Oxburgh, Trond Myklebust,
Tim Grant and Rebecca Milne**

WILEY Blackwell

This edition first published 2016
© 2016 John Wiley & Sons, Ltd

Registered Office
John Wiley & Sons, Ltd, The Atrium, Southern Gate, Chichester, West Sussex,
PO19 8SQ, UK

Editorial Offices
350 Main Street, Malden, MA 02148-5020, USA
9600 Garsington Road, Oxford, OX4 2DQ, UK
The Atrium, Southern Gate, Chichester, West Sussex, PO19 8SQ, UK

For details of our global editorial offices, for customer services, and for information
about how to apply for permission to reuse the copyright material in this book please
see our website at www.wiley.com/wiley-blackwell.

The right of Gavin Oxburgh, Trond Myklebust, Tim Grant and Rebecca Milne to be
identified as the authors of the editorial material in this work has been asserted in
accordance with the UK Copyright, Designs and Patents Act 1988.

Library of Congress Cataloging-in-Publication Data

Communication in investigative and legal contexts : integrated approaches from
forensic psychology, linguistics and law enforcement / edited by Gavin Oxburgh,
Trond Myklebust, Tim Grant & Rebecca Milne.
    pages cm. – (Wiley series in the psychology of crime, policing and law)
    Includes bibliographical references and index.
    ISBN 978-1-118-76923-2 (cloth) – ISBN 978-1-118-76922-5 (pbk.)   1. Police
questioning.   2. Interviewing in law enforcement.   3. Communication in law
enforcement.   4. Examination of witnesses.   5. Forensic psychology.
I. Oxburgh, Gavin.
    HV8073.3.C66 2015
    363.25′4–dc23

                                        2015019936

A catalogue record for this book is available from the British Library.

Cover image: © parema / Getty Images

Set in 10/12pt NewCenturySchlbk by SPi Global, Pondicherry, India
Printed and bound in Malaysia by Vivar Printing Sdn Bhd

1   2016

Contents

Notes on Editors

Gavin Oxburgh

Gavin is a Forensic and Chartered Psychologist, a Chartered Scientist and a Senior Lecturer in Psychology at Newcastle University, UK. He is the Chair and founding director of the International Investigative Interviewing Research Group (iIIRG; www.iiirg.org). He previously served with the Royal Air Force Police, specializing in the investigation of sexual offences. He has recently developed training for investigators from the International Criminal Court, the United Nations High Commissioner for Refugees and the United Nations Development Programme.

Trond Myklebust

Trond is Assistant Chief of Police with the Norwegian Police University College (NPUC), a public university conducting research in areas such as psychology, police science and law. He has a background in police work, theoretical and practical experience in forensic psychology, and has specialized in investigation and forensic psychology in Norway and internationally. He is a member of the INTERPOL Specialist Group on Crimes against Children and Deputy Director/co-founder of the iIIRG.

Tim Grant

Tim is Professor of Forensic Linguistics and Director of the Centre for Forensic Linguistics, Aston University, Birmingham, UK. He has qualifications in both linguistics and psychology and is interested in the interaction between forensic linguistics and forensic psychology. His main research interests are in forensic authorship analysis and in language use during investigative interviews. His work has involved the analysis of abusive and threatening communications in many different contexts including sexual assault, stalking, murder and terrorism.

Rebecca Milne

Rebecca is Reader in Forensic Psychology in the Institute of Criminal Justice Studies, University of Portsmouth, UK. She leads the distance learning degrees for investigators and police officers and, in 2010, opened the Centre of Forensic Interviewing. She is an Associate Editor of the *Journal of Investigative Psychology and Offender Profiling* and the *British Journal of Forensic Practice*. Rebecca works closely with police and criminal justice organizations and is the author/editor of several books.

Notes on Contributors

J. Pete Blair

Pete is an Associate Professor at Texas State University, USA. He attended Western Illinois University for a Master of Arts degree in Law Enforcement and Justice Administration. After completion of the Master of Arts degree, Pete worked as an Investigator for John E. Reid and Associates and then attended Michigan State University to earn his PhD. Pete is currently conducting research in the area of deception.

Roel Boon

Roel is a forensic psychologist at the National Police of the Netherlands. After graduating with honours in Cognitive Psychology at Leiden University, he finished the MSc Investigation at the Dutch Police Academy. He conducts experiments on witness interviews and has reviewed several criminal cases. He initiated the nationwide implementation of investigative tools (such as the Self-Administered Interview) for the Dutch police and has developed training for their investigative interviewers.

Ole Andre Braten

Ole is a specialist on security issues, primarily for government organizations and large corporations. He is dedicated to the prevention of violence and threats in society and is a keynote speaker and trainer on communication and crisis management. He is a published author and has developed national training programmes on active shooter response and crisis communication. His consultancy firm has been called upon following terror, hostage scenarios and other corporate crises.

Elisabeth Carter

Elisabeth is a Senior Lecturer in Criminology at Buckinghamshire New University, UK, and takes on consultancy work on investigative interviewing, rapport-building and understanding language as evidence. Her research focuses on the points at which language and the law intersect, and currently examines formulations and deceptions in police interviews and the interactional strategies used in scam communications. Her book *Analysing Police Interviews: Laughter, Confessions and the Tape (Continuum)* won the British Society of Criminology's 'Criminology Book Prize'.

Coral J. Dando

Coral is a reader in Applied Cognition at the University of Wolverhampton, UK, a Chartered Psychologist and Scientist, and a Forensic Psychologist. Coral completed her PhD in 2008 following a career with the Metropolitan Police, London. She has published widely in the area of witnesses/victim and suspect interviewing, and her research has attracted over £1.5 million of national and international funding. Coral has co-designed and delivered interview-training courses for security/investigative organizations worldwide.

Lorna Fadden

Lorna is a Senior Lecturer in the Department of Linguistics at Simon Fraser University in British Columbia, Canada, where she is also the coordinator of the First Nations Languages programme. Her research focuses on police interviewing and other legal discourse, and she consults in the area of forensic discourse analysis on criminal and civil cases.

Ivar Fahsing

Ivar is a Detective Superintendent and Assistant Professor at the Norwegian Police University College. He has earlier published in the field of investigative interviewing, eyewitness testimony, detective skills, detective's decision-making, knowledge management and organized crime. He is used as an expert witness in courts and has for several years conducted training of law-enforcement personnel throughout Europe and Asia. He has 15 years of experience as a homicide detective in the Oslo Police Department and at the National Criminal Investigation Service of Norway.

Ronald Fisher

Ronald is a Professor of Psychology at Florida International University, USA, and is the editor-in-chief of *Journal of Applied Research in Memory and Cognition*. Ronald co-developed the Cognitive Interview (with R. Edward Geiselman) and has published many articles, chapters and a book about the technique in addition to conducting training workshops with several law enforcement, military and investigative agencies. His research also examines alternative methods to detect deception and interpreting inconsistent witness testimony.

Yvonne Fowler

Yvonne has 20 years' experience of training public service interpreters to work in the legal system. She has designed and delivered work-based courses leading to the Diploma in Public Service Interpreting in English Law (a degree-level British qualification) and has trained over 250 interpreters to work in the Crown and Magistrates Courts, with Police and Probation Officers and in lawyers' offices. She also trains legal practitioners to communicate through interpreters.

Fiona Gabbert

Fiona is an Associate Professor in Psychology at Goldsmiths, University of London, UK. Her research aims to understand and significantly improve the reliability of eyewitness testimony. One of Fiona's areas of expertise is the psychology of investigative interviewing, in particular developing ways to improve the usability, credibility and reliability of evidence from eyewitnesses. She works with academic and practitioner colleagues to develop effective interview tools and techniques.

R. Edward Geiselman

Ed has been a Professor of Psychology at the University of California, Los Angeles, for 34 years. He co-developed the Cognitive Interview and has published over 100 research papers and written five books. Professor Geiselman has trained and advised numerous investigative agencies worldwide (e.g. FBI, US Secret Service and Singapore Police) and assists police departments to investigate cold-cases. In 2013 he received the Mary-Ellen McCormick award for his work investigating child abuse.

Andy Griffiths

Andy has recently retired from the police in the UK, where he specialized in investigation, intelligence and interviewing. He has led homicide investigations and serious crime operations and has extensive experience of criminal investigation training design, delivery and policy implementation. This includes development and delivery of specialist interview training and a significant contribution to development of strategic interview policy both in the UK and abroad, including France, Canada and South Korea.

Kate Haworth

Kate is a Lecturer in Applied Linguistics at the Centre for Forensic Linguistics, Aston University, Birmingham, UK. She was previously a practising barrister. Her research interests include all aspects of language and communication in legal contexts, especially spoken interaction and the use of language data as evidence. Her research and publications to date have focused on the discourse of police investigative interviews.

Christopher Heffer

Chris is Senior Lecturer in Language and Communication at Cardiff University, where he teaches courses on forensic and anthropological linguistics and directs the MA (in Forensic Linguistics) and PhD programmes. He has published widely on the language of the courtroom and his forensic books include *The Language of Jury Trial* (2005), *Legal–Lay Communication* (2013), *Lying in Language and Law* (forthcoming) and a monograph setting out a theory of forensic discourse (Oxford University Press, forthcoming). He lives in Wales with his wife and two daughters.

Emily Henderson

Emily usually practises as a barrister and solicitor in the New Zealand courts. She writes about the reform of cross-examination and criminal trial procedure. The NZ Law Foundation International Research Fellowship enabled her to conduct most of the interviews with English judges and advocates referred to herein and also to write this chapter. She lives in New Zealand with her husband and four children.

Georgina Heydon

Georgina is a forensic linguist at RMIT University, Melbourne, Australia. Her research is concerned with the language strategies used by participants in police interviews and uses interactional sociolinguistics and conversation analysis to provide insights into police interviewing practices. She integrates this research with contemporary models of investigative interviewing to deliver training to practitioners across a variety of justice organizations.

Lorraine Hope

Lorraine is a Professor of Applied Cognitive Psychology at the University of Portsmouth, UK. Her research interests concern the performance of human cognition in applied contexts, including memory and decision-making. Her work has focused on developing theoretically informed approaches to eliciting information in policing and security contexts (e.g. development of the Self-Administered Interview©). She has published widely on witness memory and regularly speaks at international conferences aimed at both academics and practitioners.

Mark Kebbell

Mark is a Professor of Forensic Psychology at Griffith University, Nathan, Australia. Professor Kebbell wrote the guidelines for assessing eyewitness evidence for Detectives in England and Wales (with Wagstaff) and regularly works with police around the World to improve the quality of police investigations. He edited the book (with Davies) *Practical Psychology for Forensic Investigations and Prosecutions*.

Steven M. Kleinman

Steve is a career military intelligence officer with a specialty in human intelligence, strategic interrogation and special operations and has written extensively on the science of interrogation. He holds a BA in Psychology from the University of California, Davis, CA, an MSc in Strategic Intelligence from the National Intelligence University, Washington, DC and an MSc in Forensic Sciences from National University, San Diego, CA. He is the co-founder of Operational Sciences International.

Julia Korkman

Julia is an expert within the field of child forensic psychology. Her research focuses on investigating suspected crimes against children, notably interviewing and decision-making issues. She also conducts training within the field for judges, prosecutors, lawyers, health care personnel and police officers in Finland. Julia has a position with the Forensic Psychiatry Centre for Children and Adolescents at the Helsinki University Hospital as well as the Psychology Department at Åbo Akademi University.

Marty Laforest

Marty is a Professor of Linguistics at the Université du Québec à Trois-Rivières (Canada). She specializes in discourse analysis, sociolinguistics and pragmatics. She is involved in research on forensic applications of discourse analysis since 2003. Most recently, she has conducted research on verbal detection of deceit in emergency calls to the police, with the collaboration of the Québec provincial police (Sûreté du Québec).

David La Rooy

David is a psychologist at Royal Holloway University of London, UK, and was formerly at Abertay University, Scotland. He has received specialist police training in investigative interviewing, as well as in the assessment of the quality of investigative interviews conducted with children alleging abuse. He provides specialist training to police, social workers, solicitors, lawyers, advocates, sheriffs and judges on matters related to *children and the law*. In 2014, he received the International Investigative Interviewers Research Group (iIIRG) award for Academic Excellence.

Nicci MacLeod

Nicci is a Research Associate in the Centre for Forensic Linguistics at Aston University, Birmingham, UK, where she is involved in research examining the role of language in the performance of online identities. She completed her PhD at Aston in 2010 on the language of police interviews with women reporting rape and continues to be involved in the development, delivery and evaluation of interviewer training grounded in linguistic theory. She is particularly interested in the manifestation of power and ideology through linguistic structures in legal and investigative contexts.

Ruth Marchant

Ruth works to enable children's best evidence in police investigations and in the criminal and family courts in England. Her background is in psychology and she is trained as a forensic interviewer (1992, 2011, 2012) and as an intermediary (2007). Most of her work is with children under five or children with complex communication needs. She also trains interviewers and intermediaries for Triangle, an organization working with children and young people across the UK.

Christian A. Meissner

Chris is Professor of Psychology at Iowa State University. He holds a PhD in Cognitive and Behavioral Science from Florida State University (2001) and conducts research in the area of applied cognition, including the role of memory, perception and decision processes in forensic interviewing and deception detection. He has published numerous articles and book chapters, and has received recognition for his research – including the 2013 Academic Excellence Award from the International Investigative Interviewing Research Group.

Fadia M. Narchet

Fadia is an Associate Professor in the Criminal Justice Department at the University of New Haven, USA. She earned her doctoral degree from Florida International University and has published several articles investigating the psychology of interrogations and confessions.

Brendan M. O'Mahony

Brendan is a registered Forensic Psychologist in England and Wales. He works in independent practice providing expert witness reports for the Parole Board and the criminal courts. He has been a Registered Intermediary with the Ministry of Justice, London, since 2007. He also undertakes intermediary cases with vulnerable defendants. He completed his professional doctorate at the Institute of Criminal Justice Studies, University of Portsmouth, UK, where he examined the experiences of defendant intermediaries.

James Ost

James is a Reader in Applied Cognitive Psychology at the University of Portsmouth, UK. His research focuses on the inherently context-dependent nature of remembering, specifically the ways in which false memories (or 'memory errors') can occur. He has written expert reports on memory evidence for solicitors and the UK Crown Prosecution Service and has appeared as an expert witness in court.

Gary Pankhurst

Gary is a Detective Sergeant with the Metropolitan Police, UK, and for the last 20 years has specialized in sexual crime, child abuse and child homicide investigations. He is a specialist interview adviser and is keen to promote the lessons from research reaching applied practice within investigations through regular liaison between academics and practitioners. He is currently studying the issues raised by current interviewing practices on witnesses of non-recent events and its effects on recall.

Isabel Picornell

Isabel is the Principal of QED Limited (Alderney, Channel Islands), providing forensic linguistic services to the corporate industry. She holds a PhD in forensic linguistics from the Centre for Forensic Linguistics (Aston University, Birmingham, UK) for her work on deception cues in witness statements. She is a member of the International Association of Forensic Linguists and the Association of Certified Fraud Examiners and is a regular presenter on both their conference circuits. Her website is www.qedforensics.com.

Martine Powell

Martine is a leading authority on the topic of eyewitness testimony in cases of child abuse and sexual offences. She has over 20 years of experience as a researcher in the area of investigative interviewing and in implementing and evaluating interviewer training programmes across the globe. Professor Powell's research is best described as practice-based, conducted in collaboration with industry partners to inform decisions about how to improve investigative and evidential interviewing.

Terry D. Royce

Terry teaches in the Graduate Research School at the University of Technology, Sydney (UTS), Australia. He conducts professional development workshops for the Counter Terrorism and Special Tactics Command for the NSW Police Service, in particular with the Negotiators Unit, the

CT Strategy Unit, and the Security Management Unit. He is also an adjunct doctoral supervisor at the Centre for Policing, Intelligence and Counter-Terrorism in Macquarie University, Sydney.

Melissa B. Russano

Melissa is an Associate Professor of Criminal Justice at Roger Williams University, USA. She holds a PhD in Psychology from Florida International University (2004) and her primary area of research is investigative interviewing, including the processes of interrogation and confession. She has published numerous scholarly articles and her work has been funded by the US Department of Defense and the High-Value Detainee Interrogation Group.

Lawrence M. Solan

Larry is Don Forchelli Professor of Law at Brooklyn Law School, USA. He is director of the Law School's Center for the Study of Law, Language and Cognition, and his acclaimed book, *The Language of Judges*, is widely recognized as a seminal work on linguistic theory and legal argumentation. Before joining Brooklyn Law School he was a litigator and partner in the firm of Orans, Elsen and Lupert in New York.

Alan Scoboria

Alan is Associate Professor of Psychology at the University of Windsor, Canada. He studies beliefs about the occurrence and accuracy of memory, the interplay of cognitive and social aspects of remembering, applied issues in memory and best practices in interviewing. He is a registered clinical psychologist and examines clinical aspects of remembering with his students. He teaches courses in ethical, professional, legal issues and research methods.

Michel St-Yves

Michel is a forensic psychologist with the Behavioural Analysis Service of the Quebec's provincial police force. He works as a critical-incident specialist and is actively involved in criminal investigations, both in profiling suspects and preparing police interrogations. He trains police officers in crisis negotiation techniques and is a member of the specialized intervention team. He also teaches at the Quebec Police Academy and lectures at the Department of Criminology of Université de Montréal.

Jennifer Taylor

Jennifer Taylor is currently studying towards a Masters in Forensic Linguistics at the Centre of Forensic Linguistics, Aston University, Birmingham, UK, having graduated from Durham University in Education Studies and Linguistics.

Paul Taylor

Paul is a Professor of Psychology at Lancaster University, UK, and Professor of Human Interaction at Twente University, the Netherlands. At Lancaster, he directs *Security Lancaster*, the University's centre of excellence that encompasses over 60 researchers and the latest research and training facilities. Supported by over £4m of funding, Paul's research combines experimental, archival and field methods to understand the workings of human interaction and the strategies that promote co-operation. Read more at: www.pauljtaylor.com.

Martin Vaughan

Martin completed 30 years in Gwent Police, UK. In 2001, he became the lead crime trainer and was responsible for the development and implementation of new interview programmes and the Interview Management Development Programme for the force. Martin was an ACPO Accredited Interview Adviser and has been involved in this role on numerous high-profile investigations, including child and sexual abuse, and over 70 murder investigations. He received 16 Commendations for the high quality of his work during his career.

Aldert Vrij

Aldert is a Professor of Applied Social Psychology. He has more than 450 publications mainly about (non)verbal cues to deception and lie detection. He gives invited talks and workshops on lie detection to practitioners and scholars across the world, including police, homeland security, defence, judges, solicitors, social workers, fraud investigators, insurers and bankers. He has held research grants from Dutch and British research councils and Dutch, UK and US Governments, totalling over £3 million.

Nina J. Westera

Nina is a Research Fellow at Griffith University, Nathan, Australia, whose research examines adult witness interviewing practices. She specializes in the investigative and evidential interviewing of complainants in cases of sexual and violent offending. Nina's career began as an officer in the New Zealand Police, where she investigated serious crime and implemented evidence-based policy and practice for the interviewing of witnesses and suspects. She has educated and advised police officers, lawyers and judges about investigative interviewing.

Jacqueline Wheatcroft

Jacqueline is a Chartered Psychologist and Forensic Practitioner. She is leader of the Witness Research Group in the Institute of Psychology, University of Liverpool, UK. Her interests lie in the enhancement of evidence, information and intelligence with a focus on questioning and procedural techniques in legal contexts. Her work also contributes to the Ministry of Justice's Witnesses Charter, the Advocates Gateway and the Judicial College. She advises governments, police, professional investigators and the courts.

Series Preface

The Wiley Series in the Psychology of Crime, Policing and Law publishes concise and integrative reviews on important emerging areas of contemporary research. The purpose of the series is not merely to present research findings in a clear and readable form but also to bring out their implications for both practice and policy. In this way, it is hoped the series will not only be useful to psychologists but also to all those concerned with crime detection and prevention, policing and the judicial process.

This innovative collection of chapters bridges what used to be a chasm between, on the one side, investigative interviewing (e.g. Bull, Valentine & Williamson, 2009) and, on the other side, forensic linguistics (e.g. Gibbons & Turrell, 2008). A major bridge across this chasm was made by one of this volume's editors (Tim Grant – a forensic linguist) some ten years ago when he was a Lecturer at Leicester University, when he successfully suggested to me (in my role as Director of Postgraduate Programmes in Forensic Psychology) that we make available to our students a new module/course in forensic linguistics. From this arose a greater appreciation that knowledge on the topic of the present volume (i.e. communication in investigative and legal contexts) is to be enhanced by both a psychological and a linguistic perspective. Encapsulating such diverse knowledge in the one location could present a challenge, but the editors have succeeded in achieving this.

The four editors are not only themselves very active researchers but each also is, and has been, directly involved in disseminating the valuable findings of relevant research in the form of workshops, seminars and the like. Their major contributions to and effective participation in relevant international conferences and meetings has allowed the editors to recruit as chapter authors a wide array of leading authors at various stages of their careers.

The major topics covered include communicating with (i) suspects as well as with (ii) witnesses and victims – two forms of communicating that naively used to be conceptualized as being distinct but are nowadays becoming ever more treated as being similar (Milne & Bull, 1999). On these topics huge advances are regularly being made. Another major topic covered in this book is communicating in the courtroom which, sadly, has until recently seen rather few worthwhile applications by professional practitioners of the useful, available knowledge emanating from forensic linguistics and forensic psychology. Chapters on other important topics such as truth/lie detection, hostage and crisis negotiation, and the use of interpreters and of intermediaries are also included.

As I was writing this series preface news came from the United States that a man sentenced in 1993 to life imprisonment for the rape and murder of an eleven-year-old girl had recently been awarded a wrongful conviction settlement of $20 million, a proportion of which is to be paid by those responsible for his interrogation.

Fortunately, this comprehensive collection of interrelated chapters clearly demonstrates how fast knowledge is developing on communicating in investigative and legal contexts. Now is the time for those 'professional' practitioners around the world who have been ignorant of these crucial, ecologically valid research findings to update themselves and improve not only their understanding but even more importantly their skills. Researchers and theorists need to be brave enough to avoid conducting easy, cheap research studies (e.g. lazily using young undergraduates as participants and unreal settings/scenarios) and to be willing to conduct difficult, time consuming, realistic studies. Working together, researchers and practitioners can make important leaps not only across the chasm that used to exist between forensic psychology and forensic linguistics but also across entrenched, outdated views about how best to communicate when lives/livelihoods are often at risk.

Professor Ray Bull
Fishbourne, West Sussex, May 2015

REFERENCES

Bull, R., Valentine, T. & Williamson, T. (Eds) (2009). *Handbook of Psychology of Investigative Interviewing*, Wiley-Blackwell, Chichester.

Gibbons, J. & Turrell, M. (2008). *Dimensions of Forensic Linguistics*, Benjamins, Amsterdam.

Milne, R. & Bull, R. (1999). *Investigative Interviewing: Psychology and Practice*, John Wiley & Sons, Ltd, Chichester.

1

Communication in Investigative and Legal Settings: Introduction and Contexts

Gavin Oxburgh[1], Trond Myklebust[2], Tim Grant[3] and Rebecca Milne[4]
[1] Newcastle University, UK
[2] Norwegian Police University College, Oslo, Norway
[3] Aston University, Birmingham, UK
[4] Portsmouth University, UK

INTRODUCTION

Society cannot afford investigative interviewing to be poor. This affects people's perception of the criminal justice system. The guilty get away, the innocent are convicted, justice for children and vulnerable adults is inadequate. Poor interviewing is of no value to anyone; it is a waste of time, resources and money. No one wins. People will not come forward if they have no confidence in the quality of investigators' interviewing techniques.

(Milne & Bull, 1999, p. 191)

Although some 16 years old, the above quote is still valid today. That said, there has, without doubt, been a paradigm shift within the field of law enforcement interviewing during the past two decades, from the traditional interrogation model, with its emphasis on persuading the interviewee to confess, to the investigative interviewing model

Communication in Investigative and Legal Contexts: Integrated Approaches from Forensic Psychology, Linguistics and Law Enforcement, First Edition. Edited by Gavin Oxburgh, Trond Myklebust, Tim Grant and Rebecca Milne.

emphasizing the search for accurate and reliable information. One can trace the scientific perspective on investigative interviewing back to the German scientist William Stern (1903/1904). Stern was occupied with examining techniques that achieved the most valid information from children. He was the first to introduce the important distinction between *open (bericht)* and *closed (verhör)* questions. In his research, he clearly demonstrated the superiority of *open* questions, showing that they gained more quantity and with a better quality of information compared to *closed* questions. Today, there now exists a large body of scientific research that has investigated various elements of the investigative interview, including: (i) the interviewer; (ii) the interviewee; (iii) the context of the interview (e.g. where the interview takes place) and (iv) the interplay between these factors.

There have also been many studies over the past decades that have critically evaluated police interviewing skills. These studies have considered the impact of the information gathering approach to investigative interviewing (including training), the various skills that effective interviewers display and the structure of good quality interviews with suspects (e.g. Baldwin, 1993; Cherryman & Bull, 2001; Clarke & Milne, 2001; Clarke, Milne & Bull, 2011; McGurk, Carr & McGurk, 1993) and witnesses (e.g. Ceci & Bruck, 1995; Lamb, Orbach, Sternberg, Esplin & Hershkowitz, 2002; Lamb, Sternberg, Orbach, Esplin & Mitchell, 2002; Walsh & Bull, 2010; Walsh & Milne, 2008). The amount of research cited above is purely indicative of the comprehensive dataset available and it is sometimes difficult to get an overall picture of the relevant available research and training manuals that are available across the world. Taken together, the myriad of information might appear overwhelming for the practitioner. However, since the first scientific studies by Stern, almost all the scientific efforts illuminate *potential* in the interviewing process and, as a result, they offer an opportunity to improve the quality of the interview and bridge the gap between the fields of psychology, law enforcement and (forensic) linguistics.

FORENSIC LINGUISTICS

Linguistics as a discipline involves the description of texts and linguistic interactions and involves the description and explanation of the nature of communication at a variety of levels, including at lower levels, word choice and syntax, and, at a higher level, issues of context and the functional intent of the interactants. Forensic linguistics takes the methods and insights of linguistics and applies these to forensic texts and contexts. A large part of the work and research in forensic linguistics considers language evidence, evidence of authorship, evidence of meaning and evidence of textual origin (e.g. Grant, 2008). Forensic linguists also examine written legal texts explaining the historic context of legal language and how legalese can be reformed to ensure that the widest possible section of the community can understand it (see, for example, Tiersma, 1999). Finally, forensic linguistics examines interactions associated with the forensic and judicial process. This interest can include mono- and multilingual interactions in both the civil legal processes and the criminal justice process, but there has perhaps, to date, been a greater concentration on the criminal side. Research has been carried out into the caution and explanation of rights (e.g. Rock, 2007), into police interviewing (e.g. Heydon, 2005) and into witnesses and judges in Court (e.g. Heffer, 2005). Today, as demonstrated in this book, one area where psychologists and linguists work very closely together is in the area of police and law enforcement investigations with a particular focus on the investigative interview.

PROFESSIONALIZATION OF INTERVIEWING

In many countries around the world, police interviewing, and police training per se, has undergone a transformation in terms of professionalization due, in large part, to scientific experimentation and analysis. For example, Fisher, Geiselman and Raymond (1987) observed that interviewers' level of competence directly affected their responses in interviews of adult interviewees. The authors thus recommended formal, scientifically based training of police officers at the institutional level. They also suggested that training programmes would be most successful if they were divided into intensive short, practical sessions, rather than longer sessions, with extended feedback to the individual interviewers (Fisher & Geiselman, 1992; Fisher, Geiselman & Amador, 1989; Fisher et al., 1987).

Moreover, Lamb and his colleagues argued that long-time improvement in the quality of investigative interviews are observed only when the training is distributed over time (Lamb, Sternberg, et al., 2002; Lamb et al., 2000). In their studies, the length of training varied between three to five days of initial training, with follow-up supervision and feedback (Lamb, Sternberg, et al., 2002; Orbach et al., 2000; Sternberg, Lamb, Davies & Westcott, 2001). There has been much research that has shown that complete transference of training into the workplace is rather elusive (e.g. Myklebust & Bjørklund, 2006; Powell, Fisher & Wright, 2005; Wright & Powell, 2006). Particularly difficult to sustain over time are the more complex skills (e.g. rapport, use of open questions) as opposed to more procedural interviewer behaviours (e.g. outlining persons present in the interview, giving legal rights, etc.; Griffiths, Milne & Cherryman, 2011).

Although we are unable to go into detail from every country that has undergone improvements, we have highlighted below two broad geographical areas that are indicative of such improvements.

The Nordic Countries

The Nordic countries (i.e. Denmark, Finland, Iceland, Norway and Sweden) have vastly different systems compared to other European countries, where the police are provided with shorter basic training. Across the Nordic countries, they train their police officers to become so called 'generalists' within their work as police officers. They are authorized for a multitude of responsibilities, from crime prevention via operational patrolling police duties, to profound and scientifically based detective work (Birkeland, 2007; Granhag, 2010; Ministry of Justice and the Police, 2005). Focusing on the basic 'generalist' training, the central police educational institutions in the Nordic countries are heading towards a system with Police University colleges. Norway was the first and founded the Norwegian Police University College (NPUC) in 1992, receiving their college charter in 2004. They have a three-year basic education that provides all police officers with a bachelor degree in policing. In their education programme, the students are taught about psychology, law and police tactics in communication, investigative interviewing and general policing. Methodically, the theory and practice in NPUC's interview training is based on structured interview models, such as the English PEACE model and Achieving Best Evidence in Criminal Proceedings guidelines (see Myklebust, 2010). The students also receive theoretical and practical training in the Cognitive Interview and the Self-Administrated Interview. The underlying principle is that all police officers are given basic training in methods to deal with the volume and day-to-day crime, whilst the more specialist and practical training (and evaluations) are provided during further educational programmes during postgraduate studies).

England and Wales

In England and Wales, following Clarke and Milne's (2001) national evaluation of police interviewing, a tiered structure of interviewing skills was developed, which were categorized as: (i) Tier 1: Probationer training; (ii) Tier 2: Detectives (a prerequisite to attending the Initial Crime Investigators' Development Programme (ICIDP); (iii) Tier 3: Specialist interviewers (victim/witness/suspect); (iv) Tier 4: Investigative interview supervisor/ assessor; and (v) Tier 5: Specialist interview advisor. In 2005, the Initial Police Learning and Development Programme (IPLDP) was introduced, which was designed to support student officers throughout their two-year probationary period and to meet their individual development. In 2007, investigative interview training (and the five tiers outlined above) was enhanced and incorporated into the Professionalizing Investigation Programme (PIP), which was intended to increase professionalism of all police investigators and to establish a structured, professional approach to investigations and interviewing. The IPLDP provided officers with the necessary accreditation at PIP level 1, which was for all uniformed police officers and supervisors. PIP level 2 was designed for dedicated investigators (e.g. detectives) who investigated serious and complex investigations including victims, witnesses and suspected offenders. PIP level 3 was for Senior Investigating Officers (SIOs) in cases of murder, stranger rape, kidnap or crimes of similar complexity. Finally, PIP level 4 was for SIOs and Officers in Overall Command (OIOC) who managed critical, complex or protracted and/or linked serious crime.

It is important to note that, although such enhancements in training will doubtless continue, there have been debates regarding the long-term effectiveness of interview training per se (e.g. see Griffiths & Milne, 2006; Lamb, Hershkowitz, Orbach & Esplin, 2008). However, Powell et al. (2005) outlined the elements of training that have been found to be the most successful. The core elements of success included the use of:

- Structured interview protocols;
- Multiple opportunities to practice over an extended period;
- Expert feedback and ongoing supervision;
- Internal motivation by the interviewer to enhance his or her individual performance.

Griffiths and Milne found that although training levels were higher one year after officers completed advanced training, there was a 'marked decline' (p. 187) in interviewing officers' performances (in some of the assessed criteria) between their first and last assessed interview. These authors argued that despite this 'marked decline', the advanced training had nevertheless improved the skills of officers (in their sample).

GLOBAL COHERENCE

For such improvements outlined above to continue, it is vital that training and the professionalization process is continued, not just at a national level but, more importantly, internationally. There are many organizations that do such work, including:

1. INTERPOL, whose role is to enable police around the world to work together providing (amongst other things) targeted training,

expert investigative support, relevant data, and secure communications channels.

2. The European Police College (Collège Européen de Police; CEPOL) is a European Union (EU) agency dedicated to providing training and learning opportunities to police officers on issues vital to the security of the European Union and its citizens. Training covers issues ranging from leadership to law enforcement techniques and EU cooperation to economic crime. Activities are designed to facilitate the sharing of knowledge and best practice and to contribute to the development of a common European law enforcement culture.

3. The International Police Executive Symposium (IPES) brings police researchers and practitioners together to facilitate cross-cultural, international and interdisciplinary exchanges for the enrichment of the policing profession in general. The IPES encourages discussions and writing on challenging topics of contemporary importance through an array of initiatives including conferences and publications.

4. The International Investigative Interviewing Research Group (iIIRG) is an international network of academic researchers and practitioners committed to improving investigative interviewing worldwide. They provide annual conferences and specialist masterclasses, and conduct specialist training for international organizations such as: (i) the International Criminal Court (ICC); (ii) The United Nations High Commissioner for Refugees (UNHCR); and (iii) The United Nations Development Programme (UNDP). They also have an international journal *Investigative Interviewing: Research and Practice*, from which they disseminate academic research articles and practitioner case studies on legal matters relating to investigative interviewing.

Such organizations are vital for the continued professionalization of police and law enforcement organizations regarding the complex area of communication to ensure greater engagement between academic researchers and law enforcement practitioners. Such professionalization can only help further the knowledge base in this area – this book goes some way to achieve this goal.

OUTLINE OF BOOK

The purpose of this book is to provide readers with an in-depth coverage of the complex area of communication in forensic contexts. This includes the investigative interviewing of victims and witnesses, the investigative interviewing/interrogation of suspected offenders and high-interest groups, during discourse in courtrooms and via legal intermediaries and interpreters. The book is unique in bridging the gap between the fields of psychology, linguistics and law enforcement practitioners (worldwide), with clear recommendations for best practice. Highly specialist and international teams of authors comprising psychologists, linguists and dedicated practitioners in the field from Australia, Canada, the United Kingdom, New Zealand, Scandinavia and the United States of America have written most chapters.

The chapters in this book will provide an up-to-date knowledge base on developments in the ever-changing complex area of communication in forensic and investigative contexts. Through the discussions of theoretical and methodological issues, we will attempt to bridge the gap between the fields of psychology, linguistics and law enforcement. This is a vitally important blend of integrated dialogue across the disciplines for us to move forward and fully understand the underpinning issues with regard to communication in such settings. We have separated the chapters into six domains: (i) communication, language and memory; (ii) communicating with victims and witnesses; (iii) communicating with suspects; (iv) communication in the courtroom; (v) specific communicative tasks; and (vi) conclusions and future.

Communication, Language and Memory

Chapter 2 highlights the proliferation of categorization schemes, which have mostly been developed from psychologists' understanding of the nature of linguistic interactions. Tim Grant, Jennifer Taylor, Gavin Oxburgh and Trond Myklebust demonstrate how empirical research using a Conversational Analysis approach can enrich research into the police interview and, in particular, the categorization of questions during forensic communication. As demonstrated by the authors, this requires a switch of focus from the 'words' used by interviewers in question types to the 'function' of conversational turns within interviews.

In Chapter 3, James Ost, Alan Scoborio, Tim Grant and Gary Pankhurst outline research concerning memory for events before moving on to discuss the ways in which our attempts to validate and communicate those memories can bias what is eventually reported. They then focus on some of the implications this can have for investigative interviews, specifically the problem of 'skill fade' in interviewing, the impact of implicit beliefs about memory and issues surrounding the reliability of recollections of direct speech. They conclude that appropriately structuring the retrieval context is the key to achieving best memory evidence.

Communicating with Victims and Witnesses

In the first chapter of this domain, David La Rooy, Julia Korkman, Trond Myklebust and Georgina Heydon examine 'the consensus' surrounding the complex nature of communication with children in forensic contexts and the key aspects about which all investigators should be knowledgeable. They argue that over many decades of psychological and linguistic research, an enormous amount has been learnt concerning childrens' cognitive strengths and limitations, together with their motivations and emerging abilities to communicate their experiences. They argue that over the course of several decades, steady advances made through the integration of psychological and linguistic knowledge, experimental research and field studies of forensic interviews have led to untested and sometimes dangerous interviewing approaches being replaced by practices around which there is considerable professional agreement.

Chapter 5 moves us on to interviews with adult witnesses and victims. In this chapter, Coral Dando, Ed Geiselman, Nicci MacLeod and Andy Griffiths discuss the interviewing of adult witnesses and victims with reference to how the extant psychological and linguistic literature has contributed to understanding and informing interview practice over the past 20 years. They argue that contemporary research has only scratched the surface of this important and complex topic. They introduce the PEACE model of interviewing, and describe the Cognitive Interview procedure and its development. They discuss numerous other important topics including rapport building, question types and communication style, all with reference to adult witness memory and practical interviewing. Finally, they highlight potential future areas research.

The final chapter in this domain, Chapter 6, focuses on the initial contact with a witness, whose evidence invariably plays a vital role in the investigative process. Fiona Gabbert, Lorraine Hope, Elizabeth Carter, Roel Boon and Ron Fisher explore the type of information that is typically sought at this first point of contact and how the goals of eliciting information at an early stage of an investigation differ from the goals of subsequent interviews. A range of relevant issues are explored, including factors that should be considered when eliciting an initial account, whether the format (written versus spoken) of the initial account matter and whether the quality of the initial account might affect the quality of subsequent accounts.

Communicating with Suspects

Gavin Oxburgh, Ivar Fashing, Kate Haworth and Pete Blair highlight in Chapter 7 how poor practices in interrogation and interviewing techniques have led to many miscarriages of justice around the world, undermining the reputation and trust of the legal processes and organizations involved. They provide a background and history of interrogation and interviewing, highlighting the fundamental differences in the two primary philosophies in Western countries. They then explore the ultimate purpose of interviewing and interrogation and argue that modern, scientifically backed, interviewing approaches should be used at all times, no matter the challenge or situation, as a pathway towards both the collection of accurate information and diligent adherence to the standards of international human rights.

Chapter 8 explores the sensitive area of information-gathering intelligence interviews and Fadia Narchet, Melissa Russano, Steve Kleinman and Chris Meissner set new ground by setting forth a multidimensional perspective on interrogations conducted for this purpose in support of the global war on terrorism. A series of semi-structured interviews and surveys involving practitioners yielded them unique data that provided previously undocumented insights into the process involved in the interrogation of high-value targets. Such an examination of the interrogative process from differing perspectives has generated a richer and unprecedented understanding of the respective roles, responsibilities and perceptions of an interrogation team.

Communication in the Courtroom

Questioning in common law accusatorial trials is dominated by the advocates' belief that it is a legitimate opportunity for advocacy rather than just investigation. The authors of Chapter 9 (Emily Henderson, Mark Kebbell and Chris Heffer) argue that examination of a witness is a form of story-telling, leading cross-examiners to rely heavily on rhetorical and suggestive questions that advance the preferred narrative. They further argue that empirical research suggests that this style of questioning reduces witness accuracy, reduces public confidence in the trial and deters witnesses from coming forward.

In Chapter 10, Lorna Fadden and Larry Solan discuss the interaction between lawyers and expert witnesses in adversarial systems. Focusing largely on the legal systems of Canada and the United States, they look at the laws that qualify experts and govern their responsibility to the court. They discuss the presumably complementary, but often competing, truth-seeking goals of lawyers and the experts they engage. In an adversarial system, however, the expert's best intentions can be put to the test and they explore some of the ways in which a lawyer can manoeuver towards achieving their goals and how the expert's analyses and opinions might be massaged during the preparation of a case and when they are questioned on the stand.

Specific Communicative Tasks

Specific communicative tasks covers a wide variety of topics, but, in this domain, we will focus on hostage and crisis negotiation, lie detection, vulnerability and the use of interpreters in forensic communication. Hostage and crisis negotiation is a psychological and linguistically complex domain. In Chapter 11, Ole Andre Bråten, Michel St Yves, Terry Royce and Marty Laforest argue that active shooter-scenarios, terrorist attacks and kidnapping have increased the need for effective tactical crisis communication. They discuss resolution through dialogue and argue that the models presented can change unfolding events in high-stress situations and alter presumably un-negotiable scenarios. Starting with a backdrop on the evolution of hostage and crisis negotiation, they provide an overview of contemporary approaches following a psychological, law enforcement and linguistic perspective.

Aldert Vrij, Paul Taylor and Isabel Piccornell discuss in Chapter 12 the important area of verbal lie detection and argue that speech content can be revealing about deception. Starting with a section discussing the myth that non-verbal behaviour is more revealing about deception than speech, they provide an overview of verbal lie detection tools currently used by law enforcement agencies. This is followed by an overview of interview techniques that have been recently developed and that are designed to enhance verbal differences between truth tellers or liars, and by an analysis of deceptive linguistic strategies.

Chapter 13 moves on to vulnerability and discusses how, in some instances, individuals are unable to manage the communication demands that are sometimes inherent in police interviews and/or cross-examination at court. As a consequence, the evidence required to make informed decisions is inaccurately heard, only partially heard or, worse still, not heard at all. Brendan O'Mahony, Ruth Marchant and Lorna Fadden describe, using case studies, the development of intermediary practices in England and Wales, and their use in Australia and Canada. They raise a series of questions about the boundaries and clarity of the intermediary function so that the legislation pertaining to intermediaries is more inclusive. They conclude with a discussion of the need to expand the use of intermediaries across the breadth of interviews and across the globe to help prevent miscarriages of justice.

In Chapter 14, Yvonne Fowler, Martin Vaughan and Jaqueline Wheatcroft then examine the interpreter-mediated police interview from the perspective of the linguist, the psychologist and the police officer. They document problems experienced by the police when an interview involves an interpreter and expose myths and misunderstandings associated with the interpreting process. The chapter also examines interpretation research and, from this standpoint, makes a number of recommendations as to how better to manage a variety of types of interpreter-mediated interview.

Conclusions and Future

In Chapter 15, Nina Westera, Martine Powell and Yvonne Fowler suggest that, for investigative communication to improve, research needs to take into account the diverse needs of the police/law enforcement operating environment. The authors utilize adult witness interviewing practices, specifically the cognitive interview, to explore the applicability of current methods across varying contexts common in investigative practice. They examine what is known from the research and what still needs to be discovered in relation to the varying contexts of investigative interviewing with reference to the interviewer, the witness and the type of crime.

Chapter 16 concludes the volume with a review of communication in investigative and legal contexts, highlighting the important areas that psychology, linguistics and law enforcement have impacted upon in terms of rigorous and collaborative scientific endeavours. The chapter, written by the book editors, addresses some of the areas they believe are important and of interest to the reader for further research. They discuss in detail some of the important areas that they believe require further research, including vulnerability, the use of intermediaries and interpreters, and questioning techniques.

REFERENCES

Baldwin, J. (1993). Police interview techniques: Establishing truth or proof? *British Journal of Criminology, 33*, 325–351.

Birkeland, Å. (2007). Politigeneralisten, den moderne staten og politiets legitimitet [The police officer, the modern state and the legitimacy of the police force]. In H. Gundhus, T. G. Myhrer & P. Larsson (Eds.), *Polisiær Virksomhet* (p.7). Oslo, Norway: PHS Forskning, Politihøgskolen.

Ceci, S. J., & Bruck, M. (1995). *Jeopardy in the courtroom: A scientific analysis of children's testimony*. Washington, DC: American Psychological Association.

Cherryman, J., & Bull, R. (2001). Police officers' perceptions of specialist investigative interviewing skills. *International Journal of Police Science and Management, 3*, 199–212.

Clarke, C., & Milne, R. (2001). National evaluation of the PEACE investigative interviewing course (Police Research Award Scheme Report PRAS/149, p. 187).

Clarke, C., Milne, R., & Bull, R. (2011). Interviewing suspects of crime: The impact of PEACE training, supervision and the presence of a legal advisor. *Journal of Investigative Psychology and Offender Profiling, 8*, 149–162.

Fisher, R. P., & Geiselman, R. E. (1992). *Memory-enhancing techniques for investigative interviewing: The cognitive interview.* Springfield, IL: Charles C. Thomas Publisher.

Fisher, R. P., Geiselman, R. E., & Amador, M. (1989). Field test of the cognitive interview: Enhancing the recollection of actual victims and witnesses of crime. *Journal of Applied Psychology, 5*, 722–727.

Fisher, R. P., Geiselman, R. E., & Raymond, D. S. (1987). Critical analysis of police interview techniques. *Journal of Police Science and Administration, 15*, 177–185.

Granhag, P. A. (Ed.) (2010). *Forensic psychology in context: Nordic and international approaches.* Cullompton, UK: Willan Publishing.

Grant, T. (2008). Approaching questions in forensic authorship analysis. In J. Gibbons & M. T. Turell (Eds.), *Dimensions of forensic linguistics* (pp. 215–229). Amsterdam, the Netherlands: Benjamins.

Griffiths, A., & Milne, R. (2006). Will it all end in tiers? Police interviews with suspects in Britain. In T. A. Williamson (Ed.), *Investigative interviewing: Rights, research, regulation* (pp. 167–189). Cullompton, UK: Willan Publishing.

Griffiths, A., Milne, R., & Cherryman, J. (2011). A question of control? The formulation of suspect and witness interview question strategies by advanced interviewers. *International Journal of Police Science and Management, 13*, 1–13.

Heffer, C. (2005). *The language of jury trial: A corpus-aided analysis of legal–lay discourse.* Houndmills/New York: Palgrave Macmillan.

Heydon, G. (2005). *The language of police interviewing: A critical analysis.* Houndmills/New York: Palgrave Macmillan.

Lamb, M. E., Hershkowitz, I., Orbach, Y., & Esplin, P. W. (2008). *Tell me what happened: Structured investigative interviews of child victims and witnesses.* Chichester, UK: John Wiley & Sons, Ltd.

Lamb, M. E., Orbach, Y., Sternberg, K. J., Esplin, P. W., & Hershkowitz, I. (2002). The effects of forensic interview practices on the quality of information provided by alleged victims of child abuse. In H. L. Westcott, G. M. Davies, & R. Bull (Eds.), *Children's testimony: Psychological research and forensic practice* (pp. 131–145). Chichester, UK: John Wiley & Sons Ltd.

Lamb, M. E., Sternberg, K. J., Orbach, Y., Esplin, P. W., & Mitchell, S. (2002). Is on-going feedback necessary to maintain the quality of investigative interviews with allegedly abused children? *Applied Developmental Science, 6*, 35–41.

Lamb, M. E., Sternberg, K. J., Orbach, Y., Hershkowitz, I., Horowitz, D., & Esplin, P. W. (2000). The effects of intensive training and ongoing supervision on the quality of investigative interviews with alleged sex abuse victims. *Applied Developmental Science, 6*, 114–125.

McGurk, B., Carr, J., & McGurk, D. (1993). *Investigative interviewing courses for police officers: An evaluation* (Police Research Series: Paper No. 4). London, UK: Home Office.

Milne, R., & Bull, R. (1999). *Investigative interviewing, psychology and practice.* Chichester, UK: John Wiley & Sons, Ltd.

Ministry of Justice and the Police. (2005). Stortingsmelding nr. 42 – Politiets rolle og oppgaver (White Paper No 42 – The role and duties of the Police). Oslo, Norway: Statens Forvaltningstjeneste.

Myklebust, T. (2010). Politiavhør som metode [Investigative interview as a method]. In T. Myklebust & G. Thomassen (Eds.), *Arbeidsmetoder og Metodearbeid i Politiet* [Working methods within the police]. Oslo, Norway: PHS-Forskning.

Myklebust, T., & Bjørklund, R. A. (2006). The effect of long-term training on police officers' use of open and closed questions in field investigative interviews of children (FIIC). *Journal of Investigative Psychology and Offender Profiling, 3*, 165–181.

Orbach, Y., Hershkowitz, I., Lamb, M. E., Sternberg, K. J., Esplin, P. W., & Horowitz, D. (2000). Assessing the value of structured protocols for forensic interviews of alleged child abuse victims. *Child Abuse and Neglect, 24*, 733–752.

Powell, M. B., Fisher, R. P., & Wright, R. (2005). Investigative interviewing. In N. Brewer & K. D. Williams (Eds.), *Psychology and law: An empirical perspective*. New York: Guilford Publications.

Rock, F. (2007). *Communicating rights: The language of arrest and detention*. Houndmills/New York: Palgrave Macmillan.

Stern, W. (1903/1904). *Beiträge zür Psychologie der Aussage*. Leipzig, Germany: Verlag von Johann Ambrosius Barth.

Sternberg, K. J., Lamb, M. E., Davies, G. M., & Westcott, H. L. (2001). The memorandum of good practice: Theory versus application. *Child Abuse and Neglect, 25*, 669–681.

Tiersma, P. (1999). *Legal language*. Chicago, IL: University of Chicago Press.

Walsh, D., & Bull, R. (2010). The interviewing of suspects by non-police agencies: What's effective? What is effective! *Legal and Criminological Psychology, 15*, 305–321.

Walsh, D. W., & Milne, R. (2008). Keeping the PEACE? A study of investigative interviewing practices in the public sector. *Legal and Criminological Psychology, 13*, 39–57.

Wright, R., & Powell, M. B. (2006). Investigative interviewers' perceptions of their difficulty in adhering to open-ended questions with child witnesses. *International Journal of Police Science and Management, 8*, 316–325.

Section I

Communication, Language and Memory

2

Exploring Types and Functions of Questions in Police Interviews

Tim Grant[1], Jennifer Taylor[1], Gavin Oxburgh[2] and Trond Myklebust[3]

[1] Aston University, Birmingham, UK
[2] Newcastle University, UK
[3] Norwegian Police University College, Oslo, Norway

INTRODUCTION

Most investigative interviewing chapters in the current volume begin with the wealth of psychological literature. As with any research programme, this has provided within-paradigm advances; however, there are the occasionally notes about the inadequacy of some aspects of the paradigm. One example is that many studies have attempted to define and categorize questioning, but as Cerovic (2010, p. 10) notes it can be, '…difficult to define the act of questioning as questions can perform numerous different purposes, not just information seeking.' Oxburgh, Myklebust and Grant (2010) also problematize the categorization of question types as used in police interviews, pointing out the proliferation of categorization schemes, which are mostly developed from psychologists' understanding of the nature of linguistic interactions. There is, of course, a wealth of linguistics literature in this area; Heydon (2011), for example, brings a conversation analysis approach into the

Communication in Investigative and Legal Contexts: Integrated Approaches from Forensic Psychology, Linguistics and Law Enforcement, First Edition. Edited by Gavin Oxburgh, Trond Myklebust, Tim Grant and Rebecca Milne.

field to describe the control a police interviewer exhibits over interview topics. In this chapter, we wish to give a demonstration of how research originating in this linguistic paradigm can enrich research into the police interview and in particular into the categorization of questions during forensic communication per se. As will be demonstrated, this requires a switch of focus from the 'words' used by interviews to the 'function' of conversational turns within interviews.

The research into investigative questioning is of course substantial. Police interviews in England and Wales, and indeed in many other parts of the world, are given an explicit set of functions to: (i) obtain information regarding who did what, where and when; (ii) gather evidence to assist the investigation; and (iii) seek the truth from those being interviewed (Centrex, 2004; Milne & Bull, 1999; Walsh & Oxburgh, 2008). The main functions of an investigative interview are, therefore, the eliciting of information and establishing its credibility, but questions can and do perform many other functions. From the linguistics literature, Tracy and Robles (2009) cite a number of works illustrating that in conversational turns that are apparently questions, speakers can make assertions (Sidnell, 2009), perform requests, corrections and challenges (Koshik, 2002; Monzoni, 2008; Pomerantz, 1988, 2005) and demonstrate power and control (Goody, 1978; Rogers & Farace, 1975; Wang, 2006). This wealth of complexity naturally has potential in any approach, which takes a naïve view that questions in any conversation or interview are used just to elicit information. A good example of such naivety can be found in the UK police training manual *The Practical Guide to Investigative Interviewing* (PGII) (Centrex, 2004). This manual is used as part of the UK policing's Professionalizing Investigations Programme for lower-level investigators involved mostly in the investigation of volume crime. PGII declares that there are three principle structural types of question (pp. 51–53): Open (5WH; questions commencing with 'who', 'what', 'when', 'where' and 'why'), which are best to elicit new information; Closed ("Are you? ... Did you?"), restricting information through question wording, which is useful for yes/no responses and confirming specific details (quantity, identity or selection between alternatives); and Leading questions, which suggest an answer in their wording and should be avoided. PGII also names Echo questions, which are described as 'Interviewer repetition of some words used by interviewees which may elicit elaborated responses' (Centex, 2004, pp. 51–53). As detailed in Oxburgh et al. (2010), PGII follows many writings and researchers from the psychological discipline in focusing on structure to define questions. Tracy and Robles (2009) point out that when focusing on structural categorization, the most common linguistic form-related categories do indeed include: WH interrogatives, yes–no, tags, declaratives and alternative questions.

Griffiths and Milne (2006) proposed another type of categorization, known as Productive and Unproductive questions, to allow analysis of question types within police interviews to assess the success of police interview training and its impact on continuing police interview strategy and formulation. They proposed eight question categories within their categories of productive and unproductive questions. Both include structural categories, but also make use of other functional categories available in the literature, for example they use the identified category 'probing question' as a superordinate category of the 5WH questions in an attempt to overcomes the duality of 5WH questions as both 'open' and 'closed'. Whilst this begs consideration of how many other complex categorization issues may exist within police/suspect interviews that may be resolved through the identification of functional question categories, it also raises the issue that, at the lowest level, the categorization system is based on question types identified by the words used. This occurs also in Griffiths and Milne's Productive category, which comprises: Open (TED, Questions starting with 'Tell', 'Explain' or 'Describe'), Probing (5WH) and Appropriate Closed categories. The Unproductive category consists of: Inappropriate Closed, Leading, Multiple and Forced Choice questions as well as Statements as questions. Thus, although the top of this typology is functional (and this may be considered an advance), many of the underlying question types remain defined by the words used. Another problem is that the typology includes a value judgement of inappropriate versus appropriate closed questions in order to evaluate the success of questioning in police interview contexts. Griffiths and Milne (2006) concluded that police officers found it easier during and after interview training to identify question types and their impact than other aspects of interview training, such as the structuring the topics of an interview, but it was more difficult to maintain an awareness of question types and their impact over time. Perhaps a taxonomy, which combines topic and structure, would improve this. This is not currently available and without a universal questioning taxonomy, the results of such analyses cannot be compared with other studies, making it somewhat difficult to interpret findings (Oxburgh et al., 2010) and therefore damaging to pass judgement on.

A different version of question categories is presented in the document, *Achieving Best Evidence in Criminal Proceedings* (Ministry of Justice, 2011), in which TED questions are still considered as Open questions, but 5WH questions are classed as 'Specific Closed' questions that can occasionally be framed as Open questions. This seemingly dual nature of 5WH questions supports Oxburgh et al. (2010) claims that confusion exists with the categorization of question types within the 'Open' and 'Closed' categories.

Despite the debate, linguists and psychologists agree that a question taxonomy is needed to enable greater understanding and interpretation of questions (Burger et al., 2001). Tracy and Robles (2009) and Oxburgh et al. (2010) argue that attention should be given to the function of questions, not just their linguistic form, and that further research should evaluate both form and function. Prior studies outlined by Tracy and Robles have analysed questions and answers separately, but self-evidently the '...context of suspect's answers, also dictates [questioning] strategies and sequencing' (Shuy, 1986, p. 178). It is for this reason that a Conversation Analysis (CA) methodology that observes 'sequences of actions and ways in which context forms a resource in their interpretation' (Drew & Heritage, 1992, p. 13) is appropriate to analyse the combination of question form and function. CA analyses patterns in naturalistic data, noting turn-taking behaviour such as adjacency pairs. Adjacency pairs are two linked adjacent turns in a conversation, in which the first pair part (in this case a question) primes the response as a second pair part (in our case, an answer; Levinson, 1983). A further distinction of the CA approach is that it treats the conversation that is a police interview as necessarily co-constructed between interviewer and interviewee (see, for example, Haworth, 2006). This clearly has important implications. To some extent much of the psychological contribution to the development of the investigative interview has sought to reduce or remove interviewer influence. The linguistic research, however, has a different emphasis. Linguists, in recognizing that interviewees answers are necessarily co-constructed with the interviewer, recognize also the impossibility of removing the interviewer's influence. The linguistic interest shifts to tracking the influence of both interactants on one another in the context of the interview interaction. A good example of this is Haworth's work, which recognizes the importance of examining speech in the sequence and context in which she analyses the syntactic form and function of question types in order to track the use of power and control strategies of both the interviewer and interviewee.

Data and Transcription

To provide a worked example of a CA approach and how it could influence a more traditional psychological approach to question categorization, a worked CA was carried out. Five suspect interviews were analysed taking the first four to seven minutes (excluding the official caution and reading of prepared written statements, etc.) as these approximated the 'Account' phase of the interview and provided sufficient material for this example. The Account phase comes early in a PEACE interview as used by UK police. The PEACE model of interviewing provides structure to the interaction under the headings Plan and prepare, Engage and explain, Account, clarify and challenge, Close and Evaluate. This structure is described in more detail elsewhere in this volume. The portions of interview were digitized, transcribed and fully anonymized. In three interviews, the interviewee co-operated with the police interviewer's questions. In two interviews, the interviewee provided only 'no comment'[1] responses. CA transcription is very different from standard Record of Interview transcription and in this case paralinguistic features, such as pitch and pace within the transcript, were coded, ensuring that all vocalizations were included. These prosodic features of language can be seen to have a conversational function as they fill a specific conversational slot and create context for the next utterance (Ten Have, 1999). Such detailed transcription is typical of a CA approach and one minute of taped data can take an hour or more to transcribe.

In addition to this transcription, observational notes were made of turn taking and specifically of adjacency pairs (i.e. adjacent conversational turns where the second turn is a direct response to the first). Also noted were repairs, topic introductions/change and particularly any utterances that succeeded in requesting, ordering or eliciting information from another party in the conversation. These conversational turns were identified as functioning as questions and allowed further analysis of the different types of questions in their contextual settings. Finally, these types of questions were formed into structural groups and into broad function-based categories.

Analysis

The data analysis is situated in the principle that the overarching purpose of an interview is to elicit information (Centrex, 2004) and combines the observed structure of the interview with the function of the question rather than focusing on dividing questions into eliciting new information or confirmation-seeking (Newbury & Johnson, 2006). Schegloff (2007, p. 71) posits that questions can function '... both as actions in their own right and as vehicles or formats for other actions'. The analysis produced a different categorization of question types and, in particular, the turns fell into two functional types: (i) Topic Initiation Questions and (ii) Topic Facilitation Questions. A summary of the use of these questions and the relationships between these types is provided in Figure 2.1.

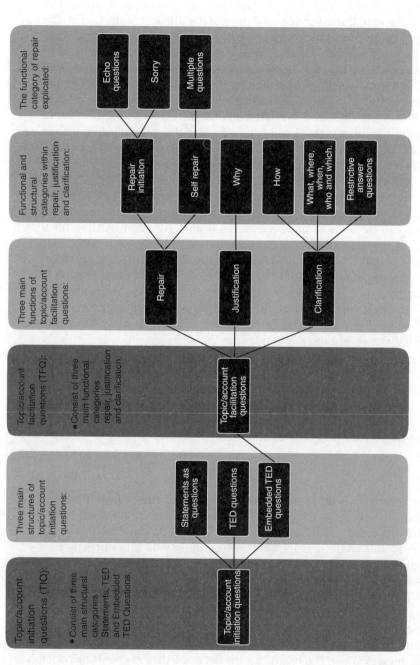

Figure 2.1 An illustration of categories of questions identified during analysis. Questions fall into two key functional areas: Topic/Account: Initiation Questions (TIQs) and Topic/Account: Facilitation Questions (TIFs). The lines indicate relationships between the categories. This structure is semi-hierarchical in nature, expanded to illustrate questions within category headings. It excludes utterances signalling continuation not treated as questions in this study.

Topic/Account Initiation Questions (TIQs)

Guidance for the PEACE interview (Centrex, 2004) states that a police interviewer should pick topics, probe and summarize to gather an account of an event, move on to the next topic and repeat these actions. This guidance assumes that questioning within the interview context will provide the framework to elicit accounts from suspects regarding specific topics. Heydon's (2011) research details the highly constrained nature of a suspect's contribution through topic initiation controlled by the police interviewer and mentions a 'range of devices' (p. 2311), which enables interviewers to introduce new topics; however, they are not fully explicated within her research. Her data indicates a cadre of question types, which are used to introduce new topics and can be categorized by their function to elicit new information in a constrained area from interviewees. These are categorized as Topic/Account Initiation Questions (TIQs) and can be further subdivided into three constructions, as outlined in Figure 2.1 and explained in further detail in Table 2.1.

Table 2.1 Examples of Topic/Account Initiation Questions (TIQs) taken from the data analysed

Question type	Examples
TED Questions	**interviewer:** ... SO [(.)] tell me about your business **interviewer:** ... tell me about where you [(X)] where you work ... describe that to me
Embedded TED Questions	**interviewer:** ... can you [(.)] in your own words and in your own time [(0.2)] errm [(.)] tell me whats happened[(.)] thats led up to you being [(0.5)] err arrested at that time [(2.0)] **interviewer:** = have you any/ [(2.0)] explanation why you have that address where you live at ADDRESS2 =
Statements as TIQ	**interviewer:** [(hh)] [(3.5)] NAME1 youre showing yourself as unemployed/ [(1.5)] **interviewer:** theres a substantial amount of cash on the premises NAME1, =

This example (and following examples) follows a standard CA transcription convention and demonstrates some of the detail that is elicited by linguistic transcription. Transcribed features here include pauses in square brackets, where possible timed in seconds; fillers such as 'errm' and overlapping talk as indicated by the equal sign. Further features include quieter speech indicted by the degrees symbol (e.g. °quiet talk°). Conversely, up arrows and capitals are used to indicate emphasized or louder talk (e.g. ^loud talk^). It is of course possible to transcribe more features using the CA conventions but a level of transcription needs to be selected (see Gibbons, 2001, for a discussion of levels of transcription).

In the data examined here, TIQs are only used by interviewers and are used to introduce new topics or initiate free recall accounts. A series of examples of TIQs from within our data are explored below. TIQs are constructed in three ways: (i) statements as questions (see Example Two); (ii) Tell, Explain, Describe (TED) questions; and (iii) embedded TED Questions (see table 2.1).

Example One: Tape 15
61 **interviewer1:** ... why dont you
62 just tell me everything ^{0}that youve done today^0 [(.)] ^{0}everything youve done to when you were
63 arrested.^{0}
64 **interviewee:** oh coz my sister gave me money to go and buy [(X)] buy some, =

TED and embedded TED questions are interpreted as first pair parts of adjacency pairs requiring an account and performing the same function: Topic/Account Initiation. In Example One, the TED question is embedded within a justification question (see below) and still elicits an account.

No comment interviews also indicate that TED and embedded TED questions aim to elicit accounts, shown by the way in which they occur at the start of topics and at any further point during police accounts of the same topic. They do not signify topic changes in these environments (see Example Two) and usually occur after police accounts, indicating that they function to elicit a response from interviewees.

Example Two: Tape 16
25 **interviewer:** ... can you [(.)] in your own words and in your own
26 time [(0.2)] errm [(.)] tell me whats happened [(.)] thats led up to you being [(0.5)] err arrested
27 at that time [(2.0)]
28 **interviewee:** err no comment [(1.0)]

Lines 39–77 Police account of events presented by interviewer
101 **interviewer:** ... | Tell me whats happened | ...
102 **interviewee:** ^{0}no comment^0

'No comment' here might be an indication that the interviewee has interpreted the interviewer's utterance as a question which requires a response (see Example Three).

Example Three: Tape 16
97 **interviewer:** ... you dont have to say anything [(.)] and youre stating no comment just to indicate that
98 youve heard the question

Statements as TIQs appear in data from 'no comment' interviews.

Example Four: Tape 23
28 **interviewer:** theres a substantial amount of cash on the premises NAME1, =
29 **interviewee:** = no comment [(1.0)]

In Example Four, the interviewee responds to a statement by the interviewer featuring topic matter not previously introduced with a 'no comment' reply. The equals sign is used to indicate that the interviewee interprets the statement as further indicating their need to respond. This exchange, even with the 'no comment' response seems to indicate that the statement is understood as functioning as a TIQ.

The examples above and in Table 2.1 demonstrate that TIQs rarely feature questioning intonation, and are less contextually constraining on the nature of response given by the interviewee, focusing on overviews rather than detail. In the more conventional categorization systems, the interviewer 'turns', whatever the structural features of the question, can be interrupted as open questions. The function of the TIQ is clearly understood by the respondent even where this function is confronted by a 'no comment' response.

The second main category of questions are, as one might expect in an Account phase of an interview, Topic Facilitation Questions (TFQs). Example TFQs are given in Table 2.2 and then in a series of shorter extracts to demonstrate individual points.

TFQs may or may not elicit new information and serve not to introduce a new topic but to progress an existing topic. Figures 2.1 and Table 2.2 show three main functions of TFQs, namely to: Clarify, Repair and Justify (a response to a previous question?). In contrast to TIQs, TFQs focus on details within a topic/account and, as such, tend to elicit shorter turns (responses by the interviewee?) than TIQs. TFQs occurred more frequently in the current dataset and are highly contextually constrained within the question itself, by reference to the surrounding co-text or as outlined in Example Five, through both.

Example Five: Tape 15
135 **interviewer:** = how long have you known him? [(1.0)]
136 **interviewee:** err I think [(3.0)] four five years ago [(0.5)] fourfive threefour fourfive yeah =

Table 2.2   Examples of Topic/Account Facilitation Questions (TFQs) taken from the data analysed

Question type	Examples
Repair Questions:	
Repair Initiation	**interviewer:** = you were no where near/ = **interviewer:** central PLACE2? **interviewer:** ^wanted to go where/ sorry?^
Self-Repair	**interviewer:** ^WHERE ABOUTS errm [(X)] where abouts are you from?^ ^where do you live?^ **interviewer:** 0but you trust him? 0 HOW LONG have you known him?
Justification Questions	**interviewer:** ... why would those items 0be in your flat\0 = ? **interviewer:** ... WHY do you need that AMOUNT of mobile phones NAME1?
Clarification Questions:	
How	**interviewer:** ... how well do you know this ^side of^ PLACE4? **interviewer:** right [(1.5)] so how does he get paid?
What, When, Where, Who and Which	**solicitor:** When you say hes senior what do you mean by he is senior? **interviewee:** = no now [(.)] I dont mean now no no what was I wearing on [(X)] on that day? [(0.5)] **interviewer:** = which sisters that.
Restrictive Answer Questions	**interviewer:** ... do you remember that at all? **interviewer:** do you remember anything at all about last night. I mean I know youve had a lot to drink didnt you? **interviewer:** is that cash YOURS?= **interviewer:** are they there errm for keeping ^that flat^ safe? =

The question structure 'how long' constrains the answer to a timescale and 'him' deictically points to an earlier discussed individual, indicating that prior utterances impact upon question formation. This question is also an example of a Clarification Question, which is explained in the next section.

Clarification Questions

Cerovic (2010) explains that interviewers often require clarification or confirmation rather than 'new information' from interviewees to achieve institutional goals (e.g. for evidential purposes). It is difficult to analyse what may be new and unknown information to participants before they take part in interviews, but it is possible to establish new information within the boundaries of a conversation during the interview. Observing the questions in the current dataset indicates that clarification questions are explicitly contextually restrictive and function to seek clarification and, in this sense, new information about a specified topic. Example Six demonstrates this.

Example Six: Tape 17
95 **interviewer:** do you know where LOCATION1 road is?
96 **interviewee:** ^{0}I know where LOCATION1 road is\\$^0$

Linguists will recognize this as the operation of one of Grice's conversational maxims. In his seminal article on the co-operative principle in conversation Grice (1975) argues for a series of necessary principles for successful conversation and 'relevance' is one such principle. The example shows that the context of the question restricts the available 'relevant; responses according to 'This is also an example of a Restricted Answer Question'.

Restricted Answer Questions (RAQs), Including Tags

From the current dataset, RAQs mostly featured in No Comment interviews and were structured in two different ways: (i) to introduce a new concept within the framework of the question that contributes to the progress of the topic (Example Six) or (ii) to act as a follow-up question to information previously provided (Example Seven). In this data, Tag questions (see Table 2.2) only feature in the No Comment interviews. RAQs in this study do appear to function similarly to a question type outlined in Pomerantz' (1988) research, which he refers to as Candidate Answer Questions. These questions incorporate a candidate, or possible, answer into their form and are useful when speakers want to guide, direct or assist a recipient in supplying relevant information. Pomerantz suggests Candidate Answer Questions may be particularly used when a speaker may not be comfortable providing this information themselves and this may also be true of RAQs. In investigative interview data, 'no comment' is clearly used to avoid answering a question. Pomerantz's observations suggest that an RAQ is more likely to be deployed following a 'no comment' answer and this is indeed found in our small dataset. Pomerantz notes that questions containing a Candidate Answer are also used to demonstrate the speaker's knowledge and familiarity with a situation. It is possible that a police interviewer facing a 'no comment' answer might wish to indicate knowledge of the interviewee's actions as a tactic to move the interviewee to provide a fuller answer.

Example Seven: Tape 17
interviewer: ... SUSPICION IS [(.)] THAT YOUVE BEEN INVOLVED IN AN A B H [(0.5)] an assault that happened on the DATE (MONTH) okay [(cough)] d- [(X)] you remember that incident =
68 **interviewee:** = yeah =

RAQs act as a follow-up to information provided in an interviewer's turn. The phrase, 'That incident' in Example Seven deictically refers to the assault mentioned in the same turn. RAQs also follow the provision of information or an account by the interviewer, functioning to request the interviewee to align to the interviewer's account (see Example Eight). However, further data are required to determine whether this is the case in other interviews.

Example Eight: Tape 16
interviewer: err they saw you stagger [(.)] b- er [(X)] back and walk into the junction with PLACE2, [(.)] still holding the bottle of wine in your hand. [(1.0)] errm [(1.0)] reading from the sergeants notes er EXHIBIT1 [(.)] er so hes [(.)] together with the :: Inspector NAME6 [(.)] err they both got out of their vehicle and approached you [(.)] errm [(.)] | as you obviously had too much to drink| [(0.5)] they took err [(X)] the err bottle [(.)] FROM you which is half full, [(.)] do you remember that at all?
interviewee: ⁰no comment⁰

As shown, the interviewer follows an account of events with an RAQ, to which the interviewee responds 'no comment'. The question provides the context through the use of 'that', a deictic marker, which makes reference to the interviewer's full account, indicating that s/he is seeking alignment (confirmation?) from the interviewee.

Other literature in this area indicates that what we have labelled RAQs are often named 'yes/no questions' within a 'Closed Question' category (see Griffiths & Milne, 2006; Oxburgh et al., 2010). Such categorizations do not take into account the impact of the question construction on topic management, the function of the type of question asked at the time of asking or the potential third 'no comment' answer. Further to this, Griffiths and Milne's categorization of Productive/Unproductive question types may be seen as making an assumption that all police interviews are likely to be co-operative interactions. The 'no comment' response can occur after any question type and is, of course, minimally productive. Given the occurrence of 'no comment' interviews, a categorization system that is based on interviewee responses seems untenable.

Who, What, When, Where, Which and How Questions

As with RAQs, WH forms of question provide contextual information within the question turn but also elicit new information rather than present information for confirmation, denial or no further comment. These question types in our data feature in interviews where the interviewee is being co-operative.

Example Nine: Tape 15
interviewer1: ... how well do you know this ^side of^ PLACE4?
interviewee: I dont know it properly thats why I asked for
    directions

The interviewee's turn is restricted to responding about their knowledge of a specified place. The length of interviewee's adjacency pair is restricted by the nature of the question and, in fact, the questions in these categories rarely afford the opportunity to provide a longer response.

These WH and How questions are not just restricted to the interviewer, however; interviewee questioning features only once in the data analysed and is met with hesitation and possible resistance (lines 119–123) by the interviewer.

Example Ten: Tape 17
interviewee: [[(what was I)] WEARING?
interviewer: well it was all [(X)] well it doesnt matter what you was
    wearing now =
interviewee: = no what was I wearing on that day
interviewer: oh
interviewee: = no now [(.)] I don't mean now no no what was I
    wearing on [(X)] on that day? [(0.5)]
interviewer: err he [(X)] he [(X)] he hasnt put a description of clothing

Solicitor questioning takes place more often and consists predominantly of clarification questions. Below is an example of a solictior closing what is called a repair loop, initiated by the interviewer. The interviewee creates a need for a conversational repair following their utterance

'He's my senior' (Tape 10 line 140). This utterance would be referred to as the trouble source turn and the solicitor's intervention at line 150 repairs the conversation to help ensure mutual understanding.

Example Eleven: Tape 10

	Question Type/Commentary
139 **interviewer:** err [(1.0)] how do you know him?	Clarification, How Question
140 **interviewee:** because hes also doing err [(X)] this [(X)] these kind of job hes my SENIOR [(1.0)]	SENIOR – Trouble Source
141 **interviewer:** right	Possible encourangement (not counted as a question – owing to response).
142 **interviewee:** thats right	Repeat's interviewer to confirm.
143 **interviewer:** hes your senior	Echo – repair initiation.
144 **interviewee:** yeah	No elaboration – unsuccessful repair.
145 **interviewer:** how do you mean =	Clarification, How Question no context – repair continues.
146 **interviewee:** = before he was working err [(X)] you know PLACE3 or [(X)] or PLACE4 [(2.0)] a::nd err we [(X)] we are	Response does not address trouble source – repair continues.
147 same thing and thats why sometime we will ask about the software about the unlocking m [(X)] mobile the	
148 err [(X)] err living now in these days [(X)] in these days hes [(X)] hes jobless	
149 **interviewer:** ⁰okay⁰ [(1.0)]	Possible encouragement (not counted as a question – owing to response) and pause, to allow a response.
150 **solicitor:** When you say hes senior what do you mean by he is senior?	Solicitor takes temporary control of interview, Clarification question provided WITH context to facilitate repair. Context enables relevent response.
151 **interviewee:** you know you know sir [(2.0)] this job I am doing four or five years but he is doing longer	
152 **solicitor:** hes more experienced?	Restrictive Answer Question, follow-up to interviewee utterance and seeks alignment with solicitor's rephrasing.
153 **interviewee:** yeah [(1.0)] more experience [(6.0)]	Alignment confirmed – repair loop closed indicated by longer pause.
154 **interviewer:** does he ever buy mobile phones for your shop?	Interviewer retake control of interview.

In Line 145, the interviewer asks a 'How' question, which does not include the context of the trouble source hindering repair. At line 150 the solicitor provides a WH question (RAQ), which includes the context of the trouble source and enables the interviewee to clarify the trouble source. This sequence of adjacency pairs is an instance of repair.

Repair Questions

Repair refers to practices for dealing with problems of hearing, speaking and understanding talk (Schegloff, Jefferson & Sacks, 1977). Distinctions are made between who initiates the problematic utterance or trouble source and who initiates the correction or repair of the problematic utterance: Self Initiated Self Repair usually occurs when a speaker corrects their own speech in the same turn; Self Initiated Other Repair occurs when the speaker initiates the repair but the hearer provides the repair; Other Initiated Self Repair occurs when the hearer initiates the repair and the trouble source speaker provides the solution to the problematic utterance; and Other Initiated Other Repair occurs when the hearer initiates and resolves the problematic utterance (Bolden, 2011, p. 238). As we have seen above, repair (Levinson, 1983) can be completed using many different types of question. Repair questions function differently to Clarification questions by initiating repair on a trouble source and seeking confirmation or expansion of prior utterances. Repair Questions fall into two categories within police interview contexts: Other Initiated Repair (usually the interviewer repairing or requesting repair on the interviewee's utterances) and Self Initiated repair on interview questions (performed by the interviewer only) (Levinson, 1983).

Echo Questions

Echo questions are only used to initiate repair on Other's utterances and are categorized as Repair Initiator Questions within the Repair category.

Example Twelve: Tape 17
interviewer: = SO where was you at half three
interviewee: about three ish in PLACE6 =
interviewer: = PLACE6. =
interviewee: PLACE6 east PLACE3

The interviewer echos 'PLACE6' resulting in the interviewee repeating and expanding the perceived trouble source highlighted by the interviewer's repetition. The data analysed indicates that the interviewer is more likely to interrupt or latch to an interviewee utterance during an account to affect an immediate repair on a perceived trouble source.

Sorry

Another examply of Other initiated repair is the use of 'sorry', usually with questioning intonation, used both by the interviewee (Example Thirteen) and interviewer (Table 2.2) to request repair on each other's utterances as shown in Example Thirteen.

Example Thirteen: Tape 17
interviewer1: ^{0}but you trust him? ^{0} HOW LONG have you known him?
interviewee: sorry? =
interviewer1: = how long have you known him? [(1.0)]

The interviewee's 'sorry' repair initiator with question intonation indicates that the interviewer's utterance in the first line contains a trouble source. The interviewer had in fact asked multiple questions, essentially 'Do you trust him and how long have you known him?' The interviewer's self-selection and repetition of just the second question indicates that the second question in the series should be the focus.

Justification Questions

Achieving Best Evidence (ABE) (Ministry of Justice, 2011) states that 'Why?' as a question can pose problems if they seek an explanation of behaviour. According to ABE, 'Why?' can also promote feelings of blame. Koshik (2003) takes this a stage further and declares that 'Why?' seeks justification, is not information seeking and can be used to 'convey negative assertions which challenge grounds for a prior claim' (Koshik, 2003, p. 59). In our data, in the initial account phase of interviews 'Why?' questions have been observed to request information alongside the requirement to provide an explanation or justification (see Table 2.2 for examples from 'no comment' interviews).

Example Fourteen: Tape 15
interviewer: ... why dont you just tell me everything ^{0}that youve done today^0 [(.)] ^{0}everything youve done to you were arrested.^{0}
interviewee: oh coz my sister gave me money to go and buy [(X)] buy some, =

The interviewee orientates to the 'Why?' question as requiring information and an explanation with 'oh coz', where 'coz' is an abbreviation of 'because', meaning 'for the reason that' (*Oxford Dictionary*). This results in the interviewee providing the start of an account as a 'reason'.

Discussion

With these worked examples, it can be seen that a CA methodology has helped identify and analyse patterns in the data that might be missed through a conventional structural question categorization. Specifically, the CA approach helps explain the blend functional and structural categorization of questioning within police/suspect interviews, encouraging the researcher's focus to remain on the data. Defining a question type remains difficult. Not all questions observed make use of a questioning intonation (e.g. TIQs), and conversely not all utterances that are structured as questions elicit information. What is clear from these data and from other linguistic studies is that the structure of an utterance alone is not enough to categorize questions. Many questions are structured in one way and function in another. TED questions can be embedded within Clarification question forms, such as Restrictive Answer Questions, and still function to elicit accounts rather than Yes/ No answers. Another example is the Restricted Answer Questions, which can be used to allow respondents to go beyond a Yes/No answer and to invite correction and elaboration. Research that evaluates the success of questioning strategies by evaluating question structure and assumed answers, such as that attempted by Wright and Alison (2004), could be damaging to police interview guidance.

Questions can be usefully categorized by an overarching function (e.g. Topic/Account Initiation, Clarification, Repair, etc.), with structure playing a part in the function of a question. The PEACE framework for investigative interviewing categorizes the stages of the interview process according to function (Centrex, 2004), with the main functional question categories (TIQ, TFQ and Clarification) resulting from the analysis coincidentally reflecting some functional stages of the PEACE model (Account and Clarification – from PGII). This demonstrates the benefit of combining function and structure within guidance to better understand the use of and response to questions.

'Challenge' (in PGII) does not feature in this question classification. The observations made in this particular dataset indicate only one incidence of the interviewee challenging an interviewer's utterance. This may be a function of having constrained the duration of the interviews analysed to the first four to seven minutes of the main body of the interview, and it is acknowledged that it may be the case that there are other question categories that have not been observed. This is supported by Griffiths and Milne (2006), who suggest that the first 6 to 24 minutes of an interview appear to cover the Account stage of PEACE, featuring more Open and Probing questions. This suggests that a fuller functional analysis using CA methods would be useful. Other specific observations from this small analysis include the fact that only the interviewers use Topic Initiation Questions and that the rarer questions of the interviewee and solicitor were all Repairs and Clarifications. Even here the acknowledged right to ask Clarification questions appears to be granted only to the solicitor – the interviewee's attempt to employ Clarification questions (as in Example Ten) is met with resistance. This is supported by Haworth's (2006) study, which indicates that the interviewer is in control of the exchange but that this does not preclude other participants from seizing control at certain points and challenging the interviewer's authority. Power, control and resistance can be demonstrated and observed in institutional interactions through the use of questions, which suggests another function of questioning: reflecting the roles of participants in interview settings (Goody, 1978; Oxburgh & Ost, 2011; Rogers & Farace, 1975; Wang, 2006, in Tracy & Robles, 2009, p. 134).

A further insight involves the use of 'Why?' questions in our data. Referred to as one of the 5WH in a number of documents and studies (Centrex, 2004; Griffiths & Milne, 2006; Ministry of Justice, 2011; Oxburgh et al., 2010), this study indicates that 'Why?' functions largely as a 'Justification' question requiring explanation of an earlier utterance. It does seem to function differently to the other WH questions, which seek only Clarification of prior utterances. Moving 'Why?' into a separate functional 'justification' category may allow for better analysis of the function of 'Why?' and allows greater understanding and interpretation of these questions.

Application to Practice

As we have seen, there are many prior examples of researchers approaching investigative interview analysis using CA. These studies and our data analysis within this chapter give rise to many good research questions and also to broader questions of police interview training and assessment. Purely as a research tool, it can be seen just from this brief data analysis that a CA approach can enrich and advance current understanding of the functions of questions in police interviews. It helps explain some of the confusion in categorization schemes, which rely on structural features of questions and avoids the circularity of defining a question in terms of its response. Further exploration of interviews using a detailed CA transcription to identify functional features of questions will be an interesting academic research pursuit that may usefully challenge some of the orthodox question typologies. From a practitioner perspective, however, this research pursuit may, at this stage, raise more questions than it answers.

On the positive side the CA approach helps bring to the fore the focus on information elicitation as the overarching function of the interview. Cauchi, Powell and Hughes-Scholes (Cauchi & Powell, 2009; Cauchi, Powell & Hughes-Scholes, 2010; Powell, Wright & Hughes-Scholes, 2011) all acknowledge the difficulty in capturing the information that is discussed during an interview, particularly because the speed of the spoken word is much faster than that of the written word (Piolat, Olive & Kellogg, 2005). A structure for recording information has proved to be more beneficial than an outline structure, which is in turn more beneficial than the linear structure used by most students (Robinson, Katayama, DuBois & DeVaney, 1998; Ruhl & Suritky, 1995). Here the 5WH questions are essential for the investigators. However, for the CA model, the focus on function may encourage the practitioner to design questions to initiate topics of (see Oxburgh, Ost & Cherryman, 2012):

- People
- Action
- Location(s)
- Item
- Temporal (dates and times).

Another benefit of classifying questions in this way may be inadvertently overcoming a police interview training issue identified by Griffiths and Milne (2006) – that police find it more difficult to structure a topic than identifies and recognizes the impact of different question types. In categorizing questions according to topic management, as in this study, question types are considered within the context of the interview setting. This typology was created as a result of observing and analysing questioning patterns in low-level crime police/suspect interview data. To produce a similar typology for training purposes, it would be recommended that a police value judgement is used to identify 'good' interviews to be analysed to assess the suitability of this typology as a best practice training tool. This is an area that would require further research and testing to fully evaluate.

On the negative side is how to effect training in such an approach, particularly to lower skilled interviewers. Training new interviewers in types of questions as expressed in structural terms (e.g. use of TED questions) may be more straightforward than asking them to consider the functions of their questions and the complexity that a statement may function effectively as a question. It may be that advanced interviewers have already drifted away from the training model to find different structures of question that are functionally useful. In these cases, some training of this sort might be effective and a reasonable reassurance. Certainly, such interviewers should not be penalized by negative assessments of their interview performance if they are effective in asking Topic Initiation Questions using a statement rather than a TED question.

CONCLUSION

This small data analysis is clearly not enough to support significant changes in current approaches to police training but it does exemplify some of the value of exploring the approach. In focusing directly on the function of questions arising from data, the questions can be grouped in new ways, which cut across the more traditional typologies. If the understanding of how questions operate in an interview is to improve this kind of classification system this approach can make a considerable contribution. It may even be possible to evaluate successful question strategies in earnest, making it possible to compare the results of many different researcher analyses of questioning strategies in the future (Oxburgh et al., 2010).

NOTE

1. In England and Wales, where a person is being interviewed in relation to a crime she/he may have committed, they have a fundamental right in law not to say anything during the interview. This is routinely called a 'no comment' interview.

REFERENCES

Bolden, G. (2011). On the organisation of repair in a multiperson conversation: The case of 'Other'—Selection in other—Initiated repair sequences. *Research on Language and Social Interaction, 44*, 237–262.
Burger, J., Cardie, C., Chaudhri, V., Gaizauskas, R., Harabagiu, S., Israel, D., ... Lin, C. Y. (2001). Issues, tasks and program structures to roadmap research

in question and answering (Q&A). National Institute of Standards and Technology. Retrieved from http://www-nlpir.nist.gov/projects/duc/papers/qa.Roadmap-paper_v2.doc, 8 December 2014.

Cauchi, R., & Powell, M. B. (2009). An examination of police officers' notes of interviews with alleged child abuse victims. *International Journal of Police Science and Management, 11* (4), 505–515.

Cauchi, R. T., Powell, M. B., & Hughes-Scholes, C. H. (2010). A controlled analysis of professionals' contemporaneous notes of interviews about alleged child abuse. *Child Abuse and Neglect, 34* (5), 318–323.

Centrex (2004). *The practical guide to investigative interviewing*. London, UK: Centrex.

Cerovic, M. (2010). Questions and questioning in Montenegrin police interviews. Retrieved from http://etheses.whiterose.ac.uk/1388/ (Accessed 11 May 2015).

Drew, P., & Heritage, J. (1993). Analysing talk at work. In P. Drew & J. Heritage (Eds.), *Talk at work: Interaction in institutional settings* (pp. 3–65). Cambridge, UK: Cambridge University Press.

Goody, E. N. (1978). Towards a theory of questions. In E. N. Goody (Ed.), *Questions and politeness: Strategies in social interaction* (pp. 17–43). Cambridge, UK: Cambridge University Press.

Grice, H. P. (1975). Logic and conversation. In P. Cole & J. Morgan (Eds.), *Syntax and Semantics* (Vol. 3, pp. 41–58). New York: Academic Press.

Griffiths, A., & Milne, R. (2006). Will it all end in tiers? Police interviews with suspects in Britain. In T. A. Williamson (Ed.), *Investigative interviewing: Rights, research, regulation* (pp. 167–189). Cullompton, UK: Willan Publishing.

Haworth, K. (2006). The dynamics of power and resistance in police interview discourse. *Discourse and Society, 17*, 739–759.

Heydon, G. (2011). Silence: civil right or social privilege? A discourse analytic response to a legal problem. *Journal of Pragmatics, 43*, 2308–2316.

Koshik, I. (2002). A conversation analytic study of yes/no questions which convey reversed polarity assertions. *Journal of Pragmatics, 34*, 1851–1877.

Koshik, I. (2003). WH-questions used as challenges. *Discourse Studies, 5*, 51–77.

Levinson, S. C. (1983). *Pragmatics*. Cambridge, UK: Cambridge University Press.

Milne, R., & Bull, R. (2006). Interviewing victims of crime, including children and people with intellectual difficulties. In M. R. Kebbell & G. M. Davies (Eds.), *Practical psychology for forensic investigations*. Chichester, UK: John Wiley & Sons, Ltd.

Ministry of Justice. (2011). Achieving best evidence in criminal proceedings: Guidance on interviewing victims and witnesses, and guidance on using special measures. Retrieved from 8 December 2014, http://www.justice.gov.uk/downloads/victims-and-witnesses/vulnerable-witnesses/achieving-best-evidence-criminal-proceedings.pdf

Monzoni, C. M. (2008). Introducing direct complaints through questions: The interactional achievement of 'pre-sequences'?. *Discourse Studies, 10*, 73–87.

Newbury, P., & Johnson, A. (2006). 'Suspects' resistance to constraining and coercive questioning strategies in the police interview. *Speech Language and the Law, The International Journal of Forensic Linguistics, 13*, 214–240.

Oxburgh, G., & Ost, J. (2011). The use and efficacy of empathy in police interviews with suspects of sexual offences. *Journal of Investigative Psychology and Offender Profiling, 8* (2), 178–188.

Oxburgh, G., Ost, J., & Cherryman, J. (2012). Police interviews with suspected child sex offenders: Does use of empathy and question type influence the amount of investigation relevant information obtained? *Psychology, Crime and Law, 18,* 259–273.

Oxburgh, G. E., Myklebust, T., & Grant, T. (2010). The question of question types in police interviews: A review of the literature from a psychological and linguistic perspective. *Speech Language and Law, The International Journal of Speech, Language and the Law, 17,* 45–66.

Piolat, A., Olive, T., & Kellogg, R. T. (2005). Cognitive effort during note taking. *Applied Cognitive Psychology, 19* (3), 291–312.

Pomerantz, A. (1988). Offering a candidate answer: An information seeking strategy. *Communication Monographs, 55,* 360–373.

Pomerantz, J. (2005). A linguistic analysis of question taxonomies. *Journal of the American Society for Information Science and Technology, 56,* 715–728.

Powell, M. B., Wright, R., & Hughes-Scholes, C. H. (2011). Contrasting the perceptions of child testimony experts, prosecutors and police officers regarding individual child abuse interviews. *Psychiatry, Psychology and Law, 18* (1), 33–43.

Robinson, D. H., Katayama, A. D., Dubois, N. F., & Devaney, T. (1998). Interactive effects of graphic organizers and delayed review on concept application. *The Journal of Experimental Education, 67* (1), 17–31.

Rogers, L. E., & Farace, R. V. (1975). Relational communication analysis: New measurement procedures. *Human Communication Research, 1,* 222–239.

Ruhl, K. L., & Suritsky, S. (1995). The pause procedure and/or an outline: Effect on immediate free recall and lecture notes taken by college students with learning disabilities. *Learning Disability Quarterly, 18,* 2–11.

Schegloff, E. A. (2007). *Sequence Organization in interaction: Vol. 1: A primer in conversation analysis.* Cambridge, UK: Cambridge University Press.

Schegloff, E. A., Jefferson, G., & Sacks, H. (1977). The preference for self-correction in the organization of repair in conversation. *Language, 53,* 361–382.

Shuy, R. W. (1986). Language and the law. *Annual Review of Applied Linguistics, 7,* 50–63.

Sidnell, J. (2009). The design and positioning of questions in inquiry testimony. In S. Ehrlich & A. Freed (Eds.), *Why do you ask? The function of questions in institutional discourse.* Oxford, UK: Oxford University Press.

Ten Have, P. (1999). *Doing conversational analysis: A practical guide.* London, UK: Sage Publications.

Tracy, K., & Robles, J. (2009). Questions, questioning and institutional practices: An introduction. *Discourse Studies, 11,* 131–152.

Walsh, D., & Oxburgh, G. E. (2008). Investigative interviewing of suspects: Historical and contemporary developments in research. Forensic Update.

Wang, J. (2006). Questions and the exercise of power. *Discourse and Society, 17,* 529–548.

Wright, A. M., & Alison, L. (2004). Questioning sequences in Canadian police interviews: Constructing and confirming the course of events. *Psychology, Crime and Law, 10,* 137–154.

3

Recall, Verbatim Memory and Remembered Narratives

JAMES OST[1], ALAN SCOBORIA[2], TIM GRANT[3] AND GARY PANKHURST[4]
[1] University of Portsmouth, UK
[2] University of Windsor, Canada
[3] Aston University, Birmingham, UK
[4] New Scotland Yard, London, UK

There is ordinarily no directed and laborious effort to secure accuracy. We mingle interpretation with description, interpolate things not originally present, transform without effort and without knowledge.
(Bartlett, 1932, p. 96).

He said that I was evil and that nobody would believe me.
(Complainant in non-recent abuse case recalling events 20 years previously)

INTRODUCTION

Accounts of memory generally argue that it can be conceived as comprising three stages: encoding, storage and retrieval. In broad terms, encoding is the process by which information 'gets into' memory, storage describes the retention of that information and retrieval

Communication in Investigative and Legal Contexts: Integrated Approaches from Forensic Psychology, Linguistics and Law Enforcement, First Edition. Edited by Gavin Oxburgh, Trond Myklebust, Tim Grant and Rebecca Milne.
© 2016 John Wiley & Sons, Ltd. Published 2016 by John Wiley & Sons, Ltd.

describes the processes involved in 'getting the information out' again. The metaphor of a computer is often invoked. For example, encoding is like typing information into a document via the keyboard, storage is like saving the file to your hard drive and retrieval is the process of searching through the files on the hard drive to find the 'file' corresponding to the event to be retrieved. This metaphor captures many features of memory that will be familiar to readers. For example, you may not remember something because you were not paying attention to it (perhaps you nodded off during the critical part of a post-lunch talk). Thus, you would be unable to recall that part of the talk because you simply failed to encode it (because you were asleep). Perhaps this is the seventh or eighth talk you have been to on a similar topic. If so, you may find it difficult to differentiate between information that was provided at the third talk from information that was provided at the fourth. Finally, you may be unable to recall precisely what was said at a particular meeting until someone reminds you that it was the meeting to which everyone brought lunch. In this case you have been provided with a cue that (may) aid your retrieval of that particular memory.

Whilst this approach to memory can be useful in communicating wider ideas about memory processing, its simplicity is also misleading. It implies that as long as you encoded an event, it should be stored and thus able to be retrieved accurately (although there is certainly evidence that a small number of people possess – or can train – extraordinary abilities in this regard, these individuals are the exception, not the rule: LePort et al., 2012; Parker, Cahill & McGaugh, 2006[1]). It also implies that memory is a passive, rather than an active process (i.e. details are just 'filed away' for later use). Finally, it does not take account of the fact that psychologists have described many different 'kinds' of memory. There are memories that represent our knowledge about the world (semantic memory), memories for how to perform actions such as riding a bicycle (procedural memory), memories for the *past events* in our lives (episodic memory; Tulving, 2002) and even memories for our future plans (Graf & Uttl, 2001). The present chapter will focus on episodic memory as this is of most relevance to legal professionals (but see Conway, 2013, for a range of memory issues that experts are sometimes required to testify about in court).

In this chapter we first introduce the notion of episodic memory and the debates surrounding how episodic memories are retrieved – are they directly accessed representations of past events or do they inevitably entail reconstructive processes? Next we focus on how retrieved information is validated and converted into observable behaviour (i.e. a memory report or the act of remembering). Here we consider the role that retrieval conditions and the strategic regulation of output have on what is remembered. We then move on to discuss the ways in which we communicate our memories and how the immediate context can have a strong influence on what we eventually report of what we 'remember'. Finally, we conclude with some continuing challenges for investigative interviews with suspects and witnesses.

WHAT IS EPISODIC MEMORY?

In short, episodic memory generally refers to our memory for past events in our lives[2] – the 'what', 'where' and 'when' (Tulving, 2002, p. 3). Behaviourally, episodic memory is the capacity to experience and describe past perceptual states in the present. The father of the concept, Endel Tulving, argued that it is a hypothetical memory system distinct from other memory systems and constitutes a uniquely human ability (Tulving, 2002). It has been characterized as the ability to travel back in time in our own minds, coupled with a subjective awareness of that 'mental time travel' (referred to as 'autonoetic awareness'; Tulving, 1972). The final essential component in this mix is that it involves a 'self' that can engage in this mental time travelling, as well as exist in the present. Not everyone was initially convinced, arguing that what appeared to be episodic memory may simply be an extension of our semantic knowledge of the world (Horner, 1990). Nevertheless, evidence from case studies of patients with organic damage to the brain suggested that these two memory systems may be, at least partly, separable. For example, there are individuals who, following injury to the brain, experience severe deficits in their ability to recall personal information about themselves (episodic memory) without a concomitant reduction in their knowledge about the world or their ability to learn new facts (semantic memory) (Tulving, Schacter, McLachlan & Moscovitch, 1988).

As noted already, early models of memory focused on different kinds of 'stores' where memories were 'held'. Over the years, many different metaphors have been used to characterize the retrieval of episodic (and other) information from such stores (Roediger, 1980). One popular and persistent metaphor is that memory works like a video-camera, accurately recording and storing information from our lives, enabling it to be 'reviewed' (remembered) at a later date (e.g. Simons & Chabris, 2011). The clear implication is that information may be stored in memory but may simply be unavailable to recall (Loftus & Loftus, 1980). Yet an established body of literature shows that our memories of past episodes can sometimes be highly error-prone and that people can report rich false memories of events that never occurred (Bernstein & Loftus, 2009). Such errors have clear implications for the legal system in terms of their impact on the reliability of witness testimony and resulting court decisions (Ost & French, in press). How are these errors to be understood? Are they the inevitable result of the organization of episodic memory? Can the science of memory offer ways to reduce the potential for such errors by designing appropriate interview protocols and questioning strategies? Before answering that question, we need to understand what the research says about: (i) how we retrieve episodic memories (are memories accessed directly or are they accessed only following an effortful, reconstructive and potentially error-prone process?) and (ii) how those retrieved memories are converted into an act of observable remembering in an interview setting.

IS THE RETRIEVAL OF EPISODIC MEMORY DIRECT OR GENERATIVE?

One recent and influential model (the Self-Memory System, or SMS; Conway, 2005; Conway & Pleydell-Pearce, 2000) emphasizes – like Tulving – the strong interconnections between memory and our sense of self. According to the SMS, remembering is a dynamic, goal-driven process in which autobiographical memories are 'transitory dynamic mental constructions generated from an underlying knowledge base (Conway & Pleydell-Pearce, 2000, p. 261). Conway and Pleydell-Pearce (2000) argue that a set of long-term memory representations, referred to as the *working self*, recruits elements of our *autobiographical memory knowledge base* (information about our past) to address remembering goals in the present (e.g. describe everything you can about the bank robbery you witnessed yesterday). As everything is filtered through the working self and its current goals, memories that are not related to those goals may be inhibited from entering awareness. According to the SMS, it is the pattern of brain activation resulting from the meshing of these two components that gives rise to a memory. Such patterns can either be *generative* (arising from controlled and strategic memory retrieval by the *working self*) or *direct* (arising from a cue, without any attempt at retrieval by the *working self*). Importantly, though, for the SMS, even in the case of direct retrieval, the working self and its goals 'operate only *after* memory construction has taken place in the knowledge base (Conway & Pleydell-Pearce, 2000, p. 275). From the point of view of SMS, the vast majority of remembering is a generative (reconstructive) process that is deliberate and effortful.

Others argue that the *generative* nature of episodic recall may have been overstated. For example, in a series of three experiments, Uzer, Lee and Brown (2012) provided evidence that some of the assumptions underlying the *generative* account of episodic recall might be due to the way in which previous experiments have been conducted. A typical pattern in such studies is that people take longer to retrieve memories cued by emotional states (e.g. *happy, sad*) than memories involving object descriptions (e.g. *car, book*). The common explanation for this finding is that object cues are more concrete and, thus, a better 'match' for information in memory than emotion words, which are more abstract. Participants take longer to retrieve memories in response to emotion words, it is argued, because they first have to convert the abstract emotional word into a more concrete and effective memory cue *before* a memory can be accessed. Uzer et al. (2012) challenged this accepted wisdom and found that, although participants reported experiencing direct retrieval (i.e. the memory just 'came to mind') more often in response to object cues than emotion cues, there were in fact no differences in response times between directly accessed and generated memories as a function of cue type. In other words, participants did not find it harder (i.e. took longer) to *generate* memories in response to emotional than object words and the previous findings may have simply been because a lot of object memories are accessed by direct retrieval, thus skewing the response time data. On this basis, they argue that the emphasis of the SMS – that the retrieval of episodic memories is a deliberate, effortful and thus inherently reconstructive and error-prone process – may have been exaggerated.

HOW ARE EPISODIC MEMORIES VALIDATED AND COMMUNICATED?

The preceding discussion has focused on the process of retrieving episodic information and, although there is clearly more research needed in this area, what is clear is that sometimes memories are directly accessed, and sometimes they are more generative. The degree to which memory reports reflect these extremes is highly dependent on how and why events are remembered. One key influence on remembering is the retrieval context, which refers to the parameters that shape the reason that the memory report is being provided – why is memory being accessed, to whom is the information being provided, what are the potential consequences of reporting or not reporting that information and so forth? In other words, once a memory has been retrieved, the next step is to convert that retrieved memory into an observable (social) act of remembering. Blank (2009) argues that this transition from the 'cognitive' to the 'social' elements of memory retrieval has largely been ignored by memory theorists, resulting in a somewhat disjointed explanatory framework (see also Nash, Wheeler & Hope, 2015). He proposes the term *remembering* to encompass an initial *memory retrieval* stage as well as two additional stages that he refers to as *validation* and *communication*.

Validating Our Recollections

In the *validation* stage, individuals attempt to assess whether what they have retrieved is a genuine memory. Blank (2009) argues that, in addition to qualities of the retrieved memory itself (e.g. the 'strength' of the memory trace), individuals rely on other sources of external information in order to make this judgement, particularly in situations of uncertainty (see also Jaeger, Cox & Dobbins, 2012, for a similar argument for recognition memory judgements). Variables such as the credibility of the source of the (mis)information (Lampinen & Smith, 1995; Scoboria, Wysman & Otgaar, 2012) or the plausibility of the event or detail (Mazzoni, Loftus & Kirsch, 2001; Pezdek, Finger & Hodge, 1997) are important factors influencing an individual's beliefs about retrieved events.

A number of lines of research address how people make decisions about the occurrence and accuracy of remembered events in circumstances in which the veracity of memories is in doubt. In research on the verification of memories, Wade, Nash and Garry (2014) asked individuals how they would go about verifying or refuting a memory that another person had told them had not occurred. They reported that people claim to seek input from social sources, seek physical evidence, seek memory cues and engage in internal cognitive processes (such as attempting to recall more details). They argued that people most frequently seek input from others when verifying memories due to the favourable balance between reliability of the verification method and the cost of accessing the method, as compared to the other verification methods, which were viewed as less reliable or more costly to access. Research on non-believed memories (vivid recollections that are no longer believed to genuinely reflect the past) demonstrates that people alter belief in existing memories due to numerous sources of information (Scoboria, Boucher & Mazzoni, 2015). These include, for example, multiple distinct types of social feedback, encountering physical evidence, coming to view an event as impossible, reattributing a memory as originating in another source, due to general beliefs about memory or because the memory is not consistent with one's view of oneself.

What this work shows is that beliefs about autobiographical events are influenced by many factors. Scoboria et al. (2014) provide evidence that *recollecting* an event and *believing* that an event occurred – often confounded in memory research – are, in fact, distinct processes. Their modelling showed measurement of the two constructs and a double dissociation where belief in the occurrence of an event, but not its recollection, was strongly predicted by the perceived plausibility of the event. In contrast, perceptual, re-experiencing and emotional features strongly predicted recollection, but not belief. Thus, it is possible to strongly believe that events have occurred without being able to recollect them (see also Mazzoni, Loftus & Kirsch, 2001; Scoboria, Lynn, Hessen & Fisico, 2007). This is a frequently reported experience, as in the examples of learning a story from family members about early childhood or learning from another person what happened on a night that cannot be recalled due to heavy drinking (Nash & Takarangi, 2011). Likewise, it is possible to clearly recollect something that you have come to decide did not happen, as in the example of non-believed memories (Mazzoni, Scoboria & Harvey, 2010). Scoboria et al. (2014) conclude that belief in the occurrence of recollected events is highly sensitive to social feedback, whether such feedback originated in oral utterances made by others or in the behaviour of others. The truth status ascribed to a memory is further influenced by whom the rememberer is interacting with at the time the memory is retrieved and communicated. This sensitivity of memory beliefs to social influence explains, in part, how it is that interviewers can come to distort memory reports. A large body of research documents that social factors such as providing negative feedback, repeating questions or pressuring individuals to provide responses to questions undermines the quality of reports (Ackil & Zaragoza, 2011; Gudjonsson, 2003).

Communicating Our Recollections

The next stage of Blank's (2009) model is *communication*, where we may choose (or are, in some contexts, required) to report our memory beliefs or recollections. At this stage, a number of additional processes come into play that impact: (i) what we select of the information we have retrieved to communicate and (ii) how we modify our memory report according to the demands of the situation. Conversational maxims (e.g. to provide relevant, reliable information) and situational demands (e.g., time pressure) shape which parts of our memory we choose to report. Likewise, the retrieval context can shape the level of detail that is provided – referred to as the 'grain size' of the response.

For example, a witness may be unsure of the fine-grained detail about whether a thief wore brown or black shoes. Rather than choose the fine-grained answer (i.e. 'brown' or 'black', with a 50% chance of being wrong), a witness may instead respond with the coarser-grained (but definitely accurate) answer 'dark shoes'.

However, witnesses may not spontaneously regulate their own output in this way unless they are told that they are allowed (or indeed expected) to do so (Goldsmith, Pansky & Koriat, 2014). Furthermore, witnesses are sometimes explicitly encouraged to provide fine-grained information that may be beyond their memorial ability (e.g. 'What colour of eyes did your assailant have?'). The more fine-grained and closed-ended questions become, the more likely that individuals will come to accept misleading cues. In such cases, linguistic opt outs (i.e. 'I don't know' or 'I did not see that') by the witness are important. However, while people use 'don't know' statements regularly in everyday discourse, they tend to favour answering questions, rather than opting out when in formal interview situations in which the interviewer holds a higher power status (e.g. police officer and witness). In formal interviews, interviewees are rarely encouraged to use 'don't know' responses (indeed, such responses are frequently discouraged; Schreiber Compo, Hyman Gregory & Fisher, 2010). This is noteworthy because a body of research shows that appropriate encouragement of 'don't know' responses enhances the quality of responding (Mulder & Vrij, 1996; Waterman, Blades & Spencer, 2004). Scoboria and Fisico (2013) found that encouraging witnesses to use 'don't know' responses increased the quality of their testimony precisely because it provided a linguistic 'opt out' that witnesses could use to regulate their own memory output (i.e. to withhold making a response if they are uncertain). Empowering witnesses to say 'don't know' is particularly helpful in avoiding erroneous responses to questions that have no answer (Scoboria, Memon, Trang & Frey, 2013; Waterman & Blades, 2011).

We also know that *who* the memory is being reported to can exert an influence on the way witnesses communicate what they remember. For example, mock witnesses focused more on *details* if they were describing an event to the police and more on *emotional content* if describing the same event to friends (Marsh, Tversky & Hutson, 2005). Observing these differences, some linguistic studies concentrate on the co-construction of witness narratives. Rock (2001) describes the process by which the free narrative recall of a witness in a serious crime is co-constructed into a usable statement including otherwise omitted detail of time and place and sequencing. These details, which might be omitted in other tellings of the story, required intervention by the investigative interviewer and, whilst such intervention was necessary, might be viewed as a potential point where there is danger of contamination of the witness' memory.

Simply stated, seemingly small changes in the retrieval context can result in notable changes in the quality of reports. There are many examples in the literature, two of which are provided here. Loftus and Zanni (1975) found that changing the indefinite article 'a' to the definite article 'the' in misleading questions led to higher acceptance of misinformation (see also Smeets et al., 2006). Scoboria and Talarico (2013) found that asking people to retrieve 'memories' versus asking them to retrieve 'events' from their past led to differences in belief in occurrence and other phenomenological features associated with the retrieved events. They conclude that participants assume that researchers are interested in memories for events that are both strongly believed to have occurred and are strongly recollected when they take part in memory studies. Such differences have little to do with the retrieval of memory per se; rather, they arise from the expectations about the purpose of the memory task that the rememberer has at the time that events are retrieved and reports are made. In sum, people provide memory reports that correspond to the environment in which the report is made.

People also tend to use language associated with remembering loosely and do not typically differentiate the specific information that they are relying on when making memory reports (Otgaar, Scoboria & Smeets, 2013). Smeets, Telgen, Ost, Jelicic and Merckelbach (2009) provide a cogent example. They asked individuals if they recalled seeing non-existent media footage for a public event (in this case the assassination of Dutch politician Pim Fortuyn). Consistent with preceding work using this method, two-thirds of those asked responded 'yes' to the question. However, when they followed up to clarify what people meant by this response, they found that 80% of these individuals did not understand the question that they had been asked. Just 10% claimed to have a clear episodic memory for the media footage. The key point here is that without taking the time to clarify the basis for the response, an interviewer would likely erroneously assume that the initial answer to the question reflected an episodic memory report. A complete understanding of memory reports requires attending to how the listener understands what it is that the person providing the report says.

PRACTICE

In this final section we outline some of the continuing challenges that investigative interviewers face when applying the principles of memory research to the practice of achieving best evidence from witnesses and suspects.

Skills Fade in Training Protocols

The fact that the retrieval context can have such a powerful effect on memory reports is one reason why investigative interviewing protocols (e.g. the cognitive interview; Fisher, Geiselman & Amador, 1989) contain components that state the conversational maxims in advance (e.g. 'Tell me in as much detail as you can', 'If you don't know, don't guess', 'Say *don't know* if I ask a question you cannot answer') and transfer control to the interviewee to allow them to self-pace their recall and legitimize them to regulate their own memory responses. One ongoing problem is this regard is the 'skill-fade' demonstrated over many studies that practitioners' use of these interviewing techniques only seems to persist for around six months following training (Clarke & Milne, 2001). One explanation for these challenges in skill acquisition and maintenance is that best practice information gathering techniques are difficult to learn because they differ from everyday conversational norms and are also different from stereotypes about the ways in which interviews are conducted. Beyond police and forensic practice, many other professions also tend to believe that interviews involve an interviewer asking pointed questions, to which interviewees provide responses (e.g. see Roter & Hall, 1987, for a discussion of medical doctors). It is challenging to shift from probative to interviewee-centered interviews. Forensic interviewers would seem to have something to learn from the interviewing techniques used by clinical psychologists, who have a long history of emphasizing the gathering of information from individuals in their own words (albeit for quite different purposes).

The Impact of Implicit Theories about Memory

Investigators hold implicit theories about memory (i.e. that it operates like a video-recorder) similar to those held by the public and other professional groups (e.g. Wise, Safer & Maro, 2011). The British Psychological Society's *Guidelines on Memory and the Law* (2008) has been available for some years, and provides clear advice on the potential areas for concern. Whilst some key points have filtered into training (mainly around inappropriate questioning styles and interrogative pressure), the research knowledge behind the key points may not have received the same attention or understanding. A potential example of conflict between investigative practice and lessons from research is set out below.

In many countries, police interviewing adheres to the PEACE model.[3] In a standard PEACE interview, information provided in an initial free recall phase is followed up with more specific questions. Each topic is then summarized, moving from the general to the specific, coarse-grain to fine-grain information. There is a pressure on the investigator to try to close gaps in an account and to seek to deal with inconsistencies at the investigation stage. They will look for the points to prove, the necessary components to prove the criminal offence. There will also be a secondary imperative to obtain information of relevance to the investigation from which new lines of enquiry may emerge. As noted already, this focus on resolving inconsistencies and obtaining additional information may encourage the witness to generate increasingly fine-grained responses that are beyond their memorial ability. In addition, the production of fine-grained details may lead to a 'trivial persuasion' effect where people make incorrect inferences about the quality of a memory report, based on the level of detail it contains (Bell & Loftus, 1989). Memory reports that contain specific details – regardless of their relevance – are more persuasive than those that do not. However, the majority of this work has examined the effects of 'trivial persuasion' on jury decision-making – its effects on investigative interviewing remain an important avenue for future research.

Memory for Conversations

One special case of an episodic memory that requires more attention in the forensic context concerns remembered conversations. The issue of direct speech is of particular concern for investigative interviewers given that it may provide a crucial element of a criminal offence. The words reportedly used by a suspect can go directly to issues of motive and intent or, in sexual offences, the issue of consent. Direct speech is often highlighted during a trial for this very reason. It is clear that the findings of memory research in this area are crucial to the understanding of the confidence that may be placed in memories of long-remembered conversations, particularly those recalled as verbatim. Woodhams and Grant (2006) summarize research considering conversations between sexual offenders and their attackers, noting that victim statements that do not report conversation are 'very rare' (p. 246). They also note that fuzzy-trace theory (Reyna & Brainerd, 1995) would suggest that while 'memory of actual words might be poor, memory for the gist of what was said is much better' (p. 251). Work reviewed by Campos and Alonso-Quecuty (2006) supports this view on the basis that the 'verbatim trace represents the item's surface form whereas the gist trace represents the semantic, relational, and elaborative properties of the stimulus' (p. 29) and thus is better recalled. In addition, some research shows that participants report what they *intended to say*, rather than what they actually said (Parks, 1997). Clearly then investigative reliance on the actual words of recalled conversation has to be subject to question (for a review see Davis & Friedman, 2007).

One linguistic critique of the standard psychological methods used in these studies into *verbatim* versus *gist* memory is that they largely ignore the interactive. That is to say, experimental conditions expose participants to auditory or video conversations and then test recall. A further critique is the lack of attention to what linguistic aspects of conversation are better recalled. Psychological studies of language comprehension (e.g. Gernbacher, 1997) suggest differential attention to different aspects of speech, for example that early words in sentences and clauses receive greater attention, that noun phrases containing indefinite articles require more processing than those containing definite articles and that certain types of sentence structure require increased processing load to comprehend. From such observations it is quite possible to develop predictions and hypotheses where different aspects of verbatim conversations might be better recalled. Clearly then, further research is required in the forensic arena around the recall of conversations.

CONCLUSION

At the outset of this chapter, we noted a few of the common metaphors about what memory 'is' (Roediger, 1980). These mostly revolve around some kind of idea of a store in which information is kept. We have hopefully convinced the reader that episodic remembering is far more than simply 'retrieving memories' from a 'store'. What we retrieve is, to a certain extent, reconstructed and subject to our current goal state. What we select and report of what we have retrieved is under strategic control (Koriat & Goldsmith, 1996), subject to metacognitive monitoring (Mazzoni & Kirsch, 2002) and sensitive to the social context (Blank, 2009). Retelling or remembering, then, is most definitely not the same as recalling or recollecting (Marsh, 2007) and appropriately structuring the retrieval context is the key to increasing the quality of witness testimony.

NOTES

1. These remarkable abilities are domain-specific however. Individuals with highly superior autobiographical memories (HSAMs) are just as likely to develop false memories in laboratory experiments (Patihis et al., 2013).

2. Not all episodic mental representations are about the past. The term future episodic thinking refers to our ability to plan ahead (i.e. to remember our appointment at the dentist) and neurological evidence shows that parts of the brain involved remembering the past are also involved in imagining the future (Schacter, Addis & Buckner, 2007).

3. PEACE is an acronym that stands for the phases of an interview – Planning and preparation, Engaging with the interviewee and explaining the interview process, gaining an Account, Closure of the interview and Evaluation (Clarke, Milne & Bull, 2011).

REFERENCES

Ackil, J. K., & Zaragoza, M. S. (2011). Forced fabrication versus interviewer suggestions: Differences in false memory depend on how memory is assessed. *Applied Cognitive Psychology, 25*, 933–942.

Bartlett, F. C. (1932). *Remembering: A study in experimental and social psychology*. Cambridge, UK: Cambridge University Press.

Bell, B. E., & Loftus, E. F. (1989). Trivial persuasion in the courtroom: The power of (a few) minor details. *Journal of Personality and Social Psychology, 56*, 669–679.

Bernstein, D. M., & Loftus, E. F. (2009). How to tell if a particular memory is true or false. *Perspectives on Psychological Science, 4*, 370–374.

Blank, H. (2009). Remembering: A theoretical interface between memory and social psychology. *Social Psychology, 40*, 164–175.

British Psychological Society. (2008). *Guidelines on memory and the law: Recommendations from the scientific study of human memory*. Leicester, UK: British Psychological Society.

Campos, L., & Alonso-Quecuty, M. (2006). Remembering a criminal conversation: Beyond eyewitness testimony. *Memory, 14*, 27–36.

Clarke, C., & Milne, R. (2001). *National evaluation of the PEACE investigative interviewing course*. London, UK: Home Office.

Clarke, C., Milne, R., & Bull, R. (2011). Interviewing suspects of crime: The impact of PEACE training, supervision and the presence of a legal advisor. *Journal of Investigative Psychology and Offender Profiling, 8*, 149–162.

Conway, M. A. (2005). Memory and the self. *Journal of Memory and Language, 53*, 594–628.

Conway, M. A. (2013). On being a memory expert witness: Three cases. *Memory, 21*, 566–575.

Conway, M. A., & Pleydell-Pearce, C. W. (2000). The construction of autobiographical memories in the self memory system. *Psychological Review, 107*, 261–288.

Davis, D., & Friedman, R. D. (2007). Memory for conversation: The orphan child of witness memory researchers. In M. P. Toglia, J. D. Read, D. R. Ross, & R. C. L. Lindsay (Eds.), *Handbook of eyewitness memory, Vol. 1: Memory for events* (pp. 3–52). Mahwah, NJ: Erlbaum.

Fisher, R. P., Geiselman, R. E., & Amador, M. (1989). Field test of the cognitive interview: Enhancing the recollection of actual victims and witnesses of crime. *Journal of Applied Psychology, 74*, 722–727.

Gernbacher, M. (1997). Two decades of structure building. *Discourse Processes, 23*, 265–304.

Goldsmith, M., Pansky, A., & Koriat, A. (2014). Metacognitive control of memory reporting. In T. J. Perfect & D. S. Lindsay (Eds.), *The sage handbook of applied memory* (pp. 481–500). Los Angeles, CA: Sage.

Graf, P., & Uttl, B. (2001). Prospective memory: A new focus for research. *Consciousness and Cognition, 10,* 437–450.

Gudjonsson, G. H. (2003). *The psychology of interrogations and confessions: A handbook.* Chichester, UK: John Wiley & Sons, Ltd.

Horner, M. D. (1990). Psychobiological evidence for the distinction between episodic and semantic memory. *Neuropsychological Review, 1,* 281–321.

Jaeger, A., Cox, J. C., & Dobbins, I. G. (2012). Recognition confidence under violated and confirmed memory expectations. *Journal of Experimental Psychology: General, 141,* 282–301.

Koriat, A., & Goldsmith, M. (1996). Monitoring and control processes in the strategic regulation of memory accuracy. *Psychological Review, 103,* 490–517.

Lampinen, J. M., & Smith, V. L. (1995). The incredible (and sometimes incredulous) child witness: Cild eyewitnesses' sensitivity to source credibility cues. *Journal of Applied Psychology, 80,* 621–627.

LePort, A. K. R., Matfield, A. T., Dickinson-Anson, H., Fallon, J. H., Stark, C. E. L., Kruggel, F., … McGaugh, J. L. (2012). Behavioral and neuroanatomical investigation of Highly Superior Autobiographical Memory (HSAM). *Neurobiology of Learning and Memory, 98,* 78–92.

Loftus, E. F., & Loftus, G. R. (1980). On the permanence of stored information in the human brain. *American Psychologist, 35,* 409–420.

Loftus, E. F., & Zanni, G. (1975). Eyewitness testimony: The influence of the wording of a question. *Bulletin of the Psychonomic Society, 5,* 86–88.

Marsh, E. J. (2007). Retelling is not the same as recalling: Implications for memory. *Current Directions in Psychological Science, 16,* 16–20.

Marsh, E. J., Tversky, B., & Hutson, M. B. (2005). How eyewitnesses talk about events: Implications for memory. *Applied Cognitive Psychology, 19,* 531–544.

Mazzoni, G., & Kirsch, I. (2002). Autobiographical memories and beliefs: A preliminary metacognitive model. In T. Perfect & B. Schwartz (Eds.), *Applied metacognition* (pp. 121–145). Cambridge, UK: Cambridge University Press.

Mazzoni, G. A. L., Loftus, E. F., & Kirsch, I. (2001). Changing beliefs about implausible autobiographical events: A little plausibility goes a long way. *Journal of Experimental Psychology: Applied, 7,* 51–59.

Mazzoni, G., Scoboria, A., & Harvey, L. (2010). Non-believed memories. *Psychological Science, 21,* 1334–1340.

Mulder, M. R., & Vrij, A. (1996). Explaining conversation rules to children: An intervention study to facilitate children's accurate responses. *Child Abuse and Neglect, 7,* 623–631.

Nash, R. A., & Takarangi, M. K. T. (2011). Reconstructing alcohol-induced memory blackouts. *Memory, 19,* 566–573.

Nash, R. A., Wheeler, R. L., & Hope, L. (2015). On the persuadability of memory: Is changing people's memories no more than changing their minds? *British Journal of Psychology, 106,* 308–326. doi: 10.1111/bjop.12074.

Ost, J., & French, C. C. (in press). How misconceptions about memory may undermine witness testimony. In P. Radcliffe, G. Gudjonsson & D. Wolchover (Eds.), *Witness testimony in sex cases.* Oxford, UK: Oxford University Press.

Otgaar, H., Scoboria, A., & Smeets, T. (2013). Experimentally evoking nonbelieved memories for childhood events. *Journal of Experimental Psychology: Learning, Memory and Cognition, 39,* 717–730.

Parker, E. S., Cahill, L., & McGaugh, J. L. (2006). A case of unusual autobiographical remembering. *Neurocase, 12,* 35–49.

Parks, T. E. (1997). False memories of having said the unsaid: Some new demonstrations. *Applied Cognitive Psychology, 11,* 485–494.

Patihis, L., Frenda, S. J., LePort, A. K. R., Petersen, N., Nichols, R. M., Stark, C. E. L., … Loftus, E. F. (2013). False memories in highly superior autobiographical memory individuals. *Proceedings of the National Academy of Sciences, 110,* 20947–20952.

Pezdek, K., Finger, K., & Hodge, D. (1997). Planting false childhood memories: The role of event plausibility. *Psychological Science, 8,* 437–441.

Reyna, V. F., & Brainerd, C. J. (1995). Fuzzy-trace theory: An interim synthesis. *Learning and Individual Differences, 7,* 1–75.

Rock, F. (2001). The genesis of a witness statement. *Forensic Linguistics: The International Journal of Speech, Language and the Law, 8,* 44–72.

Roediger, H. L. (1980). Memory metaphors in cognitive psychology. *Memory and Cognition, 8,* 231–246.

Roter, D. K., & Hall, J. A. (1987). Physicians' interviewing styles and medical information obtained from patients. *Journal of General Internal Medicine, 2,* 325–329.

Schacter, D. L., Addis, D. R., & Buckner, R. L. (2007). Remembering the past to imagine the future: The prospective brain. *Nature Reviews Neuroscience, 8,* 657–661.

Schreiber Compo, N., Hyman Gregory, A. R., & Fisher, R. P. (2010). Interviewing behaviors in police investigators: A field study of a current U.S. sample. *Psychology, Crime and Law, 18,* 359–375.

Scoboria, A., Boucher, C., & Mazzoni, G. (2015). Reasons for withdrawing belief in vivid autobiographical memories. *Memory, 23,* 545–562.

Scoboria, A., & Fisico, S. (2013). Encouraging and clarifying 'don't know' responses enhances interview quality. *Journal of Experimental Psychology: Applied, 19,* 72–82.

Scoboria, A., Jackson, D. L., Talarico, J., Hanczakowski, M., Wysman, L., & Mazzoni, G. (2014). The role of belief in occurrence within autobiographical memory. *Journal of Experimental Psychology: General, 143,* 1242–1258.

Scoboria, A., Lynn, S. J., Hessen, J., & Fisico, S. (2007). So *that* is why I don't remember: normalizing forgetting of childhood events influences false autobiographical beliefs but not memories. *Memory, 15,* 801–813.

Scoboria, A., Memon, A., Trang, H., & Frey, M. (2013). Improving responding to questioning using a brief retrieval training. *Journal of Applied Research in Memory and Cognition, 2,* 210–215.

Scoboria, A., & Talarico, J. M. (2013). Indirect cueing elicits distinct types of autobiographical event representations. *Consciousness and Cognition, 22,* 1495–1509.

Scoboria, A., Wysman, L., & Otgaar, H. (2012). Credible suggestions affect false autobiographical beliefs. *Memory, 5,* 429–442.

Simons, D. J., & Chabris, C. F. (2011). What people believe about how memory works: A representative survey of the U.S. population. *PLoS One, 6* (8), e22757.

Smeets, T., Jelicic, M., Peters, M. J. V., Candel, I., Horselenberg, R., & Merckelbach, H. (2006). 'Of course I remember seeing that film!'—How ambiguous questions generate crashing memories. *Applied Cognitive Psychology, 20,* 779–789.

Smeets, T., Telgen, S., Ost, J., Jelicic, M., & Merckelbach, H. (2009). What's behind crashing memories? Plausibility, belief, and memory of reports of having seen non-existent images. *Applied Cognitive Psychology, 23,* 1333–1341.

Tulving E. (1972). Episodic and semantic memory. In E. Tulving & W. Donaldson (Eds.), *Organization of memory* (pp. 381–403). New York: Academic Press.

Tulving, E. (2002). Episodic memory: From mind to brain. *Annual Review of Psychology, 53,* 1–25.

Tulving, E., Schacter, D. L., McLachlan, D. R., & Moscovitch, M. (1988). Priming of semantic autobiographical knowledge: A case study of retrograde amnesia. *Brain and Cognition, 8,* 3–20.

Uzer, T., Lee, P. J., & Brown, N. R. (2012). On the prevalence of directly retrieved autobiographical memories. *Journal of Experimental Psychology: Learning, Memory, and Cognition, 38,* 1296–1308.

Wade, K. A., Nash, R. A., & Garry, M. (2014). People consider reliability and cost when verifying their autobiographical memories. *Acta Psychologica, 146,* 28–34.

Waterman, A. H., & Blades, M. (2011). Helping children correctly say 'I don't know' to unanswerable questions. *Journal of Experimental Psychology: Applied, 17,* 396–405.

Waterman, A. H., Blades, M., & Spencer, C. P. (2004). Indicating when you do not know the answer: The effect of question format and interviewer knowledge on children's 'don't know' responses. *British Journal of Developmental Psychology, 22,* 335–348.

Wise, R. A., Safer, M. A., & Maro, C. M. (2011). What U.S. law enforcement officers know and belief about eyewitness factors, eyewitness interviews and identification procedures. *Applied Cognitive Psychology, 25,* 488–500.

Woodhams, J., & Grant, T. (2006). Developing a categorisation system for rapists' speech. *Psychology, Crime and Law, 12,* 245–260.

Section II

Communicating with Victims and Witnesses

4

Interviewing Child Witnesses

David La Rooy[1], Georgina Heydon[2], Julia Korkman[3]
and Trond Myklebust[4]

[1] *Royal Holloway University of London, UK*
[2] *RMIT University, Melbourne, Victoria, Australia*
[3] *Helsinki University Central Hospital, Finland*
[4] *Norwegian Police University College, Oslo, Norway*

INTRODUCTION

Given our current understanding and evidence-based approach to interviewing child witnesses, it is difficult to imagine a time when professionals were guided largely by their personal experiences of interviewing children, sometimes unrealistic beliefs about children's capabilities to remember and communicate their experiences, and authoritative pronouncements made by influential commentators. Over many decades of psychological and linguistic research we have learnt an enormous amount about children's cognitive strengths and limitations, and their motivations and emerging abilities to communicate their experiences. Many aspects of our current approach to interviewing children that are now considered *conventional wisdom*, were once bitterly contested, challenged and debated. Notably, it was previously thought that children were not capable of providing accounts of their experiences in response to 'open prompts' and therefore special

Communication in Investigative and Legal Contexts: Integrated Approaches from Forensic Psychology, Linguistics and Law Enforcement, First Edition. Edited by Gavin Oxburgh, Trond Myklebust, Tim Grant and Rebecca Milne.

diagnostic techniques were required (Ceci & Bruck, 1993; Ceci, Kulkofsky, Klemfuss, Sweeney & Bruck, 2007). Over the course of several decades, however, steady advances made through the integration of psychological and linguistic knowledge, experimental research and field studies of forensic interviews have led to untested and sometimes dangerous interviewing approaches being replaced by practices around which there is considerable professional agreement. In this chapter we will examine *the consensus* surrounding the complex nature of communication with children in forensic contexts and the key aspects about which all investigators should be knowledgeable.

DEVELOPMENTAL CONSIDERATIONS

Our approach to interviewing child witnesses is shaped by an understanding of children's emerging abilities and the numerous cognitive and developmental changes that occur throughout childhood and continue into early adulthood (Bauer & Fivush, 2014). Importantly, we should not think of 'children' simply as a single group, but rather as a set of individuals with a large range of differing capabilities across every stage from infancy, through to toddlerhood, childhood and teens. Each of these stages of development is associated with neurological developments that take place at different rates, resulting in individual and dynamic patterns of language use (Walker, 2013). Our understanding of developmental considerations has been contextualized with regard to interviewing child witnesses. Common norms and approaches have emerged that try to balance the needs of law enforcement, with the best interests of the children.

In particular, it is important to understand developmental factors surrounding memory, forgetting, reminiscence, false memory and suggestibility, as well as social and linguistic factors that impact on the dynamics of interviews and the accuracy and reliability of information that is obtained. Understanding relevant developmental considerations provides a framework within which we are able to have realistic expectations about what children are able to tell us about their experiences (Walker, 2013). Clear and realistic expectations must shape our approach to child interviewing so that children are not placed into contexts that produce unreliable information or where their credibility can be easily challenged (Lamb, Hershkowitz, Orbach & Esplin, 2008; Lamb, La Rooy, Malloy & Katz, 2011).

A common feature of many evidence-based approaches to interviewing child witnesses is that they are careful to consider children's strengths and limitations so that they are not interviewed in a manner that overreaches their mental abilities and current stage of development (Lamb et al., 2008, 2011; Poole & Lamb, 1998; Walker, 2013). It is important to emphasize that current approaches to child interviewing are thus intended to be developmentally sensitive, and although it is not possible to review all the relevant aspects of child development that are relevant for interviewing child witnesses in this chapter, we will discuss some important issues regarding language development and appropriate questioning of children.

CHARACTERISTICS OF LANGUAGE

Forensic interviewers need to be aware of several important dimensions of language when interviewing children, including phonology, vocabulary, syntax and pragmatics (De Villiers & De Villiers, 1974; Poole & Lamb, 1998; Walker, 2013). *Phonology* refers to the system of sounds that a language uses to create meaning and, consequently, a child's problems with articulation of such meaningful sounds can cause misunderstanding. In fact, the ability to produce phonemes correctly develops much more slowly than the ability to perceive them correctly. Infants can perceive differences in phonemes from as early as 10 months (Bohn, 2000), but many school-age children are unable to produce certain sounds accurately. This means that children who themselves do not differentiate between saying 'free' and 'three' can still perceive the difference in adult speech. This provides an opportunity to clarify a child's speech if the interviewer does not understand what the child is saying, but interviewers should avoid suggesting a specific interpretation as the child might acquiesce and accept the interviewer's interpretation even if it is not correct. The interviewer might instead need to follow up with a series of questions to provide clarification. Interviewers might be helped by knowing the typical phonetic characteristics of the local language in advance of the interview in order to be aware of the potentially problematic sounds they may encounter. Where a specialist in child language is consulted to provide information about pronunciation at a police station or child interviewing centre, it is important that the information is relevant to the regional language variety and accents. Phonology by its nature is specific to a particular language variety or accent and so children will also develop localized phonological patterns of errors (Vihman, 1981). Also, because articulation relies on the shape and development of the mouth and vocal organs, individual children will acquire the phonological system of their local variety at their own pace and with their own idiosyncratic pattern of pronunciation (Vihman, 1996).

It might be possible to discover some of the typical errors that an individual child makes by listening carefully to the child's speech during the preliminary stages of the interview. This would be particularly important when the interviewer does not share the child's regional variety or accent. The considerable variation in individual speech articulation makes it almost impossible to give useful advice that is relevant across regions and socioeconomic and cultural groups. As an example, for this chapter in English, there are some articulatory difficulties that children encounter that do appear to be universal for English at least and would be familiar to adult native speakers: consonant clusters, which are common to English, for instance *str/spr* (as in 'string' and 'spring') are reduced to just one or two consonant sounds, usually without the final sounds in the cluster; the interdental fricative *th* (as in 'teeth' and 'together') is commonly articulated as a labiodental fricative *f/v* (as in 'teef' and 'togever'); and the alveolar approximant *r* (as in 'real') can move towards the labialized velar approximant *w* (as in 'weal'). In most cases, these articulatory difficulties can be easily identified through the context and there is little doubt as to the intended meaning (I have *free* teddy bears/I have *three* teddy bears). However, personal names and place names can be especially problematic as the context might not provide any additional clues to the interviewer (e.g. Rhonda/Wanda). Similar articulatory difficulties and developments will be found for the different languages around the world.

Children's *vocabulary* and their semantic categorization of words develops over a long time and provides a critical building block for many other language processing abilities (Gathercole, Willis, Emslie & Baddeley, 1992). Although vocabulary is constantly developing, it has been estimated that a five-year-old child would have a vocabulary of between 5000 and 6000 words, indicating that children do have a large enough range of words to be able to describe experiences. The development of vocabulary is very much related to the *environment* in which the child lives, implying that children's linguistic abilities develop at different paces and different vocabularies will develop in different contexts (Bornstein, Haynes & Painter, 1998). A child may also understand some words in certain contexts but not in others (Wilson & Powell, 2001) and pre-school children can misinterpret a word in a new context, or appear to use words that they do not understand when they try to apply the known meaning to the new context (French & Nelson, 1985; Sandhofer & Smith, 2001).

The concept of 'time' develops with age (Friedman, 2014) and while knowing when events happened might be important in forensic

investigations, enquiries about time can be problematic when interviewing child witnesses. Children have difficulties reporting 'how many
times' or 'how long ago' something has taken place (Saywitz, Snyder &
Nathanson, 1999). Temporal terms, such as 'before' and 'after', may not
be completely understood until the age of seven (Walker, 1993, 2013)
and children have a limited capacity to identify days and times
accurately until at least ten years of age (Michel, Harb & Hidalgo,
2012; Poole & Lamb, 1998). Consequently, interviewers should avoid
questions about time terms unless they are sure that the interviewee
understands them.

Friedman (1991) showed that children as young as four years of age
were able to judge the relative recency of two events (one and seven
weeks back in time), as well as to account for the time of day the events
occurred. At the age of six years, the children were also able to tell the
day of the week, the month and the season of the event, something the
four-year-olds were not capable of doing. It is known that children
under the age of seven use different strategies for measuring time than
do older ones and that it is only at the age of ten that most children use
the same strategies as adults (Levin, Wilkening & Dembo, 1984; Michel
et al., 2012). Interviewers trying to establish the length of an event
need to keep in mind that younger children might actually describe the
intensity of the experience when talking about how 'long' something
went on (Wilson & Powell, 2001).

Nonetheless, although children do have a developing ability to
judge time accurately, we must remember than even adults have
trouble remembering specific time, days and dates. For example, most
adults would find it difficult to answer a question like 'what day of
the week were you interviewed for your first job?' When times and
dates are used to 'fact check' a child's account they can also prove
problematic and draw concerns (often unwarranted) about their credibility. Kebbell and his colleagues (2004) found that, when cross-
examining witnesses with intellectual disabilities, who, similarly to
children, may have problems with concepts related to time, lawyers
posed as many questions regarding times and dates as they did with
other witnesses. As Poole and Lamb (1998) note, it is generally considered more realistic to inquire about time by using meaningful
markers, such as asking whether the event occurred on a school day,
and to identify the time frame by asking more generally about the
context first.

Interviewers need to avoid using complex *syntax* or sentence constructions. This implies avoiding passive voice and using active sentences where possible, though there are some exceptions. Sentences
structured using a passive form have long been considered problematic

for children, as research has indicated that this grammatical structure is acquired late compared to active sentences (Maratsos, Fox, Becker & Chalkley, 1985; Romaine, 1984). However, more recent research challenges this assumption and concludes that children do acquire an abstract syntactic representation for the passive early on that is generalized to actional (e.g. *hit, touch*) and object-experiencer non-actional verbs (e.g. *frighten, upset*), but is not generalized to subject-experiencer non-actional verbs (e.g. *see*) until a later age (Thatcher, Branigan, McLean & Sorace, 2007).

Complex sentences often involve embedded clauses that separate the important parts of a sentence and require mental reconstruction by the listener. For example, adults have a tendency to separate the subject noun from the main verb with some kind of explanatory embedded clause, perhaps hoping to be more specific: *Did the car that you rode in last week during the school holidays belong to mum*? Studies have shown that simple, developmentally appropriate questions elicit the most accurate information from children and that multiple questions in one sentence as well as long and complicated sentences should be avoided (Brennan, 1995; Carter, Bottoms & Levine, 1996). For instance, Perry and colleagues (1995) showed that confusing language (including multipart questions, negatives, double negatives, complicated syntax or vocabulary) decreased the accuracy of reports by young witnesses.

The need to use developmentally sensitive language syntax in interviews is thus particularly important with pre-school children. However, older, school-aged children and even adults have difficulties understanding the type of linguistically complex questions that tend to be used in forensic proceedings (e.g. Kebbell & Giles, 2000; Kebbell & Johnson, 2000; Perry et al., 1995; Walker & Warren, 1995). Some sentence structures commonly used by police, for instance, have been shown to be almost non-existent in ordinary conversation. The subject-*then*-verb construction, as in 'The man *then* walked to the car' is almost exclusively 'policespeak', according to corpus analysis of British English (Fox, 1993) and the study from which this example is drawn demonstrated a strong tendency for police to use language that is uncommon in the speech of civilian adults. The strangeness and unfamiliarity of the language of legal processes has been well documented and its detrimental impact on the reliability and accuracy of statements made by adults and children can be considerable (Brennan & Brennan, 1988; Gibbons, 2003).

Interviewers should also mention the name of the person or the situation being referred to in order to avoid misunderstandings caused by so-called extended references, for instance by asking 'Did your *grandparents* visit you often?' instead of asking 'Did *they* visit you often?' (Carter et al., 1996; Walker, 2013). Children may also face difficulties in understanding what 'it' represents in sentences like 'Was it hot?', where 'it' on its own is an abstraction rather than a referent that is specified (Brennan, 1995). In short, interviewers should help children by asking about one concept at a time and placing the main idea early in the question. They should avoid using the passive voice and negative questions and construct questions without complex embedded clauses (Poole & Lamb, 1998).

Pragmatics refers to the social functions of language and includes understanding the social conventions of conversations (e.g. taking turns in discussions) as well as how to meaningfully use language in different social situations (Levinson, 1983). The forensic interview is a very unusual social situation for children. The questioning in a forensic interview differs greatly from the questioning that grown-ups more commonly use with children. A child is more likely to be familiar with a question–answer interaction where the grown-ups are 'testing' the child to see if he or she can produce correct answers. For example, 'what colour are daddy's shoes' is a test of a child's knowledge of colours rather than a request for information that is unknown to the grown-up. These different expectations about the interaction need to be explained and made clear to children.

Another pragmatic consideration is the way in which topics are managed across turns in an interaction. The tools we use to initiate, change or maintain conversational topics are complex, involving social rules of politeness and face. Yet topics are central to the organization of our conversations (Heritage & Watson, 1979). As these tools are only gradually acquired, young children tend to structure their conversations differently from older children and adults, and might jump from one topic to another abruptly. To maintain clarity of meaning, interviewers are advised to mention the topic repeatedly during a conversation (Poole & Lamb, 1998).

While topic structures across multiple-turn exchanges might not be fully developed in young children, children are able to understand the social pattern of questions and answers from an early age, and in general understand that questions require answers. The strong application of conversational rules like 'answer a question' can lead children to try to answer questions they have not understood (e.g. Aldridge & Wood, 1998), rather than break the conventions to request a clarification or provide a 'non-response' like 'I don't know'. Lamb and Brown (2006; see also Poole & Lamb, 1998) talk about implicit rules that guide conversations and note that if these rules are not specified, children (as well as adults) are likely to follow the rules that, in their experience, typically guide conversations.

In most conversations between adults and children, children are expected to give short and superficial answers to quite focused questions (Peterson, 1990). As mentioned above, children are familiar with situations where adults are testing their knowledge through posing questions and are used to a dialogue pattern that merely requires them to answer in a way that mirrors the presumption included in the adult's question, reflecting what the child thinks the adult wants to hear rather than what the child actually remembers (Ceci & Bruck, 1993). Instead, in forensic interviews, interviewers often have no forehand information of which there is absolute evidence; therefore they need to communicate in a way that differs from most everyday adult-to-child interaction, attempting to elicit as much and as specific information as possible from the child.

The powerful authority of a police officer can easily cause children, as well as other vulnerable groups, to accept changes to their version of events introduced by the police interviewer either in the course of the interview or during the summary phase, and this later appears as an inconsistency in the record of the interview or in cross-examination in court. In summarizing a child's contributions in an interview, some language strategies are more successful than others, and there are social and cultural factors affecting language that can have an impact on the child's capacity to respond appropriately to a question. For instance, we can expect that a police interview will present an unavoidable asymmetry in power between the police interviewer and child interviewee (Auburn, Drake & Willig, 1995; Drew & Heritage, 1992; Fox, 1993) and this is reinforced by language strategies habitually used by interviewers, like controlling the topic of conversation and designating when and for how long each participant will speak. In spite of these institutionalized practices there are opportunities to reduce this asymmetry as the interview proceeds, such as designing questions and prompts to reflect a less formal, more inclusive interaction (Heydon, 2008). In the summary phase, this means ensuring that the reformulation of the child's narrative is specifically framed as the child's own story by using phrases such as 'you told me that...' to preface a summary statement. In other parts of the interview, formality can be minimized through acknowledgement of the child's contribution as it is another important tool for reducing the distance between the participants. Neutral receipt markers or 'go on' prompts also provide reassurance that the interviewer is engaged and listening to the child's story. Neutrality in interviews is discussed further below.

PRE-SUBSTANTIVE CONSIDERATIONS

Interviewers need to be aware of the developmental level of the child's language acquisition and modify their own language use accordingly (De Villiers & De Villiers, 1974; Saywitz & Camparo, 1998; Walker, 2013). It is important to differentiate between the different aspects of communication that need to be addressed when obstacles to clear communication are identified. We need to know about issues surrounding the understanding of the particular words used and sentence structures when communicating with children (Walker, 2013). But beyond this, interviewers need to understand how children perceive the purpose, formality and pragmatics of an investigative interview. Given that we are concerned with child interviewing in a legal context, it is also crucial that the approach is framed by relevant law enforcement goals and evidentiary obligations.

Given the above concerns about the sometimes idiosyncratic development of a child's language, many interview guidelines suggest that interviewers explicitly communicate 'ground rules' to child interviewees before discussing the allegations or central concern of the interview (Lamb et al., 2008). Communication of the ground rules encourages children to feel that they are in control of the information that they provide in an interview and that they should not feel pressured to answer questions if they do not know the answers. For this reason, a common ground rule is to tell the child that if they do not know the answer to a question 'just say, I don't know'. Another important and related ground rule is to make clear to the child that they can ask interviewers to explain anything that they do not understand. Other common ground rules that investigative interviewers have found effective are communicating to the child 'don't guess – it's OK to say that you don't know' and 'correct me if I make a mistake' (Lamb et al., 2008, 2011). The ground rules are considered an important part of the pre-substantive phase of the interview because they are designed to remove implicit pressure on interviewees to guess if they are not really sure about what happened and/or to acquiesce to the interviewers suggestions by saying 'yes' (cf. Saywitz & Nathanson, 1993). The ground rules are intended to reduce the effects of suggestibility and misleading questions (e.g. see Lamb et al., 2008).

While the type of interaction prevailing in a forensic interview might seem strange to children, with the child being the informed expert and the interviewer the 'naïve partner' (Lamb & Brown, 2006), it is something that can be learned. Sternberg and her colleagues (1997) showed that if children are allowed a *practice interview* about a neutral event, conducted using open-ended prompts, they give more information in response to the first question in a subsequent investigative interview. Other authors, too, have emphasized the need for preparation and exercises to enhance the performance of children in interviews (Roberts, Brubacher & Powell, 2011; Saywitz et al., 1999; Wilson & Powell, 2001). Exercises can include practising the children's right to ask for clarification when they do not understand or a rapport-building phase using open-ended questions concerning the child's everyday life. Giving the child the opportunity to discuss a neutral topic before starting the actual investigative interview serves two primary purposes: it helps the child feel more at ease in the situation and it gives the interviewer a chance to make an informal assessment of the child's use of language (e.g. Saywitz & Camparo, 1998; Walker & Warren, 1995).

DIFFERENT TYPES OF INTERVIEWER UTTERANCE

Different types of 'interviewer utterances' including questions, requests, explanations and prompts can be used by interviewers in an attempt to elicit reliable and detailed information from a child interviewee. However, different utterances will affect the manner in which children are able to respond because interviewer utterances can target different memories and evoke different linguistic characteristics depending on their form and function (Fisher & Geiselman, 1992). Both the quality and accuracy of the child's testimony can be greatly affected by the way the interviewer seeks to elicit the information (e.g. for an overview of the research, see Lamb et al., 2008, 2011). In classifying interviewer utterances, the literature makes a general distinction between open-ended prompts, (which are also referred to as *invitations*), specific *directive* questions and closed *option-posing* yes/no questions. Suggestive questions can take many forms but characteristically either suggest an answer through their structure or delivery, or introduce information that has not already been provided by the child. We will discuss the implications of these types of interview utterances below.

Open-Ended Prompts and Invitations

Open-ended prompts are characterized by the fact that they elicit multiword responses from children and there are many reasons why they are highly recommended for interviewing child witnesses. Open-ended prompts tap free-recall memory and research has shown that the information provided in response to open-ended prompts is the most accurate (Lamb & Fauchier, 2001; Leichtman & Ceci, 1995; Orbach & Lamb,

2000, 2001; Orbach et al., 2000). Open-ended prompts also lead to clearer and more credible reports from children than more focused question types (Ghetti, Goodman, Eisen, Jianjian & Davis, 2002). Children do not contradict themselves when open-ended prompts are used across multiple situations even though children may provide new information or elaborate on previously recalled information (La Rooy, Katz, Malloy & Lamb, 2010; La Rooy, Lamb & Pipe, 2009; Orbach, Lamb, La Rooy & Pipe, 2012). Furthermore, open-ended prompts can be used irrespective of the age of the child and the length of time between the interview and the alleged events. Young children do provide fewer details to open prompts than older children and adults, but even young children are able to provide more details to open prompts than they would in response to focused direct questions (Lamb et al., 2003; Sternberg, Lamb, Orbach, Esplin & Mitchell, 2001).

Even if responses to open-prompts are initially brief, the interviewer can follow up with additional open prompts rather than resorting to closed and focused questions. In this situation, a technique that interviewers find useful is to pair information provided by the child in a previous response with an additional open prompt. For instance: 'Earlier you mentioned [person, object, or action], tell me everything about that' (Aldridge & Wood, 1998; Lamb et al., 2003, 2008; Orbach & Lamb, 2000). The narrative quality of descriptions of past events elicited in this way by open prompts is also perceived as being more truthful and credible by fact finders and juries alike and these types of accounts are much more robust to challenge and result in more guilty verdicts (Pipe, Orbach, Lamb, Abbott & Stewart, 2008).

Specific and Direct Questions

It is highly unusual to see forensic interviews with children where the interviewer does not ask specific and direct questions in an attempt to elicit and/or clarify information. Due to children's emerging cognitive abilities, specific and direct questions can, however, pose problems for some children (and even some adults). They are sometimes misunderstood and they can exacerbate miscommunication. Part of the problem with specific and direct questions is that they elicit both highly accurate as well as highly inaccurate information. Accurate information comes when the focused questions tap into semantic memory (see Lamb et al., 2008, 2011). This is memory that includes facts about aspects of our lives rather than our individual experiences located in time and space. For example, questions like 'what school do you go to?' and 'what's your sister's name?' do not involve a memory search of past experiences. However, just because children can provide impressive and accurate answers to these types of questions does not mean that they can answer all focused questions accurately. Focused questions that require the child to recall details of an event or experience (e.g. episodic memory) are likely to produce far less accurate information than questions that require the child to access semantic memory.

One problem with focused questions is that children use words before they understand them and they have emerging abilities to understand concepts that adults take for granted (Walker, 2013). For example, simple concepts like behind/in front can be understood differently by children compared with adults. If asked, adults know what is meant by the 'front' of the house but a child who plays at the back might perceive this as being the 'front' or most important side of the house. Similarly, enquiries about before/after, times/dates/ages, size/height/weight, same/different and neither/either can also prove difficult. Children will often provide answers to these questions but if they do not have sufficient understanding of the concepts underlying the questions, then misunderstandings can occur. To complicate matters, children may also acquiesce to suggested responses when they do not know the answer (Pipe, Sutherland, Webster, Jones & La Rooy, 2004).

A notable feature of specific and direct questions is that children provide answers to questions even when the information being sought was never encoded or was not remembered very well. This is especially problematic when interviews use specific and direct questions to test the 'truth' or plausibility of what is being alleged. For example, in Commonwealth countries most coins have the profile of the Queens's head on one side. Most people who have used these coins would have no trouble recognizing them but nonetheless would have trouble answering a seemingly simple question such as 'Which direction does the queen's head face?' – for most the answer would be a guess. In forensic interviews questions like 'what finger did he use?' and 'what was he wearing' may well be too specific to be answered correctly, and 'I don't know' answers to focused questions like these should not be greeted suspiciously.

Some specific and direct questions also lead to confusion due to our assumptions about the world and implied meanings that adults attach to certain words or concepts. Jones and Krugman (1986) reported a case study in which a three-year-old victim of sexual assault and attempted murder identified the colour of the suspect's car as being 'orange' when it was in fact 'black'. Thus a focused question as simple as 'what colour was the car?' can lead to a child answering from their perspective and providing the colour of the interior, whereas adults always assume the colour of a car refers to its exterior.

In grammatical terms, the use of the modal *can* modifies the verb *tell* to produce an utterance that on the surface is a yes/no question about the child's ability to tell or describe, as in 'can you tell me...' or 'can you describe for me...'. In pragmatic terms, however, these questions are generally understood as an implied (embedded) directive to tell or describe. The indirectness associated with using a yes/no question to give a directive is considered polite as it creates a semantic distance between the request and the obligation to comply. In the context of a police–child interaction, politeness features like this are often used to reduce the sense of police authority and demonstrate concern and respect for the child. Although politeness is an important function of language, with school-age children forensic interviewers are advised not to add modifiers such as 'can you' to soften the impact of the requests because it can lead to misunderstanding and children as old as 8–10 years can still interpret the question literally (Heydon, 1998, 2005) and provide a yes/no response to an embedded request for information.

Interviewers must be sensitive to the difficulties experienced by children in understanding hypothetical, multifaceted and complex sentences that connect ideas and/or use negatives such as *'You had a bruise, did you not?'* (Powell & Thompson, 1994). Furthermore, interviewers are discouraged from using questions regarding intent (Why _____? questions) as these may confuse children. Through specific and direct questions the interviewer may also implicitly point the child's responses in a particular direction that confirms the interviewer's preconceptions of the events (confirmation bias) rather than eliciting the child's uncontaminated report (e.g. Ceci & Bruck, 1995).

CHILDREN AND INSTITUTIONALIZED LEGAL LANGUAGE

Research studying children's language development has provided vital evidence to support age-appropriate questioning. Previously many professionals in the field had suspected that children were unreliable witnesses, prone to giving inconsistent and unpredictable responses to seemingly ordinary questions (Ceci & Bruck, 1993). However, research has been able to show how children can misinterpret questions, often taking a literal understanding of figurative speech, for example. Many of these issues and others that we have discussed in this chapter apply to contexts beyond the forensic interview. Complex grammatical structures and the formality of legal language combine to create obstacles for children and adults trying to communicate effectively in a police interview or courtroom.

With regard to children and the legal process, there are today two parallel legal systems for how children's testimonies are presented and used as evidence in court. First, the 'Nordic-Model' (Denmark, Finland, Iceland, Norway and Sweden), where the video of the child's interview is accepted in court as the evidence-in-chief, thus negating the need for the child to attend court, provide evidence or be cross-examined. In other words, the child's involvement in the judicial process almost always comes to an end after the interview, even if the case is appealed (Myklebust, 2012). Second, there is the legal process where the child is cross-examined in court (Henderson, 2012). Brennan (1994) discusses the difficulties experienced by child witnesses being cross-examined in court. Brennan (1994) presents findings of a study that tested children on their comprehension of various types of questions by evaluating their accuracy when they are asked to repeat the questions word for word. Brennan found that 85% of the time '... *across all ages [6 to 15 years] and ability groups ... the tested children failed to hear certain questions which were chosen from courtroom transcripts ... in terms of the sense ...*' (1994, p. 205). Critically, the study found that responses such as 'I don't know' and 'I can't remember' can indicate a failure to comprehend the question, rather than a lack of knowledge or ability to recall events. Such a failure might easily occur in the unusual surroundings of the courtroom and when the language usage is entirely unfamiliar to the child (Saywitz & Nathanson, 1993). The list of features common to courtroom language, including complex structures (e.g. embeddings, negative questions and tag questions), difficult vocabulary (legalese, jargon, archaic structures) or speaking for another (including repeating the child's words) are also commonly found in forensic interviewing (Heydon, 2013; Rock, 2007; Spencer & Lamb, 2012).

Zajac, Gross and Hayne (2003) found that, in court proceedings, children were frequently cross-examined using an inappropriate questioning style. Defence lawyers' questions included complex questions to a significant degree, which caused as much as 75% of the children to change aspects of their testimonies. In another study, Zajac and Hayne (2003) found that the accuracy of five- and six-year-old witnesses severely declined as a result of being interviewed in cross-examination style where the language was too complicated to be readily understood by the children. Brennan and Brennan (1988) found that children testifying in trials were often faced with what the authors called 'strange language', that is questions posed in such a confusing way that they could not be understood and much less appropriately answered. According to Brennan (1995), cross-examination strategies used in court deny children any possibility to come forward with their own experiences, as children are faced with questions that are hard to decode. Kebbell and Johnson (2000) further demonstrated that (adult) witnesses' accuracy was reduced when attorneys posed confusing questions. Kebbell, Hatton & Johnson (2004) showed that lawyers failed to modify their language when interviewing witnesses with intellectual disabilities, as the cognitive capacities of the witnesses would have required.

In their study, Zajac and colleagues (2003) found that defence and prosecution lawyers differed in their language use, notably in that defence lawyers used more complex and grammatically confusing language. The authors attributed this difference to the fact that prosecution lawyers were more often specialized in representing children and thus could be expected to have more knowledge on how to interview children than lawyers who are used to representing adults.

Suggestibility

There are many varieties of suggestibility that have been studied that require both psychological and linguistic perspectives to fully understand. Varieties include misleading questions, misleading information and props, repeated questions (Poole & White, 1991), social pressure, peer pressure, imagination inflation, inappropriate encouragement and praise, asking about things that did not happen, negative reinforcement and appeals to authority, to name but a few.

Suggestive questions can be particularly influential when the memory of an event is not rich or recent, when the question asked is complicated and, therefore, confusing, or when the interviewer appears to have such authority that the witness feels compelled to accept the interviewer's suggestion. There are numerous examples of children making false allegations as a result of repeated suggestive interviewing (e.g. Bruck, Ceci, Francoeur & Renick, 1995; Poole & Lindsay, 1995). Among such examples is the widely publicized McMartin Preschool Case, where seven pre-school teachers, including several elderly women, were accused of having abused many hundreds of children over a period of more than ten years. Garven, Wood, Malpass and Shaw (1998) derived a number of suggestive interviewing techniques based on the transcribed interviews used in the McMartin case and showed that by using these techniques (suggestive questioning combined with social pressure, reinforcement and removal from direct experience), 58% of the children interviewed in their experimental study made false accusations.

Younger children are more vulnerable to the deleterious effects of suggestive questions than older children (e.g. Ceci & Bruck, 1995; Goodman & Aman, 1990; Leichtman & Ceci, 1995; Poole & Lindsay, 1998; White, Leichtman & Ceci, 1997). Geddie, Fradin and Beer (2000) found that, while other child characteristics, such as metamemory ability, intellectual functioning and temperament, were helpful in predicting the accuracy of children's recall and resistance to misleading questions, the child's age remained the best predictor for the amount of information that the child recalled and for the child's suggestibility.

Fortunately, over recent decades the problems with suggestive questions have become well established and there is widespread agreement that suggestive techniques should not be used in interviews. Indeed, inspection of forensic interviews by interviewers from a variety of backgrounds reveals that suggestive questions number around 10% or below in forensic interviews. In order to avoid the problems associated with suggestive questions, interviewers should practise using question forms that eliminate suggestive elements and train themselves to rely on open prompts as much as possible.

Credibility Assessments

Many legal cases are made challenging by an absence of absolute evidence. In the absence of any reliable method of credibility assessment based on children's disclosures, assessors of CSA suspicions often need to rely on contextual information that can be assessed and validated against known facts. For example, a child might describe events occurring at a specific place, and in order to assess the credibility of the disclosure, assessors might check whether the information about the location provided by the child matches the actual location. This kind of careful assessment requires detailed and reliable information elicited during the interview with the child. In order to obtain as much information as possible, the interviewers' skill is of central importance in ensuring that the 'facts' have been obtained in a reliable way. Low-quality interviews tend to provide little or contradictory information, even when there is a strong suspicion that abuse has occurred. This is often the result of questioning strategies that rely predominantly on closed questions without any effort to utilize open prompts when seeking information.

In such cases, even when there is a strong suspicion that abuse has occurred, fact finders are often reluctant to place reliance on the information before them. This is because the questions and tactics used in low-quality interviews have also been shown to elicit erroneous information in many studies of suggestibility and false memory. Placing reliance on low-quality interviews heightens the risk that innocent persons are found guilty of child abuse, which can have profound effects on the lives of the individuals involved. Interviewers and fact finders should take into account potential pre-interview contamination when planning and assessing the interviews, but these risks are often not fully understood by fact finders and other professionals involved in the decision-making process. It is thus important to recognize the role of experts on memory and communication in being able to provide opinions in cases where children have been interviewed about their experiences.

PUTTING THEORY INTO PRACTICE

The most well-known and widely studied interviewer training system is the freely available NICHD Protocol developed by Lamb and colleagues (2000, 2007, 2008). It has been developed with reference to child development issues, including linguistic capabilities, memory and suggestibility, forensic needs, interviewer behaviour and the effects of stress and trauma by a team of researchers, interviewers, police officers and legal professionals. The purpose of the protocol has been to operationalize the 'consensus' approach to interviewing children. It is important to emphasize that the team of researchers directly involved in the development of the NICHD Protocol have drawn from a robust literature focusing on children's capabilities involving hundreds (if not thousands) of researchers worldwide concerned about issues surrounding interviewing child witnesses. More than a decade of research has shown that effective interviewer training can begin with the proper use of the NICHD Protocol because it helps interviewers (who often are not trained in issues about children memory and communication) to maximize the amount of information obtained using open-ended prompts. The NICHD Protocol requires that fewer focused questions be used and does not advocate the use of anatomical dolls and other risky techniques. The NICHD Protocol has been designed to 'dovetail' into existing interviewing systems (e.g. Ministry of Justice, 2011) and is referred to in numerous formalized interview guidelines throughout the world.

REFERENCES

Aldridge, M., & Wood, J. (1998). *Interviewing children: A guide for child care and forensic practitioners*, New York: John Wiley & Sons Ltd.

Auburn, T., Drake, S., & Willig, C. (1995). 'You punched him, didn't you?' Versions of violence in accusatory interviews. *Discourse and Society, 6*(3), 353–386.

Bauer, P. J., & Fivush, R. (2014). *The Wiley handbook on the development of children's memory* (Vols. 1 and 2). Hoboken, NJ: John Wiley & Sons, Inc.

Bohn, O.-S. (2000). Linguistic relativity in speech perception: An overview of the influence of language experience on the perception of speech sounds from infancy to adulthood. In S. Niemeier & R. Dirven (Eds.), *Evidence for linguistic relativity*. Amsterdam, the Netherlands: John Benjamins Publishing Company.

Bornstein, M. H., Haynes, M. O., & Painter, K. M. (1998). Sources of child vocabulary competence: A multivariate model. *Journal of Child Language, 25* (2), 367–393.

Brennan, M. (1994). The battle for credibility—Themes in the cross examination of child victim witnesses. *International Journal for the Semiotics of Law, 7* (1), 51–73.

Brennan, M. (1995). Cross examining children in criminal courts: Child welfare under attack. In J. Gibbons (Ed.), *Language and the law* (pp. 199–216). Harlow, UK: Longman Group.

Brennan, M., & Brennan, R. E. (1988). *Strange language: Child victims under cross examination* (3rd ed.). Wagga Wagga, Australia: Riverina Murray Institute of Higher Education.

Bruck, M., Ceci, S. J., Francoeur, E., & Renick, A. (1995). Anatomically detailed dolls do not facilitate pre-schoolers' reports of a paediatric examination involving genital touch. *Journal of Experimental Psychology: Applied, 1,* 95–109.

Carter, C. A., Bottoms, B. L., & Levine, M. (1996). Linguistic and socioemotional influences on the accuracy of children's reports: Erratum. *Law and Human Behavior, 20,* 579.

Ceci, S. J., & Bruck, M. (1993). Suggestibility of the child witness: A historical review and synthesis. *Psychological Bulletin, 113,* 403–439.

Ceci, S. J., & Bruck, M. (1995). *Jeopardy in the courtroom: A scientific analysis of children's testimony*. Washington, DC: American Psychological Association.

Ceci, S. J., Kulkofsky, S., Klemfuss, J. Z., Sweeney, C. D., & Bruck, M. (2007). Unwarranted assumptions about children's testimonial accuracy. *Annual Review of Clinical Psychology, 3,* 311–328.

De Villiers, J. G., & De Villiers, P. A. (1974). Competence and performance in child language: Are children really competent to judge? *Journal of Child Language, 1,* 11–22.

Drew, P., & Heritage, J. (Eds.) (1992). *Talk at work: Interaction in institutional settings* (Vol. 8). Cambridge, UK: Cambridge University Press.

Fisher, R. P., & Geiselman, R. E. (1992). *Memory enhancing techniques for investigative interviewing: The cognitive interview*. Springfield, IL: Charles C. Thomas.

Fox, G. (1993). A comparison of 'policespeak' and 'normalspeak a preliminary study. In J. M. Sinclair, M. P. Hoey, & G. Fox (Eds.), *Techniques of description: Spoken and written discourse, A Festschrift for Malcolm Coulthard*. London: Routledge.

French, L. A., & Nelson, K. (1985). Young children's knowledge of relationship terms. *Some if's, or's, and buts*. New York: Springer Verlag.

Friedman, W. J. (1991). The development of children's memory for the time of past events. *Child Development, 62,* 139–155.

Friedman, W. J. (2014). The development of memory for the time of past events. In P. J. Bauer & R. Fivush (Eds.), *The Wiley handbook on the development of memory* (Vol. 1). Hoboken, NJ: John Wiley & Sons, Inc.

Garven, S., Wood, J. M., Malpass, R. S., & Shaw, J. S. (1998). More than suggestion: The effect of interviewing techniques from the McMartin preschool case. *Journal of Applied Psychology, 83*, 347–359.

Gathercole, S. E., Willis, C., Emslie, H., & Baddeley, A. (1992). Phonological memory and vocabulary development during the early school years: A longitudinal study. *Developmental Psychology, 28*, 887–898.

Geddie, L., Fradin, S., & Beer, J. (2000). Child characteristics which impact accuracy of recall and suggestibility in preschoolers: Is age the best predictor? *Child Abuse and Neglect, 24* (2), 223–235.

Ghetti, S., Goodman, G. S., Eisen, M. L., Jianjian, Q., & Davis, S. L. (2002). Consistency in children's reports of sexual and physical abuse. *Child Abuse and Neglect, 26* (9), 977–995.

Gibbons, J. (2003). *Forensic linguistics: An introduction to language in the legal system*. Oxford, UK: Blackwell.

Goodman, G. S., & Aman, C. (1990). Children's use of anatomically detailed dolls to recount an event. *Child Development, 61*, 1859–1871.

Henderson, E. (2012). Alternative routes: Accusatorial jurisdictions on the slow road to best evidence. In J. R. Spencer & M. Lamb (Eds.), *Children and cross-examination: Time to change the rules?*. Oxford, UK: Hart Publishing.

Heritage, J., & Watson, D. R. (1979). Formulations as conversational objects. In G. Psathas (Ed.), *Everyday language: Studies in ethnomethodology*. New York: Irvington Publishers.

Heydon, G. (1998). Participation frameworks, discourse features and embedded requests in police V.A.T.E. interviews with children. *Monash University Linguistics Papers, 1* (2), 21–32.

Heydon, G. (2005). *The language of police interviewing: A critical analysis*. Houndmills, UK: Palgraves Macmillan Inc.

Heydon, G. (2008). The importance of being (in)formal. In K. Kredens & S. Goźdź-Roszkowski (Eds.), *Language and the law: International outlooks*. Frankfurt am Main, Germany: Peter Lang GmbH.

Jones, D. P., & Krugman, R. D. (1986). Can a three-year-old child bear witness to her sexual assault and attempted murder? *Child Abuse and Neglect, 10* (2), 253–258.

Kebbell, M. R., & Giles, D. C. (2000). Some experimental influences of lawyers' complicated questions on eyewitness confidence and accuracy. *The Journal of Psychology, 134* (2), 129–139.

Kebbell, M. R., Hatton, C., & Johnson, S. D. (2004). Witnesses with intellectual disabilities in court: What questions are asked and what influence do they have? *Legal and Criminological Psychology, 9* (1), 23–35.

Kebbell, M. R., & Johnson, S. D. (2000). Lawyers??? Questioning: the effect of confusing questions on witness confidence and accuracy. *Law and Human Behavior, 24* (6), 629–641.

La Rooy, D., Katz, C., Malloy, L. C., & Lamb, M. E. (2010). Do we need to rethink guidance on repeated interviews? *Psychology, Public Policy and Law, 16*, 373–392.

La Rooy, D., Lamb, M. E., & Pipe, M.-E. (2009). Repeated interviewing: A critical evaluation of the risks and potential benefits. In K. Kuehnle & M. Connell (Eds.), *The evaluation of child sexual abuse allegations: A comprehensive guide to assessment and testimony*. Hoboken, NJ: John Wiley & Sons, Inc.

Lamb, M. E., & Brown, D. A. (2006). Conversational apprentices: Helping children become competent informants about their own experiences. *British Journal of Developmental Psychology, 24*, 215–234.

Lamb, M. E., & Fauchier, A. (2001). The effects of question type on self-contradictions by children in the course of forensic interviews. *Applied Cognitive Psychology, 15*, 483–491.

Lamb, M. E., Hershkowitz, I., Orbach, Y., & Esplin, P. W. (2008). *Tell me what happened: Structured investigative interviews of child victims and witnesses.* Hoboken, NJ: John Wiley & Sons, Inc..

Lamb, M. E., La Rooy, D. J., Malloy, L. C., & Katz, C. (2011). *Children's testimony: A handbook of psychological research and forensic practice.* Chichester, UK: Wiley-Blackwell.

Lamb, M. E., Orbach, Y., Hershkowitz, I., Esplin, P. W., & Horowitz, D. (2007). A structured forensic interview protocol improves the quality and the informativeness of investigative interviews with children: A review of research using the NICHD investigative interview Protocol. *Child Abuse and Neglect, 31*, 1201–1231.

Lamb, M. E., Sternberg, K. J., & Esplin, P. W. (2000). Effect of age and length of delay on the amount of information provided by alleged abuse victims in investigative interviews. *Child Development, 71*, 1586–1596.

Lamb, M. E., Sternberg, K. J., Orbach, Y., Esplin, P. W., Stewart, H., & Mitchell, S. (2003). Age differences in young children's responses to open-ended invitations in the course of forensic interviews. *Journal of Counselling and Clinical Psychology, 71*, 926–934.

Leichtman, M. D., & Ceci, S. J. (1995). The effects of stereotypes and suggestions on preschoolers' reports. *Developmental Psychology, 31*, 568–578.

Levin, I., Wilkening, F., & Dembo, Y. (1984). Development of time quantification: Integration and nonintegration of beginnings and endings in comparing durations. *Child Development, 55* (6), 2160–2172.

Levinson, S. C. (1983). *Pragmatics* (Cambridge textbooks in linguistics). Cambridge, UK: Cambridge University Press.

Maratsos, M., Fox, D. E. C., Becker, J. A., & Chalkley, M. A. (1985). Semantic restrictions on children's passives. *Cognition, 19*, 167–191.

Michel, F., Harb, F., & Hidalgo, M. P. (2012). The concept of time in the perception of children and adolescents. *Trends in Psychiatry and Psychotherapy, 34* (1), 38–41.

Ministry of Justice. (2011). Achieving best evidence in criminal proceedings. *Guidance on Interviewing Victims and Witnesses, and Guidance on Using Special Measures*, London, UK: Ministry of Justice.

Myklebust, T. (2012). The position in Norway. In J. R. Spencer & M. Lamb (Eds.), *Children and cross-examination: Time to change the rules?* Oxford, UK: Hart Publishing.

Orbach, Y., Hershkowitz, I., Lamb, M. E., Sternberg, K. J., Esplin, P. W., & Horowitz, D. (2000). Assessing the value of structured protocols for forensic interviews of alleged child abuse victims. *Child Abuse and Neglect, 24*, 733–752.

Orbach, Y., & Lamb, M. E. (2000). Enhancing children's narratives in investigative interviews. *Child Abuse and Neglect, 24* (12), 1631–1648.

Orbach, Y., & Lamb, M. E. (2001). The relationship between within-interview contradictions and eliciting interview utterances. *Child Abuse and Neglect, 25*, 323–333.

Orbach, Y., Lamb, M. E., La Rooy, D., & Pipe, M. E. (2012). A case study of witness consistency and memory recovery across multiple investigative interviews. *Applied Cognitive Psychology, 26*, 118–129.

Perry, N. W., McAuliff, B. D., Tam, P., Claycomb, L., Dostal, C., & Flanagan, C. (1995). When lawyers question children: Is justice served? *Law and Human Behavior, 19*, 609–629.

Peterson, C. (1990). The who, when and where of early narratives. *Journal of Child Language, 17*, 433–455.

Pipe, M. E., Sutherland, R., Webster, N., Jones, C. H., & La Rooy, D. (2004). Do early interviews affect children's long-term recall? *Applied Cognitive Psychology, 18*, 1–17.

Pipe, M., Orbach, Y., Lamb, M., Abbott, C., & Stewart, H. (2008). Do best practice interviews with child sexual abuse victims influence case outcomes? (Final report for the National Institute of Justice). Washington, DC: National Institute of Justice. Retrieved from: http://www.ncjrs.gov/pdffiles1/nij/grants/224524.pdf.

Poole, D. A., & Lamb, M. E. (1998). *Investigative interviews of children: A guide for helping professionals*. Washington, DC: American Psychological Association.

Poole, D. A., & Lindsay, D. S. (1995). Interviewing preschoolers: Effects of non-suggestive techniques, parental coaching, and leading questions on reports of nonexperienced events. *Journal of Experimental Child Psychology, 60*, 129–154.

Poole, D. A., & Lindsay, D. S. (1998). Assessing the accuracy of young children's reports: Lessons from the investigation of child sexual abuse. *Applied and Preventive Psychology, 7* (1), 1–26.

Poole, D. A., & White, L. T. (1991). Effects of question repetition on the eyewitness testimony of children and adults. *Developmental Psychology, 27*, 975–986.

Powell, M. B., & Thomson, D. M. (1994). Children's eyewitness-memory research: Implications for practice. *Families in Society, 75*, 204–216.

Roberts, K. P., Brubacher, S. P., & Powell, M. B. (2011). Practice narratives. In M. E. Lamb, D. J. La Rooy, L. C. Malloy, & C. Katz (Eds.), *Children's testimony: A handbook of psychological research and forensic practice*. Chichester, UK: Wiley-Blackwell.

Rock, F. (2007). *Communicating rights: The language of arrest and detention*. Houndmills, UK: Palgrave Macmillan.

Romaine, S. (1984). *The language of children and adolescents: The acquisition of communicative competence*. London, UK: Basil Blackwell.

Sandhofer, C., & Smith, L. (2001). Why children learn colour words so differently: Evidence from adults learning of artificial terms. *Journal of Experimental Psychology: General, 130*, 600–620.

Saywitz, K., & Camparo, L. (1998). Interviewing child witnesses: A developmental perspective. *Child Abuse and Neglect, 22*, 825–843.

Saywitz, K. J., Snyder, L., & Nathanson, R. (1999). Facilitating the communicative competence of the child witness. *Applied Developmental Science, 3*, 58–68.

Saywitz, K., & Nathanson, R. (1993). Children's testimony and their perceptions of stress in and out of the courtroom. *The International Journal of Child Abuse and Neglect, 17*, 613–622.

Spencer, J. R., & Lamb, M. E. (2012). *Children and cross-examination: Time to change the rules?*. Oxford, UK: Hart Publishing.

Sternberg, K. J., Lamb, M. E., Hershkowitz, I., Yudilevitch, L., Orbach, Y., Esplin, P. W., & Hovav, M. (1997). Effects of introductory style on children's abilities to describe experiences of sexual abuse. *Child Abuse and Neglect, 21* (11), 1133–1146.

Sternberg, K. J., Lamb, M. E., Orbach, Y., Esplin, P. W., & Mitchell, S. (2001). Use of a structured investigative protocol enhances young children's responses to free-recall prompts in the course of forensic interviews. *Journal of Applied Psychology, 86*, 997–1005.

Thatcher, K., Branigan, H., McLean, J., & Sorace, A. (2007). *Children's early acquisition of the passive: Evidence from syntactic priming.* Reading, UK: Child Language Seminar, University of Reading.

Vihman, M. M. (1981). Phonology and the development of the lexicon: evidence from children's errors. *Journal of Child Language, 8* (2), 239–264.

Vihman, M. M. (1996). *Phonological development: The origins of language in the child, applied language studies.* Malden, MA: Blackwell Publishing.

Walker, A. G. (1993). Questioning young children in court: A linguistic case study. *Law and Human Behaviour, 17*, 59–81.

Walker, A. G. (2013). *Handbook of questioning children: A linguistic perspective.* Washington, DC: American Bar Association.

Walker, A. G., & Warren, A. R. (1995). The language of the child abuse interview: Asking the questions, understanding the answers. In T. Ney (Ed.), *True and false allegations of child sexual abuse: Assessment and case management.* Philadelphia, PA: Brunner/Mazel.

White, T. L., Leichtman, M. D., & Ceci, S. J. (1997). The good, the bad, and the ugly: Accuracy, inaccuracy, and elaboration in preschoolers' reports about a past event. *Applied Cognitive Psychology, 11* (7), S37–S54.

Wilson, C., & Powell, M. (2001). *A guide to interviewing children.* Sydney, Australia: Allen and Unwin, Crow's Nest.

Zajac, R., Gross, J., & Hayne, H. (2003). Asked and answered: Questioning children in the courtroom. *Psychiatry, Psychology and Law, 10*, 199–209.

Zajac, R., & Hayne, H. (2003). I don't think that's what really happened: The effect of cross-examination on the accuracy of children's reports. *Journal of Experimental Psychology: Applied, 9*, 187–195.

5

Interviewing Adult Witnesses and Victims

Coral J. Dando[1], R. Edward Geiselman[2], Nicci MacLeod[3]
and Andy Griffiths[4]

[1] University of Wolverhampton, UK
[2] University of California, Los Angeles, USA
[3] Aston University, Birmingham, UK
[4] Institute of Criminal Justice Studies, University of Portsmouth, UK

INTRODUCTION

Fundamental to the investigation of crime is the information provided by witness and victims[1] (Heaton-Armstrong, Shepherd & Wolchover, 1999; Milne & Bull, 1999). Witness information is typically gathered during a face-to-face interview conducted by a police officer, the objective of which is to elicit an accurate, complete and detailed account of what the witness has experienced, and to collect any other investigation relevant information (e.g. Fisher & Geiselman, 1992; Ministry of Justice, 2011). However, witness interviews are complex social and verbal interactions (see Fisher & Geiselman, 1992; La Rooy & Dando, 2010), the success of which relies heavily on effective communication by the interviewer and efficient cognition on the part of the interviewee.

To provide information about their experiences witnesses have to initiate a series of cognitively demanding processes in response to questions posed by the interviewer: they have to understand what is

Communication in Investigative and Legal Contexts: Integrated Approaches from Forensic Psychology, Linguistics and Law Enforcement, First Edition. Edited by Gavin Oxburgh, Trond Myklebust, Tim Grant and Rebecca Milne.
© 2016 John Wiley & Sons, Ltd. Published 2016 by John Wiley & Sons, Ltd.

being asked of them before the processes of searching their long-term memory for the relevant event information and verbalizing their recon-structed recollection in detail can commence (see Tulving & Craik, 2000). The interviewer's task is to support/encourage maximum remembering by asking questions and communicating appropriately, treating each witness as an individual while being cognizant of the need to gather as much investigation important information as possi-ble. This chapter will focus on the interviewing of adult witnesses with reference as to how the extant psychological and linguistic literature has contributed to understanding and informing interview practice over the past 20 years, and how it continues to support practical and procedural improvements.

Evidence provided by witnesses has been a central part of justice systems worldwide. In England and Wales, for example, the require-ment for pre-trial witness statements can be traced back almost 500 years. Yet it was only in the early 1990s that any formal consideration was given to the manner in which victims and witnesses were inter-viewed. A Home Office working party comprising psychologists and police officers (see Shepherd & Milne, 1999), formed to investigate suspect interviewing practices following persistent and significant concerns over the manner in which these interviews were conducted, found that witness interviewing practices were also extremely poor. In the light of the working party findings, and following a national review of interviewing practice, the PEACE model was formulated and intro-duced across England and Wales.

PEACE (an acronym for the stages of an interview, Planning and preparation, Engage and explain, Account, Closure and Evaluation) standardized the way in which police officers were trained to inter-view, and eventually brought about a sea change in attitude towards the purpose of an interview – that is, PEACE educated police officers in the benefits of a structured, information-gathering approach to interviewing (Williamson, 1993), steering them away from the inter-rogatory practices that dominated interviewing practice until that time. The PEACE model can be applied to all types of interviews and remains the core of British police interview techniques, and has been adopted by other countries worldwide (e.g. Canada, New Zealand and Australia). PEACE champions two primary approaches to interview-ing witnesses: (i) the cognitive approach (from here on referred to as the Cognitive Interview) as a way of obtaining an interviewee's account with 'minimal interference' and (ii) the management of conversation (from here on referred to as Conversation Management), which allows the interviewer to both control and manage an interview. Each is offered as being suitable for witnesses, but the former is advocated for cooperative witnesses, because it relies on witnesses agreeing to 'use' several mnemonic techniques, while the latter is offered for more reluctant/uncooperative witnesses. The enduring value of PEACE stems from the fact that, among other things, it clearly defines the structure of a witness interview (see Clarke & Milne, 2001; Walsh & Bull, 2010) and distinguishes the aims and differences of each of the phases within the structure in relation to questioning and retrieval techniques. As will become clear as this chapter unfolds, clarity and structure support in-depth understanding, which in turn drives improvement.

THE COGNITIVE INTERVIEW

The Cognitive Interview (CI) offers a systematic method for increasing the amount of relevant information obtained from a witness without compromising accuracy (Fisher & Geiselman, 1992; Geiselman & Fisher, 1997). In the early 1980s a constellation of factors contributed to the development and eventual refinement of the CI for investigative interviewing. First, the US Department of Justice set out to develop a protocol for interviewing victims and witnesses of crime. The most notable police procedure at the time was the Reid and Associates confrontational interrogation technique for use with suspects (Inbau, Reid, Buckley & Jayne 2001), which was unsuitable for witnesses. Second, forensic hypnosis, which was employed by law enforcement at the time, was becoming mired in legal issues (e.g. *People v. Shirley*, 1982; Sanders & Simmons, 1983). Third, the RAND Corporation (1975) reported that 85% of what police do on a daily basis is talk to citizens, but only 2% of police respondents had received any formal training on how to interview people. Fourth, two American psychologists (Ed Geiselman and Ron Fisher) were eager to steer their respective basic theoretical research programmes on memory retrieval in a more applied direction.

Following a review of the cognitive psychology literature, candidate techniques for enhancing memory retrieval were identified, resulting in the original version of the CI. Since that time, the basic set of memory retrieval aids was transformed through a progression of research into the enhanced CI (Fisher & Geiselman, 1992). The CI approach has been implemented for several years as standard practice in the conduct of criminal investigations at many federal, state and local policing agencies nationwide, as well as in other countries, notably the United Kingdom as part of PEACE. The principal elements of the CI were included in the DOJ Federal Guidelines on handling and preserving eyewitness evidence (National Institute of Justice, 1999), following which a manual for conducting the full CI was published (Fisher & Geiselman, 1992).

The CI is based on scientifically derived principles of memory and communication theory as well as extensive analyses of US law-enforcement interviews. The CI has been found in both scientific laboratory and field studies to produce significantly more information than standard police Q&A interviews, and the protocol is legally acceptable to the courts (see Köhnken, Milne, Memon & Bull, 1999; Memon, Meissner & Fraser, 2010). The CI provides a template for conducting any investigative interview and supplies the interviewer with a toolbox of techniques designed to elicit specific kinds of information. Several elements of the CI are directly relevant to a good-practice approach to investigative interviews. First, the CI relies on the witness to provide the needed information via open-ended questions and so is witness centred rather than interviewer focused, in that it is driven by the witness' recollection of events and not by the interviewer's preconceived notions of what information is important to the outcome of the investigation. Second, the CI encourages the witness to be complete in his/her report and utilizes reliable memory-enhancement techniques to achieve this goal (e.g. encourages witnesses to mentally recreate the environmental and mental context that existed at the time of the to-be-remembered event, to image and to recall the events in different temporal orders, etc.). Third, the communication elements of the CI establish a solid social foundation that is conducive to reporting information. Fourth, research has shown that the CI effectively addresses psychological stressors like those frequently encountered following a stressful incident (Fisher & Geiselman, 2010; Kunst, Rutten & Knijf, 2013).

The core elements of the CI are organized around three basic psychological processes: memory and cognition, social dynamics and communication. Some of the memory-enhancing components of the CI protocol attempt to maximize the amount of feature overlap between retrieval strategies and the witness's memory record (Flexser & Tulving, 1982) or attempt to have the witness explore multiple retrieval routes to the memory record (Tulving, 1974); for example, mentally reinstating the mental and psychological context of the to-be-remembered event, recalling the event more than once and recalling the event in a backward order (see Fisher & Geiselman, 1992; Milne & Bull, 1999). Other cognitive elements, such as encouraging focused concentration and imaging, can assist witnesses to use their cognitive resources efficiently. The communication elements include promoting extensive, detailed responses and utilizing non-verbal as well as verbal modes of expression. The social dynamics include encouraging active witness participation by using open-ended questions, which encourage more elaborate responses, not interrupting witnesses, allowing witnesses to dictate the pace of the interview and spending time building rapport immediately interviewers come into contact with witnesses (see Fisher & Geiselman, 1992; Milne & Bull, 1999).

BUILDING RAPPORT

Rapport building, which is akin to relationship building, is increasingly being viewed as fundamental to the success of most interviews (e.g. Norfolk, Birdi & Walsh, 2007; Walsh & Bull, 2012). However, for witnesses, and especially victims, rapport building is particularly important because they are often asked to give detailed descriptions of intimate, personal experiences to police officers, who are complete strangers. They must be psychologically comfortable with the interviewer as a person to go through the mental effort and emotional distress of describing crime-related details. If anything, the police investigator's official appearance (e.g. badge, uniform, gun) may create a psychological barrier between the police officer and the witness. To overcome this natural barrier, CI interviewers are taught to invest time at the outset of the interview to develop meaningful, personal rapport with the witness (Abbe & Brandon, 2013; Collins, Lincoln & Frank, 2002; Navarro & Schafer, 2001), a feature often absent in police interviews in the past (Fisher, Geiselman, Raymond & Jurkevich, 1987). Interviewers should develop a set of topics that they become comfortable in using to begin the casual conversation. One strategy is to explain to the witness, 'Before we begin, I would like to get to know you a little better – what do you do on a typical day'. The benefits of developing rapport include freeing the witness of some anxiety about being interviewed that might otherwise consume some of the witness's cognitive resources. Furthermore, the interviewer must interact with the victim not merely as a source of evidence that can be applied towards solving the crime. Rather, the interviewer should express his/her concern about the victim's plight, as a person who has undergone a potentially life-altering experience (Fisher & Geiselman, 2010).

The importance of rapport was recognized in the GEMAC model (Milne & Bull, 1999; see also the section on current training methods in this chapter) and in the formulation of PEACE. GEMAC is an acronym for a script, or series of steps, fundamental to the professional management of any purposeful conversation (Shepherd & Kite, 1988). Within GEMAC the activities of attention and active listening were described as rapport building in order to facilitate the disclosure of information, suggesting that resistant interviewees would be more likely to engage with the interview process when faced with an interviewer utilizing conversation management skills. Indeed, this approach coincides with the findings of recent research investigating the importance of rapport during adversarial interviews conducted by military intelligence and counterintelligence agents (Leps & Geiselman, 2014). No agent expressed an affinity for the use of any heavily coercive approaches to increase information revelation. Rather, every participant stated that an interviewee's refusal to speak could be countered successfully with a rapport-based approach.

However, the empirical literature suggests that police interviewers often do not fully grasp the concept of rapport or simply favour other approaches. In the aforementioned national evaluation of PEACE interviewing (Clarke & Milne, 2001) 40% of the interviews evaluated featured no rapport building at all. In a later study of detectives conducting interviews with witnesses of serious crime (such as murder) rapport building was also poorly established, with officers exercising excessive control over the direction and flow of the interview (Griffiths, Milne & Cherryman, 2011) rather than allowing the interview to develop in an interviewee-centred manner.

ASKING QUESTIONS

The *types* of questions asked by an interviewer and the position within an interview that types of questions are asked can also affect both the direction and flow of an interview and the quality and quantity of information reported by witnesses. Defining and labelling question types is, however, problematic (e.g. Oxburgh, Myklebust & Grant, 2010). While much of the current literature in the area of police interviewing focuses on the grammatical form of questions asked (e.g. open, closed, probing, multiple, etc.) and distinguishing between appropriate and inappropriate question types on this basis, a discourse analyst approaches the issue with a focus more firmly on the function of a question (i.e. what is it designed to do?). While some questions are designed to elicit informative narratives, others function merely to elicit confirmation from interviewees of interviewer-introduced information.

Professionals in the investigative interviewing context are familiar with the routine practices of the organization within which they work and are arguably more aligned to future audiences of the interview and what kinds of information are likely to be treated as relevant to the case in hand – a familiarity that is unlikely to be shared by the interviewee (see Chapter 7 in this volume). Put another way, interviewers can often be observed attaching particular inferences to interviewees' contributions based on their knowledge of the institutional framework within which they are operating. For example, in the following extract the interviewer makes obvious what he perceives to be relevant about the interviewee's report of having been 'hanging around for a bit'.

Extract 1

```
1528        IE:   I was (.) hanging around for a bit? (.) wh-
1530              I might've been looking for Nicky I might've
                  been (.) •h I don't know know what I was
                  doing but I was- I know I was (.) hang-
                  ing around for a bit (.2) •h when I f- (.3)
                  clicked on about the taxi firm round the cor-
                  ner?
            IR:   mmm=
1535        IE    =and then (.) that's when I went round that
                  corner.
            IR:   right.
                  (.7)
            IE:   °yeah°
1540              (.6)
        →   IR:   so: (.4) possibly CCTV would show you maybe
                  moving around quite a lot.
                  yea:h °possibly° yeah.
```

It seems unlikely that the possibility of CCTV footage was the interviewee's driving motivation to contribute this information, yet the interviewer treats this possibility as the most important upshot of what she has said – which, for the purposes of the investigation, there is a strong chance it is. It is thus the role of the interviewer to ensure that institutionally salient details are drawn out through appropriate questioning, while simultaneously acknowledging the interviewee's own ideas of salience, which may differ or even conflict.

One feature of question design that has taken the interest of discourse analysts is the use of particular discourse markers – 'non obligatory utterance-initial items that function in relation to ongoing talk' (Schiffrin, 2003, p. 57) and their role in prefacing questions. Discourse markers can be highly revealing of interviewer's orientations to the ongoing talk in a police interview context. For example, while prefacing a question with 'and' links it to a preceding question–answer pair and gives the question a routine character (Heritage & Sorjonen, 1994), while 'but' prefacing indicates something problematic in the preceding answer and invites a second attempt. The distinction between these forms is evident in the two extracts below.

Extract 2: 'and' prefacing in a police–witness interview

```
          IR:   so it was daylight now.
595       IE:   yeah.
                (1.5)
      →   IR:   and where were yous now?
                (1)
          IE:   on the bed still.
600             (3)
      →   IR:   and he:: what do you mean wrapped round you?
                (.)
          IE:   he had his arms round me (.) like locked
                round me. •shih
                (3)
605   →   IR:   and how did you feel then?
          IE:   ((unclear)) physically sick.
```

Extract 3: 'but' prefacing in a police–witness interview

```
          IR:   right and what kind of relationships did
                you have with the fathers?
775             (2)
          IE:   they e:rm (1) both left me for another
                woman (.) both done the same thing. •shih
                775
      →   IR:   but on the: (1) have you had long term
                relation[ships]
780       IE:   [yeah]
```

Prefacing a question with 'well' similarly indicates some kind of breakdown in communication, signalling as it does that the response just received does not fulfil the requirements of the question that was posed.

Extract 4: 'well' prefacing in a police–witness interview

```
          IR:   and how did you feel about that?
235       IE:   hh well he's married and I wasn't really (.5)
                I didn't think (.) it was nice at all. •hh
      →   IR:   well did you feel jealous or anything [like]
          IE:   [no]
```

Johnson (2002) explores the use of 'so' prefacing in the context of witness interviews, noting that *so* is a means by which the discourse is supported and rearranged to form a coherent narrative (2002, p. 97). As such, as well as contributing to a controlling tone in the interaction, *so* functions, in some environments, as an essentially empowering device. *So* prefaced questions often simultaneously function as a third-turn strategy to summarize prior talk – that is, as a formulation. We return to the matter of formulation later in the chapter.

For practitioners there exists a tension between psychological and linguistic theory in terms of what is best in laboratory settings, and the reality of investigation – notwithstanding that dealing with children or vulnerable people requires particular care. Standard texts on this subject have long advocated that open-ended questions are best (e.g. Milne & Bull, 1999). However, investigation of a crime as a whole (in contrast to obtaining uncontaminated recall of a witnessed event) requires a more sophisticated understanding of the subject and application in practice. Investigation requires not only the obtaining of information, but also its confirmation, corroboration or negation. Without these factors a lawyer or decision maker will not be able to fully judge a file of evidence.

For example, where a witness has described an offender it is important to understand whether he/she knows the person they have described or indeed has seen that person before. If this information is not forthcoming in a free recall or through open-ended questions then an interviewer *has* to ask a more direct question to establish these facts. Therefore, the correct sequencing of questions and the ability to comprehend the hierarchy of use is an essential part of the interviewer's skill set (see Shepherd & Griffiths, 2013). Skilful interviewers will adopt deliberate questioning strategies, adjusting their approach according to the particular need at that point in the interview, initiating topics with open questions and using more probing questions where necessary for extra detail or to clarify key points (Griffiths & Milne, 2006). However, a recent evaluation of real life/major crime interviews with both suspects and witnesses (Griffiths et al., 2011) observed similar strategies in both types of interview. Officers applied excessive levels of control through the utilization of more probing questions, rather than open-ended prompts, particularly in the early phases of the interviews.

MEMORY RETRIEVAL

Witness remembering can be externally supported in a number of ways, one of which is by using the CI technique (see the second section of this chapter on the cognitive interview). One of the primary CI mnemonics is the mental reinstatement of context (MRC) technique, which is based on the encoding-specificity principle (Tulving & Thompson, 1973). Encoding-specificity provides a general theoretical framework for understanding how contextual information affects memory and how memory is improved when information available at encoding (experiencing) is also available at retrieval (the interview).

Currently the MRC procedure comprises a series of individual verbal instructions designed to support a witness to mentally recreate both the psychological and physical environment that existed at the time of the to-be-remembered (TBR) event (see Home Office, 2007; Milne & Bull, 1999). The MRC technique is applied immediately prior to the all-important first free recall to facilitate the feature overlap between the event and the retrieval environment, supporting witnesses to mentally place themselves back in an experience.

The beneficial effect of mentally reinstating the context is well established in the eyewitness literature. The MRC technique significantly improves episodic remembering, typically reducing errors of omission (increasing the amount of information recalled) without a concomitant increase in errors of commission (the reporting of erroneous information). The MRC superiority effect has been found for typically developed adults (e.g. Dando, Wilcock, Behnkle & Milne, 2011; Dando, Wilcock & Milne, 2009b; Memon, Wark, Bull & Koehnken, 1997; Roebers & McConkey, 2003), typically developing children (e.g. Dietze, Powell & Thomson, 2010; Dietze & Thomson, 2006; Hershkowitz, Orbach, Lamb, Sternberg & Horowitz, 2001) and some vulnerable witness populations (e.g. older adults: Dando, 2013; Wright & Holliday, 2007). However, the MRC technique is time consuming (Dando, Wilcock & Milne, 2008) and research has consistently reported that many police interviewers either do not use the technique or do not use it correctly (Clarke & Milne, 2001; Dando & Ormerod, 2009; Dando et al., 2008, 2009b). To avoid losing the beneficial effects of the MRC technique, researchers have begun the process of modifying it, developing a Sketch Reinstatement of Context method for use in time-critical environments and with populations who, because of reduced cognitive abilities, may be less able to 'use' the current MRC technique – for example, older adults (Dando, 2013) and children with cognitive impairments (Mattison, Dando & Ormerod, 2015) for whom the demands of the procedure may outstrip the cognitive resources available (see the section of this chapter on future directions for research).

The more often witnesses search through their memories about an event, the more new details they are likely to recall (referred to as reminiscence; see Erdelyi, 1996; Payne, 1987). Interviewers can enhance witness recollection by asking witnesses to describe the event multiple times within the interview, but in ways that promote varied retrieval rather than repeating the same line of questioning. Two techniques from the original CI serve this purpose: requesting the narrative again, but this time in reverse order, and requesting the witness to change physical or conceptual perspectives on the event. These techniques are typically employed near the end of the specific-questions phase of the CI protocol. Each was taken from research on memory for stories (Anderson & Pichert, 1978; Whitten & Leonard, 1981) and is based on the concept that there are multiple access routes to memories.

Near the end of the CI protocol, the witness is asked to give the narrative a second time, but this time to begin with the last thing that happened in the incident and then to describe in detail the events moving backward in time systematically until the witness reaches the beginning of the incident. Questions such as 'What happened right before that?' and 'What were you thinking and looking at right before that?' are useful as prompts during the reverse-order recall and can elicit additional details. Reverse-order recall tends to slow down the action in the witness's mind's eye and allows for a more exhaustive search of the memory record, frame by frame. The reverse-order technique can help the witness generate information that is incidental or atypical to the target event because recalling an event in reverse order is less amenable to thematic-based recall (Geiselman & Callot, 1990). Eliciting these incidental details can be crucial for case solution. Recalling an event in reverse order is more of a frame-by-frame approach compared to recalling the event in forward order, where most often there is a clear chronology of events (Franks & Bransford, 1971). The results of a recent study suggest that the reverse-order technique should be employed only after the forward narrative report and the follow-up questioning phase have been completed (Dando, Ormerod, Wilcock & Milne 2011). Otherwise, this technique might disrupt the temporal clustering of information stored in the witness's memory.

Also near the end of the CI interview, the witness is asked to consider the different perspectives that he/she may have had on the events during the incident and/or to think about the incident again from the perspective of someone else present at the scene. Asking the witness to draw a diagram of the events, indicating where he/she was located during the incident, and to think about what he/she was able to see from each location are useful aids in enhancing the 'take' from this phase of the interview. The change-perspectives technique is a memory-jogging tool that also has been shown to increase the amount of details recalled. Throughout the interview, the witness should be cautioned against speculating or guessing, but rather to report only what he/she believes to have happened at a particular snapshot in time. One form of the change-perspectives technique (Boon & Noon, 1994) asks the witness to think about the various physical perspectives she/he may have had throughout the event. A second form of the change-perspectives technique asks the witness to consider the perspective of another person at the event (e.g. 'What do you think the cashier saw?'). With the latter application of the change-perspectives technique, a caution to the witness against guessing is recommended, especially with children or mentally challenged persons who may have difficulty taking on the perspectives of others (Saywitz, Geiselman & Bornstein, 1992).

INTERVIEWER COMMUNICATION STYLE

Footing refers to a method of describing and understanding spoken discourse in witness interviews in terms of the roles that speakers occupy and the way they position themselves in relation to the ongoing talk. Speakers can present themselves as the Principal, or authority behind the message; the Author, or party who selects the words and structure of the utterance; and lastly as the Animator, or the physical producer of the utterance (Goffman, 1981). While it is common for one speaker to occupy all three roles, this is frequently not the case. Often, for example, a person acts as a spokesperson for another – that is, they *animate* a message for which someone else retains authorship and principalship. This is clearly observable in the opening and closing stages of the police–witness interview (the Engage and explain and Closure phases of the PEACE model), where it is common to hear interviewers produce semi-scripted utterances, which make explicit that they are speaking not on their own behalf, but are animating messages on behalf of the police institution. This is particularly evident with formulaic utterances, which tend to be produced in a consistent format (see Extract 5).

Extract 5: Formulaic utterances in the opening phases[2]

```
40      IR:   yeah •hh (.2) e:rm (.) there's a couple of
              technicalities before we start what's your full
              name please?
        IE:   Becky Howard.
              (.6)
        IR:   •hh and your date of birth Becky.=
        IE:   =seventh of the eighth nineteen seventy eight.
45      IR:   and where d'you live.
        IE:   number three Whitbury Place Hesslington Square
              ((town name)).
        IR:   do you work at all?
        IE:   yeah.
        IR:   what do you do?
50      IE:   I'm a dispenser at a pharmacy in ((town name)).
```

Within the free report and crucially within the questioning phases of police–witness interactions (the Account phase of PEACE), there is a preference for interviewees to be aligned as principal and author, as well as animator, of their own accounts – that is, as far as possible, the resulting account should be in the interviewee's 'own words'. As Heydon (2005, p. 58) puts it, 'the police interviewer would, ideally, be assigned none of these roles for the duration of the information gathering'. Evidence of this preference often appears in the form of explicit promotion of the footing, such as 'would you care to tell me in your own words...'. During questioning, when it is necessary to revisit elements of the free report (which is intended to proceed uninterrupted), it is extremely common for interviewers to make use of a discursive device known as *reported speech* – the indirect quotation of interviewees' earlier utterances back to them – in order to give the impression that the interviewees retain principalship and authorship for the content of the utterances.

Extract 6: Reported speech in the questioning phases

```
210   →   IR:   (.6) okay. (.3) •h so (.4) if you think about
                when you went in to (.6) Lunar then (.7) and you
                said that this lad was still (.8) hanging about
                (.5) just describe what you mean by that.
```

However, it must be borne in mind that accurate representation of interviewees' words presents significant challenges. This is particularly important given the inherent power asymmetry, coupled with the presentation of these utterances as being the interviewees' own words. Hence, interviewees are likely to experience a great deal of pressure to agree with the propositions, even if they perceive inaccuracies with the content. The sequential positioning of these stretches of reported speech – almost invariably followed immediately by a question – presents a further obstacle for potential challenge from interviewees. On a related note, interviewers often work to maintain the preferred footing by feigning ignorance of certain facts, because they want the interviewee to answer the question on record, as though they are the owner of the 'new' information.

Extract 7: Misrepresenting the knowledge state in the questioning phases

```
1720   →   IR:   °°right°° (2.6) can you remember the first
                 time somebody spoke to you? (.) about this.
                 (.2) with your- with your dad. (1.3) did you-
                 did you ever say to your dad that you didn't
                 want to (.7) tell the police about it or-
           IE:   °yeah°
                 (.2)
           IR:   right. when was that?
```

The benefits of this are obvious, with the risks associated with packaging information as originating from the interviewer rather than the interviewee having serious implications for perceived interviewer influence, and thus for the quality of the evidence gathered. In the following extract, for example, the IR takes the lead, confidently asserting a description of the location of the events being reported, which has the potential to have a harming effect on the quality of the information gathered.

Extract 8: Risks of IR occupying all three roles

```
700        IR:   °right (.) okay° •hh cos e:rm from my memory
                 you have the Eagle Hotel in front of you (.2)
                 which you can't really miss it's a big [thing]
           IE:   [yeah] yeah.
705        IR:   •hh and then as you tu:rn (.) right you've
                 got a barrier that stops the taxis coming
                 down the high street now on the weekends?=
           IE:   =yeah.
           IR:   and then you go into e:rm (.2) what would be
                 Mile Lane?
```

There are, however, occasions when an interviewer positioning themselves as principal can have obvious positive implications for maintaining personalization and rapport with the interviewee.

Extract 9: Benefits of IR occupying all three roles

```
           IE:   it's- it takes about five or ten minutes.
220        IR:   °okay° I know the route well cos that's-
                 obviously it's near where I used to work
                 before we moved to our new police station
                 •hh so (.) do you know what time it was
                 when you got back to your flat?
```

The difference here is the sequential location of the IR-owned information – positioned as a reassuring response to the IE rather than as key information projected as known by the IE as the basis for an upcoming question, the knowledge evident in Extract 9 is far less likely to harm the quality of the final version.

The communication elements of the CI establish a solid foundation that is conducive to reporting information and address psychological stressors like those frequently encountered following a crime incident (Fisher & Geiselman, 2010). For example, victims and witnesses often will be anxious about the interview process because they are uncertain about what is expected of them and how the process will transpire. CI interviewers attempt to reduce this uncertainty by previewing the structure of the interview, and especially by explaining the witness-centered nature of the interview. Witnesses are encouraged to ask questions about the process. Foreshadowing the interview should reduce victims' anxiety about the process as it reduces uncertainty.

In addition, the CI is a witness-centred approach that relies on open-ended questions and narrative responses. The subject generates the information almost exclusively on his/her own rather than responding to leading, close-ended questions from the investigator. This approach is driven by the witness' recollection of events and not by the interviewer's preconceived notions of what information is important to the outcome of the investigation. After all, the witness has the needed information, not the interviewer. CI interviewers also encourage witnesses to be complete in their reports and to utilize reliable memory-enhancement techniques to achieve this goal. CI interviewers slow down the pace of the follow-up questioning and allow a brief pause following each answer. These communication measures attempt to increase the likelihood that the witness will search memory thoroughly.

Interviewing Resistant, Reluctant and Uncooperative Witnesses

Conversation Management (CM) is advocated for use with resistant or uncooperative interviewees because it focuses on using conversational skills (Shepherd & Kite, 1988) to build a working relationship between interviewer and interviewee to foster the disclosure of information. The CM ethos is that a successful interviewer can influence disclosure using a number of key behaviours, summed up by the mnemonic GEMAC. GEMAC summarized the effective ethical steps to facilitate disclosure from someone treated as an equal, whether they are compliant or resistant:

- Committing to the across nature of the relationship between interviewer and interviewee by managing the initial *Greeting* and behaviour across the interview.
- An *Explanation* of the purpose of the interview at its outset, a route map of subjects to be covered during the interview, any routines that the interviewer will adopt (e.g. note taking) and the expectations (e.g. explaining that the interviewee can take as much time as they need to answer questions).
- Agreeing the *Mutual activities* of active listening and productive questioning in order that detail may be obtained.
- *Closure* – summarizing to check back the detail and ensure accuracy of what information has been disclosed.

The CI has also proven valuable for interviewing police officers who have been involved in serious crimes, road traffic accidents and critical use-of-force incidents (e.g. shootings). Interviewing officers in these situations is a sensitive matter given that the officer is a witness, victim and possibly a suspect until the matter is cleared. Interviewers must understand that police officers have the same perceptual and memory systems as civilian witnesses (subject to the same human limitations). Research shows that, with some exceptions, police officers are just as affected by situational factors such as stress and weapon focus and they react to leading questions much like civilian witnesses. In the midst of a high stress encounter, such as a deadly force confrontation, perceptual distortions and exclusions caused by stress may well cause an involved officer to fail to perceive (and thus fail to recall) events that occurred in his/her immediate presence during the incident.

State of mind and ongoing threat assessment are also important with these law-enforcement witnesses, not just the material facts of the matter (Wilson & Geisleman, 2011). A CI approach is ideally suited for this circumstance given that it is an information-gathering protocol, rather than a confrontational approach, where thoughts and emotions are addressed, and so is viewed as a useful debrief tool. A confrontational approach in this context often is counterproductive and could cause the involved officer to second-guess and otherwise question his/her own memory. Under persistent and leading questioning, the officer may begin to speculate as to how the incident happened for which he/she has no clear memory. Thus, the application of the CI in this arena has been generally welcomed by policing agencies (Force Science News, 2011).

Following stressful incidents such as officer-involved shootings, a common concern is when to conduct the full investigative interview. It is common for officers to have been awake for 24–36 hours at the point where an interview could take place. Therefore, it has been recommended as a general rule that the involved officers should sleep first and give their statements later (Artwohl, 2002). If the involved officer is sleep-deprived with lingering signs of stress, it is important for interviewers to understand that the officer's recollections may be incomplete, disorganized and more open to suggestion. However, if the full investigative interview is delayed to allow for rest and for the dissipation of stress, there is a chance that details will be forgotten and the memory record will be contaminated via post-event influences. Especially if the interview is delayed, investigators should consider using a CI approach to conduct the interview. As described above, the CI protocol contains techniques for reconstructing the sensory and emotional context that existed at the time of the event as well as techniques for enhancing memory retrieval following some forgetting. These techniques have been found to circumvent certain post-event sources of contamination (Geiselman, Fisher, Cohen, Holland & Surtes, 1986; Memon, Zaragoza, Clifford & Kidd, 2010; Milne & Bull, 2003). Therefore, a CI approach goes a long way towards counteracting any negative effects on memory recall caused by a delay of the full investigative interview to allow for rest and stress reduction.

Interviewing Vulnerable Witnesses

Interviewing vulnerable witnesses/victims brings a unique set of challenges to the interview room. For example, the treatment of rape claimants has given rise to the terming of their experiences as 'rape of the second kind' (Matoesian, 1993) and 'secondary rape' (Anderson & Doherty, 2008). Historically, accusations of misogyny have often been levelled at the police institution, where displays of stereotypically masculine behaviour are expected, both by colleagues and the public at large (Page, 2008).

Research suggests that acceptance of rape myths (see Anderson & Doherty, 2008), that is prejudicial, stereotyped or false beliefs about rape, rape victims and rapists, is widespread among police officers and among society in general. However, many studies have suggested that the police hold more negative views of victims than do other professionals (e.g. Anderson & Doherty, 2008), and that acceptance of rape myth has a significant negative impact on interviewing skill (Rich & Seffrin, 2012). It is against this backdrop that special attention has been paid in recent years to improving the experiences of women who choose to report rape and sexual assault, and, in particular, the way in which they are interviewed.

One routine means by which interviewers' prejudices have been identified as coming to the fore is that of *formulation*, those points within conversation where a participant takes the opportunity to 'describe that conversation, to explain it, or characterize it, or explicate, or translate, or summarize, or furnish the gist of it...' (Garfinkel & Sacks, 1970, p. 350). *Formulating* is a recurrent practice arising from the need to clarify elements of the account for the benefit of what is termed the 'overhearing audience' – in this context, the police scribe, CPS and potentially the Court. Since the means by which this 'fixing' is achieved necessarily involves the foregrounding of elements of the account deemed to be particularly salient at the expense of other elements, which may be entirely deleted, formulations are rarely entirely neutral. Their production, therefore, has the potential to exert undue interviewer influence over the negotiated 'final version' of interviewees' accounts, as demonstrated in the text extract, where significant alterations are made to the victim's report (IE) of how the men who allegedly went on to rape her came to be in her home.

Extract 10: Risks of formulating

```
300        IE:    (.) they said "ah s- can we come back to
                  your house" (.) and I said "ok fine it's not
                  very often I get company" (.) didn't have a
                  problem with it.
                  (5)
           IR:    so how had you felt about the night so far
                  with=
           IE:    =okay (.) no problems at all.
305               (3)
      →    IR:    and you'd said yes because you were w- w-
                  enjoying the c[ompany,]
```

A good deal of information, including perhaps most importantly that it was the men who made the suggestion, is deleted from the interviewer's (IR) formulation, which instead foregrounds the victim's (IE) behaviour and her reasons for 'allowing' such a situation to present itself.

Since the late 1990s, several studies have examined whether the CI could be used effectively with children and other 'non-standard' witnesses. In some of these studies, the experimental witnesses were young children (e.g. Larsson, Granhag & Spjut, 2003; Milne & Bull, 1996), in others the witnesses were older people (Mello & Fisher, 1996) or were young adults with intellectual disabilities (Geiselman & Padilla, 1988; Milne, Clare & Bull, 1999). The patterns of results are remarkably similar to those found with typically developed adults, namely, the CI elicits considerably more information than the control interview, and at comparable or slightly higher accuracy rates. Of particular importance was the preview of the interview with these witnesses, where specific misconceptions and special concerns could be addressed: for example, clarifying that 'I don't remember' or 'I don't know' is the correct response, if that is indeed the case, and why some questions might be repeated during the interview.

Maras and Bowler (2010, 2012) and Mattison et al. (2015) have pursued workable modifications of the CI for use with children and adults with Autistic Spectrum Disorder (ASD) and older adults (Dando, 2013). Because people with ASD demonstrate difficulties in processing a stimulus in relation to its context (Gaig, Gardiner & Bower, 2008), and impaired source monitoring, current methods for mentally recreating the physical and psychological context of the to-be-remembered event, which is an important CI technique, have been found to be ineffective. For adults, physically returning to the scene of the event was necessary to achieve the benefits of this function. In the case of children, drawing to remember has proved an effective alternative to recreating the context, increasing recall performance per se and improving accuracy in line with a typically developing peer group (see Dando, 2013; Dando et al., 2009b). Similarly, older adults have exhibited significantly improved remembering when the traditional mental reinstatement of the context method is replaced by the sketching reinstatement of the context technique.

CURRENT TRAINING EFFORTS

The CI is one of the most researched and generally accepted methods for supporting and improving witness remembering, which since its inception has guided good practice in many countries. Indeed, the CI has been a fundamental element of the PEACE model in England and Wales since the early 1990s. However, following the introduction of PEACE, a national evaluation of witness interviewing (Clarke & Milne, 2001), which included an evaluation of PEACE training alongside an analysis of audio-recorded interviews with real witnesses,[3] revealed that witness interviews were still poor and of low quality. It was suggested that this was, in part, due to the majority of the training course being devoted to interviewing suspects, rather than witnesses.

Following this evaluation and building on a novel approach being developed by a number of forward-thinking UK police forces (Griffiths & Milne, 2006), witness interview training became more sophisticated, adopting a tiered approach that recognized that not all interviewers needed to be trained to the same level (Clarke & Milne, 2001). Selected officers received three days training in the Enhanced Cognitive Interview (ECI) (delivered by academics and police trainers) as a supplement to a three-week advanced suspect interview course that qualified them to interview suspects in major crime cases (Griffiths & Milne, 2006).[4] The logic underlying this was that the ECI training would enhance the previous training; turning officers into omnicompetent specialist interviewers.

Two subsequent field studies showed that the reality was somewhat different. The first reported that detectives did not use all of the cognitive techniques that they had been taught: the majority of interviews commenced with the use of context reinstatement, but officers quickly reverted to a directive approach whereby they selected the chronology and topics, using probing questions to elicit detail. The levels of control observed were contrary to the principles of the CI and officers avoided techniques such as recalling in different temporal orders, rapport building and recall from different perspectives (Griffiths & Milne, 2010). These findings replicate those of Dando et al. (2008, 2009a), who had already investigated less experienced police officers' perceptions and application of the CI following basic training and found that officers struggled to apply the procedure correctly.

The second study (Griffiths et al., 2011) examined the question strategies of the advanced interviewers in both suspect and witness interviews using a 'think aloud' procedure (Wright & Powell, 2006). Officers were found to use similar strategies in both types of interview: favouring a probing question style more suited to interviews with suspects. The order and emphasis of the training (i.e. generally suspect interview training first) appeared to have produced an overshadowing effect (Griffiths et al., 2011). As a consequence the specialist training model in England and Wales has recently changed: after completing initial PEACE training, officers can now self-select for either suspect or witness specialist training.

Each witness and situation will call for a slightly different approach for conducting an investigative interview. Consequently, it is not surprising that most investigators who have received training on the CI incorporate some, but not all, elements of the CI into any given one of their interviews (Dando et al., 2009a; Kebbell, Milne & Wagstaff, 1999). For some time now, the CI has been taught and/or implemented by several policing agencies and allied investigative agencies worldwide (Fisher & Geiselman, 1992). A manual for conducting the full CI was published in 1992 (Geiselman & Fisher, 1992) and a recommended training regimen is included in that manual. Since that time, Powell, Fisher and Wright (2005) have explored various methods to improve this training.

While training on the CI thus far has been patchy, with no coordinated effort by national and international law-enforcement and government agencies, some high-profile organizations across Europe and the United States have sponsored training. Guided by the contemporary empirical and theoretical literature, several novel interviewer-training initiatives, aimed at maximizing the efficacy of witness interviews, are being developed. One such initiative has emanated from the types of linguistic research discussed above, the piloting of which has been funded by the British Association of Applied Linguistics. The training focuses on explicating the knowledge and skills of practitioners for the benefit of their own professional practice, highlighting areas of good practice as well as instigating a general awareness of the effects of particular discursive choices. A challenge for the future is to adapt the training input to be suitable for interviewers at all levels, that is those practitioners whose day-to-day work involves the interviewing of victims in cases of sexual assault, for example. Overall, the input from participants painted a picture suggesting that sociolinguistic research had a number of important contributions to make to interview training models.

FUTURE DIRECTIONS FOR RESEARCH

With respect to future research, it is important to identify the limitations as well as the strengths of the CI for different populations and contexts, particularly in the light of recent theoretical advances in the our understanding of human memory and forensic practice. It is equally important, however, to then offer guidance and to seek solutions for those limitations. We believe the major areas of progress in the future will include (a) developing effective training programmes for investigators to learn the procedures more effectively, (b) streamlining the procedures so that police can use them more efficiently in field situations where resources are often limited, (c) developing new component techniques to expand the CI, (d) exploring the utility of the CI in other (non-criminal) investigations and (f) modifying and refining the CI for use with persons exhibiting various disorders and deficits. It is worthy of note that considerable progress is being made along each of these lines. Powell et al. (2005) have explored various methods to improve training. Dando and Ormerod (2009), Dando et al. (2011) and Dando, Wilcock and Milne (2009b) have examined ways to streamline the CI for time-constrained situations. Brock, Fisher and Cutler (1999) and Roos (2007) have examined how the CI might be used to investigate auto accidents. Finally, Maras and Bowler (2010, 2012), Mattison et al. (2015), Dando (2013) and Dando et al. (2009b) have pursued workable modifications of the CI for persons with ASD (adults and children) and older adults for whom some of the CI components are argued as being too cognitively demanding (e.g. mental reinstatement of context and reverse order recall).

Finally, it is worthy of note that an approach to the practitioner community in which there is a more equitable, symbiotic exchange of ideas would most certainly serve to improve the overall relationship for a future interface. It is apparent from the authors' work in this field that cooperation between practitioners and academics is absolutely necessary for further progress to be made. Investigative practice has changed considerably since the initial formulation of both CI and CM. Technological advances have produced the ability to conduct interviews remotely, while financial pressures experienced globally have reinforced the need to be more efficient. Therefore, research is needed into the conducting of 'remote' interviews. Global economic migration has increased the number of interviews being conducted through interpreters and therefore the need to understand and improve this procedure. These are just two of numerous issues requiring research and cooperation.

An interaction that delegitimizes the perspectives of practitioners such as police officers and military intelligence collectors through ivory tower implications seems likely to be at best unsuccessful or at worst lead to the generation of inaccurate data. We suggest that the ongoing dialogue maintains a collaborative tone and avoids the implication of ignorance that may have shaped derogatory perceptions of researchers by some in the practitioner community (Leps & Geiselman, 2014). That said, it is clear from the literature introduced in this chapter alone that productive, respectful and reciprocal relationships between practitioners and academics have existed, and do currently exist – the domain of witness interviewing has undoubtedly benefited from such relationships in a way that hitherto had not been the case. Academics have come to appreciate the complexities of working in the 'real world' and in doing so have come to better understand real world cognitive processes. Practitioners have become more knowledgeable about human cognition in witness interview settings and so have been able to access and apply methods for improving practice based on shared knowledge.

NOTES

1. From here on the term 'witness' will be used to refer to both victims and witnesses.
2. Note that in Extract 5 the description of the utterances as 'technicalities' on line 40 provides further support for them having been produced due to institutional requirements, rather than for the benefit of the IR him/herself.
3. Interviews were specifically recorded for the project as the mandatory recording of interviews is still confined to interviews with suspects.
4. Only successful graduates attended the ECI element.

REFERENCES

Ambler, C. (2005). The initial investigation of household burglary: An examination and analysis of the information gathered about burglary suspects (Unpublished Master's thesis), University of Portsmouth.

Anderson, J. R. (1983). A spreading activation theory of memory. *Journal of Verbal Learning and Verbal Behavior, 22*, 261–295.

Anderson, M. C., Bjork, R. A., & Bjork, E. L. (1994). Remembering can cause forgetting: Retrieval dynamics in long-term memory. *Journal of Experimental Psychology: Learning, Memory, and Cognition, 20,* 1063–1087.

Bergmann, M. M., Jacobs, E. J., Hoffmann, K., & Boeing, H. (2004). Agreement of self-reported medical history: Comparison of an in-person interview with a self-administered questionnaire. *European Journal of Epidemiology, 19,* 411–416.

Brown, C., Lloyd-Jones, T. J., & Robinson, M. (2008). Eliciting person descriptions from eyewitnesses: A survey of police perceptions of eyewitness performance and reported use of interview techniques. *The European Journal of Cognitive Psychology, 20,* 529–560.

Carter, E. (2011). *Analysing police interviews: Laughter, confessions and the tape.* London, UK: Continuum.

Carter, E. (2014). When is a lie not a lie? When it's divergent: Examining the interactional composition of lies and deceptive responses in a police interview. *International Journal of Language and the Law / Linguagem e Direito, 1,* 1.

Chan, J. C. K., Thomas, A. K., & Bulevich, J. B. (2009). Recalling a witnessed event increases eyewitness suggestibility: The reversed testing effect. *Psychological Science, 20,* 66–73.

Chang, L., & Krosnick, J. A. (2010). Comparing oral interviewing with self-administered computerized questionnaires: An experiment. *Public Opinion Quarterly, 74,* 154–167.

Conway, M. A., Cohen, G., & Stanhope, N. (1991). On the very long-term retention of knowledge acquired through formal education: Twelve years of cognitive psychology. *Journal of Experimental Psychology. General, 120,* 395–409.

Crown Prosecution Service. (2005). Policy for prosecuting cases of domestic violence. Retrieved from 18 May 2014, http://www.cps.gov.uk/Publications/prosecution/domestic

Crown Prosecution Service. (2011). Keir Starmer QC speech. Retrieved from 26 December 2012, www.cps.gov.uk/news/articles/domestic_violence_-_the_facts_the_issues_the_future

Dando, C. J. (2013). Drawing to remember: External support of older adults' eyewitness performance. *PloS One, 8,* e69937. doi:10.1371/journal.pone.0069937.

Dando, C. J., Ormerod, T. C., Wilcock, R., & Milne, R. (2011). Change temporal order retrieval: Help or hindrance. *Cognition, 121,* 416–421.

Dando, C., & Ormerod, T. C. (2009). Effects of change temporal order technique on eyewitness memory. In N. A. Taatgen & H. van Rijn (Eds.), *Proceedings of the 31st Annual Conference of the Cognitive Science Society.* Austin, TX: Cognitive Science Society.

Dando, C. J., Wilcock, R., Behnkle, C., & Milne, R. (2011). Modifying the cognitive interview: Countenancing forensic application by enhancing practicability. *Psychology, Crime, & Law, 17,* 491–511.

Dando, C. J., Wilcock, R., & Milne, R. (2008). The cognitive interview: Inexperienced police officers' perceptions of their witness interviewing behaviour. *Legal and Criminological Psychology, 13,* 59–70.

Dando, C. J., Wilcock, R., & Milne, R. (2009a). Novice police officers' application of the cognitive interview procedure. *Psychology, Crime, & Law, 15,* 679–696.

Dando, C. J., Wilcock, R., & Milne, R. (2009b). The cognitive interview: The efficacy of a modified mental reinstatement of context procedure for frontline police investigators. *Applied Cognitive Psychology, 23*,138–147.

Dando, C. J. Wilcock, R., Milne, R., & Henry, L. (2009). An adapted cognitive interview procedure for frontline police investigators. *Applied Cognitive Psychology, 23*, 698–716.

Dudgeon, P. (2012). Indigenous Australian mental health and racism. *Psychology Aotearoa, 4*, 85–91.

Ebbinghaus, H. (1913). *Memory: A contribution to experimental psychology.* New York: Teachers College, Columbia University (original work published 1885).

Fisher, R. P. (1996). Implications of output-bound measures for laboratory and field research in memory. *The Behavioral and Brain Sciences, 19*, 197.

Fisher, R. P., Brewer, N., & Mitchell, G. (2009). The relation between consistency and accuracy of eyewitness testimony: Legal versus cognitive explanations. In R. Bull, T. Valentine, & T. Williamson (Eds.), *Handbook of psychology of investigative interviewing: Current developments and future directions.* Chichester, UK: John Wiley & Sons, Ltd.

Fisher, R. P., & Cutler, B. L. (1995). Relation between consistency and accuracy of eyewitness testimony. In G. M. Davies, S. Lloyd-Bostock, M. McMurran, & C. Wilson (Eds.), *Psychology and law: Advances in research* (pp. 21–28). Berlin, Germany: DeGruyter.

Fisher, R. P., & Geiselman, R. E. (1992). *Memory-enhancing techniques for investigative interviewing.* Springfield, IL: Charles C. Thomas.

Gabbert, F., & Brown, C. (2015). Interviewing for face identification. In T. Valentine & J. P. Davis (Eds.), *Forensic facial identification: Theory and practice of identification from eyewitnesses, composites and CCTV.* London, UK: Wiley-Blackwell.

Gabbert, F., & Hope, L. (2013). Suggestibility and memory conformity. In A. M. Ridley, F. Gabbert, & D. J. La Rooy (Eds.), *Suggestibility in legal contexts: Psychological research and forensic implications* (pp. 63–84). London, UK: Wiley-Blackwell.

Gabbert, F., Hope, L., & Fisher, R. P. (2009). Protecting eyewitness evidence: Examining the efficacy of a self-administered interview tool. *Law and Human Behavior, 33*, 298–307.

Gabbert, F., Hope, L., Fisher, R. P., & Jamieson, K. (2012). Protecting against susceptibility to misinformation with a self-administered interview. *Applied Cognitive Psychology, 26*, 568–575.

Gabbert, F., Hope, L., Lindsay, K., Skowronska, E., & Sauer, J. (2011). Does an immediate recall test increase eyewitness suggestibility? In *The 5th international conference on memory*, August 2011, York, UK.

Garry, M., Loftus, E. F., & Brown, S. W. (1994). Memory: A river runs through it. *Consciousness and Cognition, 3*, 438–451.

Gawrylowicz, J., Memon, A., & Scoboria, A. (2013). Equipping witnesses with transferable skills: The Self-Administered Interview©. *Psychology, Crime and Law, 20*, 315–325.

Geiselman, R. E., Fisher, R. P., Cohen, G., Holland, H., & Surtes, L. (1986). Eyewitness responses to leading and misleading questions under the cognitive interview. *Journal of Police Science and Administration, 14*, 31–39.

Gever, M. (2005). The spectacle of crime, digitized: CSI Crime Scene Investigation and social anatomy. *European Journal of Cultural Studies, 8*, 445–463.

Gilbert, J. A. E., & Fisher, R. P. (2006). The effects of varied retrieval cues on reminiscence in eyewitness memory. *Applied Cognitive Psychology, 20*, 723–739.

Goldsmith, M., Koriat, A., & Pansky, A. (2005). Strategic regulation of grain size in memory reporting over time. *Journal of Memory and Language, 52*, 505–525.

Grabowski, J. (2007). The writing superiority effect in the verbal recall of knowledge: Sources and determinants. In M. Torrance, L. van Waes, & D. Galbraith (Eds.), *Writing and cognition: Research and application* (pp. 165–179). Amsterdam, The Netherlands: Elsevier.

Greater Manchester Police. (2010). Tackling domestic abuse policy and operational procedures.

Grice, P. (1975). Logic and conversation. In P. Cole & J. L. Morgan (Eds.), *Speech acts* (pp. 41–58). New York: Academic Press.

Hall, D. F., Loftus, E. F., & Tousignant, J. P. (1984). Postevent information and changes in recollection for a natural event. In G. L. Wells & E. F. Loftus (Eds.), *Eyewitness testimony: Psychological perspectives* (pp. 124–141). Cambridge, UK: Cambridge University Press.

Hashtroudi, S., Johnson, M. K., Vnek, N., & Ferguson, S. A. (1994). Aging and the effects of affective and factual focus on source monitoring and recall. *Psychology and Aging, 9*, 160–170.

Haworth, K. (2010). Police interview in the judicial process. *The Routledge handbook of forensic linguistics* (pp. 169–181). New York: Routledge.

Hester, S., & Eglin, P. (1992). *A sociology of crime*. London, UK: Routledge.

Heydon, G. (2005). *The language of police interviewing*. Basingstoke, Hampshire, UK: Palgrave Macmillan.

Hope, L., Gabbert, F., & Fisher, R. P. (2011). From laboratory to the street: Capturing witness memory using a Self-Administered Interview. *Legal and Criminological Psychology, 16*, 211–226.

Hope, L., Gabbert, F., Heaton-Armstrong, A., & Wolchover, D. (2013). Self administered witness interviews—Part IV. *Criminal Law and Justice Weekly, 177*, 60–61.

Hope, L., Gabbert, F., Fisher, R. P., & Jamieson, K. (2014). Protecting and enhancing eyewitness memory: The impact of an initial recall attempt on performance in an investigative interview. *Applied Cognitive Psychology, 28*, 304–313.

International Rehabilitation Council for Torture Victims. (2009). *Shedding light on a dark practice: Using the Istanbul Protocol to document torture*. Copenhagen, Denmark: IRCT.

Jones, E. F., & Forrest, J. D. (1992). Underreporting of abortion in surveys of U.S. women: 1976 to 1988. *Demography, 29*, 113–126.

Jönsson, L., & Linnell, P. (1991). Story generations: From dialogical interviews to written reports in police interrogations. *Text, 11*, 419–440.

Kebbell, M. R., & Milne, R. (1998). Police officers' perceptions of eyewitness performance in forensic investigations. *The Journal of Social Psychology, 138*, 323–330.

Kellogg, R. T. (2007). Are written and spoken recall of text equivalent? *The American Journal of Psychology, 120*, 415–428.

Kintsch, W., Welsch, D., Schmalhofer, F., & Zimny, S. (1990). Sentence memory: A theoretical analysis. *Journal of Memory and Language, 29*, 133–159.

Komter, M. L. (2002/2003). The construction of records in Dutch police interrogations. *Information Design Journal and Document Design, 11*, 201–213.

Koriat, A., & Goldsmith, M. (1996). Monitoring and control processes in the strategic regulation of memory accuracy. *Psychological Review, 103*, 490–517.

Koriat, A., Levy-Sadot, R., Edry, E., & De Marcas, G. (2003). What do we know about what we cannot remember? Accessing the semantic attributes of words that cannot be recalled. *Journal of Experimental Psychology: Learning, Memory and Cognition, 29*, 1095–1105.

LaPaglia, J. A., Wilford, M. M., Rivard, J., Chan, J. C. K., & Fisher, R. P. (2014). Misleading suggestions can alter later memory reports even following a cognitive interview. *Applied Cognitive Psychology, 28*, 1–9.

La Rooy, D., & Dando, C. J. (2010). Witness interviewing. In G. Towl & D. Crighton, (Eds.). *Forensic psychology*. West Sussex: Wiley Blackwell.

La Rooy, D., Lamb, M. E., & Pipe, M.-E. (2009). Repeated interviewing: A critical evaluation of the risks and potential benefits. In K. Kuehnle & M. Connell (Eds.), *The evaluation of child sexual abuse allegations: A comprehensive guide to assessment and testimony* (pp. 327–361). Hoboken, NJ: John Wiley & Sons, Inc.

Leeney, D. G., & Müller-Johnson, K. (2010). Examining the link between forensic quality and customer service quality of police call centre interviews. *International Journal of Police Science and Management, 12*, 69–80.

Leeney, D. G., & Müller-Johnson, K. (2011). Examining the forensic quality of police call-centre interviews. *Psychology, Crime and Law, 18*, 669–688.

Levy, B. J., & Anderson, M. C. (2002). Inhibitory processes and the control of memory retrieval. *Trends in Cognitive Science, 6*, 299–305.

Loftus, E. F. (2005). Planting misinformation in the human mind: A 30-year investigation of the malleability of memory. *Learning and Memory, 12*, 361–366.

Loftus, E. F., Levidow, B., & Duensing, S. (1992). Who remembers best? Individual differences in memory for events that occurred in a science museum. *Applied Cognitive Psychology, 6*, 93–107.

MacLeod, M. (2002). Retrieval-induced forgetting in eyewitness memory: Forgetting as a consequence of remembering. *Applied Cognitive Psychology, 16*, 135–149.

Marsh, E. J., Tversky, B., & Hutson, M. (2005). How eyewitnesses talk about events: Implications for memory. *Applied Cognitive Psychology, 19*, 1–14.

Mattison, M., Dando, C. J., & Ormerod, T. C. (2014). Drawing to remember: Supporting child witnesses and victims with autistic spectrum disorder to give 'best evidence'. *Journal of Autism and Developmental Disorders, 15*, doi:10.1007/s10803-014-2335-2.

McCauley, M. R., & Fisher, R. P. (1995). Facilitating children's recall with the revised cognitive interview. *The Journal of Applied Psychology, 80*, 510–516.

McPhee, I., Paterson, H. M., & Kemp, R. I. (2013). The power of the spoken word: Can spoken-recall enhance eyewitness evidence? *Psychiatry, Psychology and Law, 20*, 399–411.

Memon, A., Zaragoza, M., Clifford, B. R., & Kidd, L. (2010). Inoculation or antidote? The effects of cognitive interview timing on false memory for forcibly fabricated events. *Law and Human Behavior, 34*, 105–117.

Momenii, N. (2012). Linguistic recontextualization of police interrogation: A new approach in forensic linguistics. *International Journal of Criminology and Sociological Theory, 5*, 796–807.

Norfolk, G. A. (1999). Physiological illnesses and their potential for influencing testimony. *Medicine, Science, and the Law, 39*, 105–112.

Opdenakker, R. (2006). Advantages and disadvantages of four interview techniques in qualitative research. *Qualitative Social Research, 7*, 4. Retrieved from 12 August 2014, www.qualitative-research.net/index.php/fqs/article/view/175/391

Palmer, F., Flowe, H. D., Takarangi, M. K., & Humphries, J. E. (2013). Intoxicated witnesses and suspects: An archival analysis of their involvement in criminal case processing. *Law and Human Behavior, 37*, 54–59.

Pescod, L., Wilcock, R., & Milne, R. (2013). Improving eyewitness memory in police call centre interviews. *Policing, 7*, 299–306.

Podlas, K. (2006). 'The CSI effect': Exposing the media myth. *The Fordham Intellectual Property, Media and Entertainment Law Journal, 16*, 429–465.

Police and Criminal Evidence Act. (1984). Codes of practice D (2013). Retrieved from 12 August 2014, www.gov.uk/government/uploads/system/uploads/attachment_data/file/253831/pace-code-d-2011.pdf

Ridley, A. M., Gabbert, F., & La Rooy, D. J. (Eds.) (2013). *Suggestibility in legal contexts: Psychological research and forensic implications*. London, UK: Wiley-Blackwell.

Rubin, D. C., & Wenzel, A. E. (1996). One hundred years of forgetting: A quantitative description of retention. *Psychological Review, 103*, 743–760.

Sauerland, M., & Sporer, S. L. (2011). Written vs. spoken eyewitness accounts: Does modality of testing matter? *Behavioral Sciences and the Law, 29*, 846–857.

Sauerland, M., Krix, A. C., van Kan, N., Glunz, S., & Sak, A. (2014). Speaking is silver, writing is golden? The role of cognitive and social factors in written versus spoken witness accounts. *Memory and Cognition, 42*, 978–992.

Schacter, D. L., Norman, K. A., and Koutstaal, W. (1998). The cognitive neuroscience of constructive memory. *Annual Review of Psychology, 49*, 289–318.

Schreiber Compo, N., Evans, J. R., Carol, R., Villalba, D., Ham, L., Garcia, T., & Rose, S. (2012). Intoxicated witnesses: Better than their reputation? *Law and Human Behavior, 36*, 77–86.

Shaw, J. S., Bjork, R. A., & Handal, A. (1995). Retrieval-induced forgetting in an eyewitness-memory paradigm. *Psychonomic Bulletin and Review, 2*, 249–253.

Shepherd, E., & Griffiths, A. (2013). *Investigative interviewing: The conversation management approach*. Oxford, UK: Oxford University Press.

Shuy, R. W. (2003). In-person versus telephone interviewing. In J. A. Holstein & J. F. Gubrium (Eds.), *Inside interviewing: New lenses, new concerns* (pp. 175–193). Thousand Oaks, CA: Sage.

Sporer, S. L. (1996). Psychological aspects of person descriptions. In S. L. Sporer, R. S. Malpass, & G. Koehnken (Eds.), *Psychological issues in eyewitness identification* (pp. 53–86). Mahwah, NJ: Lawrence Erlbaum Associates.

Stokoe, E., & Edwards, D. (2008). 'Did you have permission to smash your neighbour's door?' Silly questions and their answers in police–suspect interrogations. *Discourse Studies, 10*, 89–111.

Suengas, A. G., & Johnson, M. K. (1988). Qualitative effects of rehearsal on memories for perceived and imagined complex events. *Journal of Experimental Psychology: General, 117*, 377–389.

Tousignant, J. P., Hall, D., & Loftus, E. F. (1986). Discrepancy detection and vulnerability to misleading post-event information. *Memory and Cognition, 14*, 329–338.

Tuckey, M. R., & Brewer, N. (2003). The influence of schemas, stimulus ambiguity, and interview schedule on eyewitness memory over time. *Journal of Experimental Psychology. Applied, 9*, 101–118.

Tulving, E. (1983). *Elements of Episodic Memory*. New York: Oxford University Press.

Tversky, B., & Marsh, E. J. (2000). Biased retellings of events yield biased memories. *Applied Cognitive Psychology, 40*, 1–38.

van Koppen, P. J., & Lochun, S. K. (1997). Portraying perpetrators: The validity of offender descriptions by witnesses. *Law and Human Behavior, 21*, 661–685.

van Oorsouw, K., & Merckelbach, H. (2012). The effect of alcohol on crime-related amnesia: A field study. *Applied Cognitive Psychology, 26*, 82–90.

Wagstaff, G. F., Wheatcroft, J., Cole, J. C., Brunas-Wagstaff, J., Blackmore, V., & Pilkington, A. (2008). Some cognitive and neuropsychological aspects of social inhibition and facilitation. *European Journal of Cognitive Psychology, 20*, 828–846.

Wang, E., Paterson, H., & Kemp, R. (2014). The effects of immediate recall on eyewitness accuracy and susceptibility to misinformation. *Psychology, Crime and Law, 20*, 619–634.

Watson, D. R. (1990). Some features of the elicitation of confessions in murder interrogations. In G. Psathas (Ed.), *Interaction competence. International Institute for Ethnomethodology and Conversation Analysis* (pp. 263–295). Washington, DC: University Press of America.

Yuille, J. C., Tollestrup, P., Porter, S., Marxsen, D., & Hervé, H. (1998). Some effects of marijuana on eyewitness memory. *International Journal of Law and Psychiatry, 20*, 1–23.

6

The Role of Initial Witness Accounts within the Investigative Process

Fiona Gabbert[1], Lorraine Hope[2], Elisabeth Carter[3], Roel Boon[4]
and Ronald Fisher[5]

[1] Goldsmiths, University of London, UK
[2] University of Portsmouth, UK
[3] Buckinghamshire New University, UK
[4] The National Police of the Netherlands, The Netherlands
[5] Florida International University, Miami, USA

INTRODUCTION

Forensic investigations are an attempt to recreate a criminal incident in order to understand the truth about what happened and who was involved. The goal of any successful investigation is for the police to apprehend the perpetrators and gather sufficient reliable evidence for legal proceedings. At the outset, witness evidence often directs the entire investigatory process, while in the latter stages of an investigation it plays a central role in legal decision-making and the delivery of justice (Ridley, Gabbert & La Rooy, 2013; Shepherd & Griffiths, 2013). The current chapter focuses on the role of initial

Communication in Investigative and Legal Contexts: Integrated Approaches from Forensic Psychology, Linguistics and Law Enforcement, First Edition. Edited by Gavin Oxburgh, Trond Myklebust, Tim Grant and Rebecca Milne.

accounts within the investigative process. We address the following questions:

- What are initial accounts and who elicits them?
- What should be considered when eliciting an initial account?
- How do the goals of initial accounts differ from the goals of subsequent interviews?
- Does the format of the initial account matter?
- Does the quality of the initial account affect the quality of subsequent accounts?
- Does providing an initial account inoculate against the effects of misleading questions?
- Do inconsistencies between the initial and subsequent account(s) mean that the witness is unreliable?

WHAT ARE INITIAL ACCOUNTS AND WHO ELICITS THEM?

Police emergency call handlers are often the first point of police contact for witnesses and victims of crime. Their role is to establish what has happened, to whom, when and where. They will also seek information about the presence of any weapons or dangerous substances to inform decisions on actions that should, or should not, be taken by the police and emergency services. A priority for call handlers is to determine the type of response required (police, ambulance, etc.), assign a level of urgency and then implement the response accordingly. Once the appropriate emergency response has been dispatched the call handler has the opportunity to elicit further relevant information from the caller if appropriate, including requests for information about what happened, who was involved, where the perpetrators are now, what they looked like, etc. An advantage of gathering information at this early stage is that a witness's memory of a crime is likely to be the most detailed and most accurate because of the relatively short time interval between witnessing the crime and retrieving information from memory. However, a challenge faced by emergency call handlers is to gather priority information in a very short period of time from callers who are often distressed. Some emergency call handlers are provided with scripts to help structure the interview. Scripts typically contain context-relevant prompts (about theft, vehicle crime, criminal damage, etc.) and are used to facilitate information gathering once the nature of the call has been determined. However, the use of call scripts is not standard practice across forces, or even within the same force.

In the United Kingdom, information disclosed in an initial interview with the emergency call handler may be used as evidence in court.

One area in which this is particularly pertinent is in cases of domestic violence. In 2009/2010 one in three of all domestic violence cases in the UK (over 6500) failed due to victims either retracting their evidence or failing to attend court (Crown Prosecution Service, 2011: Keir Starmer QC Speech;). In such cases – where a victim withdraws his or her statement but police pursue a prosecution – the emergency call can be used as evidence with or without the victim's cooperation (Crown Prosecution Service, 2005: Policy for Prosecuting Cases of Domestic Violence; Greater Manchester Police, 2010: Tackling Domestic Abuse Policy and Operational Procedures). To be defensible in court it is vital that these initial interviews are conducted with the same high standards as investigative interviews conducted later in the investigation by trained officers and staff.[1]

Relatively little is known about the quality of call-centre interviews, as psychological research on emergency call handling is sparse and most research focuses on obtaining evidence at later stages in the investigation process. A literature search yielded only three published studies examining call-centre calls from an interviewing perspective (Leeney & Müller-Johnson, 2010; 2011; Pescod, Wilcock & Milne, 2013) and one unpublished Master's thesis (Ambler, 2005). Leeney and Müller-Johnson (2011) examined 40 emergency calls from a single UK police force, coding the interaction between the caller and call handler, the types of questions used and the information obtained. The researchers found that 88.5% of questions asked during the calls were productive questions; these included open questions, as well as closed questions to obtain factual information (What is your phone number?, Is anyone injured?, Is an ambulance needed?). Unproductive questions accounted for 11.5% of all questions asked, consisting of inappropriate and potentially suggestive closed (yes/no) questions that introduced new information to the caller. Leading questions, forced choice and multiple questions were also observed in call handler interviews. This is of particular concern as questions of this nature can have a significant detrimental effect on witness memory, as well as the potential to mislead a police investigation or render witness evidence inadmissible in court. The call handlers in Leeney and Müller-Johnson's (2011) sample used call scripts 42.5% of the time. Interestingly, when call handlers used scripts, they relied on fewer questions to elicit the same amount of information. Specifically, call handlers using a script used more open questions to elicit information, and fewer suggestive and unproductive questions. This finding suggests that the use of call scripts is beneficial both in providing a structure for the call taker and in promoting good interview practice.

Following Leeney and Müller-Johnson's (2011) promising findings relating to the use of scripts, Pescod et al. (2013) developed a protocol for use in police call-centres using the 'Report Everything' instruction from the Cognitive Interview (Fisher & Geiselman, 1992). This was compared against 'the five Wh-questioning strategy' (where, when, who, what and why) and a control condition where participants were instructed to provide brief details of the incident. Pescod et al. found that the Report Everything instruction elicited significantly more information than the other conditions, with no significant differences in accuracy rates between the conditions. This instruction also elicited significantly more correct person description details. This is a promising finding as witnesses tend to struggle with providing police with good quality person descriptions (Brown, Lloyd-Jones & Robinson, 2008; Gabbert & Brown, 2015; Kebbell & Milne, 1998). For instance, Leeney and Müller-Johnson (2011) found that, although perpetrator details were reported in 40% of the calls in their sample, only 6.25% of the responses contained information on physical features of the perpetrator.

Once an incident has been called-in by a witness or victim, it is often the job of frontline police officers to attend and conduct interviews at the scene. During the first minutes and hours after an incident, these officers are primarily concerned with increasing the probability of apprehending the perpetrator/s and securing public safety, while other emergency responders administer first aid if required. The frontline officers may receive some information from the call-taker in the emergency control centre, but communication with witnesses at the crime scene is another direct source of information. These interviews typically focus on eliciting perpetrator descriptions and obtaining information about weapon presence and escape routes. Person descriptions in particular are often vital in the immediate stages of an investigation, especially when a search is initiated for an unknown suspect who might still be in close proximity to the crime scene. However, as with call-centre interviews, the speed of gathering information is often prioritized. Person descriptions obtained are generally poor, such that they fit a large number of people rather than distinguishing someone from a crowd (Sporer, 1996; van Koppen & Lochun, 1997). This is problematic because the more vague a perpetrator description is, the greater the chance of a false positive error when apprehending a suspect. Furthermore, in the UK, the Police and Criminal Evidence Act (1984) Code of Practice for England and Wales requires that a record must be made of the suspect's description *as first given by a witness* (PACE Code D, 2013; emphasis added). It is therefore important for the initial description of the perpetrator/s to be as detailed as possible.

The quality of investigative interview skills amongst frontline officers is a cause for concern, particularly as these officers have a relative lack of policing experience and training (Dando, Wilcock & Milne, 2008). Furthermore, there is often a lack of resources in terms of the availability of time, expertise or personnel to conduct interviews shortly after an incident has been reported. For instance, if there are multiple witnesses at a crime scene, then officers may face difficult choices in prioritizing who to interview. In direct response to this challenge, Gabbert, Hope and Fisher (2009) developed a Self-Administered Interview (SAI©) to address two important and related issues facing police investigators: (i) the serious resource challenge faced by investigators when an incident occurs for which there are numerous eyewitnesses and (ii) the need to maintain ethical, transparent, effective and responsive investigative practice in the face of budget cuts and an increased focus on cost savings. The SAI© is a generic response tool in that it is suitable for obtaining information about a wide range of different incidents. It takes the form of a standardized protocol of instructions and questions that enable witnesses to provide their own statement and is therefore ideal for use when restricted resources mean that a traditional interview is not possible. Scientific tests of the SAI© have shown that it elicits significantly more accurate and detailed information than a free-recall request. Completing an SAI© also strengthens witness memory, meaning that witnesses are protected against forgetting, and against exposure to potentially distorting post-event information (Gabbert et al., 2009; Gabbert, Hope, Fisher & Jamieson, 2012; Gawrylowicz, Memon & Scoboria, 2013; Hope, Gabbert & Fisher, 2011; Hope, Gabbert, Fisher & Jamieson, 2014). Despite being a relatively new investigative tool for officers tasked with eliciting initial witness accounts, the SAI© has been implemented effectively in a growing number of incidents involving multiple witnesses including murders, shootings, assaults and other major crime incidents (see Hope et al., 2011).

WHAT SHOULD BE CONSIDERED WHEN ELICITING AN INITIAL ACCOUNT?

First responders in forensic contexts may encounter witnesses or victims in a variety of suboptimal contexts. For instance, the immediate environment may be unsafe or unstable (e.g. ongoing threat, fire, debris from bomb or natural disaster). A primary concern of first responders should be the safety of themselves and any others nearby; therefore, no attempt should be made to elicit an initial account until a safe environment has been established. The context in which victims or witnesses are encountered may also have implications for the reliability of their initial account; for example, if the victim/witness is distressed, traumatized or intoxicated. Again, in such contexts, an immediate consideration of the first responder should be to ensure the safety and well-being of the victim/witness taking consideration of his/her personal circumstance.

Archival analysis of intoxication among witnesses and suspects suggests that while this is a common problem, investigators are inconsistent in their approach to witnesses who may be under the influence of drugs or alcohol (Palmer, Flowe, Takarangi & Humphries, 2013). Typically, police and others in forensic settings expect that the accounts provided by intoxicated witnesses are likely to be less reliable than those provided by sober individuals. Indeed, basic research on the effects of alcohol on memory tends to show memory impairment with intoxication. However, studies to date examining the effects of alcohol intoxication on witness memory produce somewhat inconsistent findings. For example, in a study designed to investigate the effect of alcohol on memory performance under controlled conditions, Schreiber Compo et al. (2012) found that mock witnesses who were intoxicated when exposed to a staged crime event did not show noticeably impaired recall and did not appear to be more vulnerable to misinformation compared to the sober and placebo groups. It is worth noting that levels of intoxication induced in laboratory studies is likely to be significantly lower (for ethical reasons) than in actual cases, where the level of intoxication is a concern for those eliciting initial accounts. Notably, in a field study conducted in bars, van Oorsouw and Merckelbach (2012) found that although the accuracy of accounts provided by intoxicated witnesses did not differ from their sober counterparts, intoxicated individuals provided significantly less information during interviews. With respect to initial interviews these results are consistent with Yuille, Tollestrup, Porter, Marxsen and Hervé (1998) finding for witnesses who had smoked marijuana prior to witnessing an incident. Specifically, the results suggest that smoking marijuana prior to witnessing a live staged incident had a temporary negative effect on the amount of information recalled (in comparison to performance in the placebo and control groups), with little effect on accuracy or recognition. It may also be worthwhile identifying whether a witness is under the influence of prescription medicines before eliciting an initial account as there is some evidence that different types of drugs prescribed for various medical and psychological conditions may affect memory performance (see the review by Norfolk, 1999). Thus, intoxication may have implications for first responders seeking to elicit detailed accounts – although further research is needed to determine the precise nature of memory deficits in applied settings.

Special care should be taken when eliciting information from people who are traumatized, including clinical intervention if necessary, depending on the degree of distress. A key initial aim in any interaction with a traumatized individual is to reduce distress levels in order to help him or her provide clearer and more complete information. In addition to intrusive thoughts/images associated with trauma memories, victims of trauma can have symptoms that interfere with communication. Additional communication barriers may also be present for those who feel their experiences are unspeakable (Dudgeon, 2012), those communicating in a second language and those afraid of the consequences of disclosing abuse (International Rehabilitation Council for Torture Victims, 2009). Due to considerations such as these, there are often delays in eliciting an initial account from witnesses. Indeed, delays in interviewing witnesses in any situational context are frequently unavoidable due to competing demands on resources. The quality of eyewitness accounts, however, is time critical. Research shows that as the delay between encoding and retrieval *increases*, the amount of information that can be recalled systematically *decreases* (Ebbinghaus, 1913/1885; Rubin & Wenzel, 1996; see also Tuckey & Brewer, 2003). The ability to remember investigatively important information such as specific details relating to descriptions, or 'who did what', also decreases over a delay, as memory becomes more gist-like with time (Conway, Cohen & Standhope, 1991; Fisher, 1996; Goldsmith, Koriat & Pansky, 2005; Kintsch, Welsch, Schmalhofer & Zimny, 1990; Koriat, Levy-Sadot, Edry & De Marcas, 2003; Schacter, Norman & Koutstaal, 1998). Any delay prior to interview also increases the risk of memory contamination, as witnesses have more time in which to encounter items of new and/or misleading postevent information (Ridley et al., 2013). For example, witnesses could encounter media coverage about the witnessed incident or discuss their memories together, which can lead to 'memory conformity', where people's memory reports become similar to one another's following a discussion and appear (falsely) corroborative (see Gabbert & Hope, 2013). Thus, conducting an initial interview in a timely manner is an important consideration as the potential consequences of delay can pose significant problems when establishing a line of enquiry. However, first responders should be aware of the potential effects of both intoxication and trauma on witness memory and, on a case-by-case basis, be sensitive to the potential trade-offs where interviews are required to be delayed for the psychological or physiological well-being of the witness.

HOW DO THE GOALS OF INITIAL ACCOUNTS DIFFER FROM THE GOALS OF SUBSEQUENT INTERVIEWS?

The amount and type of information required from witnesses by the police varies at each stage of an investigation. Once the initial response has been delivered and the investigation is under way, a door-to-door inquiry, or an appeal for witnesses, might be initiated if further information is required. Door-to-door enquiries are usually conducted in the vicinity of the crime scene whereas witness appeals are often targeted to the exact location in which the crime took place ('*Were you at this place, at this time, on this date? If so, did you see X?*'). These types of inquiries are aimed at screening the public for potential witnesses who live or work near the crime scene and might have seen or heard what happened.

Once witnesses have been identified, investigative interviews are conducted, the goals of which are to obtain potential new leads and/or to gather evidence for prosecution. The objective is therefore to secure as much reliable information from a witness's memory as possible. The interview therefore requires the use of thorough evidence-based interview techniques, with a focus not only on '*What happened?*' but also with a focus on '*Who did what?*' and '*Why?*'. The 'why' of the crime is important at this stage of the investigation because it helps legal decision makers in assessing, for example, grounds for exculpation or whether an act was deliberate. The focus on 'Who did what?' differs from earlier focus of 'Who did it?' as many legal systems require actions attributed to individuals in order to make conviction possible. The investigative interview is one of the means for the police to answer such 'Wh-questions' (where, when, who, what and why). It must be noted that the interviewer need not necessarily *ask* these 'Wh-questions': they should be *answered* during an investigation and the investigative interview is one of the means for that purpose. In fact, during the interview asking mainly open-ended questions (e.g. '*Tell me everything about the car*') is preferred to asking closed questions (e.g. '*What was the colour of the car?*') because the former questioning style usually results in more accurate responses.

Repeated interviewing of the *same* witnesses about the same incident is not unusual in criminal investigations. In fact, the witness who called the emergency room might be the same witness who is addressed by a police officer at the crime scene, and again later in an investigative interview at the police station. The goals at each stage might differ, due to the timing of the interview within the investigative process and type of information required. One reason for an investigative team to invite a witness for a second interview is the availability of new information. For example, actions previously described by a witness may appear contradictory to what happened according to newly collected video camera material. The focus of the interview in such cases is to 'problem solve' the parts of the previous account that appear to be contradictory to other available information. At any time, however, both law enforcement and investigative officers should obtain as much correct information from a witness's memory *as possible*, while minimizing the risk that other recollections may be damaged or harder to retrieve.

DOES THE FORMAT OF THE INITIAL ACCOUNT MATTER?

When considering spoken versus written formats of providing an initial account, the main areas for concern are that (i) the account is of sufficient detail and quantity, (ii) the person delivering the account is supported in the type and direction of the information, (iii) the person is protected from further harm or victimization from the process itself and (iv) the account is protected from contaminating factors. There is an overarching tension between the need for immediacy in eliciting accounts of critical events from witnesses and the need for complete accounts in order to preserve the memory of the event. This tension is exacerbated with the impracticality of achieving immediate and in-depth interviews with a large number of witnesses. Much of the literature in this area is contradictory and argues variously for the use of either *spoken* or *written* accounts for accuracy, reliability, amount and quality of information and cognitive load on participants, in either format.

McPhee, Paterson and Kemp (2013) identify difficulties in motivation that can occur in self-administered written accounts, whereby the person producing the account would be doing so without interactional feedback to motivate and structure the content. An oral interview enables the interviewer to offer support and direction to a witness while he or she provides a narrative. This can include physical feedback (hand gestures or other body movement to signal understanding) and use of social cues that encourage interviewees to elaborate or clarify their accounts (Opdenakker, 2006; Shuy, 2003). Furthermore, oral feedback, such as prompts for additional information, offer a way of gathering elaborated accounts, thereby accessing more detailed information from the interviewee (Sauerland, Krix, van Kan, Glunz & Sak, 2014; Sauerland & Sporer, 2011). Without this type of interaction and direction, written statements can end up being brief (McPhee et al., 2013). Information can also be left out as witnesses assume it might not be serious or important enough to include (Bergmann, Jacobs, Hoffmann & Boeing, 2004), or too mundane or irrelevant to a criminal investigation (Sauerland et al., 2014). This may be attributable in part to the *CSI effect*; witness statements are rarely shown to be key evidence (Gever, 2005), with DNA or other forensic clues such as ballistic evidence most often used to identify and convict the perpetrator (Podlas, 2006). In contrast, spoken accounts conducted by the police are designed to capture the information they require to satisfy the elements of an offence (e.g. 'Did you take the car without consent?', 'Were you taking any drugs?'; see Carter, 2011, for examples). They are conducted with the final audience in mind – anticipating the future use of the interview as evidence in court (Jönsson & Linell; 1991; Komter, 2002/2003) and officers will even orient away from the interviewee's talk in order to do so (Carter, 2011).

However, even the act of interviewing can have a real impact on the interviewee; in the context of the police interview the question–answer format has itself been described as a way in which power is displayed and accomplished (Carter, 2011; Watson, 1990). Grabowski (2007) and Wagstaff et al. (2008) found that the presence of an interviewer may increase cognitive load as a result of the autonomy of the speaker being compromised, and therefore diminishes the witness's capacity for memory recall. In contrast, the visual presentation of questions in written format reduces the demands on 'working memory' (Chang & Krosnick, 2010), meaning that in written conditions, event recall could be unencumbered by other cognitive demands associated with processing verbal questions. This is supported by Sauerland et al. (2014), who show that when detailed guidance that explicitly discouraged guessing was given to participants providing written accounts, this led to more relevant information being provided in written accounts, including increased accuracy and detail.

Written accounts might disadvantage people who are unmotivated or non-compliant (Hope, Gabbert, Heaton-Armstrong & Wolchover, 2013), due to the ordinary association of written accounts with non-social situations (as opposed to the potentially motivating presence of an interviewer in oral accounts). Witnesses asked to produce written accounts may also be disadvantaged by this modality if they are unaccustomed to writing or embarrassed about writing through handwriting or spelling difficulties (McPhee et al., 2013) or less able to communicate as eruditely through writing as they would orally (Hope et al., 2011; McPhee et al., 2013). Written accounts may also not be appropriate for vulnerable witnesses for whom special measures are necessary. McPhee et al. (2013) found that spoken accounts are 'less effortful' than written, and Sauerland and Sporer (2011) and Kellogg (2007) suggest that written witness statements are more cognitively demanding than their oral counterparts, due to the task involving committing memories to words on the page rather than verbalizing the same statement. This effect can be alleviated through typing, rather than writing, the account, in the case of witnesses with weaker cognitive abilities (Chang & Krosnick, 2010), although this may relate to the speed at which the account can be communicated.

In a direct comparison of written and verbal accounts, Sauerland and Sporer (2011) examined the levels of detail and accuracy between the two modes of communication in free-recall and open-ended questions in both the spoken and written conditions, with separate tasks for describing the crime (a theft) and the perpetrator. They found with regards to crime descriptions that the spoken accounts yielded more details and were more accurate in descriptions that were central to the crime and that the spoken accounts also yielded a higher quantity and accuracy with regards to key elements of perpetrator descriptions. This suggests that a written account would not be as effective as one elicited through oral interviews for the type of (critical) information an initial account would seek to gain. Kellogg (2007) also found that spoken reports were more complete and more accurate than written ones. More recently, McPhee et al. (2013) reported that both spoken and written accounts provided the same quality, the same amount of information, with the same level of accuracy, although this may have been an effect of the isolation of the participants from interviewers in the spoken condition, which prevented interviewer–interviewee interaction. Sauerland et al. (2014) subsequently concluded that written accounts yielded more quantity and detail (but not accuracy) than accounts that were spoken into a recording device. However, Sauerland et al.'s research did not allow the interviewer to deviate from the set questions asked in both spoken and written conditions, which also eliminates any potential benefit from probing questions or reformulations.

Often, oral interviews with witnesses or victims can be seen as co-constructed accounts by the interviewer and interviewee. They involve officers' reformulations of accounts produced by the interviewee, for example, by reformulating information provided by suspects into offence-specific narratives that satisfy the elements of the offence and reflecting the officer's overall objective of the interview (Stokoe & Edwards, 2008). This can also happen with witness and victim interviews; reformulations by officers can repackage the account into the appropriate format to satisfy the procedural, investigative and beaurocratic concerns of the criminal justice system (Carter, 2011), such as the court's preference for linear narratives. This active reformulating of accounts relies on the sequential interaction between the interviewer and interviewee of 'live' interaction (Carter, 2011; Hester & Eglin, 1992; Heydon, 2005; Watson, 1990), which is absent from accounts written by one party without interaction from another. Although it is possible for officers to seek clarification on descriptions, dates, times and other potentially significant details of the accounts that might be missing or unclear from the written account, this will be delayed until after the account is produced and would not form an organic part of building and developing the interview interaction. The witness would have to revisit their account, which may have an adverse effect in that they may interpret the officer's request for clarification as a signal that they have provided insufficient, inadequate or incorrect information.

In addition to the interactional differences associated with spoken and written accounts, the lack of face-to-face interaction restricts rapport-building and creating a 'natural' encounter (Shuy, 2003), but this may also mean that a witness writing an account is more likely to impart information of a more personal nature or provide more details that they may be embarrassed to talk about. Chang and Krosnick (2010) found that, without an interviewer, respondents were more likely to produce a truthful account when addressing topics that may be less socially desirable or concern sensitive issues. Chang and Krosnick (2010) also show how their empirical research reflects the wider body of work that spans a range of contexts, including medical, sexual, religious and political situations. A witness might edit their account of their role in an event to mitigate potential social judgements of the interviewer, for example, omitting socially undesirable drinking or drug-taking from their account, whereas this may be an important part of the story or an important contextualizing feature with regards to an assailant's *modus operandi* (see also Jones & Forrest, 1992).

Witnesses providing written accounts have control over the pace and content of the output (Grabowski, 2007), with less real or perceived pressure to complete the account quickly than in oral accounts to an interviewer, where the interactional structure of talk requires a response in a timely fashion, in accordance with the cooperative principle of conversation (Grice, 1975). Although witnesses should be reassured that they have plenty of time to think about their responses, they will be interactionally drawn to respond without delay (Carter, 2014). There is a flexibility embedded in the written medium that can be drawn on if needed by the witness; witnesses can spend varying amounts of time on each question to reflect or answer quickly as needed (Chang & Krosnick, 2010). This would give the witness more ownership over the account, which is a positive thing for witnesses or victims of a crime. The absence of an interviewer may also enable the witness to reflect on the event and elaborate on details without reactions from an officer or time constraints influencing or affecting them; increased pace associated with oral interviewing has an effect on the quality of the account elicited from the participant (Chang & Krosnick, 2010).

Despite the conflicting evidence pertaining to the advantages and disadvantages of spoken and written accounts, the retrieval of information and memories of an event from witnesses is time-critical (as discussed above). McPhee et al. (2013) suggest that it is better to elicit an immediate account from a witness, either spoken or written, than to wait to do so. Given that initial accounts are most likely to be enlisted following events involving large numbers of witnesses that require the elicitation of critical information, and that cognitive or in-depth interviews may not be appropriate or possible in these scenarios, it is suggested that either format would be preferable to delaying the elicitation of an account in order to seek one format over the other. One of the major benefits of written accounts is the ability to reach a large number of witnesses and gather information from them in a formulaic fashion that is advantageous in the early stages of basic data gathering for investigative purposes (of course, flexibility and detailed accounts are preferred, but are not necessarily available, as discussed above). Written accounts therefore offer more data towards the investigation on a larger scale than the Criminal Justice System would ordinarily be able to draw upon. This can only lead to better informed decisions about the case and its disposal – a key principle behind initial accounts.

The transformation that often takes place in rendering a spoken account into a written format (and specifically into a predetermined framework that these accounts must fill for evidentiary and bureaucratic purposes) has a retroactive effect on the account. This transition from a spoken to a written account is regularly performed so that a representation of the taped interview, rather than the interview itself, is heard in court. In doing so, much detail is stripped from the interaction, which is then either absent or reanimated by a police officer and prosecuting attorney (acting the parts of the police officer and the interviewed) in the manner of their choosing when it is read aloud in court. Haworth (2010) and Jönsson and Linell (1991) discuss (deliberate or accidental) transformations from a spoken to a written format and describe cases where the transformation has had serious effects on the content of the interview, which has obvious implications for the administration of justice in the courtroom. Momenii (2012) draws together research in this area and discusses the role of forensic linguistics in identifying and alleviating the associated difficulties with this practice. Whether the account is given in spoken or written format, it is evidentially best for it to remain in that format rather than be transformed to the other.

DOES THE QUALITY OF THE INITIAL ACCOUNT AFFECT THE QUALITY OF SUBSEQUENT ACCOUNTS?

Research lends support to the finding that engaging in a *high-quality* initial recall attempt facilitates an enhanced delayed recall. Specifically, repeated retrieval attempts may be facilitated by a good, and impeded by a bad, quality initial recall respectively (e.g. Hashtroudi, Johnson, Vnek & Ferguson, 1994; Marsh, Tversky & Hutson, 2005; Suengas & Johnson, 1988; Tversky & Marsh, 2000; though see McCauley & Fisher, 1995).

Theoretical models of memory suggest that an immediate *high-quality* recall may support subsequent recall attempts from episodic memory because it increases the activation levels of items in memory and the associations between them (Anderson, 1983). Thus, subsequent cued questions for target information within an investigative interview are likely to be effective, in comparison to a situation where no initial retrieval attempt has taken place. In contrast, a *poor-quality* initial recall attempt can impair later recall, because it reduces access to information not recalled initially (for retrieval inhibition, see Anderson, Bjork & Bjork, 1994; Levy & Anderson, 2002). Thus, initial accounts should be as complete as possible, as memories can be distorted or lost through an earlier incomplete retrieval (MacLeod, 2002). Shaw, Bjork and Handal (1995) demonstrated this 'retrieval induced forgetting' phenomenon using an eyewitness paradigm where participants were asked to encode details of a scene and then report what they could recall about particular target items on three occasions, such that some items became 'practised' (in that they were reported on multiple occasions) whereas others did not. When later trying to recall the scene as a whole it was found that some details had been suppressed as a direct consequence of the practised items 'overshadowing' them and making them disproportionately less accessible. MacLeod (2002) reported similar effects relating to the description of a suspect where subsets of descriptive information had been subject to repeated questioning, resulting in a limited ability to provide a description as a whole.

In a recent study, Hope et al. (2014) examined the impact of an initial account format on performance in a later interview. Mock witnesses viewed a simulated crime event and provided an initial account (using either a Self-Administered Interview (SAI©) or a Free Recall Instruction) or did not provide an initial account. One week later, all mock witnesses were interviewed with a Cognitive Interview. In the interview, mock witnesses who had provided an account using an SAI© reported more correct information and maintained higher accuracy than those who had completed a free recall (or not provided an initial account at all). An examination of consistency between the initial account and the subsequent interview suggested that the SAI© was the most effective because it preserved more of the originally recalled items (than did an initial free recall).

DOES PROVIDING AN INITIAL ACCOUNT INOCULATE AGAINST THE EFFECTS OF MISLEADING QUESTIONS?

Relevant literature suggests that a good-quality preliminary interview will strengthen a witness's memory, thus offering protection against exposure to misleading post-event information (PEI) encountered in the form of suggestive questions or from other sources such as discussions with a co-witness. This is because having a 'strong' original memory for an event increases the likelihood that individuals detect, and are therefore able to reject, discrepancies between their original memories for the event and any PEI received (Garry, Loftus & Brown, 1994; Hall, Loftus & Tousignant, 1984; Loftus, 2005; Loftus, Levidow & Duensing, 1992; Tousignant, Hall & Loftus, 1986). Geiselman, Fisher, Cohen, Holland and Surtes (1986) found that mock witnesses were less susceptible to the effects of misleading questions when a Cognitive Interview (CI) had been administered prior to the misleading questions being encountered. In contrast, a CI given after the leading and misleading questions conferred no benefits with respect to attenuating witness vulnerability to misleading questions.

Similar conclusions were reached by Memon, Zaragoza, Clifford and Kidd (2010), who gave mock-witnesses a CI either prior to or immediately after a suggestive interview, where they were encouraged to confabulate in order to provide responses to 'impossible' questions. One week later, all participants returned for a final interview. It was found that participants who had been given a CI prior to (but not following) the suggestive interview reported significantly fewer forced fabrications in their final interview, leading the researchers to conclude that a CI given prior to misleading information has protective benefits. Although Memon et al. did not draw explicitly on the notion of discrepancy detection, their findings support the idea that participants are better able to be vigilant against discrepancies if their memory for a target event is strengthened (though see LaPaglia, Wilford, Rivard, Chan & Fisher, 2014).

More recently, Gabbert et al. (2012) investigated whether an early recall opportunity, in the form of a Self-Administered Interview (SAI), protected against the negative consequences of exposure to misleading PEI. In two studies, participants viewed a mock crime event, after which half immediately recorded their account using the SAI. Control participants did not have an immediate recall opportunity. Following a delay, participants were presented with misinformation encountered either in a misleading news report (Study 1) or in the form of misleading cued-recall questions (Study 2). Study 1 found that completing an SAI shortly after witnessing an event significantly increased the amount of accurate information reported in a delayed recall test, in comparison with the performance of control participants. Almost twice as many accurate details were reported after a delay by SAI than control participants. Furthermore, SAI participants were significantly less likely than controls to errantly report items of misleading PEI that had been encountered in the news report during the delay period. Study 2 also found that participants who had an opportunity to complete an SAI after witnessing a mock-crime event had a better memory than control participants and that SAI participants were less likely to attempt to answer misleading questions by reporting confabulated responses. Both studies found a significant negative correlation between the number of accurate items of information reported and the number of items of misinformation reported.

Taken together, these studies suggest that a good-quality preliminary interview can decrease the likelihood of the undesirable effects of exposure to misinformation or suggestive questions. It is reasonable to suggest that this is because a preliminary interview can strengthen memory for the originally encoded event, thus protecting it against the negative effects of exposure to misleading suggestions. Of course, this assumes that the preliminary interview is conducted prior to exposure to potentially misleading or contaminating information.

In contrast to these findings, however, a series of studies by Chan, Thomas and Bulevich (2009) found evidence that an immediate test can actually exacerbate susceptibility to being influenced by misleading PEI. Specifically, participants who engaged in an early recall opportunity about an event, followed by exposure to a misleading narrative, were significantly more prone to reporting items of misleading PEI in a final recall test. These findings are somewhat counterintuitive based upon current memory theory, and at odds with the findings of Geiselman et al. (1986), Memon et al. (2010) and Gabbert et al. (2012). These contradictory findings may reflect an important methodological difference in the nature of the recall test used. Specifically, the studies reporting positive effects of an early recall opportunity featured participants freely reporting their memories, whereas Chan et al. (2009) used a battery of cued-recall questions to elicit an initial recall.

To explore whether the contrasting findings can be explained by the type of immediate recall test used, Gabbert, Hope, Lindsay, Skowronska and Sauer (2011) conducted an experiment where participants viewed a simulated crime incident and were immediately tested with either a free- or cued-recall test (a control group had no initial recall). Participants then listened to a summary of the event containing both accurate and misleading PEI before completing a final recall test. Participants who had completed an initial Cued-Recall test were significantly more susceptible to the misleading PEI than participants in the Free-Recall and Control conditions (who did not differ). These results, and those of Chan et al. (2009), suggest that the *type* of immediate test influences whether participants are more, or less, influenced by misleading post-event suggestions. These conclusions are partially supported by a more recent study by Wang, Paterson and Kemp

(2014), who also manipulated the type of initial recall test (free-recall, cued-recall or no test) to explore whether this can inoculate or exacerbate susceptibility to misleading PEI. Here it was found that both types of initial test, in comparison to the no-test condition, protected memory against the misleading PEI.

DO INCONSISTENCIES BETWEEN THE INITIAL AND SUBSEQUENT ACCOUNT(S) MEAN THAT THE WITNESS IS UNRELIABLE?

Witnesses are often interviewed on more than one occasion during an investigation. The consistency of information reported on each occasion can influence the perceived credibility of a witness. Witness inconsistency is sometimes incorrectly interpreted as being a diagnostic cue to witness inaccuracy on the grounds that inconsistency suggests poor memory. However, there are different types of inconsistency: *omissions* (leaving out a detail that was mentioned in a previous account), *reminiscence* (reporting new details in later interviews that had not been mentioned previously) and *contradictions* (contradicting an item of information that had been mentioned previously), and each one has a different relationship with accuracy.

Reporting new information (reminiscence) is sometimes viewed with suspicion because an increase in recall runs counter to the intuitive principle that memory decays over time. However, the psychological literature suggests that reminiscence is a common feature of repeated recall accounts (see Fisher, Brewer & Mitchell, 2009; Gilbert & Fisher, 2006; Hope et al., 2014; La Rooy, Lamb & Pipe, 2009). When witnesses are interviewed more than once, new information can be reported on later occasions for different reasons. The first is because a goal of re-interviewing is often to obtain additional information from witnesses, and so interviewers ask different questions to elicit different/new information. Recollection reflects not only the contents of the memory store but also the process of retrieval (Tulving, 1983). Thus, if the retrieval processes applied on two occasions differ (e.g. accessing the memory differently depending on which questions are asked), then the information that is reported may differ, even if the contents of memory do not change. The retrieval process is therefore partially determined by the specific question that is asked. In general, the more the retrieval cues (questions) differ across interviews, the more dissimilar the recollections will be on the two interviews (Fisher et al., 2009; Gilbert & Fisher, 2006). Reminiscence may occur, therefore, if a retrieval cue is present on the second interview, but not on the first interview.

Related to this is a second reason why witnesses report new information; the amount of information volunteered by witnesses is based upon their perceived expectations of the interviewer. Thus, if a witness is interviewed a second time he or she may feel that they did not provide enough information previously. People regulate the amount of information they report depending on their interpretation of the context (Koriat & Goldsmith, 1996). It should not be overlooked, however, that new information is sometimes reported because the witness has encountered some influential 'post-event information' from another source, such as another witness, the media or even from the police investigators. In this instance the witness's reminiscent recollections do not necessarily reflect his or her memory of the incident itself, but rather what he or she learned about the event afterwards from potentially misleading sources.

How likely is it that new information obtained in subsequent interviews is accurate? An informative piece of research designed to address this very question was conducted by Gilbert and Fisher (2006). Mock witnesses watched a three-minute videotape of a simulated bank robbery. After a short delay they were asked to write down as many details as they could remember, acting as if it was a genuine incident that they had just seen. Half of the participants were simply asked to 'describe the robbery' while the other half were given instructions to 'describe the robbery in four different ways' (e.g. in chronological order, followed by reverse order) to facilitate retrieval. Two days later participants returned to take part in a second recall task and either received the same retrieval cues as before (e.g. 'describe the robbery' on both occasions) or the alternative retrieval cues (e.g. instructions to 'describe the robbery' at the first recall attempt and to 'describe the robbery in four different ways' at the second recall attempt). The information reported across the two interviews was examined by categorizing reported details as one of four types: consistent, contradictory, reminiscent and forgotten details. Accuracy rates were examined within each category, as well as exploring how these related to the accuracy of the statement as a whole.

Gilbert and Fisher (2006) found that reminiscence was a common phenomenon; 189 out of 192 (98%) mock-witnesses made at least two reminiscent recollections in their second recall attempt. As predicted, when the retrieval cues changed from the first retrieval attempt to the second, witnesses made almost twice as many reminiscent statements (10.1) as when the same cues were given (6.1). The accuracy of the reminiscent details was 87%, indicating that a large proportion of newly reported information was accurate. In comparison, 95% of consistently reported details were accurate and 93% of the forgotten details were accurate. These findings were replicated in a recent study by Hope et al. (2014), who found that 100% of their sample reported at least one reminiscent detail in a second interview. The accuracy rates were 90% for reminiscent details and 96% for consistently reported details.

When examining the relationship between reminiscence and the accuracy of the statement as a whole, Gilbert and Fisher (2006) found that the prevalence of reminiscent details was *not* predictive of overall accuracy. Furthermore, a comparison of a sample of the *most* and *least* consistent witnesses found only minimal differences in the accuracy of their overall statements. This is because a person's memory for a complex event comprises a number of components (visual information, auditory information, temporal and contextual details, cognitive interpretations, emotional reactions, etc.). Each component of the memory can be processed independently of one another, despite being part of an associated network that collectively represents the memory as a whole (Fisher et al., 2009). Thus, witnesses who incorrectly recall the details of a perpetrator's weapon are not unduly inaccurate in recalling the perpetrator, and vice versa. In sum, if a witness fails to recall a component on one occasion, or if one component of the memory is proven to be in error, this does not mean that other components of the memory will also be incorrect.

Another type of inconsistency that can occur between an initial report and subsequent statements is when a witness contradicts him/herself (e.g. saying on one occasion that a perpetrator was clean shaven and on another occasion that he had a beard). It is obvious here that at least one of the two contradictory responses must be incorrect. As such, contradictory details tend to have a very low accuracy rate. Gilbert and Fisher (2006) found that 49% of contradictory statements were accurate. Witnesses might directly contradict a detail they reported previously because they have encountered some post-event information that has influenced their recollection or because they have simply made a mistake. However, once again, research has demonstrated that the proportion of contradictions in a repeated recall attempt is a poor predictor of overall accuracy (Fisher & Cutler, 1995; Gilbert & Fisher, 2006; Hope et al., 2014). This can be explained as before: the accuracy of recalling one component of a complex event is unrelated to accuracy in recalling other components of the same event.

In sum, when considering whether inconsistencies between the initial and subsequent accounts mean that the witness is unreliable, it is important to distinguish between different kinds of inconsistency (omissions, reminiscence and contradictions). Despite a high accuracy rate for reminiscent details, they tend not to be as accurate as either consistent or forgotten items of information; however, they are more accurate than contradictions. Witnesses who make reminiscent and/or contradictory statements may be inaccurate on those *specific statements*, but they may be accurate on the remainder of their testimony. Thus, inconsistency is diagnostic of accuracy at the level of the individual item but not at the level of the overall witness statement.

SUMMARY AND CONCLUSIONS

The current chapter has examined the role of initial witness accounts within the investigative process. While the goals of initial accounts differ from the goals of subsequent interviews, the research presented clearly highlights the benefits of obtaining a good-quality initial account for all stages of an investigation. First, the quality of the initial recall is important for subsequent retrieval attempts: it is not simply the act of engaging in retrieval at an early stage that preserves episodic memory, but the act of engaging in good-quality initial recall. Second, poor-quality initial accounts can be detrimental as recall errors made early on – perhaps made as a consequence of a poor interview – are likely to be repeated in future retrievals. Third, the act of recalling an incomplete subset of information from memory – again, perhaps as a consequence of a poor interview – can sometimes impair one's ability to subsequently recall the remaining (initially unrecalled) items of information. The format of the initial (written or spoken) account has been discussed in depth, again with the conclusion that the format is only an issue insofar as it influences the quality of the account elicited.

NOTE

1. When referring to officers throughout the chapter, we also encompass relevant non-sworn police staff.

REFERENCES

Ambler, C. (2005). The initial investigation of household burglary: An examination and analysis of the information gathered about burglary suspects (Unpublished Master's thesis), University of Portsmouth.

Anderson, J. R. (1983). A spreading activation theory of memory. *Journal of Verbal Learning and Verbal Behavior*, 22, 261–295.

Anderson, M. C., Bjork, R. A., & Bjork, E. L. (1994). Remembering can cause forgetting: Retrieval dynamics in long-term memory. *Journal of Experimental Psychology: Learning, Memory, and Cognition, 20*, 1063–1087.

Bergmann, M. M., Jacobs, E. J., Hoffmann, K., & Boeing, H. (2004). Agreement of self-reported medical history: Comparison of an in-person interview with a self-administered questionnaire. *European Journal of Epidemiology, 19*, 411–416.

Brown, C., Lloyd-Jones, T. J., & Robinson, M. (2008). Eliciting person descriptions from eyewitnesses: A survey of police perceptions of eyewitness performance and reported use of interview techniques. *The European Journal of Cognitive Psychology, 20*, 529–560.

Carter, E. (2011). *Analysing police interviews: Laughter, confessions and the tape*. London, UK: Continuum.

Carter, E. (2014). When is a lie not a lie? When it's divergent: Examining the interactional composition of lies and deceptive responses in a police interview. *International Journal of Language and the Law / Linguagem e Direito, 1*, 1.

Chan, J. C. K., Thomas, A. K., & Bulevich, J. B. (2009). Recalling a witnessed event increases eyewitness suggestibility: The reversed testing effect. *Psychological Science, 20*, 66–73.

Chang, L., & Krosnick, J. A. (2010). Comparing oral interviewing with self-administered computerized questionnaires: An experiment. *Public Opinion Quarterly, 74*, 154–167.

Conway, M. A., Cohen, G., & Stanhope, N. (1991). On the very long-term retention of knowledge acquired through formal education: Twelve years of cognitive psychology. *Journal of Experimental Psychology. General, 120*, 395–409.

Crown Prosecution Service. (2005). Policy for prosecuting cases of domestic violence. Retrieved from 18 May 2014, http://www.cps.gov.uk/Publications/prosecution/domestic

Crown Prosecution Service. (2011). Keir Starmer QC speech. Retrieved from 26 December 2012, www.cps.gov.uk/news/articles/domestic_violence_-_the_facts_the_issues_the_future

Dando, C. J., Wilcock, R., & Milne, R. (2008). The cognitive interview: Inexperienced police officers' perceptions of their witness interviewing behaviour. *Legal and Criminological Psychology, 13*, 59–70.

Dudgeon, P. (2012). Indigenous Australian mental health and racism. *Psychology Aotearoa, 4*, 85–91.

Ebbinghaus, H. (1913). *Memory: A contribution to experimental psychology*. New York: Teachers College, Columbia University (original work published 1885).

Fisher, R. P. (1996). Implications of output-bound measures for laboratory and field research in memory. *The Behavioral and Brain Sciences, 19*, 197.

Fisher R. P., Brewer, N., & Mitchell, G. (2009). The relation between consistency and accuracy of eyewitness testimony: Legal versus cognitive explanations. In R. Bull, T. Valentine, & T. Williamson (Eds.), *Handbook of psychology of investigative interviewing: Current developments and future directions*. Chichester, UK: John Wiley & Sons, Ltd.

Fisher, R. P., & Cutler, B. L. (1995). Relation between consistency and accuracy of eyewitness testimony. In G. M. Davies, S. Lloyd-Bostock, M. McMurran, & C. Wilson (Eds.), *Psychology and law: Advances in research* (pp. 21–28). Berlin, Germany: DeGruyter.

Fisher, R. P., & Geiselman, R. E. (1992). *Memory-enhancing techniques for investigative interviewing*. Springfield, IL: Charles C. Thomas.

Gabbert, F., & Brown, C. (2015). Interviewing for face identification. In T. Valentine & J. P. Davis (Eds.), *Forensic facial identification: Theory and practice of identification from eyewitnesses, composites and CCTV*. London, UK: Wiley-Blackwell.

Gabbert, F., & Hope, L. (2013). Suggestibility and memory conformity. In A. M. Ridley, F. Gabbert, & D. J. La Rooy (Eds.), *Suggestibility in legal contexts: Psychological research and forensic implications* (pp. 63–84). London, UK: Wiley-Blackwell.

Gabbert, F., Hope, L., & Fisher, R. P. (2009). Protecting eyewitness evidence: Examining the efficacy of a self-administered interview tool. *Law and Human Behavior, 33*, 298–307.

Gabbert, F., Hope, L., Fisher, R. P., & Jamieson, K. (2012). Protecting against susceptibility to misinformation with a self-administered interview. *Applied Cognitive Psychology, 26*, 568–575.

Gabbert, F., Hope, L., Lindsay, K., Skowronska, E., & Sauer, J. (2011). Does an immediate recall test increase eyewitness suggestibility? In *The 5th international conference on memory*, August 2011, York, UK.

Garry, M., Loftus, E. F., & Brown, S. W. (1994). Memory: A river runs through it. *Consciousness and Cognition, 3*, 438–451.

Gawrylowicz, J., Memon, A., & Scoboria, A. (2013). Equipping witnesses with transferable skills: The Self-Administered Interview©. *Psychology, Crime and Law, 20*, 315–325.

Geiselman, R. E., Fisher, R. P., Cohen, G., Holland, H., & Surtes, L. (1986). Eyewitness responses to leading and misleading questions under the cognitive interview. *Journal of Police Science and Administration, 14*, 31–39.

Gever, M. (2005). The spectacle of crime, digitized: CSI Crime Scene Investigation and social anatomy. *European Journal of Cultural Studies, 8*, 445–463.

Gilbert, J. A. E., & Fisher, R. P. (2006). The effects of varied retrieval cues on reminiscence in eyewitness memory. *Applied Cognitive Psychology, 20*, 723–739.

Goldsmith, M., Koriat, A., & Pansky, A. (2005). Strategic regulation of grain size in memory reporting over time. *Journal of Memory and Language, 52*, 505–525.

Grabowski, J. (2007). The writing superiority effect in the verbal recall of knowledge: Sources and determinants. In M. Torrance, L. van Waes, & D. Galbraith (Eds.), *Writing and cognition: Research and application* (pp. 165–179). Amsterdam, The Netherlands: Elsevier.

Greater Manchester Police. (2010). Tackling domestic abuse policy and operational procedures.

Grice, P. (1975). Logic and conversation. In P. Cole & J. L. Morgan (Eds.), *Speech acts* (pp. 41–58). New York: Academic Press.

Hall, D. F., Loftus, E. F., & Tousignant, J. P. (1984). Postevent information and changes in recollection for a natural event. In G. L. Wells & E. F. Loftus (Eds.), *Eyewitness testimony: Psychological perspectives* (pp. 124–141). Cambridge, UK: Cambridge University Press.

Hashtroudi, S., Johnson, M. K., Vnek, N., & Ferguson, S. A. (1994). Aging and the effects of affective and factual focus on source monitoring and recall. *Psychology and Aging, 9*, 160–170.

Haworth, K. (2010). Police interview in the judicial process. *The Routledge handbook of forensic linguistics* (pp. 169–181). New York: Routledge.

Hester, S., & Eglin, P. (1992). *A sociology of crime*. London, UK: Routledge.

Heydon, G. (2005). *The language of police interviewing*. Basingstoke, Hampshire, UK: Palgrave Macmillan.

Hope, L., Gabbert, F., & Fisher, R. P. (2011). From laboratory to the street: Capturing witness memory using a Self-Administered Interview. *Legal and Criminological Psychology, 16*, 211–226.

Hope, L., Gabbert, F., Heaton-Armstrong, A., & Wolchover, D. (2013). Self administered witness interviews—Part IV. *Criminal Law and Justice Weekly, 177*, 60–61.

Hope, L., Gabbert, F., Fisher, R. P., & Jamieson, K. (2014). Protecting and enhancing eyewitness memory: The impact of an initial recall attempt on performance in an investigative interview. *Applied Cognitive Psychology, 28*, 304–313.

International Rehabilitation Council for Torture Victims. (2009). *Shedding light on a dark practice: Using the Istanbul Protocol to document torture*. Copenhagen, Denmark: IRCT.

Jones, E. F., & Forrest, J. D. (1992). Underreporting of abortion in surveys of U.S. women: 1976 to 1988. *Demography, 29*, 113–126.

Jönsson, L., & Linnell, P. (1991). Story generations: From dialogical interviews to written reports in police interrogations. *Text, 11*, 419–440.

Kebbell, M. R., & Milne, R. (1998). Police officers' perceptions of eyewitness performance in forensic investigations. *The Journal of Social Psychology, 138*, 323–330.

Kellogg, R. T. (2007). Are written and spoken recall of text equivalent? *The American Journal of Psychology, 120*, 415–428.

Kintsch, W., Welsch, D., Schmalhofer, F., & Zimny, S. (1990). Sentence memory: A theoretical analysis. *Journal of Memory and Language, 29*, 133–159.

Komter, M. L. (2002/2003). The construction of records in Dutch police interrogations. *Information Design Journal and Document Design, 11*, 201–213.

Koriat, A., & Goldsmith, M. (1996). Monitoring and control processes in the strategic regulation of memory accuracy. *Psychological Review, 103*, 490–517.

Koriat, A., Levy-Sadot, R., Edry, E., & De Marcas, G. (2003). What do we know about what we cannot remember? Accessing the semantic attributes of words that cannot be recalled. *Journal of Experimental Psychology: Learning, Memory and Cognition, 29*, 1095–1105.

LaPaglia, J. A., Wilford, M. M., Rivard, J., Chan, J. C. K., & Fisher, R. P. (2014). Misleading suggestions can alter later memory reports even following a cognitive interview. *Applied Cognitive Psychology, 28*, 1–9.

La Rooy, D., Lamb, M. E., & Pipe, M.-E. (2009). Repeated interviewing: A critical evaluation of the risks and potential benefits. In K. Kuehnle & M. Connell (Eds.), *The evaluation of child sexual abuse allegations: A comprehensive guide to assessment and testimony* (pp. 327–361). Hoboken, NJ: John Wiley & Sons, Inc.

Leeney, D. G., & Müller-Johnson, K. (2010). Examining the link between forensic quality and customer service quality of police call centre interviews. *International Journal of Police Science and Management, 12*, 69–80.

Leeney, D. G., & Müller-Johnson, K. (2011). Examining the forensic quality of police call-centre interviews. *Psychology, Crime and Law, 18*, 669–688.

Levy, B. J., & Anderson, M. C. (2002). Inhibitory processes and the control of memory retrieval. *Trends in Cognitive Science, 6*, 299–305.

Loftus, E. F. (2005). Planting misinformation in the human mind: A 30-year investigation of the malleability of memory. *Learning and Memory, 12*, 361–366.

Loftus, E. F., Levidow, B., & Duensing, S. (1992). Who remembers best? Individual differences in memory for events that occurred in a science museum. *Applied Cognitive Psychology, 6*, 93–107.

MacLeod, M. (2002). Retrieval-induced forgetting in eyewitness memory: Forgetting as a consequence of remembering. *Applied Cognitive Psychology, 16*, 135–149.

Marsh, E. J., Tversky, B., & Hutson, M. (2005). How eyewitnesses talk about events: Implications for memory. *Applied Cognitive Psychology, 19*, 1–14.

McCauley, M. R., & Fisher, R. P. (1995). Facilitating children's recall with the revised cognitive interview. *The Journal of Applied Psychology, 80*, 510–516.

McPhee, I., Paterson, H. M., & Kemp, R. I. (2013). The power of the spoken word: Can spoken-recall enhance eyewitness evidence? *Psychiatry, Psychology and Law, 20*, 399–411.

Memon, A., Zaragoza, M., Clifford, B. R., & Kidd, L. (2010). Inoculation or antidote? The effects of cognitive interview timing on false memory for forcibly fabricated events. *Law and Human Behavior, 34*, 105–117.

Momenii, N. (2012). Linguistic recontextualization of police interrogation: A new approach in forensic linguistics. *International Journal of Criminology and Sociological Theory, 5*, 796–807.

Norfolk, G. A. (1999). Physiological illnesses and their potential for influencing testimony. *Medicine, Science, and the Law, 39*, 105–112.

Opdenakker, R. (2006). Advantages and disadvantages of four interview techniques in qualitative research. *Qualitative Social Research, 7*, 4. Retrieved from 12 August 2014, www.qualitative-research.net/index.php/fqs/article/view/175/391

Palmer, F., Flowe, H. D., Takarangi, M. K., & Humphries, J. E. (2013). Intoxicated witnesses and suspects: An archival analysis of their involvement in criminal case processing. *Law and Human Behavior, 37*, 54–59.

Pescod, L., Wilcock, R., & Milne, R. (2013). Improving eyewitness memory in police call centre interviews. *Policing, 7*, 299–306.

Podlas, K. (2006). 'The CSI effect': Exposing the media myth. *The Fordham Intellectual Property, Media and Entertainment Law Journal, 16*, 429–465.

Police and Criminal Evidence Act. (1984). Codes of practice D (2013). Retrieved from 12 August 2014, www.gov.uk/government/uploads/system/uploads/attachment_data/file/253831/pace-code-d-2011.pdf

Ridley, A. M., Gabbert, F., & La Rooy, D. J. (Eds.) (2013). *Suggestibility in legal contexts: Psychological research and forensic implications*. London, UK: Wiley-Blackwell.

Rubin, D. C., & Wenzel, A. E. (1996). One hundred years of forgetting: A quantitative description of retention. *Psychological Review, 103*, 743–760.

Sauerland, M., & Sporer, S. L. (2011). Written vs. spoken eyewitness accounts: Does modality of testing matter? *Behavioral Sciences and the Law, 29*, 846–857.

Sauerland, M., Krix, A. C., van Kan, N., Glunz, S., & Sak, A. (2014). Speaking is silver, writing is golden? The role of cognitive and social factors in written versus spoken witness accounts. *Memory and Cognition, 42*, 978–992.

Schacter, D. L., Norman, K. A., and Koutstaal, W. (1998). The cognitive neuro-science of constructive memory. *Annual Review of Psychology, 49*, 289–318.

Schreiber Compo, N., Evans, J. R., Carol, R., Villalba, D., Ham, L., Garcia, T., & Rose, S. (2012). Intoxicated witnesses: Better than their reputation? *Law and Human Behavior, 36*, 77–86.

Shaw, J. S., Bjork, R. A., & Handal, A. (1995). Retrieval-induced forgetting in an eyewitness-memory paradigm. *Psychonomic Bulletin and Review, 2*, 249–253.

Shepherd, E., & Griffiths, A. (2013). *Investigative interviewing: The conversation management approach.* Oxford, UK: Oxford University Press.

Shuy, R. W. (2003). In-person versus telephone interviewing. In J. A. Holstein & J. F. Gubrium (Eds.), *Inside interviewing: New lenses, new concerns* (pp. 175–193). Thousand Oaks, CA: Sage.

Sporer, S. L. (1996). Psychological aspects of person descriptions. In S. L. Sporer, R. S. Malpass, & G. Koehnken (Eds.), *Psychological issues in eyewitness identification* (pp. 53–86). Mahwah, NJ: Lawrence Erlbaum Associates.

Stokoe, E., & Edwards, D. (2008). 'Did you have permission to smash your neighbour's door?' Silly questions and their answers in police–suspect interrogations. *Discourse Studies, 10*, 89–111.

Suengas, A. G., & Johnson, M. K. (1988). Qualitative effects of rehearsal on memories for perceived and imagined complex events. *Journal of Experimental Psychology: General, 117*, 377–389.

Tousignant, J. P., Hall, D., & Loftus, E. F. (1986). Discrepancy detection and vulnerability to misleading post-event information. *Memory and Cognition, 14*, 329–338.

Tuckey, M. R., & Brewer, N. (2003). The influence of schemas, stimulus ambiguity, and interview schedule on eyewitness memory over time. *Journal of Experimental Psychology. Applied, 9*, 101–118.

Tulving, E. (1983). *Elements of Episodic Memory.* New York: Oxford University Press.

Tversky, B., & Marsh, E. J. (2000). Biased retellings of events yield biased memories. *Applied Cognitive Psychology, 40*, 1–38.

van Koppen, P. J., & Lochun, S. K. (1997). Portraying perpetrators: The validity of offender descriptions by witnesses. *Law and Human Behavior, 21*, 661–685.

van Oorsouw, K., & Merckelbach, H. (2012). The effect of alcohol on crime-related amnesia: A field study. *Applied Cognitive Psychology, 26*, 82–90.

Wagstaff, G. F., Wheatcroft, J., Cole, J. C., Brunas-Wagstaff, J., Blackmore, V., & Pilkington, A. (2008). Some cognitive and neuropsychological aspects of social inhibition and facilitation. *European Journal of Cognitive Psychology, 20*, 828–846.

Wang, E., Paterson, H., & Kemp, R. (2014). The effects of immediate recall on eyewitness accuracy and susceptibility to misinformation. *Psychology, Crime and Law, 20*, 619–634.

Watson, D. R. (1990). Some features of the elicitation of confessions in murder interrogations. In G. Psathas (Ed.), *Interaction competence. International Institute for Ethnomethodology and Conversation Analysis* (pp. 263–295). Washington, DC: University Press of America.

Yuille, J. C., Tollestrup, P., Porter, S., Marxsen, D., & Hervé, H. (1998). Some effects of marijuana on eyewitness memory. *International Journal of Law and Psychiatry, 20*, 1–23.

Section III

Communicating with Suspects

7

Interviewing Suspected Offenders

GAVIN OXBURGH[1], IVAR FAHSING[2], KATE HAWORTH[3] AND J. PETE BLAIR[4]
[1] Newcastle University, UK
[2] Norwegian Police University College, Norway
[3] Aston University, Birmingham, UK
[4] Texas State University, USA

INTRODUCTION

The interviewing[1] of suspected offenders (hereinafter referred to as 'suspects') is a key stage in any investigative process and its outcome is crucial for the overall investigation (Milne & Bull, 1999). Ultimately, a well-performed interview may convert information into evidence that establishes an individual's level of involvement in an offence, implicate others or exonerate innocent parties. Unfortunately, some interviews with suspects around the world involve the employment of unsound practices, coercive methods (including torture), degrading treatment, manipulation and psychologically unsafe practices (Gudjonsson, 2003). In some cases, these practices have led investigators to obtain poor-quality, misleading and unreliable information, which has caused serious miscarriages of justice on all continents of the world (see Kassin & Gudjonsson, 2004, for a review). This has damaged the reputation of the legal process and led to serious distrust of the organizations

Communication in Investigative and Legal Contexts: Integrated Approaches from Forensic Psychology, Linguistics and Law Enforcement, First Edition. Edited by Gavin Oxburgh, Trond Myklebust, Tim Grant and Rebecca Milne.
© 2016 John Wiley & Sons, Ltd. Published 2016 by John Wiley & Sons, Ltd.

involved (Fahsing & Rachlew, 2009; Leo, 2008). Therefore, it is crucial that all interviews with suspects are conducted in a professional and trustworthy manner. This chapter describes current practice in interview and interrogation, highlighting fundamental differences in approaches around the world, and examines the history of how those different positions evolved. It also explores the ultimate purpose of the interviewing and interrogation of suspects.

BACKGROUND AND HISTORY OF INTERVIEWING

The forensic history, from ancient times to the present day, shows how investigators have used a broad array of tactics to obtain information from suspects about their potential involvement in a crime. Lawyers from both the early Roman Empire and Ancient Greece promoted the outcome of torture 'as the highest form of truth' (Ross, 2005, p. 4). In the twelfth century, Roman Law was revived by officials in Italy and France to become a source of authority in civil law systems across Europe. In criminal proceedings, the testimony of two witnesses or the confession of the accused was required as 'proof' for a conviction. In this way interrogation, torture and confessions became central in the civil law system (Ross, 2005). Although torture was much more common and accepted in earlier times, the practice has always received criticism. As early as the fourth century, the Greek philosopher Aristotle recognized that 'Those under compulsion are as likely to give false evidence as true, some being ready to endure everything rather than tell the truth, while others are really ready to make false charges against others, in the hope of being sooner released from torture' (Ross, 2005, p. 163).

The first treaty prohibiting torture[2] was the European Convention on Human Rights (Article 3), which was adopted in the 1950s. In 1984, the United Nations Convention Against Torture became the first binding international instrument that obliged each Member State to 'take effective legislative, administrative, judicial or other measures to prevent acts of torture (Article 2-1). Such measures not only include clearly outlawing acts of torture but also cover the effective training of police and security personnel, and the implementation of precise guidelines on the treatment of persons deprived of their liberty (Kälin, 1998). These are summarized in the Human Rights Standards and Practice for the Police (United Nations, 2004, pp. 13–14), many of which relate directly to the interviewing of suspects:

- *Everyone has the right to security of the person.*
- *Everyone has the right to a fair trial.*
- *Everyone is to be presumed innocent until proven guilty in a fair trial.*

- *No one shall be subjected to arbitrary interference with his or her privacy, family, home or correspondence.*
- *No one shall be subjected to unlawful attacks on his or her honour or reputation.*
- *No pressure, physical or mental, shall be exerted on suspects, witnesses or victims in attempting to obtain information.*
- *Torture and other inhuman or degrading treatment is absolutely prohibited.*
- *No one shall be compelled to confess or to testify against himself or herself.*
- *Investigatory activities shall be conducted only lawfully and with due cause.*
- *Neither arbitrary, nor unduly intrusive, investigatory activities shall be permitted.*
- *Investigations shall be competent, thorough, prompt and impartial.*

Although most UN member states have officially ratified the Convention, allegations of torture and other grave systemic breaches are still being reported to Amnesty International (AI) from all continents. These reports are mapped by the Ill-Treatment and Torture Data Collection Project (ITT), as shown in Figure 7.1 (Conrad, Haglund & Moore, 2014). Although this goes wider than the interview and interrogation context, it is nevertheless a disturbing indication of widespread and ongoing malpractice at the state level in some parts of the world.

In the United States during the 1930s, the Wickersham Commission found that use of the so-called 'third degree' was widespread. This term, which can be traced back to the brutal methods employed during the Italian Inquisition in the fourteenth century,[3] has become a common term of reference, defined as 'The inflicting of pain, physical or mental, to extract confessions or statements' (Skolnick & Fyfe, 1993). The use of the third degree was technically made illegal after the Wickersham report, which was concerned with the professionalism of the police and the production of false confessions. Furthermore, the police caused serious injuries to totally innocent suspects – mainly of non-European origin. At the same time, the commission criticized the police for not dealing effectively with rapidly growing crime during the prohibition period.

In 1947, John Reid, an Irish police officer from Chicago, with no background in psychology, became known for a specialized technique for persuading suspects to confess. The officers first had to conduct an information-gathering interview (based on verbal and non-verbal cues) followed by a nine-step interrogation if they believed the person was guilty (Inbau, Reid, Buckley & Jayne, 2013). Reid willingly shared his technique and it was rapidly adopted throughout the United States. The Reid Technique of Interrogation was seemingly simple, easy to learn and appeared to work very well in that it produced confessions.

Total torture allegations 1995–2005

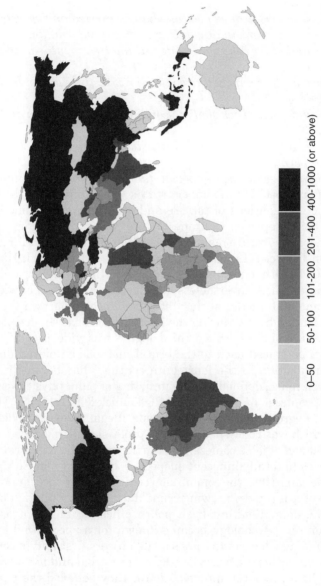

0–50　50–100　101-200　201-400　400-1000 (or above)

Based on data from Amnesty International

Figure 7.1 *Map showing the total number of torture allegations that Amnesty International made against each state between 1995 and 2005.*

Despite this historical emphasis on exerting pressure on suspects to produce a confession, a number of pioneering early studies indicated that a different approach to interviewing might be more productive. For example, academics from Sweden recommended that investigators should attempt to gain the trust of a suspect before asking relevant questions (Leche & Hagelberg, 1945). They also recommended that to get more reliable information, investigators should obtain a 'free account' of events from the suspects by asking them only open-ended questions (this topic is covered in more detail later in the chapter). They also advised that the police might benefit from knowledge of psychology and human memory to ensure they understand the natural limitations of recall and how it may be altered (perhaps inadvertently) by either the police or other subsequent events. In a slightly later study, Gerbert (1954) argued the importance of understanding that signs of nervousness were not necessarily signs of guilt; rather, they could be 'normal' reactions to the interviewer's questioning and behaviour.

Another interesting example comes in the form of Hanns Scharff, an interrogator in the German Luftwaffe during World War 2, who interrogated many hundreds of American fighter pilots who were held as prisoners-of-war (POWs) (see Oleszkiewicz, Granhag & Sebastian, 2014; Toliver, 1997). Current research into Scharff's methods suggest that he became a renowned interrogator primarily – and paradoxically – because he did not actually interrogate; rather, he was described as a true master of conversation, a man who used a very detailed and seemingly ethical method for eliciting information from his detainees (Oleszkiewicz et al., 2014; Toliver, 1997). Each of Scharff's four basic approaches was said to serve a particular purpose: (i) *friendly approach* – he used no methods or tactics that involved torture or coercion; (ii) *not pressing for information* – instead of asking many questions, Scharff told long stories in a way that offered his prisoners the opportunity and encouragement to add to them; (iii) *the 'I-already-know-it-all' illusion* – Scharff would tell the POW that it was unlikely they would be able to offer any new information to him and would then tell a detailed story suggesting that he was very well informed on the topic;[4] and (iv) *confirmation/disconfirmation* – instead of asking direct questions, Scharff used 'confirmation' and 'disconfirmation', whereby he would get the POW to confirm (or otherwise) a small piece of information (see Granhag, Montecinos & Oleszkiewicz, 2015, for further details).

Although not all of these examples can be held up as ideal, some of these early pioneering ideas first suggested in the 1930s to 1950s are recognizable in current models of interviewing best practice (Roberts, 2012). Unfortunately, however, they were not adopted at the time and development has been slow. Furthermore, in many police forces around the world, a wide range of manipulative strategies to extract confessions or self-incriminating statements are still commonplace (see Kassin & Gudjonsson, 2004, for a review). However, other countries both in Europe and elsewhere have developed a very different approach to interviewing suspects. It is, therefore, timely to explore the available recommended practices of suspect interviewing and interrogation, to highlight how and why 'search-for-the-truth' approaches to investigative interviewing arose and to remind ourselves why, even in extreme situations such as terrorism, they represent best practice.

MODELS OF INTERROGATION AND INVESTIGATIVE INTERVIEWING

As indicated above, there are different types of interviewing and interrogation models used across the world, but there are essentially only two dominant philosophies in Western countries: The *Reid Technique* of interviewing and interrogation and the *PEACE model* of investigative interviewing, both of which are explained below.

The Reid Technique of Interviewing and Interrogation

The Reid Technique is probably the most widely taught and employed interviewing and interrogation technique in the USA and some parts of Canada. It should, however, be noted that policing in the USA is extremely non-uniform, with approximately 18 000 distinct policing agencies operating throughout the country. While state laws and numerous US Supreme Court rulings provide a broad framework within which a police agency must operate, there is substantial variation both from state-to-state and department-to-department regarding what interviewing/interrogation procedures are authorized and actually used. As a result, most departments utilize a range of different techniques mostly consisting of the Reid Technique, but frequently combined with other systems. Although many investigators in the USA have not been trained in such techniques, it is helpful to identify the components of the Reid Technique because it is often referred to as the 'standard' in the USA (Blair, 2005).

The Reid Technique consists of three distinct stages. The first stage is a careful factual analysis of the case. During this phase, the investigator should review all of the available evidence. The investigator will also attempt to identify who amongst the potential suspects is most likely to be involved through assessing opportunity, access, motivation and other evidence. Additionally, the investigator will identify areas that need to be covered during the interview. In this way, the factual analysis phase is comparable to the 'planning and preparation' phase of the PEACE model (see below). The second stage is a non-accusatory, information-gathering process, which the authors of the Reid Technique (John E. Reid and Associates) refer to as an interview. Investigators are advised to take a neutral attitude towards the suspect's possible involvement in the crime and begin the interview by asking the suspect for an open-ended account about the event in question and then seek clarifying information by asking further 'open' questions (questions that are less restrictive in the type of answers they allow). Interviewers are advised to ask 'closed' questions (those that are more restrictive in terms of allowable answers) when they are needed to gather information that multiple open questions have failed to elicit. This process also includes a component known as the Behavioural Analysis Interview (BAI), which is a structured part of the interview/interrogation process whereby suspects are asked a series of questions (e.g. 'What do you think should happen to the person who did this' and 'Would you give the person who did this a break?') that are believed to provoke differential verbal and non-verbal behaviours between the innocent and the guilty. This process has been highly controversial in the social psychology literature, with critics claiming that the behavioural indicators taught by Reid are wholly inconsistent with scientific research (e.g. Blair & Kooi, 2004; Kassin & Gudjonsson, 2004; Vrij, 2008).

The third stage of the Reid Technique is the nine steps of interrogation. It should be noted that while there are nine identified steps, not all are utilized in every interrogation; nor are they always utilized in any specific order. This is because the interaction will not always unfold in the same way and the investigator will have to adapt the technique to the specifics of the situation. This process is utilized only after the non-accusatory BAI has been completed and only with suspects whose guilt is thought to be certain. The first of the Reid nine steps of interrogation is a direct accusation of guilt. The interrogator begins with a statement such as, 'We have thoroughly reviewed the evidence in this case and there is no doubt that you did it. What I want to do is sit down with you and see if we can't get this sorted out.' If the suspect still denies guilt, the interrogation enters into the second step, which is referred to as *theme development*. During this stage, the interrogator attempts to shift the suspect's perception of the situation in an attempt to overcome the suspect's resistance to telling the truth. Steps 3 to 5 give instructions about how to stop or overcome resistance on the part of the suspect. Step 3 involves overcoming denials – a denial is defined as any attempt to say that an allegation is false. Inbau et al. (2013) advise that the suspect should not be allowed to voice denials during the interrogation. The interrogator can accomplish this by dominating the interrogation and not giving the suspect time to talk. If the denial is stated, the interrogator is told to restate their confidence in the suspect's guilt and change the particular theme that was being used, as the denial is a sign that the theme is not being accepted by the subject. Step 4 deals with overcoming objections – an objection is not a direct statement of innocence; rather it is a reason why the accusation of guilt is incorrect. For example, in a case involving an armed robbery with a gun, an objection might involve the suspect stating that they do not own a gun. Inbau et al. (2013) advise that when a suspect makes an objection, the interrogator should draw the objection out, and then use it to form a new theme. In the example given above, the interrogator might say something like: 'I hope that it is true that you don't own a gun. That tells me that you aren't a violent type of person, and that you didn't want to hurt anyone. It is important that we bring this point out because a person who doesn't want to hurt anyone during a robbery is different from one that does. We don't want people to have an inaccurate picture of who you are because ....'

After the interrogator turns the objection into a theme, they are advised to use the new theme to move the suspect beyond their resistance. Step 5 relates to dealing with a suspect who stops paying attention to the interrogator. According to Inbau et al. (2013), this sometimes occurs when the suspect realizes that the denials and objections are not deterring the interrogator from continuing the interrogation. At this point, the suspect may attempt to ignore the interrogator. Inbau et al. advise that, when this happens, the interrogator should do several things to get the suspect re-engaged. Because it is difficult to ignore someone who is in your field of vision or invading your personal space, the interrogator is advised to move their chair closer to the suspect and attempt to establish eye contact. The interrogator may also ask questions that require a response from the suspect. For example, the interrogator might ask, 'You care about this don't you?' If the suspect answers such questions, the suspect is no longer ignoring the interrogator.

Step 6 is a transition towards the first admission of guilt. At this point, the suspect has stopped attempting to resist the investigator and has become somewhat passive. The investigator is advised to abbreviate their themes and begin a transition to Step 7, which is referred to as the alternative question. This question gives the suspect a choice between two reasons for committing the crime. One of the reasons is more *morally* (but not legally) acceptable than the other. For example, 'Did you steal the money to pay for *food* or *drugs*? It was food wasn't it?' is an example of an alternative question. Steps 8 and 9 deal with documenting admissions and developing corroborating evidence for the confession. Particular focus is placed on getting the suspect to give a complete account of their involvement in the crime. Investigators are advised to seek out details that can be corroborated against other case information in an attempt to assess the validity of the confession.

The Reid approach is, however, seen by many scholars as simply a psychological version of the 'third degree' in that it is equally capable of extracting a false confession through coercion and active manipulation (Kassin & Gudjonsson, 2004). Despite this, it is still the most widely used approach by law enforcement agencies in the USA and has also been sporadically embraced in some European countries. Although the Reid technique is still widely used in the USA and parts of Canada, it is extremely controversial in most of the available academic literature (e.g. Gudjonsson, 2003; Irving & Hilgendorf, 1980; Kassin, 1997; Kassin & McNall, 1991; Leo, 2008; Vrij, 2008; Wolchover & Heaton-Armstrong, 1996). Critics of the Reid Technique argue that it is highly unethical and can/has led to false confessions. Critics also often express concern that the theme development stage uses powerful psychological techniques that can pressure the innocent into making a false confession. Of specific concern, the steps that are designed to stop or overcome the suspect's resistance can far too easily cause innocent suspects to feel that resisting the interrogator is hopeless and subsequently confess to a crime they did not commit.

The PEACE Model of Investigative Interviewing

In many other countries, a rather different approach to interviewing suspects has developed. In England and Wales, after a number of public scandals linked to improper, oppressive and confession-oriented interviewing methods, a Royal Commission on Criminal Procedure (RCCP) brought about legislation paving the way for a change in approach, away from the coercive and manipulative interrogation styles that were felt to be prevalent in practice at that time (Irving, 1980). This shift, in the beginning of the 1980s, entailed a more fair, legal and scientifically based approach. The aim of the suspect interview was no longer to fulfil the detective's personal hypotheses about the case, but simply to communicate effectively and respectfully with the intent of gathering accurate and reliable information from victims, witnesses and suspects (Baldwin, 1992; Gudjonsson, 2003; Schollum,

2005; Williamson, 2006). It formed part of an integrated programme of training, research and development that resulted in the PEACE model of interviewing, which was implemented by police forces in England and Wales in the early 1990s (Soukara, Bull & Vrij, 2002). PEACE is the mnemonic acronym for the five stages involved: Planning and preparation, Engage and explain, Account, clarify and challenge, Closure and Evaluation. The 'main' stages of the interview are the E, A and C stages.

The planning stage (P) is a vital part of all investigative interviews and interviewers must first consider how the interview might contribute to the overall investigation. The interviewer/s should have a clear understanding of the purpose of the interview and should consider when and where it will take place. If there are two interviewers, they should be clear what each other's roles are within the interview, but they should also be aware of all evidence available and know at what point in the interview any evidence will be disclosed. The interviewing officer/s should also recognize what points are required to prove the offence about which they are interviewing a suspect. Before commencing the interview, she/he should make any necessary arrangements for the attendance of other persons, such as a legal advisor, an appropriate adult, intermediary or interpreter.

The engage and explain stage (E) relates to the opening of the interview and is crucial to its overall success. The importance of rapport cannot be overemphasized. Interviewers should use appropriate language and avoid legal jargon. Interviewers should be flexible in their approach and try to create a relaxed atmosphere. They should explain the reason for the interview, the procedures that will be followed, how long the interview will last and provide a basic outline of the interview, including which interviewer will ask the most questions and who will be taking notes.[5] The third phase of the interview (A) is the account, clarify and challenge step – this is where the interviewer/s obtain the person's account. Once obtained, they should divide it into a number of subsections in order to probe for further detail or clarify any details provided. The former approach would see the interviewer use several attempts to get the interviewee to recall their events using appropriate questioning techniques. During the challenge part of this phase, the interviewer/s should introduce any relevant exhibits and other evidence available (if the interview involves a suspect).

The closure of the interview (C) is equally as important as the other stages. This phase involves the interviewer/s summarizing what had occurred during the interview to ensure that there is a mutual understanding about what has taken place. This is an ideal opportunity for the interviewer/s to verify that all aspects have been sufficiently covered. The interviewer/s should also explain to the suspect what will happen after the interview is completed, including such things as what will happen to any audio/DVD recordings. Finally, if this phase is conducted appropriately, it should facilitate a positive attitude on the part of the suspect towards helping the police in the future. The final stage (E) of the PEACE model includes an evaluation of the current investigative interview, together with how much information was obtained. It also includes an evaluation of the entire investigation, giving due consideration of the information (if any) obtained during the interview. The interviewers should also evaluate their own individual performance during the interview, including whether the aims and objectives for the interview have been achieved.

Other countries around the world, including Norway, The Netherlands, New Zealand and Australia (amongst others), have embraced similar processes of change as England and Wales and have endorsed the PEACE model of interviewing (Fahsing & Rachlew, 2009; Schollum, 2005). Indeed, the PEACE model is now widely accepted as the most ethically sound and effective investigative interview model in Europe and Australia, and many States in Canada have also started using this model (Snook, Eastwood, Stinson, Tedeschini & House, 2010). The philosophy rejects the term 'interrogation' completely (see Centre for Investigative Skills, 2004) and all interviews, whether with victims, witnesses or suspects, are termed 'investigative interviews'. The PEACE model of interviewing is non-accusatory, focusing instead on the importance of honesty, the development of rapport (see Vanderhallen & Vervaeke, 2014, on the role of building rapport and a working alliance within investigative interviews), the use of empathy (see Oxburgh & Ost, 2011) and appropriate questioning (see below), in order to search for the truth.

'INTERVIEW' VERSUS 'INTERROGATION'

As illustrated above, there are fundamental differences between interrogations and investigative interviews. The investigative interview is always intended to be non-accusatory and its purpose is to gather information fairly and impartially, thereby securing the most reliable accounts from interviewees (Oxburgh & Dando, 2011). Fine-grain, relevant and reliable information will assist in the overall strategic decision-making process to decide if there is sufficient and reliable evidence to proceed with the enquiry. The *investigative* interview forms an integral part of the overall *investigative* process (College of Policing, 2013) and is, thus, a central and significant aspect of the criminal justice process (Milne & Bull, 1999; Oxburgh & Hynes, 2015). Conversely, an interrogation is always accusatory and involves active persuasion on the part of the interrogator/s and where '... the investigator is reasonably certain of the suspect's guilt' (Inbau et al., 2013, p. 5). Although not necessary by definition, history shows that interrogations may involve highly manipulative techniques; on occasion, lies and deception may also be used by the interrogator to pressure a subject into compliance (Leo, 2008).

A recent study in the USA involved a systematic review and meta-analysis of the available empirical literature, which assessed the influence of accusatorial (interrogations) and information-gathering methods of interrogation (investigative interviewing) in eliciting true and false confessions (see Meissner et al., 2014). Although the authors urge caution based on the small number of independent samples used in the analysis, they found that an information-gathering approach reduced the likelihood of false confessions. Furthermore, this approach preserved, and in some cases increased, the likelihood of true confessions. Conversely, the accusatorial approach increased both true and false confessions.

We argue that interrogation is, by definition, a guilt-presumptive process and a closed social interaction led by an authority figure who already believes in the perpetrator's probable guilt. The focus under such circumstances is on overcoming the suspect's resistance to telling the truth as the investigator perceives it. However, in relation to domestic crime investigations, the recommended standards of The European Council's Anti-Torture Committee (CPT, 2002) concludes the following:

> The questioning of criminal suspects is a specialist task which calls for specific training if it is to be performed in a satisfactory manner. First and foremost, the precise aim of such questioning must be made crystal clear: that aim should be to obtain accurate and reliable information in order to discover the truth about matters under investigation, not to obtain a confession from someone already presumed, in the eyes of the interviewing officers, to be guilty (paragraph 34).

QUESTIONING STRATEGIES

The challenge that faces investigators, then, is to develop the best possible methods of obtaining 'accurate and reliable information' in an ethical and effective way. In order to achieve this aim, practitioners are increasingly looking to academic research to provide a sound, evidence-based approach to development, training and practice. There is a wealth of pre-existing research in various academic fields that can be applied to interviewing, especially in the fields of psychology and linguistics. However, the discussion above of the history of interviewing and interrogation highlighted a number of highly relevant academic studies that were not utilized by practitioners, even when they demonstrated that the prevalent methods were not the most effective. Combining academic theory and professional practice is not an easy task, and the potential challenges are all the greater when the subject matter involves giving 'outsiders' access to sensitive personal data and police operational practice. It is, therefore, notable that practitioners and academics are now increasingly working together successfully to produce research findings that can inform and improve best practice in interviewing. This is particularly the case with psychology, which had a significant input into the development of the PEACE model (see, for example, Williamson, 2006).

One aspect that has received a great deal of academic attention is the classification of question types used in investigative interviews, much of which relates to the relative coercive nature of the question itself. A common method of categorization, for example, is to distinguish between *open* and *closed* questions (sometimes known as *appropriate* or *inappropriate* questions), focusing on the extent to which each question type limits the scope of an acceptable answer. However, question categories have become much more complex than this simple binary distinction and there is a plethora of categorization systems in the literature (see Oxburgh, Myklebust & Grant, 2010, for a summary). Some of these have formed the basis for an assessment of practitioner competence, including in terms of how different question types are deployed through the various stages of the interview (e.g. the 'Griffiths question map'; Griffiths & Milne, 2006).

Despite this focus on the structure and categorization of question turns, until recently there has been a noticeable absence of input from the discipline of linguistics (see Chapter 2), despite its obvious relevance. However, this is now changing, largely thanks to the emergence of the field of forensic linguistics, which is concerned with all aspects of language and communication in legal contexts. A number of linguists (e.g. Carter, 2011; Haworth, 2010; Heydon, 2005) have turned their attention to the investigative interview, especially interviews with suspects, and the resulting research is beginning to be picked up and utilized by various police forces, especially in England and Wales. What linguistic research shows is that there are many aspects of the investigative interview context that need to be considered if the aim of achieving best evidence is to be met. In addition, although question types are of interest, they are by no means the only facet of language and communication that must be taken into account. The following describes some of the areas in which linguistics can contribute to increasing the accuracy and reliability of interview information, while also reducing the risk of oppression and/or undue influence.

QUESTIONS AND ANSWERS

It is clear that one of the most important facets of any interview is the asking of questions. The fact that this seems like stating the obvious only demonstrates how widely the conventional question–answer format has been taken for granted. It is, therefore, worth considering why it is used and what the consequences are for the outcome. An alternative would be simply to allow a suspect to talk freely about the incident, or indeed anything else that they choose to mention. This would certainly minimize any possible pressure or coercion on the part of an interviewer. However, it is of course necessary to ensure that all relevant aspects are addressed, that any account provided is challenged and tested, and that the information necessary for the ongoing investigation process is obtained. Therefore, some institutional interference is necessary and the medium that is universally used is to ask questions. However, although this enables an interviewer to keep the interview on track, it potentially grants the person asking the questions a great degree of power over the interaction, as the following will illustrate.

At the most basic level, if one participant in a conversation asks a question, the recipient is restricted in what they can say next; that is, there is an unstated but nonetheless influential expectation that any response will hew closely to being an answer to the question (in Conversation Analysis terms, the question and answer form an 'adjacency pair'; Sacks, Schegloff & Jefferson, 1974). This means that the responder (e.g. the interviewee) is not able to start talking about a topic of their own choosing, but must restrict himself to the topic established by the nature of the question posed by the interviewer. In ordinary conversation, there are unlikely to be any consequences if a participant disobeys this 'rule', although it is likely to be socially 'marked'. However, in an investigative interview, the interviewer does have the power to sanction a non-answer; for example, they can ask the question again and keep pressing until an 'acceptable' answer is produced (this is far less likely to be tolerated in a context where the power relations are more equal, such as a casual conversation with a friend). There is, therefore, clear interactional pressure on the interviewee only to address the topics set by the interviewer. Linguistic analysis of interview interactions has revealed the extent of this topic control. Heydon (2003) comments that 'Analysis of the topic management tools used by suspects and police demonstrates that, at the level of turn-taking, suspects are in a vastly disadvantageous position when trying to support their version of events' (p. 95). This is highly problematic if we consider the purpose of the interview is to gather information from the interviewee as the format of the interaction itself makes this more difficult.

A potential way to reduce these adverse consequences is to ensure that any questions asked are as open as possible. This is why there has been such focus on the best types of question to ask. However, linguistic research in the area of pragmatics shows that, unfortunately, it is not that simple. The focus in investigative interviewing circles to date has tended to be on the *form* of questions, that is their grammatical and syntactic structure (e.g. 'what', 'why...', closed 'yes/no'). However, linguists have long been aware that meaning is derived from the underlying *function* of what we say and not necessarily from a literal interpretation of the exact words used (Austin, 1962; Searle, 1970). The fact that there is no straightforward relationship between *form* and *function* can be illustrated with the following example (see also Chapter 2). All the questions below take the form of a 'why' question, but they all have completely unrelated meanings and implications:

Why did you do it?
Why am I here?
Why don't we take the bus?
Why did the chicken cross the road?
Why don't you go and play in the traffic?

This demonstrates the difficulties of devising question categories that will adequately reflect whether or not an interviewer is being coercive, or even threatening. The problem is that we rely on indirectness and implicature[6] when we communicate. The ways in which we derive meaning from another person's words are complex and involve many different factors, many of which are highly context-dependent. What matters from a pragmatic perspective, therefore, is not the literal meaning of the words used but what a particular utterance *does*: in other words, is the underlying implication to accuse, to threaten, to persuade; to seek new information or to confirm what is already known? This is of course much harder to categorize, especially as it inevitably involves an element of personal interpretation.

However, although this might not be as neat a solution as providing a set of appropriate question types, it is a reflection of the reality of verbal communication.

The fact that meaning is so context-dependent leads to particular difficulties in a police interview context, given that the context of an investigative interview is inherently coercive. For example, a person is held against their will by an agent of the State and must remain in the interview room while questions are put to them, on the grounds that they are suspected of committing a criminal offence, which may lead to their conviction and punishment by that State. If the goal is to obtain good-quality information from the interviewee, as opposed to obtaining a confession, then the challenge for the interviewer is to offset the substantial institutional power that they have over the interviewee and the oppressive and restrictive situation in which the interviewee finds themselves, in order to create an environment in which an interviewee's own evidence can emerge unfettered (see Vanderhallen & Vervaeke, 2014). However, linguistic studies have shown that many aspects of the interactional context actively reinforce, and indeed help to create, the interviewer's dominance over the account that emerges, even when this is not intended. These can seriously undermine attempts to improve interview practice, since they result in the imposition of the interviewer's biases and assumptions directly on to the accounts produced by interviewees (see, for example, Auburn, Drake & Willig, 1995; Heydon, 2005; see also Fairclough, 1989; van Dijk, 1993, on language and power more generally). The importance of drawing attention to such features is all the greater as they are generally far less obvious than direct or physical coercion.

Alongside the topic control mentioned above, the question–answer (Q-A) turn-taking sequence also gives questioners access to particular types of utterance that are not available to responders. One such resource, which has been shown to be of particular significance in this context, is the 'formulation' (Heritage & Watson, 1979; for their role in investigative interviews see Heydon, 2005; Stokoe & Edwards, 2008; Haworth, in press). These occur after a Q-A sequence and involve a summary by the interviewer of the immediately prior verbal exchange. They thus enable the interviewer to select and highlight only those parts of the interviewee's communication that *they* (the interviewer/s) consider relevant or important and to minimize or dismiss all other aspects of what was said. The following example, which includes a formulation, encapsulates the extent of the interviewer's influence over the account produced by an interviewee, even when there is no apparent coercion or undue pressure (IR = interviewer, IE = interviewee).

Example 1

IR:	Okay just describe yourself for me. What sort of build are you	01
	and size.	02
IE:	Me I'm a little un I'm stocky. And – small and stocky yeah.	03
IR:	What sort of height.	04
IE:	I'm five foot five and a half.	05
IR:	And what do you weigh.	06
IE:	I weigh I think it's about eleven and a half stone.	07
IR:	Eleven and a half stone so you're not fat, you're not stocky,	08
	you're quite proportionate build.	09
IE:	Yeah.	10

Here, the interviewer's formulation of the prior talk (lines 8–9) directly contradicts what the interviewee actually said: 'I'm stocky' (line 3) becomes 'you're not stocky' (line 8). Presenting this as a summary of what the interviewee himself has said makes it difficult for the interviewee to challenge. Further, this formulation is presented as a statement inviting a simple confirmation, which provides further pressure for agreement. Sure enough, this interviewee simply agrees with the interviewer's version (line 10). In this particular instance the topic is innocuous enough, but it serves to illustrate the point. It is likely that the formulation is the interviewer's own opinion of the interviewee's build and size, and here it is this opinion that becomes the accepted version. The interviewer continues to exert a strong influence over what the interviewee says as this extract continues. He next asks for a description of a different person, using what would be classed as an appropriate question (line 11), but the interviewee chooses to respond by providing only the details that the interviewer sought in his immediately preceding questions.

Example 2

IR:	What about Caroline, what does she look like.	11
IE:	Caroline is, erm she's got a big build. She's five foot three cos we	12
	measured her – ourselves against each other the other day, and it	13
	was about five foot three, erm it's – it's a re – normal, it's slight,	14
	because she's trying to lose all this weight or whatever, quite	15
	slight fra – well I don't – n – no she's not slight she's kind of	16
	normal. I mean, kind of, sort of, I don't know reasonable build,	17
	reasonable height, you know?	18

Despite the appropriate framing of the question, the interviewee limits his answer only to the same details that the interviewer specifically asked him to provide about himself: build, height and weight (lines 1, 4 and 6). He does not include any other information that we might expect, such as hair or skin colour, resulting in only a partial account. This demonstrates the extent to which an interviewee is influenced by an interviewer in terms of selecting which aspects of his account to report, and even his lexical choice (especially the use of 'build': interviewer lines 1 and 9; interviewee lines 12 and 17). This simple and relatively mundane example illustrates a fundamental challenge for the investigative interview. Due to the power relations between participants, the structure of the interview as question–answer and the myriad of consequent interactional features such as formulations and topic control, an interviewer's agenda is always likely to dominate the interview. Yet this influence is unavoidable, since it is due to basic aspects of human communication. For this reason, the agenda that an interviewer takes into the interview room is crucial. If it is to ascertain guilt or, worse, to confirm presumed guilt, then the resulting evidence will inevitably be restricted and distorted by that agenda. If, on the other hand, the interviewer has a more open-minded agenda and an information-gathering aim, then the outcome is likely to be much more productive and will avoid cognitive bias (see Meissner & Kassin, 2004, for a review). That said, functional open-mindedness is not something that comes naturally to any human being, including police officers (Findley & Scott, 2006; Nickerson, 1998). To do something about this fundamental problem for any investigator, she/he must: (a) acknowledge the notion of open-mindedness and (b) apply systematic counter strategies (when required).

DISCUSSION

It is clear that the aim of modern-day investigative interviewing is to gather accurate, relevant and reliable information from the interviewee within the legal framework defined by national and international legislation. However, there are still many countries that use interrogation methods that, whilst acceptable under their own current legal framework, are psychologically and ethically questionable. In addition to the widespread concerns about the Reid Technique, courts in the USA have upheld the police investigators' use of trickery and deceit during interrogations.[7] More specifically, investigators can lie about the presence or strength of evidence, although the authors of the Reid Technique suggest that this tactic should be used only as '... an investigator's last effort to persuade the suspect to tell the truth (Inbau et al., 2013, p. 270). There are, of course, several ethical issues inherent in lying to suspects about fabricated evidence. The warning of Inbau et al. to use persuasive methods only when the police are reasonably certain of the guilt of the suspect begs the question as to what is actually the role of an investigator in the criminal justice process. Furthermore, how can an investigator really be *certain* of a person's guilt? From both a legal and science-based perspective, we suggest they simply cannot.

The very notion of an interrogation, therefore, fuels the basic problems related with tunnel vision: a premature conclusion of guilt and a seeming aversion to considering other alternatives. In the Reid Technique and other interrogative approaches, the confirmation bias is not accidental but deliberate; investigators are taught that this is the way to most expeditiously advance their investigation. The potential for confirmatory bias in interrogative approaches, then, may heighten the risk of convicting the innocent. This, in turn, may lower the probability of finding the guilty. This risk of convicting the innocent is of paramount concern in Western countries and methods that increase this risk should be avoided (Roberts, 2012). Hence, it should never be the role of an investigator to presume, or predict, guilt. Cultures, structures and methods that reinforce and operationalize this fundamental notion are clearly needed in all aspects of investigation work – both inside and outside the interview room. Because interrogative methods rely upon the presumption of guilt, we feel that they undermine the core function of the investigator and should be avoided whenever possible. We believe that modern, scientifically backed, interviewing approaches should be used at all times – no matter the challenge or situation. They contribute in an important way to an operationalization of the true role of an investigator, namely to gather accurate, reliable and relevant information whilst at the same time upholding international human rights (Fahsing & Ask, 2013; Kälin, 1998; Kassin, Appleby & Perillo, 2010; Stelfox, 2009).

CONCLUSION

This chapter has hopefully shown that interviewing of suspects is an acid test of the professionalism of the police and other law enforcement agencies. The science-based search-for-the-truth approaches to interviewing stand in contrast to other approaches and appear to maximize the information obtained whilst minimizing the risks to the interviewee (Meissner et al., 2014), the integrity of the investigative process and to the overall criminal justice system (Roberts, 2012). Moreover, investigative interviews in their myriad forms are contact points between the State and the public – their importance should not be underestimated.

NOTES

1. This encapsulates all forms of formal communication with a suspect, including 'interrogation'.
2. For the purposes of this Convention, torture means any act by which severe pain or suffering, whether physical or mental, is intentionally inflicted on a person for such purposes as obtaining from him or a third person information or a confession, punishing him for an act he or a third person has committed or is suspected of having committed, or intimidating or coercing him or a third person, or for any reason based on discrimination of any kind, when such pain or suffering is inflicted by or at the instigation of or with the consent or acquiescence of a public official or other person acting in an official capacity. It does not include pain or suffering arising only from, inherent in or incidental to lawful sanctions.
3. In his book, *A Question of Torture* (2006), historian Alfred W. McCoy describes the use of the *strappado*, a rope device that suspended a victim by the arms in five increasing degrees of both duration and severity. According to McCoy, the 'third degree' of this process has maintained fluency in modern times as a term used to refer to harsh police interrogation.
4. Scharff did, in fact, possess comprehensive knowledge about the topics he pursued (air order of battle), in large part due to the fact that he only interrogated US air crewmen who were operating out of air bases in the United Kingdom.
5. A common practice within the PEACE model is to have two investigators involved in the interview, with one taking the lead in questioning a subject and the other serving in a support role with the important responsibility of taking notes.
6. Implicature is a term drawn from the subfield of linguistics known as pragmatics and refers to a phenomenon where what is suggested through an utterance is understood despite the fact that the underlying meaning was neither expressed nor implied.
7. *Frazier v. Cupp*, 394 US 731, 89 S. Ct. 1420 (1969).

REFERENCES

Auburn, T., Drake, S., & Willig, C. (1995). 'You punched him, didn't you?': Versions of violence in accusatory interviews. *Discourse and Society, 6* (3), 353–386.

Austin, J. L. (1962). *How to do things with words*. Oxford, UK: Clarendon Press.

Baldwin, J. (1992). Video-taping of police interviews with suspects: An evaluation. Police Research Series: Paper No.1, Home Office, London.

Blair, J. P. (2005). What do we know about interrogation? *Journal of Police and Criminal Psychology, 20*, 44–57.

Blair, J. P., & Kooi, B. K. (2004). The gap between research and training in the detection of deception. *International Journal of Police Science and Management, 6,* 77–83.

Carter, E. (2011). *Analysing police interviews: Laughter, confessions and the tape.* London, UK: Continuum.

Centre for Investigative Skills (CFIS). (2004). *Practical guide to investigative interviewing.* England, UK: Central Police Training and Development Authority.

College of Policing. (2013). Investigative interviewing. Available at: http://www. app.college.police.uk/app-content/investigations/investigative-interviewing/.

Conrad, C. R., Haglund, J., & Moore, W. H. (2014). Torture allegations as events data: Introducing the Ill-treatment and torture (ITT) specific allegation data. *Journal of Peace Research, 51,* 429–438.

CPT. (2002). European Committee for the Prevention of Torture and Inhuman or Degrading Treatment or Punishment. Paragraph 34, 12th General Report [CPT/Inf. (2002)15].

Fahsing, I. A., & Rachlew, A. A. (2009). Investigative interviewing in the Nordic Region. In T. Williamson, R. Milne & S. Savage (Eds.), *International developments in investigative interviewing.* Cullompton, UK: Willan Publishing.

Fahsing, I., & Ask, K. (2013). Decision making and decisional tipping points in homicide investigations: An interview study of british and norwegian detectives. *Journal of Investigative Psychology and Offender Profiling, 10* (2), 155–165.

Fairclough, N. (1989). *Language and power.* London, UK: Longman.

Findley, K. A., & Scott, M. S. (2006). The multiple dimensions of tunnel vision in criminal cases. *Wisconsin Law Review,* 291–397.

Gerbert, K. (1954). The psychology of expression and the technique of criminal interrogation. *Jahrbuch fuer Psychologie und Psychotherapie, 2,* 85–98.

Granhag, P. A., Montecinos, S. C., & Oleszkiewicz, S. (2015). Eliciting intelligence from sources: the first scientific test of the Scharff technique. *Legal and Criminological Psychology, 20* (1), 96–113.

Griffiths, A., & Milne, R. (2006). Will it all end in tiers? Police interviews with suspects in Britain. In T. A. Williamson (Ed.), *Investigative interviewing: Rights, research, regulation.* Cullompton, UK: Willan Publishing, pp.167–189.

Gudjonsson, G. (2003). *The psychology of interrogations and confessions: A handbook.* Chichester, UK: John Wiley & Sons, Ltd.

Haworth, K. (2010). Police interviews as evidence. In M. Coulthard & A. Johnson (Eds.), *Routledge handbook of forensic linguistics.* London, UK: Routledge.

Haworth, K. (in press). The discursive construction of evidence in police interviews: Case study of a rape suspect. *Applied Linguistics.*

Heritage, J., & Watson, D. (1979). Formulations as conversational objects. In G. Psathas (Ed.), *Everyday language: Studies in ethnomethodology.* Irvington Publishers.

Heydon, G. (2003). Now I didn't mean to break his teeth': Applying topic management to problems of power asymmetry and voluntary confessions. In S. Sarangi & T. van Leeuwen (Eds.), *Applied linguistics and communities of practice.* London, UK: Continuum.

Heydon, G. (2005). *The language of police interviewing: A critical analysis.* Palgrave.

Inbau, F. E., Reid, J. E., Buckley, J. P., & Jayne, B. C. (2013). *Criminal interrogations and confessions*, 4th ed. Burlington, UK: Jones & Bartlett.

Irving, B. L. (1980). Police interrogation: A case study of current practice. Research Study Number 2, Royal Commission on Criminal Procedure, Her Majesty's StationaryOffice, London.

Irving, B. L., & Hilgendorf, L. (1980). *Police interrogation: The psychological approach. Royal commission on criminal procedure* (Research Study Number 1). London, UK: Her Majesty's Stationary Office.

Kälin, W. (1998). The struggle against torture. *International Review of the Red Cross, 38*, 433–444.

Kassin, S. M. (1997). The psychology of confession evidence. *American Psychologist, 52*, 221–223.

Kassin, S. M., Appleby, S. C., & Perillo, J. T. (2010). Interviewing suspects: Practice, science, and future directions. *Legal and Criminological Psychology, 15*, 39–55.

Kassin, S. M., & Gudjonsson, G. (2004). The psychology of confessions: A review of the literature and issues. *Psychological Science in the Public Interest, 5*, 33–67.

Kassin, S. M., & McNall, K. (1991). Police interrogations and confessions: Communicating promises and threats by pragmatic implication. *Law and Human Behavior, 15*, 233–251.

Leche, E., & Hagelberg, V. (1945). *Förhör i Brottmål*. Stockholm, Sweden: P.A. Nord-stedt & Söners Förlag.

Leo, R. A. (2008). *Police interrogation and American justice*. Cambridge, MA: Harvard University Press.

McCoy, A. W. (2006). *A question of torture: CIA interrogation, from the cold War to the War on terror*. New York: Metropolitan Books.

Meissner, C. A., & Kassin, S. A. (2004). You're guilty, so just confess! *Perspectives in Law and Psychology, 20*, 85–106.

Meissner, C. A., Redlich, A. R., Michael, S. W., Evans, J. R., Camilletti, C. R., Bhatt, S., & Brandon, S. (2014). Accusatorial and information-gathering interrogation methods and their effects on true and false confessions: A meta-analytic review. *Journal of Experimental Criminology*. Published on-line 28 June 2014. doi: 10.1007/s11292-014-9207-6.

Milne, R., & Bull, R. (1999). *Investigative interviewing: Psychology and practice*. Chichester, UK: John Wiley & Sons, Ltd.

Nickerson, R. S. (1998). Confirmation bias: A ubiquitous phenomenon in many guises. *Review of General Psychology, 2* (2), 175–220. doi: 10.1037/1089-2680.2.2.175.

Oleszkiewicz, S., Granhag, P. A., & Sebastian, C. M. (2014). The Scharff-technique: Eliciting intelligence from human sources. *Law and Human Behavior, 38*, 478–489.

Oxburgh, G. E., & Dando, C. J. (2011). Psychology and interviewing: What direction now in our quest for reliable information? *British Journal of Forensic Practice, 13*, 135–144.

Oxburgh, G. E., & Hynes, I. (2015). Investigative practice. In P. Radcliffe, G. Gudjonsson, & D. Wolchover (Eds.), *Witness testimony in sexual cases investigation: Law and practice*. Oxford, UK: Oxford University Press.

Oxburgh, G. E., Myklebust, T., & Grant, T. (2010). The question of question types in police interviews: A review of the literature from a psychological and linguistic perspective. *International Journal of Speech, Language and Law, 17*, 43–64.

Oxburgh, G. E., & Ost, J. (2011). The use and efficacy of empathy in police interviews with suspects of sexual offences. *Journal of Investigative Psychology and Offender Profiling, 8*, 178–188.

Roberts, K. (2012). Police interviewing of criminal suspects: A historical perspective. *Internet Journal of Criminology*, 1–17.

Ross, J. (2005). A history of torture. In K. Roth, M. Worden, A. D. Bernstein & Human Rights Watch (Organization) (Eds.), *Torture: Does it make us safer? Is it ever OK?: A human rights perspective*. New York: New Press.

Sacks, H., Schegloff, E. A., & Jefferson, G. (1974). A simplest systematics for the organization of turn-taking for conversation. *Language, 50*, 696–735.

Schollum, M. (2005). *Investigative interviewing: The literature*. New Zealand Police Department, Office of the Commissioner of Police.

Searle, J. R. (1970). *Speech acts: An essay in the philosophy of language*. Cambridge, UK: Cambridge University Press.

Skolnick, J. H. & Fyfe, J. J. (1993). *Above the law: Police and the excessive use of force*. New York: Free Press.

Snook, B., Eastwood, J., Stinson, M., Tedeschini, J., & House, J. C. (2010). Reforming investigative interviewing in Canada. *Canadian Journal of Criminology and Criminal Justice, 52*, 203–217.

Soukara, S., Bull, R., & Vrij, A. (2002). Police detectives' aims regarding their interviews with suspects: Any change at the turn of the millennium? *International Journal of Police Science and Management, 4*, 101–114.

Stelfox, P. (2009). *Criminal investigation: An introduction to principles and practice*. Cullompton, UK: Willan Publishing.

Stokoe, E., & Edwards, D. (2008). 'Did you have permission to smash your neighbour's door?' Silly questions and their answers in police–suspect interrogations. *Discourse Studies, 10*, 89–111.

Toliver, R. (1997). *The interrogator*. Atglen, PA: Schiffer Publishing.

United Nations (2004). *Human rights standards and practice for the police. Expanded pocket book on human rights for the police* (Professional training series no. 5/3). New York/Geneva, Switzerland: Office of the United Nations High Commissioner for Human Rights.

van Dijk, T. (1993). *Elite discourse and racism*. Sage.

Vanderhallen, M., & Vervaeke, G. (2014). Between investigator and suspect: The role of the working alliance in investigative interviewing. In R. Bull (Ed.), *Investigative interviewing*. New York: Springer, pp. 63–90.

Vrij, A. (2008). *Detecting lies and deceit: Pitfalls and opportunities*, 2nd ed. Chichester, UK: John Wiley & Sons, Ltd.

Williamson, T. (2006). Investigative interviewing and human rights in the war on terrorism. In T. Williamson (Ed.), *Investigative interviewing: Rights, research and regulation*. Cullompton, UK: Willan Publishing, pp. 3–22.

Wolchover, D., & Heaton-Armstrong, A. (1996). *Wolchover and Heaton-Armstrong on confession evidence*. London, UK: Sweet and Maxwell.

8

A (Nearly) 360° Perspective of the Interrogation Process: Communicating with High-Value Targets

FADIA M. NARCHET[1], MELISSA B. RUSSANO[2], STEVEN M. KLEINMAN[3]
AND CHRISTIAN A. MEISSNER[4]

[1] University of New Haven, West Haven, Connecticut, USA
[2] Roger Williams University, Bristol, Rhode Island, USA
[3] Operational Sciences International, Monterey, California, USA
[4] Iowa State University, Ames, Iowa, USA

INTRODUCTION

Until recently, most research on interrogation has focused on the interrogator's role, actions and perceptions in the criminal law enforcement setting. However, in the past decade, due to a resurgence in the role of interrogation as a means of gathering intelligence in the 'War on Terror', which regrettably included several high-profile cases (e.g. Abu Ghraib) involving the use of infamous interrogation tactics, an increasing number of researchers have begun empirically studying intelligence interviewing. The differences between interrogations in law enforcement and military or intelligence settings have been recently described elsewhere (Evans, Meissner, Brandon, Russano &

Communication in Investigative and Legal Contexts: Integrated Approaches from Forensic Psychology, Linguistics and Law Enforcement, First Edition. Edited by Gavin Oxburgh, Trond Myklebust, Tim Grant and Rebecca Milne.
© 2016 John Wiley & Sons, Ltd. Published 2016 by John Wiley & Sons, Ltd.

Kleinman, 2010; Hartwig, Meissner & Semmel, 2014). However, one of the key differences is that criminal interrogations are focused on obtaining a confession from a suspect whereas human intelligence (HUMINT) interrogations[1] are focused on procuring reliable, actionable information from the target. In a study conducted by Russano, Narchet, Kleinman and Meissner (2014), this sentiment was expressed by an interrogator with high-value target (HVT) experience who stated that the purpose of an interrogation is to '...get to the truth of something. You're eliciting information. You're getting information. What you do with that information may be against the interests of the person you're interviewing, or it may be on their behalf. You may be using that information to go arrest somebody, or to disrupt some sort of a terrorist activity or to arrest them, or to put them under surveillance. You're not sure. But you're gathering information.' Another key distinction between a criminal and HUMINT interrogation is the frequent and direct involvement of an analyst and an interpreter in the intelligence collection process (although in both cases the interrogator plays the central role in the interview process). Interpreters facilitate communication between the interrogator and the target, whereas analysts support an interrogation through an assortment of tasks, including compiling background information about the target and vetting (i.e. fact checking) and corroborating information elicited from the target (Russano, Narchet & Kleinman, 2014).

Until recently (see Russano, Narchet & Kleinman, 2014; Russano, Narchet, Kleinman & Meissner, 2014), the supporting role of analysts and interpreters as substantial and irreplaceable contributors to the interrogative process has largely been ignored by the research community. Russano and her colleagues sought to gain a better understanding of the multidimensional interrogative process by conducting semi-structured interviews with 17 HVT interrogators, 25 highly experienced non-HVT interrogators and 12 intelligence analysts to explore broad topic areas such as training, perceived effectiveness of interrogation techniques and attributes specific to working with HVTs. Moreover, 27 interpreters were also asked to respond to a similar series of questions using a survey format. In this fashion, the researchers sought to explore the interrogative process from differing perspectives to gain a better understanding of the respective roles, responsibilities and perceptions of each member of the interrogation team (Russano, Narchet & Kleinman, 2014; Russano, Narchet, Kleinman & Meissner, 2014).

In this chapter, we explore the communication process with HVTs from the perspective of the interrogator, the analyst and the interpreter. Relying primarily on interviews and surveys conducted by Russano, Narchet, Kleinman and Meissner (2014) and Russano,

Narchet and Kleinman (2014),[2] we present an exploratory qualitative analysis of issues surrounding the HVT interrogation communication process. It is our hope that such an exploratory examination will stimulate future research on this unique and seldom explored topic.

INTERROGATOR PERSPECTIVE

Definition of an HVT

When asked to define an HVT by Russano, Narchet, Kleinman and Meissner (2014), one of the common themes among interrogators was to conceptualize an HVT as someone who has information that may threaten national security (see Table 8.1). One element of the HVT interview widely reported by interview respondents was the focus not only on past events but also on collecting information about any current or possible future acts. Overall, it appears that interrogators converged on the notion that a high-value target is a term that, while surprisingly not formally defined in US Government doctrine or legal statute, is commonly used to describe an individual who holds a leadership position or serves as a technical expert with a terrorist organization. The target refers to the fact that this individual has been targeted for capture or termination based on the substantial threat they pose to Western or allied national interests.

Russano, Narchet, Kleinman and Meissner (2014) also asked interrogators to compare HVT interrogations to non-HVT interrogations. Although HVT interrogations were perceived not to differ in terms of

Table 8.1 Exemplar remarks of HVT interrogators' definitions of an HVT

'High-value target would be somebody who has information of either strategic value, meaning it would actually shape policy at a very high level. Or as a real critical nature, because there's going to be an event that can happen in a very reasonably short period of time that needs to be prevented. Without this information, the cost of life and property would be high.'

'... a high-value means that this person is intimately involved in some kind of a criminal act or a terrorism group, or intelligence operation, that we have a degree of confidence that this person is involved, is somebody we're interested in, and has information.'

'A high-value detainee for me is someone who has played a significant role in, whether it's in a government organization or has extremely valuable information that benefits the U.S. Government. Someone who has committed an extremely heinous or violent crime, that crime received a lot of attention and scrutiny and as a result it was viewed as very significant.'

the methodology of the preparation process and the interrogative approaches used, they *did* differ to the extent that, given the high-stakes nature of the cases, there was heightened scrutiny of the case and pressure on the interrogator to produce results (Russano, Narchet, Kleinman & Meissner, 2014). Most HVT interrogators did not believe that the skills necessary to conduct a successful interrogation of an HVT were substantially different than those needed to conduct a non-HVT interrogation. One theme that emerged from the interview responses was that the key to a successful interview seems to lie in the interrogator's motivation and/or ability to adequately prepare for the interrogation (see Table 8.2). Specifically, the guiding principle of a successful interrogation, according to interrogators, appears to be that the more information an interrogator has about a target prior to an interrogation, the more likely it is that the interrogation will be productive and successful, in that pre-interrogation knowledge about the target directs the line of questioning and informs how the interrogation is subsequently conducted. Interrogators also suggested that these guiding tenets do not differ depending upon whether they were interviewing an HVT or a non-HVT.

Table 8.2   Exemplar responses of HVT interrogators regarding keys to a successful HVT interrogation

'I don't think the keys are [different]…I don't think at the fundamental level. It's more how it's orchestrated. Just with a high value target, everything is going to take longer and needs to be developed, and it's just…nothing is going to be simple.'

'I mean to me, in my experience, the keys to success are … the preparation that goes into the interrogation. And no, it's not any different, but with a higher-value person you would tend to put a lot more in. And I even was guilty of that, and I learned my lesson from that. I was halfway through my time in Iraq, I did an interrogation of an individual that I took for granted. So I went into this interrogation with the idea he was going to confess to all of that and of course implicate others for those atrocities. I didn't have a lot of time to prepare, and I took it for granted… And I didn't give it the preparation that I should've. Thirty, forty minutes into it, I realized that I was in way over my head with him…I walked away very disappointed. So [I] went back several weeks later, because I still needed that information, plus I wanted to correct myself. Same subject, same approach, same interrogator, same room, same everything else; the preparation though that I went into it was 100 times different. I knew everything about him by then. I had prepared so much I had…probably went a little overboard just because my ego needed it and I realized what his vulnerabilities were…we were only 45 minutes into it, he broke down, and he cried like I had never seen an adult male cry. And the only difference was the preparation that went into it.'

Training and Necessary Skills for HVT Interrogators

When asked about what type of training HVT interrogators need, most respondents stated that interrogators needed more subject-matter expertise training (e.g. about the HVT's culture, religion, region, political viewpoints, etc.) (see Table 8.3). This sentiment seems intertwined with the issue of preparedness for effective communication; in fact, being prepared was often presented as synonymous with being or becoming a subject-matter expert. HVT interrogators also suggested that on-the-job training was an invaluable experience builder; such activities encompassed a wide variety of experiences, ranging from observing others to allowing others to observe and provide feedback to an interrogator about his performance (oftentimes in the context of a mentorship relationship) to spending time in the target's country to learn about the culture.

Interrogators most often cited excellent interpersonal skills, the ability to adapt to different situations and maturity as qualities and skills of a 'good' interrogator (see Table 8.4). Overall, HVT interrogators thought that the skills needed to be a 'good' HVT interrogator did

Table 8.3 Exemplar responses of HVT interrogators concerning training to work with HVTs

'I would say that they should know everything that can be known about the particular target that they're focused on, the group that they're involved in, the level of engagement in that group. The history of that particular person, and their involvement and what they've done...'

'I think probably people interviewing high-value detainees should have done some traveling on cases, maybe some temporary duty assignments to some of our liaison offices overseas or at least kind of served on squads that do a lot of extraterritorial type cases, so they're comfortable going to a foreign country doing interviews and working with foreign services. And they understand working with foreign services, kind of the dos and don'ts of that...I mean, it's a world unto itself with all sorts of different entities in there. You need to have a general idea of who does what so, I think on-the-job doing interviews, number one. Number two, having done some traveling, kind of operationally, to understand the dynamics.'

'That's what I'm trying to figure out here on a daily basis. I believe that each person is different so you can't have a cookie-cutter approach for your interrogators. You can't train them all the same because everybody's personality is different; what works for me isn't going to necessarily work for someone else. So my perception or my thought is providing interrogators kind of that, the broad skill set and then allowing them to fine tune that to fit their individual personalities and capabilities. And that's where, by doing it over and over, you develop an individual to become ready to do a high-value interrogation. So giving them a good baseline of training.'

Table 8.4 Exemplar responses of HVT interrogators regarding necessary skills for conducting HVT interrogations

'I mean, I think you have good knowledge and background, information, cultural sensitivities. Good rapport-building. Good ability to build a good, solid team, to work with people, work with other people beside you as well as parlay that team effort...to have an effective communication back and forth. I mean, this would go for any interview, really, but I think that the stakes are a little bit higher, so I think you have to be on the tip-top of your game...'

'Those skills that are important to be a good interrogator, they have to be refined as you become focused on a high-value subject. It's the experience that develops you to that point. So that's as important as evolving those unique skill sets. While you can be the most skilled person, if you don't have the experience you're not, in my opinion, going to have success. So it's a combination of the two.'

'Patience, preparation, flexibility, insight, perception, ability to talk about a range of subjects, sensitivity to the subject and the subject's condition, curiosity about how they got where they got, flexibility in terms of understanding the value of taking time to build rapport, and leverage that. Leverage the things you learn about their personality and values.'

not differ substantially from those needed to be a 'good' interrogator, more generally. They primarily emphasized the need for HVT interrogators to have patience, display a high level of maturity and have superior interpersonal skills. Another recurrent theme is the importance of using highly experienced interrogators for HVT interrogations, which may relate to the observation that a successful interrogation is dependent on an interrogator's ability to be flexible in stressful situations. Ross (2013) reported that experienced interrogators were better able to deal with time constraints, work with naturalistic elements, work with ambiguous information and verbalize more flexibility with their interrogative approach as compared to less experienced interrogators.

Planning and Preparation

Prior to interviewing the target, the interrogator and his/her team must prepare for the interrogation. The majority of HVT interrogators stated that although, in theory, the preparation process for HVT interrogations did not differ from non-HVT interrogations, in practice, there were higher stakes, increased pressure and therefore a more thorough preparation process associated with interviewing an HVT (Russano, Narchet, Kleinman & Meissner, 2014). When asked how they prepared for an interrogation, HVT interrogators emphasized the need to acquire as much information as possible about the individual prior to starting the

Table 8.5   Exemplar remarks from HVT interrogators regarding preparation[3]

'I would do all of my research on the individual that I'm going to interview. Their background, any kind of intelligence or law enforcement information that's out there about them, their family, their education; anything you can get so you can understand where they're coming from. If you can, read up what they have said in the past. As well as if they were arrested, try to find out, not only where and the circumstances of their arrest, but try to get as much as you can about things that were recovered, phone books, computers, anything like that. Facts that you can have when you go into the interview, so you can test them throughout the interview to see how honest they're being.'

If you don't know the basic concepts of what makes somebody become a radical terrorist or join a terrorist organization, you should know some of the tenets of why he joined or what the philosophy is of whatever terrorist group that person happens to be, so at least when you're talking, you can discuss things with that person. If you don't know anything about it, that person will pick up on it, and he'll lose interest in you as an interrogator. If you don't know enough about the subject matter, he can lead you off into tangents that could take months literally, and you will never hit the crux of what you want to find out, unless you can bring him back on track. So you have to do your homework and become almost a subject-matter expert in the area of this person.'

'First thing we're going to do is we're going to get everything we know about this person, and figure out what we don't know. And then, what we don't know, we're going to go find out that. We're going to nail down an interview plan. Specifically, what do we want from him? What are we trying to get from him? And we're going to know everything we need to know about that. We're going to get experts, photographs, pictures, imagery, intelligence, anything we can.'

interrogation (see Table 8.5). The concept of preparation also involved having some basic knowledge of the target's culture and philosophies. Possessing a substantial degree of knowledge about the target provides the interrogator with not only insight into the personality and motivations of the target, but also with the ability to corroborate information elicited during the interrogation (very often in collaboration with an analyst). In other words, good preparation serves not only to inform the progress of an interrogation, but it also allows for some insight into the inner workings of the target.

Interrogation Setting

The interrogation setting may provide a supporting backdrop to a successful interrogation (Goodman-Delahunty, Martschuk & Dhami, 2014) (see Table 8.6). Russano, Narchet, Kleinman and Meissner (2014) reported that interrogators emphasized placing the target at ease.

Table 8.6 Exemplar statements from HVT interrogators regarding their ideal interrogation setting

'So, setting would be, you don't want too many people. A lot of these interviews, everybody wants to participate or sit in the room, and that's just not very conducive, so I think the least amount of people that you need in the room. If you need a translator, then hopefully you've worked with one in the past or you have a relationship with [one], or you at least have a clear understanding of how that should go, so that you're not in the room with the subject explaining to a translator who's supposed to be on your same team kind of how that works. Making sure you have that good relationship with the translator, obviously is important...Yeah, in terms of a table, no table. I want as less between us as possible.'

'Setting is so overlooked, I think. The problem with setting in most interrogations – they're driven by security first. Because they're in a prisoner of war camp or a detention center, that is designed and managed by people with security interests, not by intelligence interests. And so it's not easy to create a positive, compelling rapport with somebody when they're shackled to the floor. I can understand the security of it, but a lot of it's not thought out.'

'So I guess I would say just in general, in a room that's fairly comfortable. Some chairs that are fairly comfortable, and just kind of a non-threatening room. Maybe a window...I would say you want the temperature to be somewhat comfortable, not cold, not hot. So I would say probably a limited number of people as well, so the person is not overwhelmed. Maybe yourself, a translator if one is necessary, kind of a backup investigator who is taking notes or switching off with you taking notes. Maybe that's it, you know, three people. I would want to provide refreshments, some water, soda, whatever. A place where you can sit and talk comfortably, and the person is not incredibly uncomfortable.'

HVT interrogators generally believed the interrogation setting should be comfortable and relaxed in nature. For example, many HVT interrogators noted that the number of individuals in the interrogation room should be kept to a minimum and that an environment should be created that mimics a relaxed conversation between individuals rather than an environment that encourages an adversarial relationship associated with a stereotypical interrogation (e.g. uncomfortable chairs, target shackled). Goodman-Delahunty et al. found that a comfortable physical environment was more conducive to greater cooperation from HVTs, in that an inviting physical environment appeared to encourage rapport and decrease resistance. When the physical environment of the interrogation was uncomfortable, interrogators report that HVTs are less likely to provide information or make incriminating statements (Goodman-Delahunty et al., 2014). This amiable environment is a preference, although not always possible, according to some of Russano et al.'s HVT interrogators – interrogators must work within and adapt to the constraints of the situation. As a case in point, one interrogator aptly offered the following in response to the question about the ideal interrogative setting, 'You don't have much control over the setting. If you're in Gitmo, you're in Gitmo. You're going into a box.'

Interrogation Techniques

Kelly, Miller, Redlich and Kleinman (2013) proposed that interrogation techniques can be categorized into one of six domains. *Rapport and Relationship Building* tactics centre on facilitating a respectful relationship between the interrogator and the target (e.g. finding commonalities; expressing concern for the target's situation), while *Context Manipulation* involves the physical and temporal manipulation of interrogation space for the purpose of influencing behaviour (e.g. conducting the interrogation in a small room; making the interrogation room more neutral). *Emotional Provocation* techniques are designed to manipulate a target's emotions and perceptions, especially in terms of the outcomes associated with cooperation or resistance (e.g. exaggerate the fears of the target; compliment the target). *Confrontation/Competition* techniques tend to create an adversarial dynamic by setting the interrogator and the target against one another. Examples include insulting the target, continually asking the target the same question and emphasizing the authority the interrogator holds overs the target. Techniques in the *Collaboration* domain encourage cooperative interactions between the interrogator and the target. Offering tangible objects (e.g. cigarettes, candy) and/or psychological feedback (e.g. praise in response to providing desired information) are prominent examples. Finally, *Presentation of Evidence* techniques involve the use of evidence to convince a target to cooperate (i.e. confront the target with actual evidence of involvement; confront the target with unsubstantiated evidence of involvement). In a subsequent project, Redlich, Kelly and Miller (2014) examined the frequency and perceived effectiveness of interrogation techniques among military and federal interrogators. They found that relationship and rapport-building techniques were the most commonly used tactics and that these techniques were perceived as the most effective at eliciting information when compared with techniques from the other domains.

Using the Kelly et al. taxonomy, Russano, Narchet, Kleinman and Meissner (2014) reported a significant difference between the perceived use of and the effectiveness of interrogative techniques used by HVT interrogators as compared to their non-HVT counterparts. HVT interrogators were more likely to report most commonly using rapport-based, collaborative and evidence-based approaches than non-HVT interrogators. HVT interrogators were also more likely than non-HVT interrogators to cite relationship and rapport-building techniques as being most effective at eliciting information from a target.

Goodman-Delahunty et al. (2014) examined the perceived use and effectiveness of interrogative strategies when working with HVTs, and their data are quite consistent with the responses provided by Russano, Narchet, Kleinman and Meissner (2014) HVT interrogators. Specifically, Goodman-Delahunty et al. reported the frequent use of rapport-building techniques for gathering information from HVTs. They suggest that practitioners should refrain from employing aggressive and confrontational interrogative tactics because it diminishes cooperation. Furthermore, their data suggest that evidence should be presented in a respectful and non-confrontational manner that allows the HVT to recount their recollection of events. They also contend that accusatorial interrogative strategies were less effective and increased resistance among HVTs. Goodman-Delahunty and colleagues maintain that to increase HVT cooperation, interrogators should use non-coercive social influence strategies to secure cooperation and elicit information, while coercive tactics and physical intimidation were found to result in less reliable information or increased silence from HVTs.

As noted above, the vast majority of HVT interrogators asserted that relationship and rapport-building techniques are most effective at eliciting reliable information. Although there seems to be a lack of consensus regarding the exact definition of rapport – it ranges from forming a productive working relationship (Russano, Narchet, Kleinman & Meissner, 2014) to being friendly and treating targets with respect (Alison, Noone, Elntib & Christiansen, 2013) – there *is* consensus regarding the importance of rapport as a foundation for the ability to elicit reliable information from targets. Recently, Abbe and Brandon (2012) posited that rapport is a necessary component for the exchange of information in any task-oriented interaction. In Russano, Narchet, Kleinman and Meissner (2014) study, one interrogator simply stated that 'Rapport is the lubrication that makes approaches work...rapport is the lubrication for the exploitation' (p. 5). A number of other studies have found support for the effectiveness of rapport-based approaches for eliciting information. For instance, Redlich et al. (2014) reported that rapport and relationship building techniques were perceived to be most effective at eliciting information from a target. Similarly, Alison et al. (2013) suggested that treating targets with respect, dignity and integrity was an effective interrogative strategy and Goodman-Delahunty et al. (2014) found that displays of respect and politeness towards targets were used to successfully garner cooperation from targets.

As stated by most HVT interrogators, no one technique is 100% effective because the successful approach is dependent on, and tailored to, the target. Although developing rapport has emerged as an interrogative approach championed by both practitioners and researchers, HVT interrogators appear mindful that a successful interrogation is a dynamic interaction based on the tone and focus of the interrogation and the target (Evans et al., 2010; Russano, Narchet, Kleinman & Meissner, 2014).

SUPPORTING COMMUNICATION THROUGH INTERPRETERS

All of the interrogators in Russano, Narchet, Kleinman and Meissner (2014) sample worked with interpreters for at least some of their interrogations. One HVT interrogator stated, 'I really like to spend a lot of time with anybody else that's going to be in the room. So I really like to know my interpreter.' According to experienced interrogators, an interpreter can either facilitate communication between the interrogator and the target or hinder the interaction between the two parties. Although the critical importance of interpreters has been acknowledged, very little research has been conducted to examine their role and perceptions of the interrogation process. Russano, Narchet and Kleinman (2014) sought to close this knowledge gap by surveying a sample of highly experienced interpreters with interrogation experience[4] about their beliefs about and experience with the interrogation process. When asked to define their role during an interrogation, interpreters claimed that their primary function was to facilitate communication between the interrogator and the target. However, they did not perceive themselves as a simple mouthpiece or 'translation machine'; rather, they also served as a sort of 'cultural ambassador' (see Tribe & Lane, 2009) who could provide knowledge and expertise about the target's culture (e.g. regarding language, region, religion, etc.). Relatedly, there was a trend that interpreters with HVT interrogation experience were more likely to believe it was important for interrogators to understand the target's culture in order to be an effective interrogator as compared to those without HVT experience.

Definition of an HVT and Perceived Differences between HVT and Non-HVT Interrogations

When asked to define an HVT, the most common response was someone who possessed information about a potential threat to national security (Russano, Narchet & Kleinman, 2014). One interpreter noted that an HVT '...possesses or has access to the person/information vital to the related investigation of high importance...', while another noted that their '...knowledge of attack plans and methodologies could enable law enforcement authorities to disable or disrupt such plans.' Interpreters with HVT experience viewed HVT interrogations as involving higher stakes and therefore more pressure on the interrogation team as compared to non-HVT interrogations.

Interrogation Tactics and Successful Interrogations

Consistent with interrogators' perceptions of the interrogative process (Goodman-Delahunty et al., 2014; Redlich et al., 2014; Russano, Narchet, Kleinman & Meissner, 2014), Russano, Narchet and Kleinman (2014) reported that interpreters perceive relationship and rapport-building techniques as the most effective strategies for eliciting accurate, useful information from targets. When asked to identify those interrogation tactics that were perceived as least effective, the interpreters reported techniques from the confrontation/competition domain (e.g. threats and intimidation) as least effective at eliciting reliable information. Furthermore, when asked what distinguishes successful interrogations from less successful ones, interpreters emphasized having a well-prepared team, in conjunction with a highly skilled interrogator and a highly skilled interpreter.

SUPPORTING INFORMATION ELICITATION THROUGH ANALYSIS

Russano, Narchet, Kleinman and Meissner (2014) found that the majority of interrogators had received analytic assistance during at least some of their interrogations. According to interrogators, analysts support the interrogation process by serving as subject-matter experts about the target or group, providing 'big picture' context beyond target-specific information and providing auxiliary services such as fact-checking information a target provides. Russano, Narchet and Kleinman (2014) found that analysts purport similar beliefs about their role and the services they typically provide when supporting interrogations – they emphasize their role in preparing the interrogator for the interrogation by providing him/her with background information about the target/group, setting intelligence priorities for the interrogation and corroborating elicited information.

Definition of an HVT and Perceived Differences between HVT and Non-HVT Interrogations

In the Russano, Narchet and Kleinman (2014) study, all but one of the analysts had experience supporting HVT interrogations. When asked to define an HVT, the most common response was someone who has valuable information regarding national security and who has information that has the potential to impact strategic decision-making (see Table 8.7).

Analysts were asked to provide their opinions on certain aspects of the HVT interrogation process, including whether HVT interrogations differed from non-HVT interrogations (see Table 8.8). Like other interrogation team members, analysts report a difference in the nature of an HVT interrogation, but not the process. Specifically, analysts report heightened pressure to produce results during an HVT interrogation due to the high-stakes nature of the case (Russano, Narchet & Kleinman, 2014).

Table 8.7 Exemplar remarks from the analysts regarding their definition of an HVT

'Somebody who has information that will save lives, prevent attacks essentially, or affect strategic decision-making against groups or nations.'

'I'd define a high-value target as someone that can provide intelligence value that's substantial enough to possibly deter a threat or provide information on people that possibly pose a threat to the U.S. or its allies.'

'They don't necessarily have to be the person on top, but they might have access to the person on top or they might have access to the cell leader. Or they might have access to the person who's training them. Or they might have access to the financier or they might know about how that gets done in an organization. They might have access to knowledge about the group overall or knowledge about the group's intentions.'

Table 8.8 Exemplar remarks from analysts regarding differences between HVT and non-HVT interrogations

'Yes and no. When you're working with high-value people, there's a whole lot more pressure on you to get something new, useful, timely, whatever. They're not different in terms of [much else], anytime you interrogate somebody for intelligence purposes, you want something useful.'

'The stress level is going to be different. The biggest difference when it's a high-value individual is the amount of attention that's going to be paid to it and the number of people that are going to want their fingers in the pot.'

'Not really. I mean, it was a different flavor of ice cream, if you will. We knew that what we were doing was a big deal. Because there was no confusing those guys with anything other than what they are. You know, they're mass murderers, some of the most dangerous men on the planet. However, the process was essentially the same.'

Preparation, Planning and Interrogation Tactics

Analysts were asked to provide their thoughts on the preparation process, as well as the most and least effective techniques for seeking information. Preparing for an HVT interrogation was perceived as more intense and stressful when compared to a non-HVT interrogation. One analyst stated, 'You want a lot of time to prepare, to digest all the information, and then knowing the information, to plan for how you're going to conduct that interrogation.'

Like interrogators (Goodman-Delahunty et al., 2014; Redlich et al., 2014; Russano, Narchet, Kleinman & Meissner, 2014) and interpreters, analysts perceived relationship and rapport-building techniques as the most effective way to elicit reliable information from both HVT and non-HVT targets (i.e. being friendly; treating them with respect). In the words of one analyst, 'I think across the board, if we participate in or have seen the rapport-based approach be successful a lot ...whether it's that guy or this guy [HVT or non-HVT], it hasn't mattered.'

When asked to provide their opinions on the least effective techniques for eliciting reliable information, most analysts cited interrogation techniques from the confrontation/competition domain (e.g. yelling; insulting the target; Russano, Narchet & Kleinman, 2014). One analyst noted, 'Yeah, well, you can't scare those guys. You can't belittle them. You're not going to be able to guilt them into anything. I mean, these are the best of the best. And so confrontational stuff is going to be a waste of time. And most of the tricks and lies aren't going to work either. You just can't intimidate or frighten those guys. Because regardless of what happens in that interrogation room, they've seen worse. They've done worse, first of all, and they've had worse things done to them. I mean, these are guys that were in jail in Egypt, you know, in the 80s, you know? They weren't gentle with those guys. "Oh, are you going to beat the soles of my feet with a stick for the next six hours? No? All right, well, I guess it's not going to be as bad as it's been." So you're not going to intimidate them or push them around. And to try to would just be a waste – it would be insulting.'

A (NEARLY) 360° PERSPECTIVE

Capturing the self-reported beliefs and opinions of the interrogators themselves provides an unprecedented insight into the perspectives that ultimately shape how individuals plan, conduct and assess their interrogation efforts. While there is not yet sufficient data to examine how closely those reports reflect actual performance, it nonetheless offers a uniquely objective assessment of a fundamentally subjective set of beliefs. This leads to a number of compelling questions. How, for example, might the perspectives of experienced interrogators differ from those who only recently completed basic interrogation training? Similarly, how might the perspectives of experienced interrogators in the field differ from experienced interrogators serving as instructors at various training centres? Moreover, how do perspectives change over time and experience? Similar questions might be posed regarding the perspectives reported by interpreters and analysts.

What is arguably of most value in examining the far-ranging perspectives across a single discipline (e.g. among interrogators or among interpreters) *and* across the three separate disciplines is that a nearly 360° perspective of the interrogation process is available for the first time. The reports of the interrogators offers data to explore how beliefs, expectations, past experiences and even biases can inform how an interrogation might be conducted. Reports from interpreters not only offer data on the vital communication component – both linguistic and cultural – that is very often key to a successful interrogation, but also an unrestricted, 'frontline' observation of how interrogators actually go about their work. The reports from analysts can also provide a strategic perspective on both the competition for information that is an integral part of any interrogation, as well as the value (i.e. accuracy, comprehensiveness and timeliness) of the information gleaned from a subject.

The self-reported reflections of the targets themselves would complete this circle, providing not only additional data but also an additional layer or dimension to the phenomenon. While collecting data about the interrogation experience directly from a subject or detainee might sound incomprehensible, there are real-world precedents that support the contention that such an option may, in fact, be possible. In his book, *Slow Burn: The Rise and Bitter Fall of American Intelligence in Vietnam*, CIA contract interrogator Orrin Deforest chronicles the use of standardized psychological testing of Viet Cong prisoners, the results of which informed the varied interrogation strategies that were reportedly successful in eliciting valuable intelligence information (Kleinman, 2006a).

With or without the perspective of the target, the availability of data from the interrogator, interpreter and analyst offers the opportunity for a multirater assessment. Although not currently used as part of the interrogation/interrogator evaluation process employed within the US military, multirater – or 360° – evaluations are commonplace in a broad cross-section of other activities in both the public and private sectors. According to Carlson (1998), the potential value to be derived from a multirater assessment is supported by three key assumptions: (i) observations from multiple sources offer a more robust portrait of both strengths and weaknesses; (ii) the comparison of self-perception with the perceptions offered by others can serve to enhance self-awareness; and (iii) the most effective performers often possess a self-view that parallels the views of others.

In the absence of data to assess the differential between self-reporting and actual performance, there remains the opportunity to compare the self-reported perspectives of interrogators *about an interrogation* with the self-reported perspectives of individuals who are immediately involved in those interrogations (i.e. the interpreter and analyst). Such a comparison might be viewed as a somewhat unconventional yet nonetheless useful form of multirater assessment. What we find in this regard is a remarkable symmetry among this triad; that is, there is a strong consistency found among the 'assessments' of all three 'raters' (interrogator, interpreter and analyst). This is especially true when it comes to the interrogator's definition of a high-value target and the central role of rapport and relationship building as a strategy for eliciting cooperation and reliable information. Similarly, there was broad consensus that pointed to confrontational or competitive interrogation tactics as being least effective at eliciting reliable information. Whether such information, when revealed to interrogators, would enhance the self-awareness that Carlson finds of value is yet to be determined.

TOWARDS A LEARNING ORGANIZATION

During the course of the War of Terror, the West's adversaries have shown a remarkable ability to learn from experiences in a manner that informed the evolution of their tactics. Perhaps the most notorious example involves the employment of improvised explosive devices that, according to a *Washington Post* accounting, have tragically killed more than 2500 US servicemen and women in the wars in Iraq and Afghanistan (http://apps.washingtonpost.com/national/fallen/causes-of-death/ied/). Less definitive, yet often referred to in the media, have been the changes in counterinterrogation strategies employed by detainees held in US facilities. In response to the former, the US Department of Defense created the Joint Improvised Explosive Device Defeat Organization in 2006. Yet, while there has been a major emphasis placed on learning lessons from operational experience – as evidenced by the long-standing Center for Army Lessons Learned managed by the US Army Combined Arms Center at Fort Leavenworth, KS – there is little to suggest the Army Field Manual (2006) that governs interrogation operations (Field

Manual 2.22-3, Human Intelligence Collector Operations) has been revised based on the field experiences of interrogators and support personnel, despite the years of extensive field experiences. The results of the interviews and surveys designed to capture the perspectives, beliefs and reflections of these individuals could be of material value to a systematic learning effort. This is especially true in an emerging effort known as research to practice (the adaptation of evidence-based interrogation methods to formal interrogation training and operations).

Training creates mental models that, ideally, reflect the most effective means of achieving a specified end (e.g. the successful elicitation of reliable information from a subject). That mental model will, in turn, be shaped – for better or worse – by a series of experiences as the interrogator begins to actually operate in the real world as well as by the feedback she/he receives from supervisors and peers. The prevailing mental model, both the individual and collective, might be accurately described as the sum total of a series of formal and informal lessons learned and both conscious and unconscious responses to experiences. As a result, the comparison of the mental models – as constructed from the responses to the aforementioned interviews and surveys – that exist during various points in an interrogator's development would offer unparalleled insights into how training, experience and both formal and informal feedback will directly inform not only the professional culture and standards of behaviour with the larger cadre of interrogators but also how formal doctrine is ultimately applied on the action end of the training pipeline. In essence, it opens a window into the systemic nature of the interrogation process.

We have previously described the importance of *systems thinking* in interrogation, one that recognizes the process of gleaning information from a subject as a complex, dynamic system with capabilities, potential and functions that cannot be predicted simply by deconstructing that process into discrete elements (Kleinman, 2006b). Senge (2006), who has written extensively about the necessary attributes of a learning organization, offers a resonate view of systems, 'You can only understand the system…by contemplating the whole, not any individual part of the pattern' (p. 34).

Senge (2006) additionally offers an exceptionally useful systems-based framework that serves as a vehicle for better understanding the overarching interrogation process and how that process might be enhanced through organizational learning. Central to this approach is the requirement that we should not 'focus on snapshots of isolated parts of the system, and wonder why our deepest problems never seem to get solved' (p. 34). To examine only the perspectives of the interrogator while the overall process is also materially impacted by the perspectives of the interpreter and analyst (perspectives that form the basis for decision-making and action-taking) would, in line with this thinking, prevent us from solving the 'deepest problems' that undermine optimal effectiveness in the interrogation room.

It is intriguing to note that each of the five 'disciplines' that, together, form Senge's (2006) framework for creating a learning organization – systems thinking, personal mastery, mental models, shared vision and team learning – are reflected in the responses among interrogators, analysts and interpreters. To create a true learning organization, every individual involved must understand his or her role in a much larger, very complex system. Every individual must pursue personal mastery in his or her respective niche. Every participant must gain awareness of his or her personal mental models, as well as understand and appreciate, to the extent possible, those held by others in the system. Individual mental models should also embrace a vision shared by all in the process. Finally, team learning is an ongoing emergent property made possible by these other disciplines.

Inherent in each of these disciplines is perspective, and this explains why it is vital to not only know what an interrogator (or interpreter or analyst) actually does but also what they *think* about what they (and others) do. Perspective is critical to creating a learning organization and the continued evolution of the practice of interrogation.

ACKNOWLEDGEMENT

This work was funded by the High-Value Detainee Interrogation Group contract (J-FBI-10-009) awarded to Melissa Russano at Roger Williams University (subcontracts 26-3001-8961 and 26-3002-4132) through the University of Texas at El Paso. Statements of fact, opinion and analysis in the paper are those of the authors and do not reflect the official policy or position of the FBI or the US Government.

NOTES

1. We recognize that the terms 'interview' and 'interrogation' and 'interrogators' and 'interviewers' have various connotations depending on the agency and/or context. For the purpose of this chapter, we define the term interrogation to mean 'The systematic questioning of an individual who is thought to possess information of law enforcement or intelligence value. The individual being questioned may not respond co-operatively during certain phases of

the interaction and typically presents some degree of resistance to answering questions and/or answering questions to the best of their knowledge. In response, specific methods, strategies, or themes are traditionally employed to foster co-operation.'

2. Unless otherwise noted, all quotes presented in this chapter were culled from the data collected by Russano, Narchet, Kleinman and Meissner (2014) and Russano, Narchet and Kleinman (2014).

3. Please note that these observations are not specific to working with HVTs, but reflect an HVT interrogator's preparation process generally.

4. All of the interpreters in Russano, Narchet and Kleinman's (2014) sample were affiliated with the Federal Bureau of Investigation. Fourteen of the 27 respondents had experience with HVT interrogations.

REFERENCES

Abbe, A., & Brandon, S. E. (2012). The role of rapport in investigative interviewing: A review. *Journal of Investigative Psychology and Offender Profiling.* Published online, doi: 10.1002/jip.1386.

Alison, L. J., Alison, E., Noone, G., Elntib, S., & Christiansen, P. (2013). Why tough tactics fail and rapport get results: Observing rapport-based interpersonal techniques (ORBIT) to generate useful information from terrorist. *Psychology, Public Policy, and Law, 19*, 411–431. doi: 10.1037/a0034564.

Carlson, M. S. (1998). 360-degree feedback: The power of multiple perspectives. *Popular Government,* Winter 1998, 39–48.

Evans, J. R., Meissner, C. A., Brandon, S. E., Russano, M. B., & Kleinman, S. M. (2010). Criminal versus HUMINT interrogations: The importance of psychological science to improving interrogative practice. *Journal of Psychiatry and Law, 38*, 215–249. Faces of the Fallen: U.S. service member deaths caused by ied in Operation Iraqi.

Freedom and Operation Enduring Freedom, Washington Post. Retrieved from: http://apps.washingtonpost.com/national/fallen/causes-of-death/ied/.

Goodman-Delahunty, J., Martschuk, N., & Dhami (2014). Interviewing high value detainees: Securing cooperation and reliable disclosures. *Applied Cognitive Psychology.* Advance online publication. doi: 10.1002/acp3087.

Hartwig, M., Meissner, C. A., & Semmel, M. D. (2014). Human intelligence interviewing and interrogation: Assessing the challenges of developing an ethical, evidence-based approach. In R. Bull (Ed.), *Investigative interviewing* (pp. 209–228). New York: Springer.

Kelly, C. E., Miller, J. C., Redlich, A. D., & Kleinman, S. M. (2013). A taxonomy of interrogation methods. *Psychology, Public Policy, and Law, 19*, 165–178. doi: 10.1037/a0030310.

Kleinman, S. M. (2006a). KUBARK counterintelligence interrogation review: Observations of an interrogator – lessons learned and avenues for future research. In R. Swenson (Ed.), *Educing information – interrogation: Science and Art.* Washington, DC: National Defense Intelligence College Press.

Kleinman, S. M. (2006b). Barriers to success: Critical challenges in developing a new educing information paradigm. In R. Swenson (Ed.), *Educing information – interrogation: Science and Art.* Washington, DC: National Defense Intelligence College Press.

Redlich, A. D., Kelly, C. E., & Miller, J. C. (2014). The who, what, and why of human intelligence gathering. Self-reported measures of interrogation methods. *Applied Cognitive Psychology*. Advance online publication. doi: 10.1002/acp.3040.

Ross, A. B. (2013). Assessing naturalistic decision making by experienced and inexperienced interrogators in high stakes interviews (Unpublished Master's thesis), University of Texas at El Paso, Texas.

Russano, M. B., Narchet, F. M., & Kleinman, S. M. (2014). Analysts, interpreters, and intelligence interrogations: Perceptions and insights. *Applied Cognitive Psychology*. Advance online publication. doi: 10.1002/acp.3070.

Russano, M. B., Narchet, F. M., Kleinman, S. M., & Meissner, C. A. (2014). Structured interviews of experienced HUMINT interrogators. *Applied Cognitive Psychology*. Advance online publication. doi: 10.1002/acp.3069.

Senge, P. M. (2006). *The fifth discipline*. New York: Doubleday.

Tribe, R., & Lane, P. (2009). Working with interpreters across language and culture in mental health. *Journal of Mental Health, 18*, 233–241. doi: 10.1080/09638230701879102.

US Department of Defense. (2006). Joint Improvised Explosive Device Defeat Organization (Directive 2000.19E). Washington, DC: Office of the Deputy Secretary of Defense.

US Department of the Army. (2006). Human intelligence collector operations (Field Manual 2-22.3). Washington, DC: Headquarters, Department of the Army.

Section IV

Communicating in the Courtroom

9

Courtroom Questioning and Discourse

Emily Henderson[1], Christopher Heffer[2] and Mark Kebbell[3]
[1] Barrister, New Zealand
[2] Cardiff University, Cardiff, UK
[3] Griffith University, Nathan, Queensland, Australia

> Examination in chief is where the witness gives the evidence. Cross-examination is where I give the evidence and the witness says 'yes' or 'no'.
> (English QC teaching young barristers to cross-examine children, 2013)

INTRODUCTION

In an ideal world only honest and reliable witnesses would be called to give evidence in court. Relatively few crimes are committed, however, in front of disinterested, sober, upright members of the public... . The unenviable task of the jury in such cases is to assess the witnesses and to try to pick out those parts of their evidence that are truthful and reliable.
> (*R v. Camberwell Green Youth Court*, 2005)

Communication in Investigative and Legal Contexts: Integrated Approaches from Forensic Psychology, Linguistics and Law Enforcement, First Edition. Edited by Gavin Oxburgh, Trond Myklebust, Tim Grant and Rebecca Milne.
© 2016 John Wiley & Sons, Ltd. Published 2016 by John Wiley & Sons, Ltd.

Every justice system faces the problem of how to test witnesses' accounts to ensure that decision-makers undertake their 'unenviable task' with what the English call 'best evidence': a complete and accurate picture of the witness's recollections, veracity and competence (*R v. Barker*, 2010).

This chapter discusses the process in England and a related group of what we will, for convenience's sake, call 'accusatorial' systems: Australia, New Zealand and Canada. Although, of course, there is no strict division between so-called accusatorial and inquisitorial systems[1] (Spencer, 2005), witness examination remains an area where procedural and theoretical differences do exist.

Broadly, in more inquisitorial systems, witnesses may testify at trial, but their pre-trial statements also have the force of evidence. At trial, a judge, duty-bound to seek the truth, takes the lead in questioning. Prosecutors and defence advocates may ask questions, but more in a supplementary capacity. In more accusatorial systems, there is a heavier emphasis on live, oral evidence, and it is the parties – or, almost always, their advocates – who take charge of questioning. The judge and any jury remain virtually passive (Spencer, 2005). The judge can ask further questions or even, exceptionally, call witnesses (*R v. Haringey Justices*, 1996; *R v. Wellingborough Justices*, 1994), but only to clarify or ensure fairness. Accusatorial judges are process guardians, never investigators (*Jones v. National Coal Board*, 1957).

Accusatorial lawyers argue that a neutral investigator cannot be trusted to probe the evidence as closely as an interested party, nor, having acted as investigator, to maintain enough distance to make an unbiased ruling. Further, they believe only a committed partisan advocate can be trusted to facilitate the defendant's right to test evidence fully, a right they consider demands a personal say in both the direction and the directing of the testing. Thus, in accusatorial trials, just as the investigation overall is divided betwixt the parties, so also is witness examination. First, the advocate for the party 'calling' the witness undertakes an 'examination in chief', eliciting all evidence favourable to their client's case. Next, the advocate for the opposing party 'cross-examines' the witness to reveal flaws in the evidence in chief or to draw out contrary evidence supporting their client's case. The original advocate may then 're-examine' to repair any damage done during cross-examination. Accusatorial lawyers are deeply proud of this system, especially cross-examination, regarding it as a superb means of ensuring accurate evidence while protecting the defendant's rights (*Mechanical & General Inventions Co. Ltd v. Austin*, 1935).[2]

There are real advantages to strong partisan-controlled examination. Theoretically, it should ensure that any contested evidence is thoroughly challenged. For this reason Italy adopted a more accusatorial process in the mid-1980s after the Neapolitan *Camorra* trials, where the courts convicted hundreds of *cammoristi* on the basis of the essentially unchallenged evidence of other mafiosi turned state's evidence, only to find that they had been badly misled (Jacquemet, 1996). However, despite its strengths, strong partisan control also has adverse impacts upon the quality and reliability of the evidence, especially when witnesses are young or impaired, but, as we discuss, even when the witness is a robust adult.

The essential issue, we argue, is that while partisan-controlled questioning protects defendants' rights to test, partisan advocates feel compelled to exploit any chance to advance the client's wider interest in persuading fact-finders in their favour. Hence, cross-examination is used not just to test evidence but to present it so as to enhance the case, by controlling witnesses tightly so that they give only useful answers and by using questions to "speak" directly to the fact finders (Ellison, 2001; Heffer, 2005, 2012; Henderson, 2001, 2003; Pennington & Hastie, 1986, 1991). Witnesses in an accusatorial trial are more than evidential sources: they are the tools through which counsel tells a story (Stone, 1995).[3] Unfortunately, the tactics this attitude causes advocates to adopt can undermine the reliability of the evidence.

Consequently, there is now a strong movement to reform cross-examination practice, but that practice has proven extremely resilient. Recent advances in England suggest that the key is to address that which drives advocates to excess, namely their belief that in cross-examination investigation is subservient to advocacy.

PROBLEMS WITH CROSS-EXAMINATION

While accusatorial lawyers revere cross-examination, ever since the late 1800s (Cairns, 1999; Langbein, 2003; Spencer & Flin, 1993), and especially over the last thirty years (Plotnikoff & Woolfson, 2012; Spencer, 2012a), it has been subject to intense criticism, first of its forensic safety and second of the trauma to witnesses. While no one questions that defendants' rights to a fair trial are sacrosanct, critics argue that a fair trial can include a greater degree of accuracy and respect for witnesses' dignity.

Forensic Safety

This section examines three problems undermining cross-examination as an effective testing methodology, namely its use of suggestive questions, its efficacy in revealing deception and its traumatic impact upon some witnesses.

Testing or Suggesting?

The first problem with cross-examination is its reliance on suggestive questions, which critics argue can amount to coercion, particularly with children and impaired adults. Cross-examination almost invariably involves a high proportion of suggestive questions. The standard advice in training manuals is to use a wide variety of such questions, including affirmative and negative tag questions, closed option-posing questions and various questioning strategies, including repetition, abrupt shifts between subjects and a rapid pace, designed to reduce the witness's resistance and maximize their suggestibility. Advocates are advised to 'lead the witness forcefully on one point after another, keeping maximum control over him and his testimony, (Stone, 1995; see also Eichelbaum, 1989), and to exert psychological authority over witnesses to increase their vulnerability to suggestions.

> Above all, make sure the witness understands and feels your attitude about the facts of the case and your expectations in your answers '... *it will usually have a significant impact in obtaining the answers you want*'. (Eichelbaum, 1989, p. 209) (DuCann, 1993; Stone, 1995)

Part of the explanation for this is that the rules on examination are based on false assumptions about the dynamics of memory and suggestibility. The belief is that honest, accurate witnesses remember events easily, even months or years later. Thus, they only comply with suggestion if they are inaccurate, dishonest or colluding with the advocate making the suggestions because they are biased in favour of the advocate's client. Ergo, the rules usually[4] ban leading questions in examination in chief, since witnesses are presumed biased in favour of the side calling them and, so, liable to collusion. Conversely, cross-examination witnesses are presumed hostile to the examiner and therefore suggestive questions are a safe and effective test of their accuracy and veracity (*Bastin v. Carew*, 1824; *Clarke v. Saffery*, 1824).

The courts do recognize that some questioning is so 'oppressive' or overbearing that it should be stopped lest even a hostile witness be coerced into agreement. Unfortunately, since the belief is that most people are still very resistant to suggestion, the courts' concept of 'oppression' is so extreme that they rarely find the threshold exceeded.[5]

The assumptions underlying the rules are outdated. Empirical research establishes conclusively that memory is extremely friable (Loftus, 1996; Wells, Memon & Penrod, 2006), that even robust adults are highly suggestible and that children and vulnerable adults even more so (Gudjonsson, 2003; Kebbell & Hatton, 1999). Multiple studies that have tested cross-examination-type questions on children (e.g. Zajac & Cannan, 2009; Zajac & Haynes, 2003, 2006) and on robust adults (see, for example, Ellison & Wheatcroft, 2010; Kebbell, Evans & Johnson, 2010; Kebbell & Johnson, 2000; Valentine & Maras, 2011; Wheatcroft & Ellison, 2012; Wheatcroft & Wood, 2010) have shown that they often make witnesses less, rather than more, accurate. Moreover, extensive research on the dynamics of false confession (Cutler, Findlay & Moore, 2014; Kassin & Gudjonsson, 2004; Snook, Eastwood & Barron, 2014) shows that questioning similar to conventional cross-examination – authoritarian, controlling and very challenging questioning – exacerbates suggestibility, especially in the young and the impaired (Cutler et al., 2014; Roper & Shewan, 2002; Zajac & Cannan, 2009). This is particularly so when questioning takes place in an intimidating setting (Cutler et al., 2014; Zajac & Cannan, 2009), which a courtroom certainly can be.

However, these false factual assumptions are only part of the reason accusatorial examination has developed in this way. Lawyers are vividly aware of the risks of suggestive interrogation in police interrogations and the courts regularly take police or evidential interviewers to task (*Ibrahim v. The King*, 1914; *Lam Chi-ming v. The Queen*, 1991; *R v. Mushtaq*, 2005; *R v. Prager*, 1972; *Saunders v. United Kingdom*, 1996). The full answer is that lawyers see suggestion as a legitimate part of cross-examination because it forwards their overall aim of persuading the fact finders.

> ...Janus-faced, a cross-examiner has to look in two directions – at the witness and at the court. He seeks to induce the witness to give certain testimony, and he wishes to persuade the court that a certain version of the facts is true....
>
> (Stone, 1995, p. 121)

Fundamentally, cross-examiners use suggestive questions because they *want* to manipulate witnesses and they also regularly exploit questioning to comment upon the evidence (Heffer, 2005). 'Comment' is, in theory, prohibited (*Hardy's Trial*, 1794), but the rule is almost universally ignored, although it is a point of style not to make them in too obviously theatrical a manner (Henderson, 2001, 2003, in press-b). Recent research suggests that the advocate's instinct that cross-examination presents a rhetorical opportunity is correct and a 'speech in questions' can be effective in persuading jurors (Klemfussi, Quas & Lyon, 2014).

Cross-examination is also sometimes regarded as an opportunity for a symbolic confrontation between accuser and accused. While this is more popular in the United States (*Coy v. Iowa*, 1988) and has been comprehensively rejected by the English courts (*R v. Camberwell Green Youth Court*, 2005), it still has a shadowy half-life where lawyers sometimes accept that defendants expect advocates to use cross-examination to denounce the witness publically. Therefore, there is a certain tolerance of an element of symbolic denunciation, lest the defendant feel cheated of a fair trial (Henderson, in press-b). Further, although few advocates want to actually bully witnesses into agreement, the perception that cross-examination is more than an interrogation means that they do not see themselves as having a strong responsibility to *avoid* coercion. There is a strong element of wilful blindness in their approach to suggestibility. Manuals on examination are replete with examples where the clear implication is that the accuracy of the evidence elicited from the witness is not of concern. There is, for example, considerable advice available as to how to block unfavourable evidence emerging, regardless of its accuracy. Advocates are also taught to ask a series of questions from which a favourable inference can be drawn, but never to ask the witness to draw that inference in case the witness provides some further inconvenient fact that undermines the preferred conclusion (Eichelbaum, 1989[6]; Munkman, 1991; Stone, 1995). The concern is not about whether the witness has been coerced or misled, but merely whether the fact-finders will notice (Stone, 1995[7]). Provided the advocate is not violating the minimal safety standards in the professional code of ethics by putting forward something he or she actually knows to be untrue, accuracy is irrelevant: impression is everything.

Communication
The second major complaint against conventional cross-examination practice concerns its comprehensibility. Significant empirical evidence shows that cross-examiners regularly use complex language inappropriate for child or impaired adult witnesses (e.g. Hanna, Davies, Crothers & Henderson, 2011; O'Neill & Zajac, 2013; Plotnikoff & Woolfson, 2012; Zajac & Cannan, 2009; Zajac & Hayne, 2003, 2006) and also confusing for ordinary adults (Ellison & Wheatcroft, 2010; Kebbell et al., 2010; Kebbell & Johnson, 2000; Valentine & Maras, 2011; Wheatcroft & Ellison, 2012; Wheatcroft & Wood, 2010). The empirical evidence suggests that previously accurate witnesses are likely to become less accurate under conventional cross-examination questioning as a result. Linguistic confusion is also associated with increased suggestibility (Clare & Gudjonsson, 1993; Ellison, 2001; Ellison & Wheatcroft, 2010).

This complexity results more from ignorance and ineptitude rather than intention (Henderson, in press-c), although a few do deliberately exploit a witness's communication weaknesses (Henderson, 2003). More often, there is simply little concept that advocates bear much responsibility for ensuring that witnesses understand questions, bar some mild pruning of the more obvious legalese (Heffer, 2005).

The assumption is that witnesses must adapt to the court, not the court to the witnesses. Thus, any confusion raises issues not about the suitability of the questions but rather about the witness's competence and/ or veracity (*R v. Malicki*, 2009; *R v. Powell*, 2006; cf. *R v. Barker*, 2010).

Ineffective Cross-examination
In addition to criticisms of its potential for contaminating and confusing evidence, research also suggests that cross-examination is ineffective in revealing unreliable witnesses. While the audience of fact-finders encourages advocates to adopt a potentially misleading style of questioning, their presence can also limit the extent to which advocates are prepared to push their investigations. Fear of giving witnesses an opportunity to say something damaging in front of the jury discourages advocates from asking questions if they fear the answer might be unfavourable or delivered in too convincing a manner. If a witness used a question to introduce inadmissible evidence, a judge may instruct a jury to disregard it; common sense and research suggest that they are not always able to do so (Edmond, 2012). These fears restrict the questioning, potentially depriving the court (and the client) of a full investigation and full evidence. Further, even with assertive advocates, empirical research suggests that cross-examination is not terribly effective in revealing liars. Not only do witnesses who were accurate before cross-examination become less accurate during it, but most studies show that it does not increase the accuracy of previously inaccurate witnesses either (Ellison & Wheatcroft, 2010; Kebbell et al., 2010; Kebbell & Johnson, 2000; Valentine & Maras, 2011; Wheatcroft & Ellison, 2012; Wheatcroft & Wood, 2010).

Research also shows that the traditional accusatorial reliance on witness demeanour as a clue to deception[8] is mistaken. The accusatorial system's insistence on live oral examination is based on the assumption that the witness's behaviour while testifying is itself of great forensic value.[9] However, deception research over many decades shows that people are both very good at lying and very poor at detecting lying (Vrij, 2008). Many studies have shown that even professional lie detectors – police, judges and advocates – are able to detect lies at only just above the level of chance (Kassin & Gudjonsson 2004; Kebbell et al., 2010; Snook et al., 2014; Strömwall & Granhag, 2003; Wheatcroft, Wagstaff & Kebbell, 2004; Wheatcroft & Wood, 2010; Zajac & Cannan, 2009). Thus, the courts' preoccupation with witness 'demeanour' is misguided; it is virtually impossible for a fact-finder to determine from merely *observing* a witness whether or not they are telling the truth.

The likelihood of making a valid observation diminishes further when one factors in the extent to which cross-examiners also strive to manipulate the witness's emotional state to make them appear less credible or less sympathetic (Henderson, 2015[10]).

There are, however, more effective alternatives. Recent research suggests that better than the conventional cross-examiner's reliance on closed leading questions is using more open questions to seek further information (Vrij et al., 2009). Since the most stable correlate of deception is 'cogniative load' (Vrij et al., 2008), the more factual questions are asked, the more a liar has to remember previous answers and this becomes increasingly difficult. Conversely, conventional cross-examination tactics do not increase cognitive load and are much easier for a liar to manage (Heaton-Armstrong, Shepherd, Gudjonsson & Wolchover, 2006). There is as yet no research on this in a trial context and it would greatly challenge conventional practice, which aims to limit and control the emergence of information. However, it has merit as a possible approach.

Examining Expert Evidence

Research suggests that cross-examination is even less effective as a tool for testing experts than it is as a test of ordinary witness's evidence (Edmond, 2012; National Research Council of the National Academies, 2009; Neufeld, 2005). There is very extensive evidence that jurors, judges and lawyers alike are very poor at evaluating expert evidence, especially statistical or highly technical evidence (see the review in Henderson & Seymour, 2013). Instead, people tend to make crude assessments based on the expert's credentials, demeanour and their own prior assumptions (Spencer, 1992). Indeed, using demeanour to assess an expert may be even less reliable than with an ordinary witness since many experts are experienced and skilled courtroom performers (Henderson & Seymour, 2013)

Further, many advocates lack the necessary knowledge to question experts effectively and may even be unfit to assess whether to challenge them. This has prompted widespread calls for advocates to be trained to evaluate scientific evidence (Edmond, 2012; National Research Council of the National Academies, 2009) and also for the adoption of alternative measures for taking expert evidence, including 'hot-tubbing', where experts are cross-examined concurrently in a panel discussion situation, enabling them to critique each other's evidence without relying on lawyers (Blaumire-Brown, 2011; Genn, 2012; Rares, 2012).

Even the division of examination into two halves – the positive and then the negative – may impede decision-makers' ability to evaluate expert evidence. Research suggests that people assess evidence by constructing stories out of it, with the most convincing story winning

(Edmond, 2012; MacDonald & Tinsley, 2011; Pennington & Hastie, 1986, 1991). In a story-telling competition, the advocate calling the expert has a great advantage over the cross-examiner, since evidence in chief can more easily be woven into the narrative of the case theory ('test X shows that the bloodstains that officer Z found in the bedroom were from the victim'), while cross-examination of expert evidence tends to be highly technical and purely negative ('test X failed to take into consideration factor Y') and thus less easy to incorporate into a narrative (Edmond, 2012; Young, Cameron & Tinsley, 1999). Hence, studies suggest that cross-examining an expert generally has little or no impact upon juries, whose minds are made up during examination in chief (Cutler & Penrod, 1995; Diamond, Casper, Heiert & Marshall, 1996; Kovera, 2008; Kovera, Levy, Borgida & Penrod, 1994; Levett & Kovera 2008; Sanders, 2003).

Another issue is 'adversarial bias'. Studies show that merely by appointing witnesses to one side or the other may bias even neutral people in favour of their 'team' (Sanders, 2003). Where witnesses already hold strong opinions, the fear is that a partisan appointment may persuade them to a still stronger position. Cross-examination may exacerbate this because some witnesses react to criticism by adopting more extreme or more entrenched positions than they would normally espouse (*GMC v. Meadow*, 2006).[11]

Given the difficulty of non-expert advocates interrogating expert evidence, special efforts are made to insulate experts from adversarial bias. Although they are called by a party, they have a special ethical obligation to consider themselves neutral witnesses of the court. Some even urge that they be appointed only by the court. Many jurisdictions require opposing experts to discuss their differences and create a joint statement describing areas of agreement and disagreement (Henderson & Seymour, 2013). While these efforts to increase the reliability of expert evidence are laudable, there is currently little attention given to whether the same issues might arise with other witnesses.

Re-balancing the Accusatorial Trial: Judicial Intervention and Re-examination

The accusatorial trial does contain safeguards against cross-examination distorting the evidence, in particular the judge's power to intervene when advocates breach the rules and the advocate's re-examination after cross-examination. Increasingly, the English courts encourage judicial intervention (Henderson, 2014a in press-a; *Wills v. R*, 2011[12]) and this message has been reinforced with a specific Practice Direction and other recent guidance (Judicial College, 2013; Plotnikoff & Woolfson, 2012).

However, prior to these changes, studies show a very low level of intervention (Hanna et al., 2011; O'Kelly, Kebbell, Hatton & Johnson, 2003; Plotnikoff & Woolfson, 2009, 2012) and the question remains whether judges will change their practice. Their underlying attitude is still very cautious (*R v. McFadden*, 1975[13]). Although judges can ask questions to clarify evidence elicited in cross-examination, the case law emphasizes that they must limit their interventions so that it does not appear that they are either biased or taking over the role of one or other party (Henderson, 2014b).

English trial judges in a recent study described intervention as 'one of the hardest tasks' of judging. Even with child witnesses, they fear the jury might conclude they are biased against the party on whom they intervene. Judges are also reluctant to stop what might be a legitimate inquiry and they fear censure on appeal (Henderson, in press-a). Accordingly, 'you wait until you are absolutely certain that you are going to have to' intervene and, even then, interventions should be as minimal as possible.

> ...The starting point is as much as possible to shut up: the more I intervene the more likely I have an impact on proceedings over the evidence....
> (Henderson, in press-a)

As another judge commented, the judicial preference for passivity '...is such a powerful instinct, and sometimes it gets the better of the rules...' (Henderson, in press-a).

Meanwhile, the opposing party's counsel will usually be slow to intervene (Hanna et al., 2011), fearing that the fact-finders will perceive the intervention as an attempt to deflect legitimate criticism and conceal a witness's frailties or unreliability. Nor will they necessarily intervene to protect a distressed witness. Judges and advocates tend to see hurt as an unavoidable side-effect of examination, not only when the case involves humiliating or traumatic events but because they assume the advocate must put the witness under pressure in order to test them. They believe, as a barrister told the first author recently, 'a little bit of torture is inevitable'. Some may not even appreciate when witnesses are distressed. While judges are eager to protect vulnerable witnesses from overly aggressive cross-examination, most also say that aggression is rare, whereas witnesses' own assessments, as reported in the studies below, are very different. Other judges commented that their colleagues can become blind to witness stress (Henderson, in press-a, in press-c). Thus, while judges and advocates may want to protect witnesses from trauma, they may notice and define it differently from the way in which it is experienced by witnesses.

The second remedy for a distorting cross-examination is re-examination by the advocate who called the witness. However, in the first author's experience it can be difficult to achieve a satisfactory re-examination, again due to the advocates' concern to present a convincing narrative. Advocates worry that the jury's attention span will not stand much more time spent in questioning. Thus, even where there are numerous issues the advocate may only address one or two. Further, tired and disorientated witnesses are difficult to direct to the relevant issues, especially since leading questions are prohibited in re-examination. Even then, if the witness cannot summon the energy to give a crisp explanation of, for example, an apparent contradiction, the re-examination may even reinforce the jury's impression that a damaging concession has been made. If the advocate is unsure why a witness has made an unfavourable concession, he or she may prefer to leave the issue unresolved rather than risk further admissions. Advocates especially fear re-examining expert witnesses for this reason (Henderson & Seymour, 2013). Further, advocates know that a well-phrased comment by a cross-examiner can leave an indelible impression on the jury, regardless of the witness's response (Henderson, 2001, 2003; Klemfussi, Quas & Lyon, 2014). Re- examination rarely has the same impact. As a result, it often seems wiser to stay silent than to attempt salvage.

In summary, not only can an accusatorial witness examination result in evidence being distorted or confused but the main safeguards provided during the trial are sometimes not adequate to the challenge of clarifying and correcting false impressions.

Trauma and Witness Participation

Another major criticism of conventional cross-examination is that it traumatizes witnesses, especially sex offence complainants. This is not only undesirable per se but is a major issue for the reliability of the evidence, since stress is known to impede recall and increase suggestibility in children (Plotnikoff & Woolfson, 2012) and vulnerable and robust adults alike (Cutler et al., 2014; Snook et al., 2014).

Cross-examination can be very challenging, even where the advocate's manner is not aggressive, often involving repeated, pointed rejections of the witness's evidence and aspersions on their character. The more important the witness's evidence (as in a he said/she said conflict without corroborating evidence, as in many sex trials), the more likely it is that the cross-examiner will challenge the witness's veracity, character and, not uncommonly, sanity (Ellison, 2001; Spencer & Flin, 1993; see, for example, *H v. R*, 2014). Not only is it assumed that suggestive questions make for good interrogation but the rules oblige advocates to 'put the case' or give witnesses opportunities to answer any adverse allegations in the party's case (*Brown v. Dunn*, 1893) (although recently the English courts introduced some exceptions for vulnerable witnesses; see *R v. Barker*, 2010). While the rule is intended to assist witnesses, advocates often undermine it by turning the obligatory questions into strong rhetorical statements – 'The truth is that you are lying, aren't you?' – often obstructing or obscuring the answer.

While, obviously, not every witness – even when vulnerable – is distressed by cross-examination (Kebbell, O'Kelly & Gilchrist, 2007; Wade, 2002), many studies suggest that adult rape complainants especially find testifying extremely stressful (Ellison, 2001; Lees, 1996; MacDonald & Tinsley, 2011; Temkin, 2000), as do many children (Cashmore & Trimboli, 2005; Eastwood & Patton, 2002; Hanna et al., 2011; Plotnikoff & Woolfson, 2009; Quas et al., 2005; Whitehead, 2000). Rape complainants have described it as 'worse than the rape' (Ellison, 2001) and commentators label it 'revictimization' (Matoesian, 1993). The English media recently highlighted several trials in which rape complainants were severely distressed by cross-examination, including two separate cases in which complainants committed suicide shortly after testifying (Norfolk, 2013; Surrey County Council Safe-guarding Adults Board, 2014).

There is little research on the stress experienced by ordinary adult witnesses in examination, although there are some indications it can be high (Ellison & Wheatcroft, 2010). One wide-scale UK survey found that while 48% of all witnesses and complainants felt that they had been treated courteously and were able to say everything needful, 28% disagreed (Whitehead, 2000). There is also considerable anecdotal evidence that expert witnesses often find cross-examination extremely unpleasant (Henderson & Seymour, 2013).

In principle, as already discussed, the system contains safeguards against oppressive cross-examination. In practice, however, the rules are rarely enforced or the threshold is set too low to make much difference. The end result is that cross-examination is often traumatic, most particularly, but not exclusively, for the witnesses least able to withstand trauma. Given the implications of stress for accuracy and recall, more research is needed.

Deterrence

Not only is cross-examination detrimental to some individuals, but there are long-running concerns that the fear of cross-examination deters victims from laying complaints and witnesses from testifying, particularly about sex assault (Davies & Westcott, 1992; Ellison, 2001), but also about other offences, such as domestic violence (Lininger, 2005). Researchers point to the fact that many rape complainants drop charges, some explicitly citing fear of trial as their reason (Ellison, 2001; Lininger, 2005). There are also long-standing concerns that police and prosecutors drop some legitimate complaints, particularly of sex assault, due to fears the complainants will not withstand cross-examination (Brown, 2011; Ellison, 2001; MacDonald & Tinsley, 2011).

Several studies have also asked actual witnesses whether they would be prepared to give evidence again. The results vary, but a significant minority of witnesses say they would refuse. In 2009, Plotnikoff and Woolfson found that of 172 British child witnesses in criminal trials of all types, 33% would not give evidence again, while 65% would testify 'only if I absolutely had to' (Plotnikoff & Woolfson, 2009). Eastwood and Patton's survey of child witnesses in sexual abuse trials in various Australian states found that 17% of Western Australia child witnesses, 39% of Queensland child witnesses and 56% of those in New South Wales said they would never testify again, regardless of the outcome of the trial in which they had appeared (Eastwood & Patton, 2002). Tellingly, they also found that of their interview sample, only 18% of Queensland barristers, 33% of New South Wales barristers and 46% of Western Australia barristers would allow their own children to testify (Eastwood & Patton, 2002[14]).

Concerns about witness reluctance have led the UK government to conduct several large-scale 'Witness Satisfaction Surveys' (Whitehead, 2000). The first and widest-ranging, in 2000, found that 21% of all witnesses, 25% of all complainants and 36% of all children would refuse to testify again (Whitehead, 2000). The most recent 2012 survey only considered adult witnesses and excluded sex offences, domestic violence and crimes resulting in death, but still found that 16% would not testify again (Franklyn, 2012). The reasons identified are wider than just cross-examination but it does appear to be a factor. Similarly, many commentators warn that conventional cross-examination deters expert witnesses from testifying, and numerous anecdotal accounts support this (Henderson & Seymour, 2013).

However, self-report studies such as these should be treated cautiously: jurors, for example, often self-report understanding jury instructions (Thomas, 2010; Zander & Henderson, 1993) despite strong evidence that they do not (Thomas, 2010; Young et al., 1999). Similarly, witnesses in the immediate aftermath of a trial may well say that they will not testify again but may later consent in the right circumstances. What these surveys *do* show, though, is that witnesses are very dissatisfied with the process. While more research is needed, there are obvious costs to any society where fear of the court process deters complainants and witnesses from participating in trials.

Achieving Reform: Achieving Cultural Change

In this chapter we argue that the fundamental problem with accusatorial cross-examination is that partisan advocates, intent on the larger task of advancing their clients' best interests, are strongly motivated to use examination to persuade the fact-finders to find for their clients rather than merely to investigate the evidence. The accusatorial system's insistence that witnesses' evidence be presented orally in front of an audience of fact-finders then creates an opportunity to exercise that partisan fervour.

Accusatorial lawyers believe fervently that their examination method still produces reliable evidence. However, the research suggests that cross-examination is frequently coercive, confusing and obstructive and, moreover, not terribly effective at unmasking deceptive witnesses. Nonetheless, despite the research and a considerable body of critical commentary, accusatorial examination has remained largely immune to reform (Spencer, 2012a). The most major incursions have been into examination-in-chief, although even then only in aid of some vulnerable witnesses. Recognition of the damage done to vulnerable witnesses' memories and to their emotional health by the long delays endemic in the trial system and of the general unfitness of the courtroom as an environment for eliciting their evidence has led to some sweeping changes. It is now general practice across Britain, Australia, New Zealand, Canada and South Africa for trained interviewers to examine children and, increasingly, vulnerable adults 'in chief', in special facilities designed to be less intimidating and for that evidence to be pre-recorded for replay at trial (Henderson, 2012; Hoyano & Keenan, 2010). However, cross-examination and the examination-in-chief of other witnesses are almost untouched.

Virtually the only reforms affecting cross-examination directly are limited to a particularly vulnerable group, namely sex assault complainants. Most accusatorial jurisdictions now require the defence to apply to cross-examine rape complainants about their sexual past and ban the few self-represented defendants from cross-examining rape complainants in person (Brown, 2011; Hoyano & Keenan, 2010; see Temkin, 2000). Otherwise, all that has been done is to ameliorate some of the more stressful surrounding practices, such as the requirement to testify in open court, to face the defendant directly or be named in the press and, again, only for witnesses recognized as especially vulnerable.

A very few states allow cross-examination as well as examination in chief to be pre-recorded, but most resist (Henderson, 2012; Jackson, 2012). Although these are all important reforms, the fact that they are all that has been achieved underlines cross-examination's special status in accusatorial legal culture.

For example, in 2013, there was major public outcry in England over the brutal cross-examination of teenage complainants in a sex-offence trial, cross-examinations that included multiple demeaning accusations and extended into weeks, involving upwards of ten cross-examiners (Norfolk, 2013). The ministerial response was to announce the long-delayed pilot of legislation allowing cross-examination to be pre-recorded, a measure that, while welcome for its impact on delay (Spencer & Lamb, 2012), does not address questioning methodology (Bowcott, 2013).

The central issue is that cross-examination carries such cultural significance for accusatorial advocates and judges that they are insulated from criticism, even where it is supported by strong empirical evidence. As those same judges and advocates have near-total control over the conduct of trials (unless one or other party exercises their right of appeal), it is almost impossible to shift practice without their cooperation. There is a long history of all sorts of reforms of trial practice foundering where the reformers have been unable to convince practitioners that their cultural attachments to the practice were wrong (Henderson, 2012; Spencer & Flin, 1993; Zuckerman, 1996). Thus, to shift practice we must first shift practitioners' attitudes (Henderson, 2012; Plotnikoff & Woolfson, 2012; Zuckerman, 1996). As the then Lord Justice Sir John Thomas – now the Lord Chief Justice of England and Wales – once said of failures to implement government policy and legislative special measures for child witnesses:

> ...[T]he real need [is] – not yet more initiatives and reforms, but the cultural change that is necessary to make the new framework a reality....
> (Plotnikoff & Woolfson, 2009, pp. i–ii)

The situation suggests the joke about the number of psychologists it takes to change a light bulb: 'only one, but the light bulb has to *want* to change'. As Professor Darbyshire said recently of the slow progress in implementing case management reforms in England and Wales, 'changing this culture is taking a long time' (Darbyshire, 2014, p. 49).

Disillusionment over the pace of change has led some to conclude that the only way to achieve an evidence-based examination methodology is to wrest it from the lawyers, replacing partisan investigation with a neutral specialist interrogator working under counsels' direction

(Hanna, Davies, Henderson & Hand, 2012; Henderson, 2012), which is similar, perhaps, to that in Norway (Myklebust, 2012). However, in 2010, the senior judiciary in England and Wales began a bold initiative to reform vulnerable witnesses' cross-examination, issuing a series of rulings to bring practice closer to the empirical research on safe forensic interrogation. Crucially, the decisions include a carefully articulated reframing of the theory of cross-examination, emphasizing reliability or the achievement of 'best evidence' and rejecting the conventional view of it as an opportunity for advocacy (*R v. Barker*, 2010; *R v. Edwards*, 2011; Henderson, 2014b; *R v. W & M*, 2010; *R v. Wills*, 2011). Advocates, the Court declared, must ensure that their language is comprehensible to the witness, does not risk contaminating their evidence through suggestive questions and is not laden with comment (*R v. Barker*, 2010). Moreover, advocates should not confront the witness with stressful accusations or 'put the case' where doing so is likely to result in a compliant and therefore unreliable response. The new model makes it clear that examination should be seen as separate from advocacy.

As the outgoing Lord Chief Justice later declared, these decisions are nothing short of 'revolutionary' (Judge, 2013, p. 1). However, the revolution has its roots in groundwork laid a few years before during initiatives to reduce the length and cost of criminal and civil trials, initiatives that explicitly identified overzealous partisan advocacy as a major cause of the problems (e.g. The Woolf Report (Woolf, 1996)), and sought to inculcate in the legal profession a more balanced sense of its duties to the court system as a whole. Consequently, the senior judiciary have sought to rein in partisanship by encouraging greater judicial case management (*R v. Butt*, 2005; *R v. Chaaban*, 2003; *R v. Jisl & Tekin*, 2004) and also promulgated the *Criminal Procedure Rules*, new statements of the objectives of trial reiterating the 'overriding obligation' on all participants to 'deal with cases justly', a concept that includes, *inter alia*, accurate decision-making.

While the response to these reforms was slow (Derbyshire, 2014), the response to the cross-examination reforms has been remarkably quick. While the profession's plans to re-train its members advance slowly (Advocacy Training Council, 2011), the Judicial College (the judges' education body) immediately seized on the Court of Appeal's decisions, promoting them to the judiciary. Recent interviews suggest that trial judges in particular are accepting and even enthusiastic about the changes and that advocates are following suit (Henderson, in press-a, in press-b, in press-c). They are responding to the recognition that the Court of Appeal's changes have made it possible to get good-quality evidence from witnesses who would not otherwise have been capable of participating in trials. (Henderson, in press-b, in press-c). In short,

England and Wales show that it is possible, against all the odds, to change the culture of advocacy.

This has significant implications for the future. Already, helped by practical advice from communication experts or 'intermediaries', the English courts have begun to accept innovative practices that were unimaginable only a few years ago. They appear to be developing a whole new model of cross-examination for vulnerable witnesses, challenging even the conventional reliance on suggestive questioning (Plotnikoff & Woolfson, 2013; for examples of innovation see Marchant, 2013; Plotnikoff, 2014; Plotnikoff & Woolfson, 2012). Further, the Court of Appeal intimated recently that its reforms apply to robust adult witnesses also, opening the prospect of reform on a broader scale than previously contemplated (*H v. R*, 2014; Judge, 2013; *R v. Farooqi*, 2013).

The consequence of these remarkable advances is that the next section of this chapter, discussing future reform, is far more optimistic about what can be achieved within the conventions of the accusatorial trial than would have been the case had it been written even a year or so ago. The English example offers real hope that the accusatorial system may yet create a reliable, evidence-based method of examination that still preserves the advantages of a strong partisan presence in the investigation without radical systemic change.

WHERE TO FROM HERE? REFORM OPTIONS

Currently, most proposals for reform are based around the idea of erecting shields around particular groups of people to protect them from conventional practice. There are, for example, proposals for specialist sex offence courts, separate representation for complainants in particularly sensitive cases to intervene where the questioning becomes abusive (MacDonald & Tinsley, 2011), education programmes to prepare witnesses to cope with cross-examination (Ellison & Wheatcroft, 2010; Wheatcroft & Ellison, 2012) or intermediaries to monitor, translate or buffer inappropriate questioning (Henderson, 2012).

These options are worthy of serious consideration. Any justice system, for instance, will always need specialist assistance if witnesses have serious communication deficits and the English system of registered intermediaries is particularly impressive in this regard (Plotnikoff & Woolfson, 2004, in press). However, concentrating on shielding vulnerable people can mask the fact that the problems with cross-examination are far wider and breed an unhelpful complacency about its effectiveness with other more robust witnesses.

We suggest that it would also be useful if experts in forensic interrogation, experimental psychologists and linguists were to engage with the courts to assist them to develop a new methodology for examination generally. As a starting point, on the basis of current research, we suggest that all witness examinations should use a relatively simple, everyday vocabulary and uncomplicated syntax and eschew the current heavy reliance on suggestive questioning. Advocates need to minimize the possibility of coercion by adopting a less challenging manner of questioning and a slower pace. The courts could also explore ways of reducing the possibility of intimidation by reducing courtroom formality, allowing witnesses to give evidence from locations outside court and explicitly instructing witnesses that they can seek clarification if they are unsure about anything. Our suggestion is that these changes would not only make cross-examination a more reliable method of interrogation but they would also deal with much of the stress witnesses experience at the moment without requiring major changes to the accusatorial trial system.

Removing the Audience: Pre-recording Cross-examination

Another possibility would be to remove or reduce the pressures created by the presence of the fact-finders. As mentioned, most common law countries already pre-record children's and some vulnerable adults' evidence in chief, but most then still require the witnesses to come back to court to be cross-examined, often much later (Henderson, 2012; Plotnikoff & Woolfson, 2012; Spencer, 2012a). During the 1970s, several US states allowed ordinary adults' entire evidence to be pre-recorded (Henderson, 2012). This fell into disuse, but since 1992 Western Australian courts have allowed children's examination in chief and cross-examination to be pre-recorded. So successful has this been – from the perspective of defence advocates as well as prosecution counsel – that a number of Australian states have followed Western Australia's lead (Henderson, 2012) and, as already mentioned, England is currently piloting the process (Bowcott, 2013).

While pre-recording is primarily aimed at preserving children's evidence from the effects of lengthy delays between charge and trial, Australians say that the absence of the jury reduces witness stress and frees advocates and judges from some of the constraints created by the jury's presence (Cashmore & Trimboli, 2005; Eastwood & Patton, 2002; Henderson, 2012; Henderson, Hanna & Davies, 2012; Jackson, 2012; Spencer, 2012a). Pre-recording frees advocates to explore material they might otherwise fear to discuss in front of the jury because the recording could be edited of prejudicial, inadmissible answers or irrelevancies

(Henderson, 2012; Henderson et al., 2012; Jackson, 2012; Spencer, 2012a). It may also enable better use to be made of re-examination. For example, before re-examining an expert witness where the advocate is unsure of technical issues raised in cross-examination, the ability to break to consider the notes of evidence or even consult another expert could make a huge difference.

Further, given that the jury's presence is a major barrier to judges intervening in cross-examination, pre-recording a hearing to take place before a judge alone may increase their willingness to act, since their interventions can be edited out. Anecdotal reports suggest that judges in the English pre-recording pilot are already noticeably more interventionist.[15] Moreover, at present, if the witness appears to retract under cross-examination, the court will often be faced with applications to discharge the jury immediately and will have to make an immediate decision. Pre-recording gives the court time to review the recorded evidence in detail before making a decision, without the pressure created by the knowledge that rejecting the evidence will mean aborting a full trial and inconveniencing the jury and the other witnesses (Henderson et al., 2012). Pre-recording the examination would also allow the defendant to seek a different judge for trial if it was felt that the original judge had been too interventionist or shown bias, thus preserving the integrity of the actual trial and avoiding the delay and cost of appeals and retrials.

Holding the examination away from the jury may also reduce the temptation to 'play to the gallery', which currently has such a distorting impact on advocates' behaviour. Anecdotally, advocates tend to examine in a more moderate manner before a judge alone, because they believe judges are less swayed by theatrics. As a barrister once commented:

> ...[C]ross-examination in front of a jury is different from before a single judge. There is more emphasis in front of the jury [on] the way you deliver a question. . . . I remember once cross-examining [before a judge alone] in a very theatrical fashion and [he] interrupted me and said 'oh, look, brilliant in front of a jury: brutal in front of a jury,. . . but look, just give us the answer, will you?....
>
> (Henderson, 2015)

While advocates will still try to anticipate the jury's reaction at the later trial, the lack of their actual presence may moderate some of counsel's enthusiasm.

There are issues with pre-recording evidence, not least the lack of public oversight. However, the potential gains in quality of evidence are considerable.

Limitations

Ultimately, despite the authors' hopes for a truly evidence-based cross-examination model, the bipartisan structure of the accusatorial examination is likely to prevent the accusatorial trial system accepting certain reform measures, at least in the medium term. The main casualty in this will be the detection of deceptive behaviour. The evidence suggests (see above) that the best method of revealing deception is not, as in conventional cross-examination, closed directive questions but instead to seek additional evidence to test the witness's ability to maintain a consistent account. Lawyers brought up in a partisan model may baulk at allowing witnesses the necessary freedom to give both favourable and unfavourable evidence.

However, if it were the only realistic way to obtain evidence, it is foreseeable that the accusatorial criminal courts might, in extreme circumstances – as with a very young child or severely impaired adult – employ a neutral expert to examine the witness on behalf of both sides of the dispute, as currently happens in the semi-accusatorial jurisdiction of Norway (Myklebust, 2012). There is a long-standing proposal by the influential English Pigot Commission to allow such a measure and there have been recent calls in England for its introduction (Henderson et al., 2012; Spencer, 2012b).

At the other end of the spectrum of witness competence, it also seems sensible to consider allowing opposing expert witnesses in criminal trials be 'hot-tubbed' or examined concurrently, as they are, increasingly, in civil matters. Both hot-tubbing and the Pigot method make conventional cross-examination almost impossible. They remove counsel's ability to use cross-examination as rhetoric; they destroy the advocate's control of the discussion, hugely restricting opportunities for the advocate to control, coerce and obstruct the witness's evidence. Nevertheless, in certain cases, it is possible – remarkably – to see at least the English accusatorial courts tolerating the incursion.

CONCLUSION

A robust, reliable mechanism for testing witnesses' accuracy and veracity is essential to any justice system. We can never lose sight of the fact that some completely honest witnesses are nonetheless completely wrong, while others set out deliberately to deceive. Accusatorial cross-examination has great strengths. It recognizes and protects the defendant's right not only to have the evidence properly examined but also to participate in that examination and to exercise a measure of self-determination in the investigation. However, the dominance of partisan advocates as examiners has led to the adoption of practices that carry significant risks both for the reliability of the evidence and, increasingly, public confidence in the trial process. It is difficult, when dealing with a venerated institution, to persuade practitioners to reform their practice. However, recent developments in England and Wales show that even the most entrenched cultural beliefs can change when the senior judiciary offers strong leadership and a coherent alternative vision.

This could indeed spell, as the Lord Chief Justice Judge said, a 'revolution' in cross-examination theory and practice. Ultimately, however, whether the revolution fulfills its promise may depend on whether lawyers can see viable alternatives to their current methods. Lawyers need assistance from experts in interrogation to develop new tactics if they are to feel confident in abandoning their current arsenal of techniques. We end this chapter with the hope that this help will be in progress.

ACKNOWLEDGEMENT

The first author is very grateful to John R. Spencer, Professor Emeritus of Law, University of Cambridge, and Joyce Plotnikoff for reviewing a draft of this paper. Of course, any remaining errors are ours alone.

NOTES

1. Another way to describe them is as 'common law' jurisdictions, meaning that they have a shared body of judge-made law and consider each other's courts' decisions relevant to their own courts' judgements.
2. As the English House of Lords declared in 1935, 'Cross-examination is a powerful and valuable weapon for the purpose of testing the veracity of a witness and the accuracy and completeness of his story.' <rom 2>
3. As one manual on advocacy puts it, in a trial: 'Belief or disbelief in a story is the ultimate test for most practical purposes ... . For an advocate, his witnesses are the principal medium by which he tells his story.'
4. Unless the witness proves hostile or the information is uncontested (i.e. the witnesses' name or job).
5. For recent examples of what the English court has held *not* to be improper, see *R v. Hamilton* (2014) concerning the extremely aggressive cross-examination of a teenage rape complainant with mental health problems and also *R v. Jisl & Tekin*, 2004; *R v. Farooqi*, 2013; *R v. Randall*, 2002.

6. As Eichelbaum (1989) says (p. 205): '[A]void asking the last question that explicitly drives home your point. Instead your cross-examination will merely suggest the point. During your final submission you can rhetorically pose that last question and answer it the way you want it answered when the witness is not around to give you a bad answer.'
7. Stone (1995) says (pp. 121–122): '[T]here is no point in eliciting testimony on which the Court is unwilling to rely because of the way in which it was obtained. … Consequently, a cross-examiner's strategy must maintain a balance between manipulating the witness and presenting the case to the Court.'
8. More formally known as the principles of orality and immediacy (Spencer, 2005).
9. As one senior English judge commented to the first author recently, '[W]e must be careful … not to underestimate the importance of [challenging the witness in examination] … it is important for witnesses to get the opportunity to answer allegations against them and for the jury to see their reactions.'
10. As one QC said recently to the first author, regarding cross-examining rape complainants: 'All the time you employ little tricks: you want the witness to blow their top.'
11. Said the English Court of Appeal in *GMC v. Meadow* (2006, p. 207): '… The line and pace of the questioning may leave little time for calm analysis by an expert witness … . In that, sometimes, fevered process, mistakes can be made, ill-considered assertions volunteered or analogies drawn by the most seasoned court performers, whatever their role….'
12. In *Wills v. R* (2011) the English Court of Appeal said (p. 38): '…in cases where it is necessary and appropriate to have limitations on the way in which the advocate conducts cross-examination, there is a duty on the judge to ensure that those limitations are complied with….'
13. In *R v. McFadden* (1975) the Court said that before intervening '[t]he judge should consider his position most carefully. It requires great experience and a considerable exercise of tact for such a court to be effective and constructive, instead of destructive of the climate needed to foster fairness to all concerned in the trial.'
14. Eastwood and Patton (2002) hypothesize that one major factor in the higher level of comfort amongst children (and advocates) in Western Australia (WA) is due to the relatively short pre-trial delays in WA because of the use of pre-recorded cross-examination. Anecdotally, another possible factor is the reputation of the WA Bar for a relatively non-confrontational style of advocacy compared to that, for instance, in New South Wales (NSW).
15. Personal communication between the first author and Joyce Plotnikoff and the first author and registered intermediaries.

REFERENCES

Bastin v. Carew (1824). Ry & Mood 126; 171 ER 516.
Blaumire-Brown, C. (2011). Hot-tubbing: Cutting costs and time. *The Times,* October, 3, 2011, http://www.in presssonline.co.uk/2011/03/hot-tubbing-cutting-costs-and-time/ (accessed 26 January 2013).
Bowcott, O. (2013). Pre-recording to spare vulnerable victims court ordeal. *Guardian*, 10 June 2013.

Brown, J. (2011). We mind and we care but have things changed? Assessment of progress in the reporting, investigating and prosecution of allegations of rape. *Journal of Sexual Aggression, 17*, 1–10.

Brown v. Dunn (1893). 6 R 67 (HL).

Cairns, D. (1999). *Advocacy and the making of the adversarial criminal trial 1800–1865*, Oxford Studies in Modern Legal History. Oxford, UK: Clarendon Press.

Cashmore, J., & Trimboli, L. (2005). *An evaluation of the NSW Child Sexual Assault Specialist Jurisdiction Pilot*. Sydney, Australia: NSW Bureau of Crime Statistics and Research.

Clare, I., & Gudjonsson, G. (1993). Interrogative suggestibility, confabulation and acquiescence in people with mild learning disabilities. *British Journal of Clinical Psychology, 32*, 295.

Clarke v. Saffery (1824). Ry & Mood 126; 171 ER 966.

Advocacy Training Council (2011). *Raising the Bar: The Handling of Vulnerable Witnesses, Victims and Defendants in Court*. London, UK: ATC.

Coy v. Iowa (1988). 487 US 1012 per Scalia J.

Cutler, B., Findlay, K., & Moore, T. (2014). Interrogations and false confessions: A psychological perspective. *Canadian Criminal Law Review, 18*, 153–160.

Cutler, B., & Penrod, S. (1995). *Mistaken Identification: The Eyewitness, Psychology, and the Law*. New York: Cambridge University Press.

Darbyshire, P. (2014). Judicial case management in ten Crown Courts. *Criminal Law Review*, 30–50.

Davies, G., & Westcott, H. (1992). Videotechnology and the child witness. In H. Dent & R. Flin (eds), *Children as witnesses*. Chichester, UK: John Wiley & Sons, Ltd.

Diamond, S., Casper, J., Heiert, C., & Marshall, A. (1996). Juror reactions to attorneys at trial. *Journal of Criminal Law and Criminology, 87*, 17.

DuCann, R. (1993). *The Art of the advocate*, 2nd ed. London, UK: Penguin.

Eastwood, C., & Patton, W. (2002). The experiences of child complainants of sexual abuse in the criminal justice system, trends and issues in crime and criminal justice (Research Paper Series Paper No. 250). Canberra, Australia: Australian Institute of Criminology.

Edmond, G. (2012). Is reliability sufficient? the Law commission and expert evidence in international and interdisciplinary perspective (part 1). *The International Journal of Evidence and Proof, 16* (1), 30–65.

Eichelbaum, T. (1989). *Mauet's fundamentals of trial technique*. Auckland, New Zealand: Oxford University Press.

Ellison, L. (2001). *The adversarial process and the vulnerable witness*. Oxford, UK: Oxford University Press.

Ellison, L., & Wheatcroft, J. (2010). Could you ask me that in a different way? Exploring the impact of courtroom questioning and witness familiarisation on adult witness accuracy. *Criminal Law Review*, 823–826.

Franklyn, R. (2012). *Satisfaction and willingness to engage with the criminal justice system. Findings from the witness and victim experience survey, 2009–10*, Ministry of Justice Research Series 1/12. London, UK: Ministry of Justice.

Genn, H. (2012). *Manchester concurrent evidence pilot: Interim report*. London, UK: UCL Judicial Institute.

GMC v. Meadow (2006). EWCA Civil 1390.

Gudjonsson, G. H. (2003). *The psychology of interrogations and confessions*. Chichester, UK: John Wiley & Sons, Ltd.

H v. R (2014). EWCA Crim 1555.

Hanna, K., Davies, E., Crothers, C., & Henderson, E. (2011). Questioning child witnesses in New Zealand's criminal justice system: Is cross-examination fair? *Psychiatry, Psychology and Law, 19*, 530–546.

Hanna, K., Davies, E., Henderson, E., & Hand, L. (2012). Questioning child witnesses: Exploring the benefits and risks of intermediary models in New Zealand. *Psychiatry, Psychology and Law, 20*, 527–542.

Hardy's Trial (1794). *Cobbett's State Trials, 24*, 523.

Heaton-Armstrong, A., Shepherd, E., Gudjonsson, G. H., & Wolchover, D. (2006). *Witness testimony: psychological, investigative and evidential perspectives.* Oxford, UK: Oxford University Press.

Heffer, C. (2005). *The language of jury trial: A corpus-aided analysis of legal–Lay discourse.* Basingstoke, UK: Palgrave Macmillan.

Heffer, C. (2012). Narrative navigation: Narrative practices in forensic discourse. *Narrative Inquiry, 22* (2), 267–286.

Henderson E. (2001). Mapping the theory of cross-examination in relation to children. In H. Westcott, G. Davies, & R. Bull (eds), *Children's Testimony: Psychological Research and Forensic Practice.* Chichester, UK: Wiley Publications.

Henderson, E. (2003). Psychological research and lawyers' perceptions of child witnesses in sexual abuse trials. In R. Bull & D. Carson (eds), *Handbook of psychology in legal contexts.* Chichester, UK: Wiley Publications.

Henderson, E. (2012). Alternative routes: Other jurisdictions on the slow road to best evidence. In J. R. Spencer & M. E. Lamb (eds), *Children and cross-examination: Time to change the rules.* Oxford, UK: Hart Publishing.

Henderson, E. (2014a). Judges as cross-examiners. *Archbold Review, 5*, 3–4.

Henderson, E. (2014b). All the proper protections – the Court of Appeal rewrites the rules for the cross-examination of vulnerable witnesses. *Criminal Law Review, 2*, 93–108.

Henderson, E. (2015). Bigger fish to fry? Should the reform of cross-examination be expanded beyond vulnerable witnesses? *International Journal of Evidence and Proof,* April, *19* (2), 83–99.

Henderson, E. (in press-a). Taking control of cross-examination: judges, advocates and intermediaries discuss judicial management of the cross-examination of vulnerable people. *Criminal Law Review.*

Henderson, E. (in press-b). Theoretically speaking: judges and advocates discuss the changing theory of cross-examination. *Criminal Law Review.*

Henderson, E. (in press-c). Communicative competence? Judges, advocates and intermediaries discuss communication issues in the cross-examination of vulnerable witnesses. *Criminal Law Review.*

Henderson E., Hanna, K., & Davies, E. (2012). Pre-recording children's evidence: The western Australian experience. *Criminal Law Review,* 3–14.

Henderson, E., & Seymour, F. (2013). *Expert witness under examination in the New Zealand criminal and family courts,* Published Project Report, School of Psychology. Auckland, New Zealand: University of Auckland.

Hoyano, L. (2014). What is balanced on the scales of justice? In search of the essence of the right to a fair trial. *Criminal Law Review,* 4–29.

Hoyano, L., & Keenan, C. (2010). *Child abuse.* Oxford, UK: Oxford University Press.

Ibrahim v. The King (1914). AC 599.

Jackson, H. (2012). Children's evidence in legal proceedings – the position in western Australia. In J. R. Spencer & M. E. Lamb (eds), *Children and cross-examination: Time to change the rules.* Oxford, UK: Hart Publications.

Jacquemet, M. (1996). *Credibility in court: Communicative practices in the camorra trials*. Cambridge, UK: Cambridge University Press.

Jones v. National Coal Board (1957). 2 QB 55.

Judge, I. (2013). The Rt Hon Lord Judge, The evidence of child victims: The next stage, Bar council annual Law reform lecture, 21 November 2013. Retrieved from: http://www.barcouncil.org.uk/media/241783/annual_law_reform_lecture_rt_hon_the_lord_judge_speech_2013.pdf.

Judicial College (2013). Equal treatment bench book. Retrieved from: https://www.judiciary.gov.uk/wp-content/uploads/JCO/Documents/judicial-college/ETBB_all_chapters_final.pdf.

Kassin, S., & Gudjonsson, G. (2004). The psychology of confessions: A review of the literature and the issues. *Psychological Science in the Public Interest, 5*, 33–67.

Kebbell, M., Evans, L., & Johnson, S. (2010). The influence of lawyers' questions on witness accuracy, confidence, and reaction times and on mock jurors' interpretation of witness accuracy. *Journal of Investigative Psychology and Offender Profiling, 7*, 262–272.

Kebbell, M., & Hatton, C. (1999). People with mental retardation as witnesses in court. *Mental Retardation, 3*, 179–187.

Kebbell, M., & Johnson, S. (2000). The influence of lawyers' questions on witness confidence and accuracy. *Law and Human Behavior, 24*, 629–641.

Kebbell, M. R., O'Kelly, C. M. E., & Gilchrist, E. (2007). Rape victims' experiences of giving evidence in English courts: A survey. *Psychiatry, Psychology and Law, 14*, 111–119.

Klemfussi, Z., Quas, J., & Lyon, T. (2014). Attorneys' questions and children's productivity in child sexual abuse criminal trials. *Applied Cognitive Psychology, 287*, 780. doi: 10.1002/acp.3048.

Kovera, M. (2008). The effectiveness of opposing expert witnesses for educating jurors about unreliable expert evidence. *Law and Human Behavior, 36*, 363.

Kovera, M., Levy, R., Borgida, E., & Penrod, S. (1994). Expert testimony in child sexual abuse cases: effects of expert evidence type and cross-examination. *Law and Human Behavior, 18*, 653.

Lam Chi-ming v. The Queen (1991). 2 AC 212.

Langbein, J. (2003). *The origins of the adversary trial*, Oxford Studies in Modern Legal History. Oxford, UK: Clarendon Press.

Lees, S. (1996). *Carnal knowledge: Rape on trial*. London, UK: Penguin.

Levett, L., & Kovera, M. (2008). The effectiveness of opposing expert witnesses for educating jurors about unreliable expert evidence. *Law and Human Behavior, 32*, 363.

Lininger, T. (2005). Bearing the cross. *Fordham Law Review, 74*, 1353–1364.

Loftus, E. F. (1996). *Eyewitness testimony*. Cambridge, MA: Harvard University Press.

MacDonald, E., & Tinsley, Y. (2011). *From 'Real Rape' to real justice: Prosecuting rape in New Zealand*. Wellington, New Zealand: Victoria University Press.

Marchant, R. (2013). How young is too young? The evidence of children under five in the English criminal justice system. *Child Abuse Review, 22* (6), 432–445.

Matoesian, G. M. (1993). *Reproducing rape: Domination through talk in the courtroom*. Cambridge, UK: Polity Press.

Mausip, J., & Herrero, C. (2013). What would you say if you were guilty? Suspects' strategies during a hypothetical behavior analysis interview concerning a serious crime. *Applied Cognitive Psychology, 21*, 60–70.

Mechanical & General Inventions Co. Ltd v. Austin (1935). AC 346 (HL).

Munkman, J. (1991). *The technique of advocacy.* London, UK: Butterworths.

Myklebust, T. (2012). The position in Norway. In J. R. Spencer, & M. E. Lamb (eds), *Children and cross-examination. Time to change the rules?* Oxford, UK: Hart Publishing Ltd, pp. 147–170.

National Research Council of the National Academies (2009). *Strengthening forensic science in the United States: A path forward.* Washington, DC: The National Academies Press.

Neufeld, P. (2005). The (near) irrelevance of Daubert to criminal justice: and some suggestions for reform. *American Journal of Public Health, 95,* 107–113.

Norfolk, A. (2013). Abuse trials shamed the British legal system. Humiliation in Court: How the law treated abuse victims. *The Times,* 23 May 2013. Retrieved from http://www.thetimes.co.uk/tto/law/article3772512.ece and http://www.thetimes.co.uk/tto/law/article3772541.ece.

O'Kelly, C. M. E., Kebbell, M. R., Hatton, C., & Johnson, S. D. (2003). When do judges intervene in cases involving people with learning disabilities? *Legal and Criminological Psychology, 8,* 229–240.

O'Neill, S., & Zajac, R. (2013). The role of repeated interviewing in children's responses to cross-examination-style questioning. *British Journal of Psychology, 104,* 14–38.

Pennington, N., & Hastie, R. (1986). Evidence evaluation in complex decision making. *Journal of Personality and Social Psychology, 51*(2), 242–258.

Pennington, N., & Hastie, R. (1991). A cognitive theory of juror decision making: the story model. *Cardozo Law Review, 13,* 519–557.

Plotnikoff, J. (2014). A more flexible approach to vulnerable witnesses and defendants, Judicial College Serious Sex Offences Seminar, The Advocates Gateway. Retrieved from: http://www.theadvocatesgateway.org/resources.

Plotnikoff, J., & Woolfson, R. (2004). *In their Own words: The experiences of 50 young witnesses in criminal proceedings.* London, UK: NSPCC.

Plotnikoff, J., & Woolfson, R. (2009). Measuring Up? evaluating implementation of government commitments to young witnesses in criminal proceedings, NSPCC and Nuffield foundation, London. Retrieved from: www.nspcc.org.uk/measuringup.

Plotnikoff, J., & Woolfson, R. (2012). Kicking and screaming: The slow road to best evidence. In J. R. Spencer & M. E. Lamb (eds), *Children and cross-examination: Time to change the rules.* Oxford, UK: Hart Publishing.

Plotnikoff, J., & Woolfson, R. (2013). Toolkits, The Advocates' gateway. Advocacy training council. Retrieved from: http://www.theadvocatesgateway.org/toolkits.

Plotnikoff, J., & Woolfson, R. (in press). *Changing communication in the criminal justice system: The role of intermediaries with vulnerable witnesses and defendants.* Bristol, UK: Policy Press.

Quas, J. A., Goodman, G. S., Ghetti, S., Alexander, K. W., Edelstein, R. S., Redlich, A. D., Cordón, I. M., & Jones, D. P. H. (2005). Childhood sexual assault victims: Long-term outcomes after testifying in criminal court. *Monographs of the Society for Research in Child Development,* Serial No. 280, 70(2), vii–145.

R v Butt (2005). EWCA Crim 805.

R v. Barker (2010). EWCA Crim 4.

R v. Camberwell Green Youth Court (2005). UKHL 4.

R v. Chaaban (2003). EWCA Crim 1012.

R v. Edwards (2011). EWCA Crim 3028.

R v. Farooqi (2013). EWCA Crim 1649.

R v. Hamilton (2014). EWCA Crim 1555.

R v. Haringey Justices (1996). *ex pte DPP* QB 351.

R v. Jisl & Tekin (2004). EWCA Crim 696.

R v. Malicki (2009). EWCA Crim 365

R v. McFadden (1975). 62 Cr App R 187.

R v. Mushtaq (2005). 1 WLR 1513 (HL).

R v. Powell (2006). EWCA Crim 3.

R v. Prager (1972). 1 WLR 260.

R v. W & M (2010). EWCA Crim. 1926.

R v. Wellingborough Justices (1994). *ex pte Francois* 158 JP 813.

R v. Wills (2011). EWCA Crim. 1938.

Rares, S. (2012). Using the 'hot tub' – how concurrent expert evidence aids understanding issues. Federal Court of Australia, Judges Speeches. Retrieved from: http://www.fedcourt.gov.au/publications/judges-speeches/justice-rares/rares-j-20131012.

Roper, R., & Shewan, D. (2002). Compliance and eyewitness testimony: Do eyewitnesses comply with misleading 'expert pressure' during investigative interviewing? *Legal and Criminological Psychology, 7*, 155–163.

Sanders, J. (2003). The merits of the paternalistic justification for restrictions on the admissibility of expert evidence. *Seton Hall Law Review, 33* (4), 881–941.

Saunders v. United Kingdom (1996). 23 EHRR 313.

Snook, B., Eastwood J., & Barron W. (2014). The next stage in the evolution of interrogations: The PEACE model. *Canadian Criminal Law Review, 18*, 219.

Spencer, J. R. (1992). Court experts and expert witnesses – do we have a lesson to learn from the French? *Current Legal Problems, 45*, 216–236.

Spencer, J. R. (2005). Introduction. In M. Del-Marty, & J. R. Spencer (eds), *European criminal procedures*, Cambridge Studies in International and Comparative Criminal Law. Cambridge, UK: Cambridge University Press.

Spencer, J. R. (2012a). Introduction. In J. R. Spencer, & M. E. Lamb (eds), *Children and cross-examination: Time to change the rules?* Oxford, UK: Hart Publishing.

Spencer, J. R. (2012b). Conclusion. in J. R. Spencer, & M. E. Lamb (eds), *Children and cross-examination: Time to change the rules?* Oxford, UK: Hart Publishing.

Spencer, J. R., & Flin, R. (1993). *The evidence of children*. London, UK: Blackstone Press.

Spencer, J. R., & Lamb, M. (2012). *Children and cross-examination: Time to change the rules?* Oxford, UK: Hart Publishing.

Stone, M. (1995). *Cross-examination in criminal trials*. London, UK: Butterworths.

Strömwall, L., & Granhag, P. (2003). How to detect deception? arresting the beliefs of police officers, prosecutors and judges. *Psychology, Crime and Law, 9*(1), 19–36.

Surrey County Council Safe-guarding Adults Board (2014). The death of Mrs A: A serious case review. Retrieved from: http://www.surreycc.gov.uk/_data/assets/pdf_file/0011/815384/FINAL-Mrs-A-full-report-26.03.14.pdf.

Temkin, J. (2000). Prosecuting and defending rape: Perspectives from the Bar. *Journal of Law and Society, 27*(2), 219–239.

Thomas, C. (2010). *Are juries fair?* Ministry of Justice Research Series 1/10. London, UK: Ministry of Justice. Retrieved from http://www.justice.gov.uk/

downloads/publications/research-and-analysis/moj-research/are-juries-fair-research.pdf.

Valentine, T., & Maras, K. (2011). The effect of cross-examination on the accuracy of adult eyewitness testimony. *Applied Cognitive Psychology, 25* (4), 554–561.

Vrij, A. (2008). *Detecting lies and deceit: Pitfalls and opportunities*. Chichester, UK: John Wiley & Sons, Ltd.

Vrij, A., Leal, S., Granhag, P. A., Mann, S., Fisher, R. P., Hillman, J., & Sperry, K. (2009). Outsmarting the liars: The benefits of asking unanticipated questions. *Law and Human Behavior, 33* (2), 159–166.

Vrij, A., Mann, S., Fisher, R., Leal, S., Milne, B., & Bull, R. (2008). Increasing cognitive load to facilitate lie detection: The benefit of recalling an event in reverse order. *Law and Human Behavior, 32*, 253–265.

Wade, A. (2002). New measures and new challenges: children's experience of the court process. In H. L. Westcott, G. M. Davies, & R. H. C Bull (eds), *Children's testimony: A handbook of psychological research and forensic practice*. Chichester, UK: John Wiley & Sons, Ltd.

Wells, G. L., Memon, A., & Penrod, S. (2006). Eyewitness evidence: Improving its probative value. *Psychological Science in the Public Interest, 7*, 45–75.

Wheatcroft, J., & Ellison, L. (2012). Evidence in court: Witness preparation and cross-examination style effects on adult witness accuracy. *Behavioural Sciences and the Law, 32*, 821–840.

Wheatcroft, J., Wagstaff, G., & Kebbell, M. (2004). The influence of courtroom questioning style on actual and perceived eyewitness confidence and accuracy. *Legal and Criminological Psychology, 9*, 83–101.

Wheatcroft, J., & Woods, S. (2010). Effectiveness of witness preparation and cross-examination non-directive and directive leading question styles on witness accuracy and confidence. *The International Journal for Evidence and Proof, 14* (3), 187–207.

Whitehead, E. (2000). *Witness satisfaction: Findings from the witness satisfaction survey*, Home Office Research Study 230. London, UK: Home Office Research, Development and Statistics Directorate.

Wills v. R (2011). EWCA Crim 1938.

Woolf, L. J. (1996). *Access to justice: Final report to the Lord Chancellor on the civil justice system in England and Wales*. London, UK: Lord Chancellor's Department.

Young, W., Cameron, N., & Tinsley, Y. (1999). *Juries in Criminal Trials: Part Two: A Summary of Research Findings*. Wellington, New Zealand: NZLC.

Zajac, R., & Cannan, P. (2009). Cross-examination of sexual assault complainants: A developmental comparison. *Psychiatry, Psychology and Law, 16*, 36–54.

Zajac, R., & Hayne, H. (2003). I don't think that's what *really* happened: the effect of cross-examination on the accuracy of children's reports. *Journal of Experimental Psychology, 9* (3), 187–195.

Zajac, R., & Hayne, H. (2006). The negative effect of cross-examination style questioning on children's accuracy: older children are not immune. *Applied Cognitive Psychology, 20*, 3–16.

Zander, M., & Henderson, P. (1993). *Crown court study*, Royal Commission on Criminal Justice, Research Study No. 19, HMSO, London, UK.

Zuckerman, A. A. S. (1996). Lord Woolf's access to justice: *plus ca change*. *Modern Law Review, 59*, 773–796.

10

Expert Witness Communication

LORNA FADDEN[1] AND LAWRENCE M. SOLAN[2]
[1] Simon Fraser University, British Columbia, Canada
[2] Brooklyn Law School, New York, USA

INTRODUCTION

When a party in a civil litigation, or either the government or the defendant in a criminal prosecution, calls an expert to testify, competing goals come into play, creating a complex dynamic. First, the legal system has its own goals. Expert testimony is permitted when the expert's specialized knowledge assists the judge or jury in understanding technical issues in a case.

From the legal system's perspective, the testimony must meet the substantive standards of its field and be on a topic relevant to the case. It is up to judges to police the offer of expert testimony to ensure that the expert's contribution will meet these standards, a task that sounds simple but which has created great controversy in many instances.

The goals of the lawyer and the goals of the expert overlap, but are not identical. The lawyer wants to win the case, playing within the

Communication in Investigative and Legal Contexts: Integrated Approaches from Forensic Psychology, Linguistics and Law Enforcement, First Edition. Edited by Gavin Oxburgh, Trond Myklebust, Tim Grant and Rebecca Milne.
© 2016 John Wiley & Sons, Ltd. Published 2016 by John Wiley & Sons, Ltd.

rules. From the lawyer's perspective, the case will benefit most if the expert (1) presents a credible analysis; (2) does so in a way that is maximally comprehensible and accessible to the judge and/or jury (depending on the legal system); (3) presents an analysis that is as strong as possible for the lawyer's case; and (4) understands that as a team player, the expert is to defend the position as well as possible in the teeth of cross-examination.

The expert, in contrast, shares the first goal, but after that, things get more complicated. An expert may be of a mixed mind when it comes to sacrificing the scientific precision of a technical vocabulary for a general sense of the analysis that lay people can understand. The expert will also often feel a tension between the lawyer's goal of encouraging the expert to present an analysis that gives the lawyer's position the benefit of the doubt and the sense of intellectual neutrality that is the hallmark of good science. Defending a position under attack is commonplace for experts in science and social science, but doing so as part of an obligation to a team that hired the individual is not.

When these three sets of goals and values come together in a single case, they result in a kind of tug of war at the margins over how an expert should communicate. We say 'at the margins' because, at least most of the time, the expert is likely to have developed an analysis that is relevant to the case and that the expert believes to be a defensible position. Yet close cases are won and lost at the margin, and it is there that decisions about what and how to communicate come into play. Moreover, this combination of expertise and sincerity, however, leaves considerable space for spin when it comes to responses to hard questions during cross- examination and decisions about how energetically alternative positons that seem reasonable but not quite as persuasive as the expert's own opinion should be discussed.

In this chapter, we discuss what some of those decisions are and how they result from tensions among the overlapping but non-identical goals of, first, the legal system, next the lawyer and finally the expert. Our analysis looks at expert communication in both Canada and the United States, with brief reference to UK practice to the extent that we perceive differences to be instructive. The very nature of the adversarial system in these countries presents unique challenges to the law and procedures designed to ensure objectivity when experts and expert evidence is admitted. Legal systems operating within the civil law tradition are not discussed in this chapter. In these systems, experts are frequently appointed by the court and written reports are more significant than testimony (see Broeders, 2003; van Kampen, 2003). These differences make comparison of communication practices between the two systems difficult, except at the most general level.

WHAT THE LEGAL SYSTEM ASKS OF EXPERTS

In 1975, the US adopted the Federal Rules of Evidence. Rule 702 governs the admissibility of expert testimony. That rule, in its current, amended form, says:

> A witness who is qualified as an expert by knowledge, skill, experience, training, or education may testify in the form of an opinion or otherwise if:
> (a) the expert's scientific, technical, or other specialized knowledge will help the trier of fact to understand the evidence or to determine a fact in issue;
> (b) the testimony is based on sufficient facts or data;
> (c) the testimony is the product of reliable principles and methods; and
> (d) the expert has reliably applied the principles and methods to the facts of the case.

The language of the rule reflects in part a series of three decisions made by the US Supreme Court in the 1990s. The first, and most important of these cases, was *Daubert v. Merrell Dow Pharmaceuticals, Inc.*, decided in 1993. The issue there was whether Bendectin, a drug used to treat nausea during pregnancy, caused birth defects in Mrs Daubert's child. Most of the scientific literature suggested that it did not, but Mrs Daubert attempted to have an expert present animal studies that suggested a causal relationship between the drug and the birth defects.

In affirming the rejection of her expert, the Supreme Court articulated four non-exclusive criteria for deciding whether scientific evidence should be admitted into evidence: whether the theory offered has been tested; whether it has been subjected to peer review and publication; the known rate of error; and whether the theory is generally accepted in the scientific community. The last of these criteria reflects the holding in a 1923 court of appeals case, *Frye v. United States*. That case rejected the admission of a lie detector test into evidence. The *Frye* standard dominated the admissibility of scientific evidence until *Daubert*. Since then, all federal cases apply the *Daubert* standard, of which the *Frye* rule is only one part. Some states, however, which have always used the *Frye* standard, have continued to do so, leading to a division of methods employed by courts in the US.

It is not entirely clear that the replacement of *Frye* with *Daubert* has made a substantive difference in what expert testimony is admitted into evidence in American Courts (Cheng & Yoon, 2005). Nonetheless, taken together, Rule 702 and *Daubert* reflect an effort to ensure that

scientific evidence be scientific. Presumptively, it should not be adequate for an expert to opine basing that expert's confidence in his or her own experience, thus absenting some showing of how likely it is that the opinion is actually valid.

The most difficult of the *Daubert* criteria to meet is often the known rate of error. Critics argue that while *Daubert* promotes scientific values in many instances, it also has the effect of asking more of science than science has to offer. Epidemiologists cannot be sure that a toxin caused a particular plaintiff to contract cancer, even if there was a statistically significant increase in cancer following a chemical emission (see Berger, 1997).

In Canada

In Canada, four criteria set out in *R v. Mohan* (1994) comprise the law pertaining to the admission of expert evidence. During the 1990 trial in which Dr Mohan was tried for the sexual assault of four female teen patients in his care, the defense called a psychiatrist who testified that the accused did not possess the set of characteristics consistent with the type of sexual offender that he allegedly was, and therefore it was unlikely that he assaulted the four victims. In the 1996 appeal case of Dr Mohan's sexual assault conviction, Justice Sopinka revisited the criteria by which the psychiatric expert's evidence would be admissible and, in this case, ruled that expert evidence must be:
(a) Relevant
(b) Necessary
(c) Absent of exculpatory rule
(d) Delivered by a properly qualified expert.
The intent behind these criteria is similar to those set forth by *Daubert*, pertinently, that the expert must supply an understanding about key evidence that the judge and jury could not reasonably arrive at unassisted by themselves.

It is worth noting that more so than *Daubert*, *Mohan* is explicit regarding the risk of expert evidence distorting or skewing the fact-finding process. As Justice Sopinka cautions, an expert who brings with her an impressive set of credentials and experience can give evidence which is 'apt to be accepted by the jury as being virtually infallible and having more weight than it deserves'. Several cases reiterate this point, including *R v. Béland and Philips* (1987), in which Justice La Forest rules that 'such evidence should not be admitted by reason of "human fallibility in assessing the proper weight to be given to evidence cloaked under the mystique of science"' and *R v. Melaragni* (1992), in which Justice Moldaver urges the court to ask:

(1) Is the evidence likely to assist the jury in its fact-finding mission, or is it likely to confuse and confound the jury?

(2) Is the jury likely to be overwhelmed by the 'mystic infallibility' of the evidence, or will the jury be able to keep an open mind and objectively assess the worth of the evidence?

As such, Adair (2004) advises trial lawyers to ask themselves and judges to determine whether 'the probative value of the evidence is overborne by its prejudicial effect' (p. 350).

Canadian courts are also wary of cases that become, in effect, a contest of experts. In situations where both sides have retained experts who bring divergent interpretations of the evidence, the jury is placed in the position of having to decide which expert's report and testimony are superior, yielding two possible outcomes. The experts' competing testimonies simply cancel each other out in terms of their usefulness to the fact-finding process or the more self-assured witness may be more compelling, regardless of the scientific merit of his or her testimony (Bradfield & Wells, 2000; Solan, 2010). The jury, in any case, has no way of knowing whether they properly weighed the experts' contributions.

The notion that the court must address the risk that an expert and his or her testimony might be given more credence than it deserves has been addressed, particularly in cases where experts might be asked to 'give an opinion on the very issue before the court, the so-called ultimate issue. For example, in an insanity case, can the psychiatric expert say that this person was indeed insane, at the material time and therefor qualifies for a defense of not guilty by reason of insanity?' (Glancy & Bradford, 2007, p. 352). At this time, whether such an opinion is to be considered is left to the trial judge. However, allowing the expert to communicate yes or no on the ultimate issue, insanity for example, can mean her testimony will effectively prescribe a verdict.

Strong criteria must be met in order for an expert and his or her opinion to be admissible, and the system must safeguard against its overuse and the possibility that it could do more harm than good. Canadian courts are moving towards a reined-in, conservative approach to expertise in the courtroom.

A Note on Expert Evidence in the United Kingdom

In the United Kingdom, the courts admit expert opinion for the same reason that it is admitted in Canada and the US, specifically to 'furnish the court with scientific information which is likely to be outside the experience of a judge or jury' (*R v. Turner*, 1975: 841). However, in recognizing the possibility of an expert's bias, both the Civil Procedure Rules and the Criminal Procedure Rules require experts to certify in their reports that they have acted in a neutral manner. Thus experts must recognize that:

1. It is the duty of an expert to help the Court on matters within his expertise.
2. This duty overrides any obligation to the person from whom he has received instructions or by whom he is paid.

(Civil Procedure Rule 35.3)

The Criminal Procedure Rules read essentially the same and include a requirement that all parties and the court be informed should the expert's opinion change from that which is served as evidence (Criminal Procedure Rule 33.2). In addition, experts testifying on behalf of the prosecution have a duty to disclose to the defendant any tests conducted by the expert that may assist in the defence's efforts (Richardson, 2014, p. 1218).

Other rules and standards require similar certification (see Solan, 2010, for a discussion). We are not aware of empirical work testing the effectiveness of the UK approach. Its intuitive appeal, however, is striking in its addressing the tension between the needs of the legal system, the efforts of the attorneys to win their case and the expert's uncomfortable position, caught between these competing goals. As in the Canadian legal system, UK courts are concerned with the potentially disproportionate weight an expert's opinion might carry.

HOW LAWYERS WISH THEIR EXPERTS TO COMMUNICATE

In the United States

Handbooks and materials used to teach law students and lawyers how to be good trial advocates often include instructions on how to present expert testimony. A leading American text on trial advocacy (Mauet, 2013, p. 382) teaches that good experts have four basic characteristics: 'they are knowledgeable, well prepared, impartial, and dynamic'.

The first two are self-evident. It is the last two characteristics that are especially relevant for our purposes, and they are in tension with one another. Below is what Mauet says about impartiality:

[G]ood experts are impartial. They don't reflexively favor one side or the other, or have a preconceived view of things. Beware the expert who testifies frequently, who always testifies for the plaintiff or the defendant, or who always comes to the same conclusion on a particular subject. Jurors are sensitive to obvious bias and interest.

This is quite a minimal standard when it comes to impartiality. Yet other texts are even more relaxed about it. An online treatise called *Trial Communication Skills* advises: 'The ability to project sincerity is one of the major attributes of a good expert witness. The witness must appear to be free of bias and to honestly believe what he is saying' (Aron, Fast & Klein, 2013, para. 31.4).

Aron, Fast and Klein are being quite candid. Expert testimony is proffered precisely because it helps a party's case. The last thing most lawyers want is an impartial expert, unless the expertise involves some kind of objective measurement (e.g. blood type) that is helpful in its own right. What they really want is an expert whose views will help the case and who will work as a team member to write a report that is as strong as the facts will permit and who will try to stave off difficult questions during cross-examination. As Aron et al. (2013) put it:

> Experts, particularly those from universities and medical schools, are often too willing to see the other side of the story. They have enough experience to know that nothing is 100 per cent certain. They are also used to showing deference to opinions held by colleagues. These professionals frequently make terrible witnesses. They tend to be wishy-washy on direct and to crumble on cross-examination (para. 31.5).

Experts sense this concern. Those who venture into the legal system either understand in advance that the lawyers who hire them have an agenda that either falls short of or goes beyond truth-seeking.

To be of any real help in a case, the expert must be a good communicator. Mauet (2013) comments:

> [G]ood experts must be good communicators. They are dynamic, confident, and communicate clearly. Lawyers often put too much emphasis on impressive-sounding credentials, and too little emphasis on finding experts who are good communicators. Jurors, by contrast, put more weight on good communication skills than on paper credentials. ... The more complex and unfamiliar the subjects on which the experts testify, the more jurors decide which expert to believe through circumstantial cues such as which expert is more likeable, testifies in a simple, straightforward manner, and has no apparent bias or interest.

Mauet's warning about the risks of presenting excessively complex testimony is confirmed by the experimental psychological literature. Cooper and Neuhaus (2000) found that people distrust experts in mock trial scenarios when the expert is highly paid and testifies frequently. However, the level of distrust diminishes significantly when the expert testifies in clear language that the participants could understand. In another set of studies, Oppenheimer (2006) presented half of his participants with a version of an essay for admission to graduate school written using long words and the other half a simplified version in which the words were shorter. The result was that participants thought the authors of the simpler versions were more deserving of admission into the graduate program. The same result held when he gave subjects two translations of an obscure essay by René Descartes. Some subjects were told that the essay was written by a philosopher but did not identify the author by name. Those who read the simpler translation judged the philosopher as more intelligent than those who read the more complex version. Other subjects were told that Descartes wrote the piece. Remarkably, those individuals judged Descartes more highly intelligent than did those who read the more complex version.

Another trial skills manual (Lubet, 2013, pp. 169–176) instructs lawyers, in bringing out their expert's testimony, to humanize the witness; use plain language; avoid narratives (which can be long and boring); use examples and analogies; make sure that the first thing that the jury hears is the most important; use visual aids; use leading questions; encourage powerful language; and use enumeration ('there are three basic problems with the other side's study'). Among the specific advice is: 'Caution experts to avoid language that unintentionally qualifies or hedges their results, using instead wording that emphasizes accuracy and certainty' (p. 175). As for humanizing the expert, Lubet advises:

> Many experts from scientific, technical, or financial backgrounds may appear aloof, intimidating, or even arrogant to jurors who do not share their special expertise. It is therefore important to humanize these witnesses as much as possible in the course of the direct examination. If permitted in your jurisdiction, this can be done by bringing out personal and family background information and by allowing the witness to talk about more than strictly professional matters.
>
> (Lubet, 2013, p. 169).

On the one hand, then, the expert must not be biased. On the other, the expert must come across as being credible more by virtue of the expert's style than by virtue of the substance of the expert's opinion. This tension is at the heart of what makes the communication of expert witnesses so problematic.

Lubet is well aware of this tension and instructs lawyers and experts accordingly in a book on expert testimony that he and Elizabeth Boals co-authored:

> Most lawyers understand and accept [the assumption] that expert witnesses are independent of retaining counsel and that they testify

sincerely on an intellectual level. Still, in the heat of adversary battle, it is not unknown for lawyers to seek, shall we say, to broaden or expand an expert's opinion in just the right direction. This is wrong. It is no more acceptable for a lawyer to push an expert into altering her opinion than it would be to convince an eyewitness to change his account of the facts.

(Lubet & Boals, 2009, p. 164)

The tension could not be more overt: lawyers need their experts to testify in a way that will help their case, but they must draw the line when it comes to how far to push the experts in that direction. The more successful the lawyer in making the expert a team player, the easier it becomes for the lawyer to accomplish his or her goal while remaining within the rules. We return to the effects of such efforts below.

In Canada

The tension between lawyers' advocacy and experts' impartiality found in the American legal landscape also permeates the interactions between the same professions in Canada and, generally, trial manuals advising Canadian practitioners closely mirror those described above for their American counterparts. While the Canadian perspective appears less adversarial in some respects, it, too, acknowledges the fact that advocates come to court to win their cases and will want to enlist experts who are most likely to be helpful.

The Advocates' Society (2014), an arm of the Law Society of Upper Canada, which provides continuing education for Ontario lawyers, offers a set of guidelines for its members when working with experts. Lawyers who engage experts are advised to make their expert aware that his or her role is to assist the court fairly and objectively, and that the lawyer must refrain from 'communicating with an expert witness in any manner likely to interfere with the expert's duties of independence and objectivity' (p. 6). Further, the lawyer is told he 'must be particularly careful not to persuade, or be seen to have persuaded, an expert to express opinions that the expert does not genuinely share or believe' (p. 6). One would expect that discussion to stop there; however, it does not, and the advocate is also advised to 'not abandon the preparation of an expert report or affidavit entirely to an expert witness, and instead [s/he] can have appropriate input into the format and content of an expert's report or affidavit before it is finalized and delivered', and that it is common for there to be a considerable exchange between the lawyer and his expert during the preparation of any report.

Guidelines such as these, which are mirrored elsewhere in trial and case management manuals, would seem contradictory from the point of view of the expert, who is charged with the task of supplying an objective report intended to answer questions of legal significance, *for the court*. Taking into consideration a lawyer's input or feedback during the preparation of a report as it is readied for submission, might leave the expert feeling like her work is being massaged and manipulated in ways that do not truthfully reflect the conclusions arrived at through the methods and analytical tools standard in her field and the expert might find herself in a position of having to resist such pressure or yield to it.

That lawyers might have a bit too much input on experts' reports and testimony in the preparation of a case may be leading to a recent tendency for Canadian courts to rely less on experts. In their rulings, provincial judges have outwardly admonished experts – and counsel who engage them – for submitting reports and testifying in ways that cross the line brazenly into advocacy. In one of the more scathing rulings in which an expert's report and testimony were rejected, Justice Gropper in *Warkentin v. Riggs* (2010) rebukes one doctor whose CV boasts "'Expert Medical Legal Consultant providing opinions on behalf of patients with chronic pain who are seeking legal remedies", indicates that he does not consider his role as an expert to be that of an objective advisor to the court'.

The Supreme Court of Canada also has, since *R v. Sekhon* (2014), effectively halted the use of experts, in particular those whose training and skills arise from experience (e.g. police experts). In the initial trial, the judge had admitted a police expert who testified that after overseeing a thousand or more trafficking cases, he was not aware of a single case where a so-called 'blind courier' could not have known he was transporting drugs. The Supreme Court, however, found this type of testimony to not meet the standards of *Mohan*, that it is unacceptable and unfair inference, and that it '[usurps] the trial judge's role in resolving the issue of guilt or innocence'. The judge further mocked the use of the expert, comparing him to a 'stolen goods investigator testifying that he or she has never seen a case of innocent possession of stolen property....The inherent danger of admitting such evidence is obvious'.

While these are but two of the more egregious examples, it suggests that at least some lawyers have been less than conscientious in choosing experts who will adhere to their academic or professional principles more so than a sideline career in expert witnessing, and in being a good team player for the side who hires them, a concept we expand on below.

It would seem that the court itself appointing experts, or joint experts who would be cross-examined by both of the litigating parties, is a reasonable avenue to avoid the potential for experts behaving as advocates, and indeed such is an option in provincial courts across the country. As appealing as that is from the point of view of objectivity, that is that neither side has commissioned the work and much less interaction takes place between lawyers and experts, it does not appear to be a fact-finding tactic that the court applies with any frequency. Speculation as to why this is ranges from one or both parties not wishing to take a chance on genuine objectivity to the court not having the budget to pay for it in financially lean times. Similar efforts in the US to add to the objectivity of expert testimony (see, for example, Robertson, 2010) have also failed to alter the landscape substantially notwithstanding their substantive merit.

In the United Kingdom

One difference between the US and Canadian jurisdictions and the UK is the strength of regulation against the coaching of witnesses by lawyers and these rules apply equally to expert witnesses. The UK Barristers' Code of Conduct is explicit stating baldly that 'A barrister must not... rehearse, practise or coach a witness in relation to his evidence' (para. 705). Further reinforcement of this principle is found in strong case law. Lord Justice Judge (in *R v. Momodou*, 2005, EWCA Crim 177) makes the point that rules against coaching are not just proscribing witnesses or lawyers malpractice, rather these rules are also there to prevent the innocent contamination of witness evidence:

> The witness should give his or her own evidence, so far as practicable uninfluenced by what anyone else has said, whether in formal discussions or informal conversations. The rule [against coaching] reduces, indeed hopefully avoids any possibility, that one witness may tailor his evidence in the light of what anyone else said, and equally, avoids any unfounded perception that he may have done so. These risks are inherent in witness training. Even if the training takes place one-to-one with someone completely remote from the facts of the case itself, the witness may come, even unconsciously, to appreciate which aspects of his evidence are perhaps not quite consistent with what others are saying, or indeed not quite what is required of him. An honest witness may alter the emphasis of his evidence to accommodate what he thinks may be a different, more accurate, or simply better remembered perception of events.

Although this judgement strictly applies just to criminal cases, the UK Bar Council guidance suggests that it should also apply in civil contexts.

THE EXPERT'S DILEMMA OVER WHAT TO SAY
AND HOW TO SAY IT

There are two communication streams at work when an expert is engaged in a legal matter. The first involves the communication between the lawyer and the expert as the case is being built and the expert is supplying her analyses and opinions. The second happens when (if) the expert takes the stand and is questioned by both her retaining lawyer and the one who cross-examines her. We address the interactional linguistics at work for these distinct communicative settings.

In the Office

As a case develops, there often is a great deal of communication between the lawyer and the expert, as the lawyer provides the expert with the details and evidence that she will analyse and the expert starts to shape her conclusions and opinions. A conversation of this nature belongs to a category of talk called institutional discourse (see Drew & Heritage, 1992, for an introduction), wherein some sort of 'work' is being performed through the act of speaking; in this instance, the lawyer is learning about the expert's field in order to incorporate it into the case and the expert is learning about the evidence in order to conduct her analysis.

Essentially, the two carry out their work in a speaking style appropriate for their professions, but the high degree of literacy and communicative skill required for each to accomplish the tasks in their respective fields does not guarantee communicative ease when the two must work together. The differences stem in large part from the primary roles played by each in case preparation and in court – advocacy versus objectivity – and indeed many have noted the difficulty for experts in maintaining their scientific objectivity towards the evidence at hand when a lawyer is striving hard to make the best possible case for their client. Interestingly, the very principles that many linguists study, that is the rules by which conversation manifests as a cooperative social endeavor, are the same principles that make it difficult for an expert to communicate his or her work in an objective fashion.

As speakers, we are strongly compelled to be polite and accommodating with one another in order not to undermine or threaten relationships (Tannen, 1986), and professional contexts such as these are no exception. Furthermore, it has long been acknowledged that, in order to establish a successful working relationship, facilitate the flow of information and remove any social barriers to communication, some degree of solidarity or rapport must be built up between the two (Tannen, 1994). So naturally, where an expert's findings align well with the theory advanced by the lawyer, no problems arise, the two are in agreement over details and the case can advance to the lawyer's satisfaction. Where the expert's findings do not fully serve the lawyer's theory, a situation arises where the two must manoeuver in order to find a way to resolve the discord, restore the solidarity, facilitate further conversation and allow the working relationship to continue. A range of conversational strategies can be used to achieve this, such as highlighting common ground, backgrounding disputed information, joking, and even more nefariously perhaps, suggestion and coercion, among others (see Brown & Levinson, 1987). These types of conversational finessing are found in casual and professional discourse alike, but given the dynamic between the two interactants – the expert engaged to do a job and the lawyer managing the case – it is here that the expert might find herself bending her objectivity.

And bend it will unless the expert's opinion is based upon a validated and reliable methodology that takes the analysis out of the realm of being susceptible to manipulation at the margins. This is because we are all subject to cognitive biases that cause us to value information that confirms our hypothesis above information that challenges it. Psychologists refer to this tendency as the confirmation bias (see Nickerson, 1998; Simon, 2004). In a classic study illustrating the bias, Darley and Gross (1983) showed subjects a video of a teenage girl taking a standardized test. During the test, she spent some time writing and other time looking around. Half the subjects were provided with information that she was from a poor neighbourhood. The other half saw her as coming from an upper middle class environment. Sure enough, participants construed her conduct as confirming their understandings of how people in different socioeconomic groups perform on academic tests. Those who believed she came from a wealthier family concluded that she performed better on the test than did those who believed that she came from a less wealthy family.

In legal settings, the confirmation bias is well known as a problem when police and prosecutors commit to a theory during early stages of an investigation and ignore evidence that someone other than the person under investigation may have committed the crime (see, for example, Brown, 2005, p. 1600). The same dynamic applies to experts who are apprised of the case from the point of retention, establish an intellectual position and are in the process of developing it, knowing that it will later have to be defended in court. This propensity is familiar to scholars on scientific evidence (ee, for example, Faigman, 2008, pp. 990–991; Risinger, Saks, Thompson & Rosenthal, 2002).

The communicative dynamic described above is bound to compound the confirmation bias in many cases of expert/lawyer interaction. Moreover, while it is unethical in each of the legal systems we discuss for a lawyer to tell an expert what the expert's opinion must be, there are effective communicative strategies that enable the lawyer to exert some influence without crossing an ethical line. Given the ubiquity of the confirmation bias, a lawyer who successfully builds a team spirit between herself and her expert will likely succeed in making the expert all the more committed to analysis that will be more helpful to the lawyer's case. In the interest of disclosure with respect to the discussion that follows, both of the authors of this piece have been engaged by lawyers as experts in the field of linguistics and both are well acquainted with the tightrope act that comes from working with a lawyer and being in effect being 'part of the team'. Moreover, one of us practised law before joining the academic community and candidly acknowledges his role in bringing experts onboard by speaking to them intermittently as independent thinkers whose expertise was valued on its own terms, and as team members who are part of a mission to see to it that the system of justice does not make a mistake by permitting the other side – which is wrong – to win.

On the Stand

On the stand, an entirely different set of communicative rules, comes into play because of the tightly constrained question and answer sequence that characterizes courtroom testimony (Drew, 1992; Heffer, 2005; Wodak, 1980). Because lawyers select the topics and ask the questions, witnesses – expert or lay – are left in a position of only responding, and the nature of the questions dictates how much and the quality of information those witnesses will be allowed to provide. The expert will have to respond both to questions from the side that hired her under direct-examination and from opposing parties under cross-examination. Lawyers characterize the different styles of questioning as non-leading ('When did you get home?') or leading ('You arrived home at 4 a.m., right?'). Linguists have a more nuanced taxonomy, referring to the former type of question as 'wh-questions' and to many different forms of leading questions (see, for example, Sidnell, 2010). Under either condition, the expert, who often holds a teaching position of some sort, and who is probably well-accustomed to presenting complicated work in a long-form manner, may find herself feeling hamstrung and unable to present her opinions and conclusions in a way that she feels adequately represents them.

Quite naturally, we would expect that under direct-examination, the lawyer who engaged the expert will ask pointed but open-ended questions that allow the expert to provide full, well-grounded answers that make her testimony effective. The lawyer and the expert will have had considerable opportunities to prepare for the expert's testimony. In this context, the lawyer (at least the effective lawyer) acts as teacher, helping the expert to make decisions about how to present her opinion in a manner that is comprehensible and interesting on the one hand and technically valid on the other. It is here that the consequences of team identity can create problems for the expert. For if an expert, whether to please the lawyer who hired her or because loyalty to the position she is assisting has clouded her professional judgment, offers an opinion that exceeds what the expert would have said in a more neutral setting, it is likely to create both discomfort within the expert's psyche and provide fuel for the other side to discredit the expert in cross-examination.

During cross-examination, the lawyer often restricts questions to those eliciting a yes or no response, which prevents the expert from explaining details or otherwise qualifying her answers in a way that still accurately represents her analyses. The same trial practice manuals that teach lawyers about how to deal with their own experts also teach lawyers how to deal with opposing experts. It is the obligation of an opposing lawyer to diminish the value of the expert's report and testimony as much as possible. There are many ways to do this, each of which puts pressure on an expert who wishes to finish the day's testimony with her sense of self-respect intact.

One thing a skilled cross-examiner knows how to do is to discover ways in which the expert's position differs from the position of the side offering the expert's testimony and to exploit these gaps. Perhaps the lawyer has argued that three provisions in a contract are ambiguous, but the expert (either in linguistics or in the subject matter of the contract) opines about only two. A natural inference is that the expert is at odds with the position of the party that hired her on the third claim of ambiguity. To say so, however, is disloyal to the team and it feels uncomfortable for the expert to be so disloyal. Obviously, the expert must do so anyway, for to attempt to rescue the situation by hedging not only will reduce her credibility but will also be less than fully honest. Yet it would also be dishonest for most people who testify as experts not to admit that such possibilities cross their minds, and in fact their academic training will likely have prepared them to consider alternate analyses. The very fact that one must reject such 'spin' indicates that loyalty competes with disinterested professional integrity as values in our lives. When we are not being questioned sharply on the witness stand, most of us would be perfectly happy to tell others that we are both loyal friends and honest actors, regarding both traits as virtues.

Making the decision easier is the fact that that team that hired the expert is sitting at their table in the court room, not able to participate in the decision. But what if that changes? What if, during cross-examination, there is a lunch break, for example. In the US, it is not unethical for lawyers to speak with their witnesses at such times, unless the judge has ordered them not to do so. Let's say that the lawyer suggests that the expert not express disagreement about the third ambiguity – returning to our hypothetical case – but rather say that the third case is outside the scope of the report, but seems ambiguous in a different way, as stated in the friendly party's written submissions. The lawyer will not tell the expert to lie. Rather the lawyer would ask, 'Can you be comfortable saying ...?' and the lawyer will probe the expert's comfort zone until the answer is yes.

This is a very awkward position for the expert to find herself. On the one hand, the opposing lawyer is trying to discredit her. On the other, the lawyer whose side she is purportedly on is pushing her to say things which, while not lies, are certainly not the way she would want to put them if left to her own devices. Here again, the expert must not cave to the temptation to be a good team player. However, once the lawyer presents a communicative option that is at the very least not dishonest, the expert will need a great deal of moral strength and self-confidence as an independent actor to stand her ground. If she does not stand her ground, perhaps she will be made to look foolish conceding that her stance, or some portion of it, is weak or perhaps she will succeed in supporting a position in which she does not believe. Neither outcome is desirable and both are possible, likely even, when questioning tightly constrains what the expert can say.

Even more difficult for the expert is the portion of the cross-examination in which the opposing lawyer wishes to demonstrate that the expert should not be believed because of bias and because the expert is flat-out wrong about important aspects of what she says. Most academics are accustomed to being questioned about the results of research. Sometimes this probing can be harsh, but most of the time it maintains the tone of a conversation about the best way to solve an intellectual problem. Not so during cross-examination. The lawyer's only goal is to complete the questioning with the satisfaction that the judge or jury has far less respect now for the expert's views, or the expert herself, than they did when the testimony began.

This discursive antagonism can take on another dimension when experts from the same discipline are hired by both sides, in which case, each expert in direct-examination will be probed on the weaknesses of her colleague's analysis and in cross-examination each expert will be defending her own analysis in the light of what she knows about the position her colleague presents. Rebutting another expert, even if one is committed to presenting her critique objectively, will undoubtedly come across much less collegially than a dispute carried out in an academic context because, in order to keep his expert on-task, questions will almost necessarily lead the expert to throw her colleague under the bus. Even in cases where opposing experts agree on elements of an analysis, lawyers will only lead their experts to present that which makes their case look strongest, despite the significance of the additional evidence from the expert's point of view.

Such relentless attack resides outside the discourse norms with which most experts are accustomed, apart from experts who have testified multiple times and have seen it all before. Tone of voice and the direction of intonation contours play a big role in this effort intonation (Gaines, 2001). The lawyer will frequently ask questions with an incredulous voice that oozes disrespect, hoping that the judge or jury will assume that such a tone is reserved only for those who deserve it. The lawyer will also ask questions in a manner to suggest any answer to the contrary can only be false: 'You can't really say for sure whether that conclusion would be reached unanimously in your field, can you?', spoken with falling intonation. Questions about prior testimony – too much, too little or for the same sort of party – will be asked to suggest that the expert cannot be trusted. Challenges from the expert's own written work or the written work of others will suggest inconsistencies of various types. Through all of this, the expert needs to maintain a dispassionate tone, admitting what should be admitted, without regard to the consequences of these admissions to the outcome of the case or the overall effectiveness of the expert's role in it. That is not the expert's problem, though, with luck, she will be given the opportunity to qualify her position on redirect.

This sort of combative discourse, however, is unnatural to most people. The temptation is to express answers with more certainty and less nuance that the expert feels. As noted earlier, trial practice manuals encourage such self-confidence tempered with dispassion. At the end, the expert often has difficulty deciding whether the testimony was successful because she did not give up the position she committed to taking or because she maintained the intellectual distance from the fray with which she is most comfortable as a scientist (or other such expert).

CONCLUSIONS

It is tempting, but too simple, to regard communication between experts and lawyers as a battle between the truth seekers on one hand and advocates on the other. In fact, the legal system sides with the experts in wishing expert testimony to produce helpful learning, but permits the lawyers to act aggressively in bringing out their side of the story, and indeed they have an obligation to do so for their clients. Moreover, experts enter the fray not as innocents, but rather as people with their own built-in biases and loyalties, whether to positions they take or parties for whom they have agreed to testify, creating much more of a mixed picture as the judge, the expert and the lawyers attempt to play out their roles within a process purportedly designed to get at the truth.

Most significantly, the amplitude of the dilemma facing experts about how best to communicate their views bears an inverse relationship to the reliability of the methods used to generate the expert's opinion as an initial matter. The firmer the methodological basis of the expert's opinion, the fewer the crucial decisions about how to communicate them, whether in direct testimony or in rebuffing cross-examination. A lab technician will require little training to testify clearly and convincingly that the blood found at the scene of the crime is Type A positive, and how she came to that conclusion. By the same token, it is also the case that the less reliable a field's methods, the more room for 'spin' in either direction and the more important the decisions about how the testimony should be styled. Legal writers have noted these issues both as a matter of ethics for expert witnesses (Sanders, 2007) and the ability of science to resolve legal problems generally (see, for example, Haack, 2014). In the short run for some fields and the long run for others, however, communicative decisions among the various players are key to both the legitimacy and the effectiveness of expert testimony in the legal system.

ACKNOWLEDGEMENT

The authors thank Nicholas Adamson, Kate Haworth, Jennifer Glougie and Benjamin Schaer for valuable suggestions that have been incorporated into this chapter.

REFERENCES

Adair, G. (2004). *On trial: Advocacy skills, law, and practice* (2nd ed.). Markham, Ontario, Canada: LexisNexis Butterworth.
Aron, R., Fast, J., & Klein, R. B. (1996/2013). *Trial communication skills*. New York: Clark Boardman Callaghan.
Berger, M. A. (1997). Eliminating general causation: Notes towards a new theory of justice and toxic torts. *Columbia Law Review, 97*, 2117–2152.

Bradfield, A. J., & Wells, G. L. (2000). The perceived validity of eyewitness identification testimony: A test of the five Biggers criteria. *Law and Human Behavior, 24*, 581–594.

Broeders, T. (2003). The role of the forensic expert in an inquisitorial system. In P. J. van Koppen & S. D. Penrod (Eds.), *Adversarial versus inquisitorial justice: Psychological perspectives on criminal justice systems* (pp. 245–253). New York: Springer.

Brown, D. K. (2005). The decline of defense counsel and the rise of accuracy in criminal adjudication. *California Law Review, 93*, 1585–1645.

Brown, P., & Levinson, S. (1987). *Politeness: Some universals in language usage*. Cambridge, UK: Cambridge University Press.

Cheng, E. K., & Yoon, A. (2005). Does Frye or Daubert matter?: A study of scientific admissibility standards. *Virginia Law Review, 91*, 471–513.

Cooper, J., & Neuhaus, I. M. (2000). The 'hired gun' effect: Assessing the effect of pay, frequency of testifying, and credentials on the perception of expert testimony. *Law and Human Behavior, 24*, 149–171.

Darley, J. M., & Gross, P. A. (1983). A hypothesis-confirming bias in labeling effects. *Journal of Personality and Social Psychology, 44*, 20–33.

Daubert v. Merrell Dow Pharmaceuticals, Inc. (1993) 509 U.S. 579.

Drew, P. (1992). Contested evidence in courtroom cross-examination: The case of a trial for rape. In P. Drew & J. Heritage (Eds.), *Talk at work: Interaction in institutional settings* (pp. 470–520). Cambridge, UK: Cambridge University Press.

Drew, P., & Heritage, J. (1992). Analyzing talk at work: An introduction. In P. Drew & J. Heritage (Eds.), *Talk at work: Interaction in institutional settings* (pp. 3–65). Cambridge, UK: Cambridge University Press.

Faigman, D. L. (2008). Anecdotal forensics, phrenology, and other abject lessons from the history of science. *Hastings Law Journal, 59*, 979–1000.

Frye v. United States (1923). 293 F. 213 (D.C. Cir. 1923).

Gaines, P. (2001). Intonation as a marker of illocutionary force in legal examination tag questions. In A. Wennerstrom (Ed.), *The music of everyday speech* (pp. 161–164). Oxford, UK: Oxford University Press.

Glancy, G., & Bradford, J. (2007). The admissibility of expert evidence in Canada. *Journal of the American Academy of Psychiatry and the Law, 35*, 350–356.

Haack, S. (2014). *Evidence matters*. New York: Cambridge University Press.

Heffer, C. (2005). *The language of a jury trial: A corpus-aided analysis of legal–lay discourse*. Basingstoke, UK: Palgrave Macmillan.

Lubet, S. (2013). *Modern trial advocacy: Analysis and practice*. Boulder, CO: National Institute for Trial Advocacy.

Lubet, S., & Boals, E. I. (2009). *Expert testimony: A guide for expert witnesses and the lawyers who examine them* (2nd ed.). Boulder, CO: National Institute of Trial Advocacy.

Mauet, T. A. (2013). *Trial techniques and trials* (9th ed.). New York: Wolters Kluwer Law & Business.

Nickerson, R. S. (1998). Confirmation bias: A ubiquitous phenomenon in many guises. *Review of General Psychology, 2*, 175–220.

Oppenheimer, D. M. (2006). Consequences of erudite vernacular utilized irrespective of necessity: Problems with using long words needlessly. *Applied Cognitive Psychology, 20*, 139–156.

Richardson, P. J. (2014). *Archbold: Criminal pleading, evidence and practice*. London, UK: Sweet and Maxwell.

Risinger, D. M., Saks, M. J., Thompson, W. C., & Rosenthal, R. (2002). The Daubert/Kumho implications of observer effects in forensic science: Hidden problems of expectation and suggestion. *California Law Review, 90*, 1–56.

Robertson, C. T. (2010). Blind expertise. *New York University Law Review, 85*, 174–257.

R v. Béland and Philips (1987). 2 SCR 398.

R v. Melaragni (1992). 73 C.C.C. (3d) 348 (Ont. Gen. Div.).

R v. Mohan (1994). 2 SCR 9.

R v. Momodou (2005). EWCA Crim 177.

R v. Sekhon (2014). SCC 15.

R v. Turner (1975). QB 834.

Sanders, J. A. (2007). Expert witness ethics. *Fordham Law Review, 76*, 1539–1584.

Sidnell, J. (2010). The design and positioning of questions in inquiry testimony. In A. F. Fred & S. Ehrlich (Eds.), *'Why do you ask:' The function of questions in institutional discourse*. New York: Oxford University Press.

Simon, D. (2004). A third view of the black box: Cognitive coherence in legal decision making. *University of Chicago Law Review, 71*, 511–584.

Solan, L. M. (2010). The expert linguist meets the adversarial system. In M. Coulthard & A. Johnson (Eds.), *The Routledge handbook of forensic linguistics*. Abingdon, UK: Routledge.

Tannen, D. (1986). *That's not what I meant: How conversational style makes or breaks your relations with others*. New York: William Morrow.

Tannen, D. (1994). *Gender and discourse*. New York: Oxford University Press.

The Advocates' Society. (2014). Principles governing communication with testifying experts. Retrieved from http://www.advocates.ca/assets/files/pdf/The_Advocates_Society-Principles_Governing_Communications_with_Testifying_Experts_3_sep18.pdf.

UK Barrister Code of Conduct, Part 2. Retrieved from https://www.barstandardsboard.org.uk/media/1663630/bsb_handbook_complete.pdf.

van Kampen, P. T. C. (2003). Expert evidence: The state of the law in the Netherlands and the United States. In P. J. van Koppen & S. D. Penrod (Eds.), *Adversarial versus inquisitorial justice: psychological perspectives on criminal justice systems* (pp. 209–234). New York: Springer.

Warkentin v. Riggs (2010). BCSC 1706.

Wodak, R. (1980). Discourse analysis and courtroom interaction. *Discourse Processes, 3*(4), 369–380.

Section V
Specific Communicative Tasks

11

Hostage and Crisis Negotiation, Perspectives on an Interactive Process

OLE ANDRE BRATEN[1], MICHEL ST-YVES[2], TERRY D. ROYCE[3]
AND MARTY LAFOREST[4]

[1] Corporate consultant, Norway
[2] Sûreté du Québec, Université de Montréal, Canada
[3] University of Technology, Sydney, Australia
[4] Université du Québec à Trois-Rivières, Canada

FROM HOSTAGE TO CRISIS NEGOTIATION

A trained negotiator[1] can influence a static hostage situation through the principles of reciprocity, liking and authority (Cialdini, 2009). The oldest is the rule of give and take, where the negotiator leverages the conversation with bargaining techniques. Establishing report and building it throughout the interaction is a second way of utilizing the trust built in the 'artificial relationship' – using techniques like 'active listening' presented in this chapter. The third principle, authority, exploits the human need to follow guidance from people in power – here the hostage negotiator. The art of influence is subtle communication without the need to raise awareness. Tools of persuasion can be both verbal and non-verbal, where a thorough analysis of the situation can pinpoint the optimal communication with regard to the degree of 'elaboration likelihood' (Chaiken,

Communication in Investigative and Legal Contexts: Integrated Approaches from Forensic Psychology, Linguistics and Law Enforcement, First Edition. Edited by Gavin Oxburgh, Trond Myklebust, Tim Grant and Rebecca Milne.

Gruenfeld & Judd, 2000; Petty & Cacioppo, 1996). The verbal message approach, called the central route of persuasion, needs both the attention and motivation of the person we try to persuade. First of all, the attention can be hampered and aggression increased due to alcohol intoxication, the use of narcotics, psychological disorders or simply the high degree of bodily and cognitive stress (Braten, 2011). The person might also lack the motivation to evaluate the verbal message. Law enforcement on the scene can then rely on non-verbal communication, the peripheral route of persuasion. The mere presence of uniformed officers on the perimeter might both increase the motivation towards paying attention to the negotiator on the phone, as well as demonstrating the ability to increase this show of force. When the situation moves towards a deadline or the situations is getting out of hand, officers in charge can increase the elaboration likelihood by launching a tactical assault. Facing SWAT officers moving towards the situation, facial expressions, direct gaze, swift movements and bodily contact (Argyle, 1998) increase the degree of persuasion further. Hostage situations were negotiated successfully in a number of high-profile cases throughout the 1970s and 1980s. The first responding officers cordoned off the scene, waiting for the arrival of SWAT (special weapons and tactics) officers and trained negotiators. Upon arrival, SWAT officers assumed vantage positions and the negotiators initiated communication. Use of the tactical solution was the last resort, putting communication fourth as a truly powerful weapon. With the decrease of hostage situations in the 1980 and 1990s, communication as a tactical tool was further implemented in routine calls, labelled 'crisis communication'. Individuals under the influence of alcohol, narcotics, psychological disorders or the high degree of stress associated with conflict situations are at risk of using violence and/or threatening with such behaviour (Braten, 2011). Negotiation is truly a demanding process, requiring a number of different skills (Ury, 1993; Fisher & Shapiro, 2005).

First, we will investigate if all negotiations share the same dynamics and stages, which is an important approach towards gaining increased situational awareness (SA) (Endsley, 1995, 2000) in the offset of hostage and crisis situations. The officer in contact with an individual in a negotiation scenario needs to be aware that the situation is indeed a negotiation scenario (SA 1) and have an understanding of the elements present that might interact (SA 2) and an understanding of where the situation might be heading in the minutes to come (SA 3). Throughout the chapter you will be presented with contemporary approaches to increase both individual and shared SA for both individuals and teams in a law enforcement context. Two approaches to the stages that will develop in a negotiation are presented to raise awareness.

Traditional Stages in Hostage and Crisis Scenarios

In the literature on hostage/crisis negotiations there are some interesting models that have attempted to capture some sense of the stages that negotiations, showing them as negotiated interactions moving towards an agreed resolution. Two well-known approaches to staging, both of which interpret it primarily from the point of view of the negotiator, are important here: the first takes a forensic psychology perspective, while the second contextualizes it in law enforcement and corrections. The forensic psychology perspective taken by Call (2003, 2008) proposes that hostage/crisis negotiations may move through five distinct stages or 'strategic steps':

1. Intelligence gathering: develop strategy(s) for approach to the crisis and prepare for any potential or unforeseen problems.
2. Introduction and relationship development: after an initial attempt to build rapport or some kind of relationship. Action on instrumental demands until rapport is evident and established needs to be deferred.
3. Problem clarification and relationship development: with rapport established negotiate (bargain) 'normatively' rather than by using 'brinkmanship'.
4. Problem-solving: based on the developing rapport, start to advance proposals to solve the situation and seek compliance.
5. Resolution: with continuing rapport maintenance, carefully organize steps for any hostage release, and steps for an efficient and safe surrender.

McMains and Mullins (2001), writing about the stages of a hostage/crisis negotiation police training and correctional contexts, suggest that they can be characterized as passing through four distinct, and unfolding stages:

1. Pre-crisis: those involved in a potential crisis carry on their normal daily activities.
2. Crisis/defusing: intense emotional excitation is triggered in the subject by some event, unpredictability and uncertainty increases, and a course of action is chosen leading to police involvement and initial attempts to defuse the crisis.
3. Accommodation/negotiation: the subject begins to be open to alternative suggestions, emotional excitation decreases and rational thinking increases (often in connection with discussions related to instrumental purposes).
4. Resolution/surrender: the subject can start to visualize solutions and a possible clear path for alternative choices, agrees with and tests new ideas and makes clear moves towards a conclusion.

Table 11.1   The stages in Operation Terrall (adapted from Royce, 2009, pp. 36–38)

Stages	Processes	Exchanges and instances
Pre-crisis	**Intelligence-gathering**	• Incidents in town (visiting town, bank, police station wearing armed body IED and guns) • Police interview (with person who knows POI) • Police intelligence on property (carrying guns while patrolling perimeters; general paranoid behaviours)
Crisis	**Containment** and **isolation**	N: *'POI' You are under arrest. Stop immediately, and stay exactly where you are ... . There are police all around you, ... You will be safe if you stay exactly where you are, and do exactly as I ask.* N: *We know you've been going into town with a bomb and there's a lot of people very worried about that... .* P: *Well that's only if I was attacked... .* N: *... but no-one wanted to attack you, no-one wants to go near you, ... very worried about the bomb ... .*
Crisis-defusing	**Expressive**	P: *Now listen, this is absolutely bloody ridiculous.* P: *Well certainly I'm going to keep my weapons, I've had them for most of my life.* N: *I know that, I know that, but police have to make sure that the bomb is disarmed.* P: *Rightio, well what are you going to do?* N: *Well I need you to take off your overalls ....* P: *Then what do you intend to do?* ... P: *Well what about my property and everything? .... what do you intend to do with my weapons? ... my land, my bike ... selling my land? ... getting out of the country? ... The pistol ....* N: *Well they are your property ...*

Table 11.1 (*Continued*)

Stages	Processes	Exchanges and instances
Negotiation and accommodation		**N**: *... but you just can't go into town with a bomb.*
		P: *What I've got is absolutely safe, that's the only problem. ...*
		N: *Well I know that you've got it really well made and I know it's as safe as it can be ....*
	instrumental (bargaining)	**P**: *I was worried you were attacking me on my land to get my weapons which I've had for years, because you've all gone bloody well mad. ...*
		P: *OK I'll leave my things here on the road. ...*
		N: *And if you feel you could, if you can disarm it* [the IED] *easily.*
		P: *It is disarmed now. ... Rightio, I'll even disconnect the battery from it. ...*
		N: *Yes, I can guarantee that that* [the money] *will be returned to you. ...*
		P: *But you're giving me a guarantee that I can definitely get out of this country?*
		P: *Rightio, now you want me to walk down toward the armoured personnel carrier?*
Resolution/ surrender	**Surrender ritual**	**N**: *Please, if you could just place the phone there .... And if you do that you'll be absolutely safe. ...*
		N: *Just keep walking towards them ... until they call out to you.*
		P: *This is wonderful. ...*

The view taken by McMains and Mullins stresses that a crisis is an unfolding process, with 'predictable stages through which people move [and that] each stage has different issues with which negotiators must deal and requires different skills that are valuable in dealing with the issues of that particular stage' (McMains & Mullins, 2001). This view of the interaction as unfolding is an interactive, process-based view, and is one where the stages unfold as the interlocutors involved draw upon various interactive processes. An instance where these understandings are adapted and drawn upon can be seen in Royce's (2009) analysis of the discourse staging in a crisis negotiation in Australia. This can be seen in Table 11.1.

Resolution through Dialogue

In the excerpt above bargaining techniques are used, effective when controlling the perimeter. Even so, barricade and hostage-taking situations were not so long ago resolved by the use of force (Bahn, 2003), with options usually limited to verbally persuading the individual in crisis into surrendering or using force, including weapons. This offensive intervention brings a quick end to the crisis (action–reaction), but also leads to high numbers of dead and injured among the hostage-takers, hostages and police. Thanks in part to the pioneering work of Harvey Schlossberg and Frank Bolz, an approach based on peaceful intervention through communication – i.e. 'as long as no immediate threat to life exists, negotiations are acceptable' (McMains & Mullins, 2001) – was developed. This new approach is not only more efficient, and safer, than the use of force, but can significantly reduce the number of injuries and deaths among all parties (Leviton & Greenstone, 2002; Michaud, St-Yves & Guay, 2008a, 2008b; St-Yves & Collins, 2012). In 95% of hostage-taking incidents, this approach prevents the death of both the hostages and the hostage taker (Blau, 1994; McMains & Mullins, 2001). Today, most police negotiators are trained to resolve conflicts through the remarkably effective weapon of communication. Even famous intervention teams proudly display mottos such as 'Talk to me'"(NYPD, New York), 'L'écoute est notre arme' (RAID, France) and *Pax per conloquium* (Latin for 'resolution through dialogue') (FBI). These mottos demonstrate just how important communication now is in police responses to crisis situations (St-Yves & Collins, 2012).

Some experts have long argued that within the context of conflict interaction, communication functions to create conflict, define conflict and resolve conflict, thereby becoming the very essence of conflict (Folger, Poole & Stutman, 1993). It is through verbal and non-verbal communication that the author of the crisis situation and the law enforcement negotiators engage in a transactional 'dialogue'. Here each party is seeking to define the interaction, exert control and influence over the other, manage the relational parameters of trust and power, project their desired image and achieve their desired outcome. As such, crisis/hostage negotiation is a communicative event (Rogan, 2012).

The term 'negotiation' evokes concepts of compromise, concession, flexibility and agreement. Negotiation thus requires both parties to be willing to cooperate and 'put a little water in their wine'. This communication is framed as a sort of contract. It is most appropriate when the person or entity it represents acts in a 'rational' way. However, this is far from true in the majority of police interventions – the vast majority of which in fact involve mentally disturbed individuals (Noesner, 1999; St-Yves & Tanguay, 2009). Crisis situations are characterized by psychological distress, impulsive reactions and violent and self-destructive behaviours. One of the first functions affected by mental health problems is judgement. The loss of efficiency in this faculty, of the ability to reason and take thoughtful decisions, largely explains why these crises are highly volatile and may at any time become irreversible tragedies. Unlike so-called 'free' negotiations, in which the parties voluntarily decide to come together to find a solution and are free to withdraw at any time they wish, a 'captive' negotiation is a negotiation in which 'voluntary' aspects and 'freedom' are limited. The parties are trapped in the same problem, without the possibility of withdrawing without losing everything. These situations are the most common forms of crisis interventions (St-Yves & Veyrat, 2012).

Negotiation in High-Stress Situations

Although they obey the same basic rules as ordinary negotiations, crisis negotiations have their own set of specific traits, particularly the variable rationality of the individuals in crisis, who range from individuals known to be mentally disturbed to those who are rational and determined. The approach to the former is the neutralization of armed and dangerous individuals, with the focus on psychological aspects. The second are persons who, while certainly in a temporary state of limited rationality – since they can be mentally disturbed by the crisis situation – are perfectly aware of how to sustain a show of force.

In crisis situations the individual in crisis typically moves through three classic stages: (1) the acute stage (generally emotional); (2) the problem-resolution stage (more rational and focused on solving the problem); (3) acceptance or resignation (including the ability to accept and face consequences). Most crisis intervention models follow this pattern and have been developed in accordance with these natural – indeed universal – stages of human crises, which are often set off by deep psychological distress. Most models of crisis intervention call for a communication strategy that closely mirrors the dynamics of the crisis. This strategy calls for the use of open-ended questions and active listening to understand the individual in crisis and allow them to express their distress, which will help them become more rational. This should be followed by the exploration of possible solutions and encouragement of the individual in crisis to choose solutions that are acceptable for both sides. The ultimate goal of such strategies is, of course, surrender. To preserve the individual's dignity and facilitate exit, negotiators must strengthen their resolve to surrender voluntarily to the police. Negotiators must often become more directive and encourage subjects to think of the future: 'We've come a long way together and there's just one little step left.' They must never skip steps and must accompany the individual in crisis through the various stages of the crisis, from the acute phase until the surrender (voluntary, whenever possible). Often in a hurry to defuse the crisis and obtain surrender, negotiators sometimes jump too quickly into 'problem-solving' or even 'surrender' mode while the individual in distress is still in 'crisis' mode. This classic error often plays out as follows: after just a few minutes of conversation with the individual in distress, the negotiator switches to 'problem-solving' mode or 'surrender' mode, while the individual in crisis is still in the emotional 'crisis' mode. When this occurs, it does not just slow the progress down, there is a risk of the situation degenerating (St-Yves, Tanguay & St-Pierre, 2001).

Most crisis intervention models share many features with therapeutic approaches: active listening, empathy and building rapport. Some models are more oriented towards the search for agreement, usually where each party makes concessions and seeks to make the most of the situation. This is often termed 'constructive conflict management'. This type of approach, which incorporates the principles of barter, is suitable for situations where the individual negotiating is rational and has the desire to achieve a common solution (St-Yves & Veyrat, 2012).

There are several models of 'principled negotiation', but one of the best known is the 'win–win' model, which aims at producing a satisfactory and lasting agreement between people who have different interests, but also interests in common. Influence techniques (e.g. reciprocation, authority, liking and scarcity) are often used to influence the outcome of the negotiation (see Cialdini, 1993; Webster, 2012). Communicating with an individual who has a mental disorder is probably the most difficult part of the job of a police negotiator. Understanding people with mental illnesses is one of the foundations of crisis negotiation (Schlossberg, 1974). The objective is to better understand how others communicate and how to communicate with them. The parties must adapt to each other, decode the others' messages and find some way to communicate. If the individual in crisis exhibits an intention to commit suicide, it will primarily be in the form of an expression of despair. Negotiators should seek to create hope. If the person expresses anger, negotiators must help them find a suitable and safe way to break their cycle of suffering.

The Role of Speech

When an individual in crisis tells a negotiator, 'I'm giving you 15 minutes to get my girlfriend on the phone, or else ...', he not only is setting a deadline and making an implicit threat, he is also defining the interaction as conflictual and asserting that he is in control (Hammer, 2007; Rogan & Hammer, 2006). If the individual in crisis has lost contact with reality, they may have auditory hallucinations – it is important to be patient and consider their perception of the situation. These voices actually exist for them. Although communication is more difficult, it is nevertheless still possible, as long as the delusional symptoms are taken into account and the individual's perceived reality is understood. Often individuals in this state may communicate, but differently. Sometimes all that is required is that negotiators adjust their speech to the individual: speak more slowly, repeat words or messages, use simple and short sentences, avoid abstractions. If the individual in crisis is not communicating, negotiators may have to try other channels of communication. Sometimes listening to negotiators is all that is necessary. At other times, saying nothing may be the best intervention (Schlossberg, 1979). Despite all these obstacles, police negotiators succeed in establishing contact with individuals in crisis in four out of five cases (Michaud et al., 2008a, 2008b).

In the context of captive negotiations, it is often the police who 'impose' its aid or 'forces' communication in the face of a hostile reaction or of no reaction at all. According to Michaud and St-Yves (2006), only 55% of barricaded individuals immediately respond to the police and almost 20% take more than an hour to respond to police calls. In a crisis, the communication strategy must also take into account another parameter: security. Most of the time, and especially when the individual in crisis is armed, communication is over some distance, usually by phone or megaphone. Listening is thus much more important than the non-verbal cues on which much of communication is often based. It is through listening that negotiators must assess the point of view of the other, observe, analyse, express themselves correctly and develop a relationship with the individual in crisis. 'This is basically the quality of the relationship that generates the quality of communication' (Abric, 2003, p. 155). According to Donohue and Roberto (1996), negotiators and suspects engage in a 'relational dance' as they strive to manage the dynamics of their relationship, and these implicit relational dynamics have implications for the outcome of explicit negotiations.

The dynamic nature of communication ensures that police negotiators try to change the individual in crisis' perception of reality, in order to lead them to see a 'new reality' that is less hostile. The police also try to induce the individual to adopt behaviour that can turn a crisis into a problem to be solved (Donohue & Roberto, 1996). Listening skills play a key role in the communication techniques used during a negotiation. Whatever the situation, it must be borne in mind that listening is more important than speaking and that communicating allows others to express themselves (Strentz, 1995a, 1995b, 2006). The police negotiator must analyse the individual in crisis' choice of words, try to decode the individual's message and see if their problems are real or imaginary (Wargo, 1990). As a negotiating tool, speech has an important role to play and is not merely a question of words and meaning. Inflection, tone and rhythm all play an important role (Divasto, 1996; Wargo, 1990). For example, the word 'problem' should be avoided and replaced by the word 'difficulty'. Similarly, 'hostage' should be replaced by the victim's first or last name (St-Yves & Veyrat, 2012).

How Can We Adapt a Coherent Communication Strategy?

To communicate, police negotiators must not only adapt their communication strategy to the individual in crisis' mental state but must also decipher the behaviour of individuals whose cultural schemata may be different from theirs (Giebels & Taylor, 2009). If the negotiator's cultural norms differ from those of the individual in crisis, each may interpret a given situation differently (see Pettigrew, 1979). This mismatch will occur whenever each party tries to explain the other's behaviour on the basis of what they expect, rather than on the basis of the social, cultural and contextual factors specific to the other person (Giebels & Taylor, 2009). Similarly, in situations involving extremists or terrorists, ideologies and beliefs (which are not always rational) must be identified, because the fundamental issues (and the solution) can often be found there (see Derocher, 2012).

Police interventions in crisis situations have evolved considerably since the 1970s. The role of the police has gradually evolved into that of a social worker or a mediator, and interventions now increasingly rely on a remarkably safe and effective weapon – communication. Moreover, crisis negotiation has been described as one of the most important advances in decades in policing. Meanwhile, ways of communicating have greatly changed. We have progressed from the megaphone and telephone to the Internet and text messaging. However, these new forms of communication all serve the same objective of crisis intervention: peaceful resolution of the situation through communication. The FBI's Crisis Negotiation Unit developed 'The Behavioural Change Stairway Model' (Vecchi, Van Hasselt & Romano, 2005) as a tool for crisis resolution.

How Can the Negotiator Change Behaviour?

The Behavioural Change Stairway Model (BCSM) is an interpersonal model that provides a representation of the relationship-building processes involved between a negotiator and a subject, culminating in the desired peaceful settlement. The model represented in Figure 11.1 consists of five stages, which are active listening, empathy, rapport, influence and behavioural change, and it clearly places the use of active listening initially, and pre-eminently, as the required entry activity for the process of resolving a hostage/crisis situation. The progression of a negotiation through these stages occurs both sequentially and cumulatively, such that 'the negotiator proceeds in sequence from Stage 1 (active listening) to Stage 5 (behavioural change). However, in order to establish rapport (Stage 3) with the subject, active listening skills (Stage 1) and empathy (Stage 2) must first be demonstrated (and maintained throughout) by the negotiator' (Vecchi et al., 2005).

In terms of case studies investigating how active listening is used in actual hostage/crisis negotiations and interpreted in the professional development of serving police negotiators, there is work with the New South Wales Police Service (NSWP) in Australia. Royce (2005) examines the usage of active listening in establishing rapport in the first 4 minutes of a successful crisis negotiation, while Royce (2012) discusses the

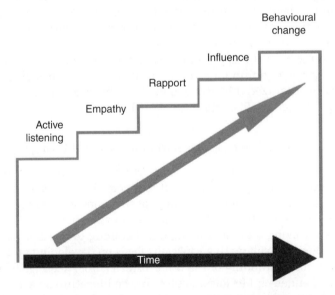

Figure 11.1 Behavioural Change Stairway Model (from Vecchi et al., 2005, p. 542).

NSWP's more verbal skills approach in the professional development training workshops it offers to its serving police negotiators. These closely follow most of the FBI's listings, but some psychologically derived terms are introduced, such as *association* and *interpreting* (Royce, 2012, p. 6). These verbal skill are:

1. Attending (being physically or vocally there for a subject)
2. Paraphrasing (statements which exactly/closely mirror the subject's words)
3. Reflection (helps the subject understand that negotiator understands his/her feelings)
4. Summarizing (clarifies the subject's meanings and shows the negotiator is listening)
5. Association (building rapport through sharing feelings, attitudes, opinions, etc.)
6. Probing (open-ended questions to get the subject to express more ideas)
7. Interpreting (drawing upon ideas expressed and re-framing them for the subject)
8. Confrontation (using questions/statements to clarify avoided feelings or states).

The BCSM model is an interesting representation of the unfolding process of building, in a sense through stages, of interpersonal rapport and the expected, anticipated and resultant changes in the behaviours of the subject being talked to; this view accords with the principles of communication assumed in a functional, communicative view of language (derived from Systemic Functional Linguistics, or SFL), whereby all communication, in any context, written or spoken, can be interpreted in terms of an understanding that it unfolds through time and is generally organized into and can be described according to recognizable stages (Eggins, 1994; Halliday, 1978).

Active Listening as the Start of Behavioural Change

The concept of 'active listening' is both taught and employed to professionals across a variety of contexts. It is a very important interpersonal skill, and the way it is defined and interpreted depends on how it is used and the reasons for its use. Across these contexts, it is generally interpreted as involving an empathizing and listening to another person (or persons) constructively, with a conscious focus on developing and demonstrating an understanding of the other interlocutor's feelings (Cambria, DeFilippo, Louden, & McGowan, 2002). In the literature on active listening, a sampling of these various contexts might include dispute/conflict resolution and mediation (Potter, 1995), marital, religious, self-help, parenting and even educational counselling or advice (*Active Listening*

Skills, 2012; Charles, 2007), journalism, sales and management (Romano, 2002) and suicide prevention (*Listening Skills: A Powerful Key to Successful Negotiating*, 2000). An alternative interpretation has emphasized the building of empathy between interlocutors and has thus been referred to as 'empathetic listening. This, according to Pickering (1986) relates to the desire or aims of the listener to be other-directed and non-defensive, to envisage the roles, perspectives or experiences of the other person and to listen to understand or appreciate, rather than trying to instrumentally agree on some transaction or to influence the other person to change his/her behaviour or attitude is some way.

In the literature specifically focusing on hostage or crisis negotiation, however, active listening has been typically defined as 'the ability to see a circumstance from another's perspective and to let the other person know that the negotiator understands his [or her] perspective' (Lanceley, 1999). In may be useful to juxtapose two of the more well-known of these major classifications: Noesner and Webster (1997) approach the issue by interpreting active listening in terms of specific verbal skills that are recommended for use by FBI negotiators, while McMains and Mullins (2001) take a more generalized approach, which collects these under more generalized, superordinate groupings (which subsume the verbal skills developed by Noesner & Webster, 1997). Table 11.2 lists these interpretations.

Table 11.2 Active listening classifications

Noesner and Webster verbal skills (1997, *FBI Law Enforcement Bulletin*)	
Labelling	Emotion labelling (*you sound…, I hear…*)
Silence/pausing	The use of silence/pausing to encourage a subject to talk
Back-channelling	The use of back-channelling or minimal encouragers (OK, *oh…, I see…, really?*)
'I' messages	The use of 'I' messages or first person singular by the negotiator (I know that …; *I feel.. xx … when you …*)
Questions	Open-ended questions that do not encourage yes/no answers (*how, when, what, where, why, who, … ,* etc.)
McMains and Mullins groupings (2001)	
Paraphrasing	A response in which the negotiator gives the subject the essence of his message in the negotiator's words
Reflecting feelings	A response in which the negotiator mirrors back to the subject the emotions the subject is communicating (mirroring)
Reflecting meaning	A response in which negotiators let the subject know they understand the facts and the feelings the subject is communicating
Summative reflections	A response in which the negotiator summarises the main facts and feelings that the subject has expressed over a relatively long period

Active listening, therefore, as an interpersonal skill in hostage/crisis negotiations, should be used to 'thoughtfully communicate with the hostage taker, defuse the conflict, and work toward establishing a level of rapport that allows them to explore problem-solving options and progress to a nonviolent resolution' (Noesner, 1999). It is an interactive strategy to be used for lowering subjects' degrees of emotional excitation, for soothing, lessening and defusing antagonistic feelings, and for increasing the probability of the subjects resorting to more rational ways of dealing with the situation. A core tenet is to build 'trust and rapport by demonstrating understanding of and concern for subjects', with the result that 'negotiators should specifically demonstrate through word and expression that they understand the issues that are important to or bother subjects [their stories] and how subjects respond to those issues [their feelings]' (Noesner, 1999). The building of rapport and the subsequent establishment of a trusting relationship then provide the context and circumstances for non-violent problem-solving alternatives to be introduced and explored; once this occurs further agreeable behaviours can be developed, compliance with requests increased, with the result that the situation can result in a successful, non-tactical resolution (Rogan, Hammer & Van Zandt, 1997). Insights from the contextual and linguistic perspective on hostage and crisis negotiation can bring us further towards peaceful resolution, providing two perspectives into how we can analyse the situation and tailor our communication (verbal or non-verbal) to the highest elaboration likelihood. The importance of this swift analysis will be presented with an active-shooter scenario.

A Negotiation as a Communicative Event

While the exchanges between a negotiator and a suspect can and should be viewed interactively from the point of view of the use of active listening and its unfolding discourse staging, another important aspect is the role of context in generating both the use of utterances to build rapport and in activating the unfolding stages of a negotiation. A central assumption in the above-mentioned functional, communicative view of language is the understanding that all communication (no matter what type) occurs in some kind of context of situation (Halliday, 1978) and that this context also plays a very important role for realizing verbal message choices. Verbal exchanges do not occur context-free, or in isolation, but are very much the results of previous interactions in differing contexts that have differing contextual features. In this SFL view of communication, one can say that the 'context is in text' via the choices that the interactants make through time and in the response or reaction to previous utterances (Eggins, 1994). Here, the context *activates* the choices made by the interlocutors and the relationship between the context and a verbal text is viewed as a dialectic or 'dialogic exchange' (Matthiessen, 1995), whereby a text is both activated by the context in which it occurs and at the same time works to construe it (Halliday, 1978).

According to an SFL view of communication, each context of situation (or register) can be described in terms of three variables, referred to as *Field*, *Tenor* and *Mode* (Halliday, 1994). Field refers to the social activity for which language is being used and what is being talked about, and is reflected in the choices of content words – words that connect to the subject matter (a discussion about available finances between a married couple will lead to the use of words such as *budget*, *money*, *payments*, *deposits*, *expensive*, etc., but the insertion of *crocodiles* will of course be out of that particular field, unless the discussion was about buying crocodile leather shoes!). Tenor deals with the roles and relationships of the interlocutors, where, for example, a negotiator's choice of utterance involves a choice between a statement, command or question (and all the other subtle variations within those – e.g. a question can also be a request). The choices made here by the speakers will be affected by the nature of the relationship between them (a good example being a police officer to a speeding driver and vice versa). Mode refers to the channel of communication chosen, whether the language is written or spoken, and with regard to the latter, whether it is face-to-face or more remote (by police phone or megaphone, for example).

Apart from drawing upon the immediate contextual knowledge that might arise as an interactional exchange develops and unfolds, a negotiator can in certain circumstances also utilize contextual knowledge that may have been gathered prior to the crisis occurring – this might occur despite the fact that the vast majority of hostage/crisis situations have a certain immediacy to them in that they can arise quite quickly from a proximate, stimulating situation. The notion that no negotiation occurs in isolation (at the time of the interaction there are other communications that occur simultaneously and feed into it) and that no text is an isolate that has no background history or sourcing to it, draws upon the theoretical understanding that besides being the realization of the immediate context of situation, a negotiation as a communicative event is also influenced by other related interactions, meaning that a text has an interactive history and a context of creation (Hasan, 1996). Here also Fairclough's (1992) notion of 'manifest intertextuality' is relevant: to Fairclough, manifest intertextuality refers to 'the case where specific other texts are overtly drawn upon within a text" and where 'other texts are explicitly present in the text under analysis: they are "manifestly » marked or cued by features on the surface of the text, such as quotation marks'; or it can mean that 'a text may "incorporate » another text without the latter being explicitly cued: one can respond to another text in the way one words one's own text' (Fairclough, 1992). Some examples of these may be earlier police reports gathered about a suspect that are sourced from legal sources, such as police on-line databases, possible immediate causes of the excitation drawn from interviews with connected people, operational notes provided by the initial attending officers or via tactical intelligence gathering (see Royce, 2013, for an instance of this).

The Linguistic Perspective Can Enhance Negotiations

The issue of negotiations in a crisis situation from a linguistic perspective has received relatively little attention. However, given that the very material of negotiation is language, linguistics – and, more specifically, discourse analysis – can considerably enrich the debate on how a crisis evolves and is resolved, since it allows for a particular critical examination of the interaction between a perpetrator and a negotiator. This section begins by presenting the bases of a suitable theoretical framework for the sociopragmatic analysis of negotiation discourse, which has already been profitably used to study verbal violence (Laforest & Moïse, 2013). The most useful concepts for analysing such negotiation situations are subsequently presented. The sociopragmatic trends of discourse analysis are rooted in a performative concept of language that maintains that 'saying is doing', a concept that has developed and become widespread since the founding work of Austin (1962). In keeping with Bakhtin (1929, 1986), those analysing discourse from this perspective adhere to the idea that talk-in-interaction constitutes the real substance of language and that, as a result, the speech act is not conceived independently of an immediate reaction; no-one speaks alone, and it is in the interaction that meaning occurs and is transformed. The point of view of the hearer is therefore essential. It is the hearer who, for example, interprets such and such a statement as a complaint (not as an observation) and who, through his reaction to this perceived complaint, more or less determines the rest of the interaction. This signifies that meaning does not exist prior to the interaction, but is gradually constructed thanks to the combined actions of all participants. Sociopragmatic discourse analysis also owes a debt to Goffman (1959), who makes the preservation of each speaker's social image, or 'face', an imperative that contributes significantly to the shape of the discourse. In short, talk-in-interaction is seen here as a progressive construction by all those engaged in it and as a way to constantly negotiate both meaning (which does not pre-exist the interaction) and identities (whether based on family, profession, etc.). When examining a crisis negotiation, therefore, we must keep in mind that underlying the object of the (macro) negotiation itself, which is the very reason for the interaction between a law-enforcement officer and a person holding hostages or threatening to end his days (for example), there is a (micro) negotiation of the meaning of most utterances: Is such and such a statement a request or an order? Is another statement a joke or an insult? Now, this identification of the act accomplished through words – not to mention the fact that the participants agree on this identification – is essential to the establishment of proper communication and, consequently, to optimal crisis resolution.

Discourse analysts employ a qualitative approach founded on a detailed analysis of what is accomplished by one or the other interact-ant (see, for example, Agne, 2007). This analysis consists of retracing the meaning attributed to the statements formulated by each partici-pant by building on the identifiable features, in discourse, of the accomplishment of such and such a speech act. The analysis of these actions is based on the postulate that insofar as they are accom-plished through language, they are linguistically analysable – that they present phonetic, lexical, grammatical and prosodic 'observables' for the linguist (see Gumperz, 1982). The use of a particular type of adjective or adverb or of a particular tense or modal verb, the tone of voice, the presence of certain forms of names and the choice of certain syntactic structures, of certain pronouns and certain verbs (e.g. 'can' rather than 'must') are examples of such observables and their study always reveals underlying issues. We consider, therefore, that speech act X has been carried out (regardless of the participant's intention) when it generates reactions associated with this act; thus, the pres-ence of excuses, bravado, denial, justification, counterattacks, etc., allows us to interpret a statement as an act of condemnation (e.g. an act of complaint or accusation). The more or less direct or allusive character of these acts, along with their intensity, can be assessed because they are marked by the linguistic (or prosodic) elements mentioned above.

Three key concepts of discourse analysis are particularly relevant for an analysis of conflict negotiation: frame, face-threatening acts and facework. Because the last two are very closely interlinked, they will be discussed together. For discourse analysts, frame (Goffman, 1974; Tannen, 1993; Tracy, 1997)[2] refers to how each participant views the interaction and the corresponding expectations (notably as regards the behaviour of the other) or, in Agne's words (2007, p. 551), 'what people think they are doing, or what they think is going on, in a situation (e.g. joking, fighting, arguing, playing). [...] Having a frame involves an implicit or explicit name for the situation or interaction (e.g. "negotiation").' For Goffman (1974), frame is about values and implicit social norms. It is easy to understand that interaction can lead to conflict when the participants are not operating within the same frame (see Tracy, 1997). Agne (2007) thus shows that the institutional frame of the FBI negotiators during the siege at Waco in Texas (1993) was incompatible with the religious frame of the head of the Davidian sect. Frame is rarely explicit in the interaction, but the observable characteristics of incompatibility or, at least, of differences in frames include persistent disagreements, failed attempts by a participant to impose a theme or change the subject of conversation and a refusal to submit to the discursive authority of the other (i.e. to recognize a participant's leadership in the interaction). Reframing is not always possible since it sometimes hinges on an entire value system that a participant cannot be made to abandon.

As mentioned above, the preservation of each participant's social image – that is, the need to save face (or save the face of one's interlocutor) – is an imperative that contributes significantly to the shape of the discourse, as demonstrated by Goffman (1959). Inspired by this Goffmanian notion of face and the importance of saving face during an interaction, Brown and Levinson (1987) define a face-threatening act, or FTA, as an act challenging the face wants of a participant in an interaction. The threat inherent in these speech acts always targets one's 'face'.

The FTA family is a large one. It includes all directive speech acts (Searle, 1969) by which a speaker attempts to have his hearer act in a certain way and encompasses a broad continuum of acts, ranging from the suggestion to the order (for in all these cases, a refusal on the part of the addressee threatens the speaker with loss of face). As well, it includes all acts that can be construed as condemnation (Laforest & Moïse, 2013) – e.g. disapproval, criticism, reprimands, accusations, insults, etc. – and that indicate 'at least potentially, that the speaker's wishes do not correspond to those of the hearer' (Brown & Levinson, 1987). We can substitute 'expectations' for Brown and Levinson's 'wishes', and such expectations involve respect for the set of norms governing linguistic or social behaviour. Furthermore, although the threat is always about loss of face, the latter nevertheless varies depending on the situation: face threatened by an FTA may be personal, social, professional, etc. It can be said that crisis negotiation basically rests on such face-threatening acts and hence

the importance of this concept. Indeed, what the law-enforcement officer in charge of the negotiation communicates in essence to his hearer (a hostage taker, for example) may be summed up roughly as follows:
– You did X, which violates society's expectations/prescriptions;
– You now have to do Y (e.g. give yourself up/free the hostages);
– If not, then Z1 and/or Z2 and/or Z3.
Regardless of the many speech acts the negotiator accomplishes in order to learn more about the situation and about his listener or to build a relationship of trust with him, the fact remains that these three key acts constitute the core of the negotiation process and both participants know this.

The form given by the negotiator to statements that allow him to accomplish these acts can strongly influence the hearer's way of reacting to them. Given the context of a crisis, an observation such as 'you did X' is easily interpreted as an accusation; any question formed as 'why are you doing/did you do X?', even if the speaker views it as a simple act of request (for information), will be interpreted as a complaint, as this is precisely one of its canonical forms (Laforest, 2002). Statements in the form of 'if X, Y' may be presented as information, but will be decoded as a threat.

The concept of facework comes into play at precisely this point. A key research by Rogan and Hammer (1994) effectively demonstrates that facework (everything that, according to Goffman, helps lower the level of threat in a face-threatening act, e.g. saying 'would you kindly do X' instead of 'do X', i.e. using interrogative and conditional verb forms rather than the imperative) plays a key role in the negotiation process. Accordingly, allowing one's listener to save face is essential to success and the linguistic signs of this facework are known and easy to identify. By highlighting both their presence and absence in the words exchanged by the two participants, one understands the meaning each of them has given to the statements of the other, and therefore how each person positions himself in the interaction and the evolution of these positionings. Discourse analysis cannot offer negotiators a prescriptive or predictive model of linguistic behaviour. It can, however, help clarify certain aspects of the negotiation process, highlight the characteristics of statements that have generated a favourable or unfavourable reaction from the hearer and that have, as a result, helped or hindered the desired conclusion to the negotiation. An analysis of this kind can subsequently prove effective in encouraging negotiators to develop a reflective practice approach to their activity.

To Negotiate the Unnegotiable

Active shooter scenarios has been regarded non-negotiable since 1966. In that year, Charles Whitman hauled a marine footlocker – heavy with supplies, weapons and ammunitions – to the observation tower of the University of Texas. From his elevated position he opened fire, creating havoc for 96 minutes, leaving 13 dead and 31 wounded. This incident caused the US law enforcement community to implement SWAT (special weapons and tactics) nationwide, keeping at the ready better trained and armed police officers to take on the Whitmans alike (Stair, Dwight, Shapiro, & Tang, 2012). The problems handling these incidents were first visible to the public at Columbine High School in 1999. Responding officers isolated the high school following reports of multiple shots fired. Responding officers waited for SWAT officers to arrive at the scene. The preferred choice arrived after 45 minutes, with first responders waiting outside the school. The first responding unit on the scene in active shooter scenarios mostly intervene as soon as they arrive, so that no more lives are lost (Davidson, 2002). Trained negotiators will not even be in position for the entry – and negotiation is traditionally ruled out. First of all the offender will most likely commit suicide following the rampage, as well as the short timeframe will make it impossible to gain a vantage point for containment and negotiation (Hess, Orthmann & Cho, 2011).

Multiple incidents with active shooters on and off campus have challenged tactical communication as the vital tool law enforcement had developed it to be. In the period 1992–2011 the US alone suffered 40 active shooter scenarios on campus (International Association of Chiefs of Police (IACP), 2011) – the perpetrator in 95% of the profiled cases being a fellow student (Secret Service and United States Department of Education, 2002). New training programs have reduced the injuries inflicted by the perpetrator(s) (LaRaia & Walker, 2009), stressing the need for immediate action by the first responder(s), simultaneously securing the scene for the EMS services (Maniscalo & Christen, 2011). Throughout the 1990s we have seen such incidents both in Europe and Scandinavia, making school shooting an international threat. Off campus the term workplace violence has seen an increase, since a post office in Oklahoma was targeted by a disgruntled employee in 1986. A fellow colleague entered his workplace with a weapon and killed 14 of his peers. Prior to the confrontation he was to be terminated from his position (Rugala & Isaacs, 2001). These incidents are very difficult to anticipate by the organizations targeted (Devlin, 2007). Terrorist groups have also adopted the active shooter format. The latest high-profile scenarios include Besland in Russia in 2004 and Mombai in

India in 2008. While these situations can be compared both with regard to the use of SWAT and possible solutions for negotiation (Mahadevan, 2012), in Besland the terrorists seized a school – displaying elements of traditional hostage situations as the target was static and response typically would be orchestrated by SWAT officers. In Mombai the perpetrators were on foot attacking public places where soft targets would be attainable – they attacked a train station, a coffee shop and a hotel, places that are especially vulnerable to active shooter attacks (Jenkins, 2009). The incident in Mombai has raised awareness. There is, even so, a hope that traditional active shooter training should pay off if ordinary patrol officers are confronted even with widespread terrorist attacks (LaRaia & Walker, 2009). In situations without police presence isolating the crime-scene, negotiation is the only available tool. We are confronted with the same intense need for implementing negotiations as a powerful tool where our citizens are kidnapped for ransom abroad. The problem in both lone assailant and terrorist attacks, domestic and abroad, is the lack of containment. Abroad the tactical solution is seldom present; in domestic scenarios law enforcement capabilities might struggle to reach the crime scene before the attack is over.

An active shooter scenario in Norway on the 22 July 2011 stresses the need to quickly apply effective hostage and crisis negotiation techniques like the approaches presented in this chapter. Prior to the attack the perpetrator had detonated a car bomb in the city centre of Oslo, aimed towards the Norwegian government administration. Posing as a police officer he escaped the site and drove to a deserted island (Utoya Island) used as the site for the traditional summer camp of the Norwegian Labour party. Armed with semi-automatic weapons, under the pretence to secure the island after the alleged terrorist attack, he started targeting the youth at random. The first shot was fired at 17:21 when an off-duty police officer was shot dead. The perpetrator called the police at 18:01 (first call) and at 18:26 (second call; see Table 11.3).

We have moved considerably from the belief that a trained negotiator single-handed will defuse the situation at hand. Presented hostage/crisis situations and other scenarios on a high conflict level (Braten, 2011), with the pending risk of violence and (risk of) fatalities, will affect both the individual officer, law enforcement teams and leaders on all organizational levels (Braten, 2013). They will all need to gain a high degree of situational awareness in regard to the level in the negotiation process they intercept. In the presented phone call the dispatch was the contact point of negotiation and the scene was not secured. The perpetrator was arrested one minute after he hung up on the second call, when a national SWOT element arrived on the scene at the remote island by boat. There were 66 casualties on the island, mainly

Table 11.3   The second call from Utoya Island

N: *Police emergency hotline.*
P: *Hallo, my name is Anders Behring Breivik.*
N: *Yes, hallo. ....*
P: *I am a commander in The Norwegian resistance movement.*
N: *Yes, hallo. ....*
P: *Can you patch me through to the incident commander to the Delta?*
   (Delta is the nickname of the Norwegian national SWAT-element,
   implemented after the 1972 siege)
N: *Yes.. What is your connection to Delta and what is this about?*
P: *I am at Utøya.*
N: *You are at Utøya. ....*
P: *I have completed my mission so I wish to...surrender. ....*
N: *You wish to surrender, ok. ....*
P: *Yes.*
N: *And what was your name again. ....*
P: *Anders Behring Breivik.*
N: *And you are a commander in?*
P: *The name of the organisation is Knights Templar Europe, but we are*
   organised in...the anticommunist and the Norwegian resistance
   movement against Islamisation of Europe and Norway.
N: *Yes. ....*
P: *We have just now conducted a mission on behalf of Knights Templar.*
N: *Yes. ....*
P: *Europe and Norway.*
N: *Yes. ....*
P: *As our operation is complete it is acceptable to surrender to Delta.*
N: *You which to surrender to Delta?*
P: *Yes, can you patch me through to the incident commander for Delta?*
N: *You are talking with someone now who is in charge.*
P: *Ok, just sort out what you need to and then call me back on this phone,*
   ok?
N: *Hmm, but what phone number?*
P: *Thanks a lot, by for now.*
N: *I don't have the phone number! Hallo!*

youngsters. Tactical crisis communication is a vital tool for the global law enforcement community and other organizations facing potential high-level conflict and crisis scenarios.

CONCLUSION

In this chapter, we have presented an overview on hostage and crisis negotiation, from traditional and static hostage negotiation to high-intensity confrontations like active shooter scenarios. We believe that this chapter provides knowledge to prevent and handle complex conflict and crisis scenarios, addressing the vigilance needed for resolution through dialogue.

NOTES

1. In this text, the masculine gender is used solely for convenience and includes the feminine.
2. The term must be clearly defined, as this notion may assume a different meaning, more cognitive than social, in another discipline such as psychology (see Putnam & Holmer, 1992).

REFERENCES

Abric, J. C. (2003). *Psychologie de la Communication: Théories et Méthodes.* Paris, France: Éditions Colin.

Active Listening Skills. (2012). Utah State University Academic Resource Center Idea Sheets: Active listening skills. Retrieved from http://www.usu.edu/arc/idea_sheets/pdf/active_listening.pdf

Agne, R. R. (2007). Reframing practices in moral conflict: Interaction problems in the negotiation standoff at Waco. *Discourse Society, 18,* 549–578.

Argyle, M. (1998). *Bodily communication.* London, UK: Routledge.

Austin, J. L. (1962). *How to do things with words.* Oxford, UK: Oxford University Press.

Bahn, C. (2003). Sieges and their aftermath. In R. Rosner (Ed.), *Principles and practice of forensic psychiatry* (2nd ed.). London, UK: Arnold.

Bakhtine, M. (V. N. Voloshinov) (1929, 1986). *Marxism and the philosophy of language.* Cambridge, MA: Harvard University Press.

Blau, T. H. (1994). *Psychological services for law enforcement.* New York: John Wiley & Sons, Inc.

Braten, O. A. (2011). *Handbook of conflict management: Prevention of harassment, threats and violence.* Oslo, Norway: Cappelen Damm Academic Press (in Norwegian).

Braten, O. A. (2013). *Handbook of Crisis Management.* Oslo, Norway: Cappelen Damm Academic Press (in Norwegian).

Brown, P., & Levinson, S. C. (1987). *Politeness. Some universals in language use.* Cambridge, UK: Cambridge University Press.

Call, J. A. (2003). The evolution of hostage/barricade crisis negotiation. In H. V. Hall (Ed.), *Terrorism: Strategies for intervention.* New York: Haworth Press.

Call, J. A. (2008). Psychological consultation in hostage/barricade crisis negotiation. In H. V. Hall (Ed.), *Forensic psychology and neuropsychology for criminal and civil cases.* Boca Raton, FL: CRC Press.

Cambria, J., DeFilippo, R. J., Louden, R. J., & McGowan, H. (2002). Negotiation under extreme pressure: The 'mouth marines' and the hostage takers. *Negotiation Journal – On the Process of Dispute Settlement, 18* (4), 331–343.

Chaiken, S. L., Gruenfeld, D. H., & Judd, C. M. (2000). Persuasion in negotiations and conflict situations. In M. Deutsch, & P. T. Coleman (Eds.), *The handbook of conflict resolution: Theory and practice.* San Francisco, CA: Jossey-Bas Publisher.

Charles, L. L. (2007). Disarming people with words: Strategies of interactional communication that crisis (hostage) negotiators share with systemic clinicians. *Journal of Marital and Family Therapy, 33* (1), 51–68.

Cialdini, R. B. (1993). *Influence: Science and practice.* New York: Harper Collins.

Cialdini, R. B. (2009). *Influence, science and practice.* Boston, MA: Pearson.

Davidson, T. N. (2002). *To preserve life: Hostage-crisis management.* Indianapolis, IN: Critical Incident Management Agency, Inc.

Derocher, L. (2012). Police intervention in religious cults. In M. St-Yves, & P. Collins (Eds.), *The psychology of crisis intervention: For Law Enforcement Officers.* Toronto, ON, Canada: Carswell, pp. 299–337.

Devlin, E. S. (2007). *Crisis management, planning and execution.* Boca Raton, FL: Aurebach Publications.

Divasto, P. V. (1996). Negotiating with foreign language-speaking subjects. *FBI Law Enforcement Bulletin*, June 1996, 11–15.

Donohue, W. A., & Roberto, A. J. (1996). An empirical examination of three models of integrative and distributive bargaining. *International Journal of Conflict Management, 7*, 209–229.

Eggins, S. (1994). *An introduction to systemic functional grammar.* London, UK: Pinter Publishers.

Endsley, M. R. (1995). Toward a theory of situational awareness in dynamic systems. *Human Factors, 37* (1), 32–64.

Endsley, M. R. (2000). Theoretical underpinnings of situational awareness: A critical review. In M. R. Endsley & D. J. Garland (Eds.), *Situational awareness analysis and measurement.* Mahwah, NJ: Lawrence Erlbaum Associates.

Fairclough, N. (1992). *Discourse and social change.* Oxford, UK: Polity Press.

Fisher, R., & Shapiro, D. (2005). *Beyond reason. Using emotion as you negotiate.* New York: Penguin Group.

Folger, J. P., Poole, M. S., & Stutman, R. K. (1993). *Working through conflict: Strategies for relationships, groups, and organizations.* New York: Harper Collins.

Giebels, E., & Taylor, P. J. (2009). Interaction patterns in crisis negotiations: Persuasive arguments and cultural differences. *Journal of Applied Psychology, 94*, 5–19.

Goffman, E. (1959). *The presentation of self in everyday life.* New York: Doubleday.

Goffman, E. (1974). *Frame analysis.* New York: Harper Colophon Books.

Gumperz, J. (1982). *Discourse strategies.* Cambridge, UK: Cambridge University Press.

Halliday, M. A. K. (1978). *Language as social semiotic.* London, UK: Edward Arnold.

Halliday, M. A. K. (1994). *An introduction to functional grammar.* London, UK: Edward Arnold.

Hammer, M. R. (2007). *Saving lifes: The S.A.F.E. Model for resolving hostage and crisis incidents.* Westport, CT: Praeger.

Hasan, R. (1996). In C. Cloran (Ed.), *Ways of saying, ways of meaning: Selected papers of Ruqaiya Hasan.* Cassell.

Hess, K. M., Orthmann, C. H., & Cho, H. L. (2011). *Police operations, theory and practice* (5th ed.). New York: Delmar.

International Association of Chiefs of Police (IACP). (2011). Guide for preventing and responding to school violence. Retrieved from http://www.theiacp.org/portals/0/pdfs/schoolviolence2.pdf

Jenkins, B. M. (2009). *Lessons learned from the Mumbai attacks*. Testimony presented before the Senate Homeland Security and Governmental Affairs Committee on January 28. Santa Monica, CA: Rand Corporation. Retrieved from http://www.rand.org/pubs/testimonies/CT316.html

Laforest, M. (2002). Scenes of family life: Complaining in everyday conversations. *Journal of Pragmatics, 34*(10), 1595–1620.

Laforest, M., & Moïse, C. (2013). Entre reproche et insulte, comment définir les actes de condamnation?, In B. Fracchiola, C. Moïse, C. Romain, & N. Auger (Eds.), *Violences verbales*. Rennes, France: Presses Universitaires de Rennes.

Lanceley, F. J. (1999). *On-scene guide for crisis negotiators*. Boca Raton, FL: CRC Press.

LaRaia, W., & Walker, M. C. (2009). The siege in Mumbai: A conventional terrorist attack aided by modern technology. In M. R. Haberfeld & A. Von Hassel (Eds.), *A New understanding of terrorism: Case studies, trajectories and lessons learned*. Dordrecht, The Netherlands: Springer.

Leviton, S. C., & Greenstone, J. L. (2002). The hostage and crisis negotiator's training laboratory. *Journal of Police Crisis Negotiations, 2* (2), 21–34.

Listening Skills: A Powerful Key to Successful Negotiating. (2000). The apocalypse suicide page, HealthyPlace.com, Inc. Retrieved from http://www.healthyplace.com/depression/articles/listening-skills-a-powerful-key-to-successful-negotiating/

Mahadevan, P. (2012). *The role of SWAT units* (IFS Insights No. 3), November 2012. Oslo, Norway: Norwegian Institute for Defence Studies.

Maniscalo, P. M., & Christen, H. T. (2011). *Homeland security, principles and practice for terrorism response*. Sudbury, ON, Canada: Jones and Bartlett Publishers.

Matthiessen, C. (1995). *Lexicogrammatical cartography: English systems*. Tokyo, Japan: International Language Science Publishers.

McMains, M. J., & Mullins, W. C. (1996). *Crisis negotiations: Managing critical incidents and hostage situations in law enforcement and corrections*. Cincinnati, OH: Anderson.

McMains, M. J., & Mullins, W. C. (2001). *Crisis negotiations: Managing critical incidents and hostage situations in Law enforcement and corrections*. Cincinnati, OH: Anderson.

Michaud, P., & St-Yves, M. (2006). Analyse des situations de crise survenues entre 1990 et 2004 sur le territoire desservi par la Sûreté du Québec (Unpublished).

Michaud, P., St-Yves, M., & Guay, J. P. (2008a). Predictive modeling in hostage and barricade incidents. *Criminal Justice and Behavior, 35*, 1136–1155.

Michaud, P., St-Yves, M., & Guay, J. P. (2008b). Analyse descriptive des situations de prise d'otages et de barricade au Québec. *Revue Internationale de Criminologie et de Police Technique et Scientifique, 61*, 133–150.

Noesner, G. W. (1999). Negotiation concepts for commanders. *FBI Law Enforcement Bulletin, 68* (1), 6–14.

Noesner, G. W., & Webster, M. (1997). Crisis intervention: Using active listening skills in negotiations. *FBI Law Enforcement Bulletin, 66* (8), 13–19.

Pettigrew, T. F. (1979). The ultimate attribution error: Extending Allport's cognitive analysis of prejudice. *Personality and Social Psychology Bulletin, 5*, 461–476.

Petty, R. E., & Cacioppo, J. T. (1996). Attitudes and persuasion. *Classic and contemporary approaches*. Dubuque, IA: Brown.

Pickering, M. (1986). Communication. *Explorations: A Journal of Research of the University of Maine, 3* (1, Fall), 16–19.

Potter, B. (1995). *From conflict to cooperation: How to mediate a dispute*. Berkeley, CA: Ronin Publishing.

Putnam, L. L., & Holmer, M. (1992). Framing, reframing, and issue development. In L. L. Putnam & M. E. Roloff (Eds.), *Communication and negotiation*. Newbury Park, CA: Sage.

Rogan, R. G. (2012). The communicative dynamics of crisis negotiation: Research, theory and application. In M. St-Yves & P. Collins (Eds.), *The psychology of crisis intervention: For Law Enforcement Officers* (pp. 55–81). Toronto, ON, Canada: Carswell.

Rogan, R. G., & Hammer, M. R. (1994). Crisis negotiations: A preliminary investigation of facework in naturalistic conflict discourse. *Journal of Applied Communication Research, 22*, 216–231.

Rogan, R. G., & Hammer, M. R. (2006). The emerging field of crisis/hostage negotiation: A communication-based perspective. In J. Oetzel & S. Ting-Toomey (Eds.), *Handbook of conflict communication*. Thousand Oaks, CA: Sage.

Rogan, R. G., Hammer, M. R., & Van Zandt, C. (1997). *Dynamic processes of crisis negotiation*. Westport, CT: Praeger.

Romano, S. J. (2002). Communication survival skills for managers. *FBI Law Enforcement Bulletin, 71* (9), 14–16.

Royce, T. D. (2005). The negotiator and the bomber: Analyzing the critical role of active listening in crisis negotiations. *Negotiation Journal, 21* (1), 5–27.

Royce, T. D. (2009). Critical incidents: Staging and process in crisis negotiations. *Journal of Policing, Intelligence and Counter Terrorism (JPICT), 4*(2), 25–40.

Royce, T. D. (2012). The analysis of police crisis negotiations: Important interactional features. *International Journal of Law, Language and Discourse, 2*(3), 1–24.

Royce, T. D. (2013). Serving a high-risk warrant: The role of context in police crisis negotiations. In Z. Mohd Don & A. De Rycker (Eds.), *Language and crisis*. Amsterdam, The Netherlands: John Benjamins Publishing Company.

Rugala, E. A., & Isaacs, A. R. (2001). *Workplace violence, issues in response*, National Center for the Analysis of Violent Crome. Quantico, VA: FBI Academy.

Schlossberg, H. (1974). *Psychologist with a Gun*. New York: Coward, McCann & Geogegan.

Schlossberg, H. (1979). Police response to hostage situations. In J. T. O'Brien & M. Marcus (Eds.), *Crime and Justice in America*. New York: Pergamon.

Searle, J. (1969). *Speech acts*. Cambridge, UK: Cambridge University Press.

Secret Service and United States Department of Education (2002). *The final report and findings of the safe school initiative: Implications for the prevention of school attacks in the United States*. Washington, DC: United States Secret Service and United States Department of Education.

Stair, R. G., Dwight, A. P., Shapiro, G. L., & Tang, N. (2012). *Law enforcement responder. Principles of emergency medicine, rescue and force protection.* Sudbury, ON, Canada: Jones and Bartlett Publishers.

Strentz, T. (1995a). Negotiating with extremists. U.S. Negotiator – 1995 Year, in review special edition, 6–7, 42.

Strentz, T. (1995b). The cycle crisis negotiation time line. *Law and Order, 43* (3), 73–75.

Strentz, T. (2006). *Psychological aspects of crisis negotiation.* Boca Raton, FL: CRC Press.

St-Yves, M., & Collins, P. (2012). *The psychology of crisis intervention: For Law Enforcement Officers.* Toronto, ON, Canada: Carswell.

St-Yves, M., & Guay, J. P. (2008). Predictive modeling in hostage and barricade incidents. *Criminal Justice and Behavior, 35,* 1136–1155.

St-Yves, M., & Tanguay, M. (2009). The psychology of crisis negotiation. In M. St-Yves & M. Tanguay (Eds.), *The psychology of criminal investigations: The search for the truth.* Toronto, ON, Canada: Carswell, pp. 295–329.

St-Yves, M., Tanguay, M., & St-Pierre, J. (2001). SINCRO: Le rythme de la crise. Article décrivant le modèle de négociation développé par la Sûreté du Québec. *Revue Interpol, 401,* 4–9.

St-Yves, M., & Veyrat, J. P. (2012). Negotiation models for crisis situations. In M. St-Yves & P. Collins (Eds.), *The psychology of crisis intervention: For Law Enforcement Officers.* Toronto, ON, Canada: Carswell, pp. 23–53.

Tannen, D. (1993). What's in a frame? Surface evidence for underlying expectations. In D. Tannen (Ed.), *Framing in discourse.* New York: Oxford University Press, pp. 14–56.

Tracy, K. (1997). Interactional trouble in emergency service requests: A problem of frame. *Research on Language and Social Interaction, 30,* 315–343.

Ury, W. (1993). *Getting Past No. Negotiating your way from confrontation to cooperation.* New York: Bantam Books.

Vecchi, G. M., Van Hasselt, V. B., & Romano, S. J. (2005). Crisis (hostage) negotiation: Current strategies and issues in high-risk conflict resolution. *Aggression and Violent Behavior, 10* (5), 533–551.

Wargo, M. G. (1990). Communication skills for hostage negotiators. *Police Marksman,* March/April 1990, 52.

Webster, M. (2012). The role of influence in crisis negotiation. In M. St-Yves & P. Collins (Eds.), *The psychology of crisis intervention: For Law Enforcement Officers.* Toronto, ON, Canada: Carswell, pp. 373–390.

12

Verbal Lie Detection

ALDERT VRIJ[1], PAUL TAYLOR[2] AND ISABEL PICORNELL[3]
[1] *University of Portsmouth, UK*
[2] *Lancaster University, UK*
[3] *Aston University, Birmingham, UK*

IMPORTANCE OF VERBAL COMMUNICATION IN LIE DETECTION

Sources that claim that non-verbal behaviour is very revealing about deception vary from TV series (e.g. *Lie to Me*) to police manuals (Inbau, Reid, Buckley, & Jayne, 2013). Research findings shed a pessimistic light on the relationship between non-verbal behaviour and deception. DePaulo et al.'s (2003) meta-analysis, based on 116 articles, included 32 non-verbal cues that were examined in five or more deception studies. Of these 32 cues, six (19%) showed a significant relationship with deception. The average effect size (d) of these six significant cues was 0.19; d values of around 0.20 represent a barely perceptible difference, such as the difference in height between 15- and 16-year-old girls (Cohen, 1988).

Two factors may contribute to this myth about the importance of non-verbal behaviour in lie detection. First is the often-used quote that

Communication in Investigative and Legal Contexts: Integrated Approaches from Forensic Psychology, Linguistics and Law Enforcement, First Edition. Edited by Gavin Oxburgh, Trond Myklebust, Tim Grant and Rebecca Milne.

'according to various social studies as much as 70% of a message communicated between persons occurs at a nonverbal level' (Vrij, 2014). The studies authors then refer to are from the psychologist Albert Mehrabian (1971), summarized in his book *Silent Messages*. Mehrabian's research dealt with the communication of positive or negative emotions *via single spoken words*, like 'dear' or 'terrible'. Obviously, if someone does not say much, verbal behaviour cannot have much influence on the impression information. This means that Mehrabian's findings cannot be applied to police interviews or any other interview setting where interviewees say considerably more than single words.

A second factor that may contribute to the myth about the importance of non-verbal behaviour in lie detection is the notion that it is more difficult to control behaviour than speech. Four factors contribute to this idea (DePaulo & Kirkendol, 1989; Vrij, 2008b). First, there are certain automatic links between emotions and non-verbal behaviour (e.g. the moment people become afraid, their bodies jerk backwards), whereas automatic links between emotions and speech content do not exist. Second, people are more practised in using words than in using behaviour, and this practice makes perfect. Third, people are more aware of what they are saying than of how they are behaving. Fourth, verbally people can pause and think what to say, whereas non-verbally people cannot be silent. These are valid reasons, but they do not imply that behaviours are more revealing than speech in terms of cues to deceit. These reasons seem to underestimate the difficulty of telling a detailed and plausible lie and ignore the fact that investigators can make lying verbally very difficult by using the right interview techniques. In the next section we will discuss verbal lie detection methods that examine specific types of detail. This will be followed by a section outlining interview techniques that enhance existing differences in details between truth tellers and liars or will elicit such differences.

VERBAL LIE DETECTION TOOLS

Criteria-Based Content Analysis

The first verbal lie detection tool to be discussed, Criteria-Based Content Analysis (CBCA), originates from Sweden (Trankell, 1963) and Germany (Undeutsch, 1967) and was designed to assess the statements of children in alleged sexual abuse cases. CBCA is the core of Statement Validity Assessment (SVA), and SVA assessments are accepted as evidence in court in several West European countries including Germany, the Netherlands and Sweden (Vrij, 2008a). CBCA is a list of 19 verbal criteria that are assumed to occur more frequently in truthful than in deceptive accounts (Köhnken & Steller, 1988; Steller & Köhnken, 1989; Vrij, 2015b). According to CBCA theory, some criteria are likely to indicate genuine experiences because these criteria are typically too difficult to fabricate (Köhnken, 1996, 2004). Therefore, statements that are coherent and consistent (*logical structure*), in which the information is not provided in a chronological time sequence (*unstructured production*) and contains a significant amount of detail (*quantity of detail*) are more likely to be true. Other indicators of truthfulness include when the witness describes his or her feelings or thoughts experienced at the time of the incident (*accounts of subjective mental state*) or describes their interpretation of the perpetrator's feelings, thoughts or motives during the incident (*attribution of perpetrator's mental state*).

Other criteria are said to be more likely to occur in truthful statements for motivational reasons. It is assumed that, compared with truth tellers, liars will be keener to construct a report that they believe will make a credible impression on others and will leave out information that, in their view, will damage their image of being a sincere person (Köhnken, 1996, 2004). As a result, a truthful statement is more likely to contain information that is inconsistent with the stereotypes of truthfulness. The CBCA list includes five of these so-called 'contrary-to-truthfulness-stereotype' criteria (Ruby & Brigham, 1998), including: *spontaneous corrections* (corrections made without prompting from the interviewer) and *admitting lack of memory* (expressing concern that some parts of the statement might be incorrect: 'I think', 'Maybe', 'I am not sure', etc.).

The CBCA has been widely researched and more than 50 empirical CBCA studies have been published to date (Vrij, 2008a). First, in support of the method, truth tellers typically obtained significantly higher CBCA scores than liars (this occurred in 16 out of 20 studies (80%) in which total CBCA scores were computed). Second, regarding the individual criteria, Criterion 3, *quantity of details*, received the most support. In 22 out of 29 studies in which it was measured (76%) truth tellers included significantly more details in their accounts than did liars. Third, in 24 studies the extent to which CBCA analyses can discriminate liars from truth tellers was examined. The average accuracy rate in these studies was 71%. In summary, there is evidence that CBCA can be effective in discriminating between truths and lies.

Reality Monitoring

A second verbal lie detection approach is Reality Monitoring (RM), which is used by researchers rather than by professionals. RM is based on memory theory. The core of RM is that memories of experienced events differ in quality from memories of imagined events (Johnson & Raye, 1981, 1998). Memories of real experiences are obtained through perceptual processes and are therefore likely to contain, among other things, *perceptual information* (details of sound, smell, taste, touch or visual details) and *contextual information*: spatial details (details about where the event took place and about how objects and people were situated in relation to each other, e.g. 'He stood behind me') and temporal details (details about the time order of events, e.g. 'First he switched on the video-recorder and then the TV' and about the duration of events). These memories are usually clear, sharp and vivid. Accounts of imagined events are derived from an internal source and are therefore usually vaguer and less concrete. Although RM is not developed for lie detection purposes, it is used as such by researchers. Their claim is that 'experienced events' reflect truth telling whereas 'imagined events' reflect deception. Obviously, this is not always the case. A person who gives a false alibi by describing something she/he truly experienced, albeit at a different time from the time she/he claims to have done so, is also describing an experienced event when she/he lies. Nevertheless, when Masip, Sporer, Garrido, and Herrero (2005) and Vrij (2015b) reviewed the Reality Monitoring deception research, they found that lie and truth accuracy rates were similar to those obtained with CBCA research; that is, in the 10 studies in which RM was used to discriminate liars from truth tellers, the average accuracy rate was 69%. In terms of individual criteria, in particular the idea that truth tellers recall more perceptual information and contextual embeddings received support. In sum, research findings suggest that RM can be effective in discriminating between truths and lies.

Scientific Content Analysis

A third verbal lie detection tool is Scientific Content Analysis (SCAN), developed by Avinoam Sapir, a former Israeli police lieutenant and polygraph examiner. SCAN is popular amongst practitioners but there is not much research into this tool (Nahari, Vrij & Fisher, 2012). In the SCAN procedure, the examinee is asked to write down in detail all his/her activities during a critical period of time in such a way that a reader without background information can determine what actually happened. The handwritten statement is then analysed by a SCAN expert on the basis of a list of criteria. Sapir (1987/2000) claims that some SCAN criteria are more likely to occur in truthful than in deceptive statements (e.g. denial of allegations, use of self-references), whereas other criteria are more likely to occur in deceptive than in truthful statements (e.g. change in language, missing information), but does not provide a theoretical rationale for his assumptions.

SCAN users refer to Driscoll's (1994) field study as evidence that SCAN works. However, a serious limitation of the study was that the ground truth could not be established; that is, it was unknown who of the examinees were actually truth tellers and who were actually liars. Nahari et al. (2012) tested the efficiency of SCAN in a laboratory experiment. Truth tellers truthfully wrote down their activities during the last half hour, whereas liars were asked to fabricate a story. The statements were analysed with SCAN and, by way of comparison, also with RM. SCAN did not distinguish truth tellers from liars above the level of chance but RM did. With RM analyses 71% of truth tellers and liars were correctly classified.

There is some overlap between SCAN and CBCA in the criteria that are examined. For example, the criteria 'spontaneous corrections', 'lack of memory' and 'extraneous information' appear on both lists. Intriguingly, the predictions about how these criteria vary between truth tellers and liars differ. In CBCA the occurrence of those cues are perceived as indictors of truth whereas in SCAN the same criteria are seen as indicators of deceit. Research regarding these individual criteria gives support only to the CBCA assumptions (Vrij, 2008a). In sum, although SCAN is popular amongst practitioners and widely used, there is no evidence that it works.

The Verifiability Approach

A fourth approach we discuss here is a new approach and called the verifiability approach. Although the approach has to date only be studied in one lab, the findings coming out of that lab are promising. Central to the verifiability approach are two assumptions. First, as we mentioned before, truth tellers typically include more detail into their accounts than liars (Vrij, 2008a). Observers seem to be aware of this, as the richer an account is perceived to be in detail, the more likely it is to be believed (Johnson, 2006). As a result, liars will be inclined to provide many details in order to make an honest impression on observers, and such a strategy was reported in Nahari et al. (2012). Second, liars prefer to avoid mentioning too many details out of fear that investigators can check such details and will discover that they are lying (Masip & Ces, 2011; Nahari et al., 2012). Those two assumptions put liars in a dilemma. On the one hand, they are motivated to include many details so that they make an honest impression and, on the other hand, they are motivated to avoid providing details to minimize the chances of being caught. A strategy that compromises between these two conflicting motivations is to provide details that cannot be verified. When attempting to make an honest impression, liars may choose to provide details that are difficult to verify (e.g. 'Several people walked by when I sat there') and may avoid providing details that are easy to verify (e.g. 'I phoned my friend Fred at 10.30 this morning'). If so, liars may report fewer details that can be checked than truth tellers. In experiments testing the verifiability approach, it was found that liars provided fewer perceptual, spatial and temporal details that could be verified than truth tellers (Nahari & Vrij, 2014; Nahari, Vrij & Fisher, 2014a, 2014b; Nahari et al., 2014).

Intriguingly, the effect became stronger when interviewees were informed about the lie detection method. In Nahari et al. (2014b), truth tellers truthfully wrote down their activities during the last half hour, whereas liars were asked to fabricate a story. Half of the examinees were informed that the investigator would read their statement carefully and check whether or not the details they provided could be verified. To avoid confusion they were also told what checkable details are (e.g. phone calls, presence at places with closed-circuit television, activities that were carried out together with another identified person (such as a friend, Liberian, lecturer) or that were witnessed by another person who can be identified and consulted). Truth tellers who received this instruction included more verifiable details into their account than truth tellers who did not receive this instruction, whereas this instruction had no effect on liars. As a result the difference between truth tellers and liars in providing checkable details was the largest in the condition where the participants were told that the investigator would look for verifiable detail.

This experiment thus showed that informing examinees about the lie detection technique that is used improved their ability to discriminate among truth tellers and liars. Typically, in lie detection research it is assumed, sometimes wrongly (cf. Aguinis, Pierce & Quigley, 2006), that informing examinees about the lie detection method impairs the efficacy of that method, because examinees will then be able to fool the examiner by employing effective countermeasures (responding in such a way that makes them appear convincing). Indeed, CBCA, RM and SCAN are probably less effective in this context because informed liars are capable of providing different types of detail (e.g. contextual embeddings, reproduction of speech, perceptual information), but, because no distinction is made between detail that can or cannot be verified, there is no assessment of the quality of such details. As a result, when informed about the working of CBCA and RM, liars can successfully adapt their stories and can include CBCA and RM criteria into their accounts that make their stories sound similar to truth tellers' stories. For example, as part of an alibi someone can give a detailed description of an interaction with another person who cannot no longer be traced. If an interviewee knows that the investigator is examining details that can be verified, which happens in the verifiability approach, the only way to convince such an investigator is to include more detail that can be verified. Truth tellers should often be able to include such details in their statement but most liars do not have such evidence to provide. Therefore, when informed about the working of the verifiability approach it should still be effective in discriminating between truth tellers and liars. In fact, it becomes *more* effective because truth tellers will start thinking about verifiable details and are able to come up with verifiable details they fail to mention if they are not instructed to include such details.

INTERVIEWING TO DETECT DECEPTION

In this section we present four new interview techniques that have in common that they enlarge verbal differences between truth tellers or liars or elicit such differences. The four techniques make lying more difficult and, as a result, verbal cues related to thinking hard, such as lack of detail in the answers, implausible answers and inconsistencies, occur in liars. See Vrij (2015a) and Granhag and Hartwig (2008) for more information about these interview techniques.

Imposing Cognitive Load

Many sources, including fMRI 'brain' research, have indicated that in interviews lying is more difficult than telling the truth (Vrij, Fisher, Mann, & Leal, 2008a). Several reasons contribute to this increased mental effort (Vrij et al., 2008a). First, formulating the lie itself is cognitively taxing if the lie is not prepared in advance. Liars need to make up their stories whilst monitoring their fabrications so that they are plausible and adhere to everything the investigator knows or might find out. In addition, liars must remember their earlier statements and know what they told to whom, so that they appear consistent when re-telling their story. Liars should also avoid making slips of the tongue and should refrain from providing new leads to investigators. Second, liars are typically less likely than truth tellers to take their credibility for granted, in part because truth tellers typically assume that their innocence will shine through. As such, liars will be more inclined than truth tellers to be conscious of, and hence monitor and control, their demeanour so that they will appear honest to the investigator. Monitoring and controlling one's own demeanour is cognitively demanding. Third, because liars do not take their credibility for granted, they may monitor the investigator's reactions more carefully in order to assess whether they are getting away with their lie. Carefully monitoring the investigator also requires cognitive resources. Fourth, liars may be preoccupied with the task of reminding themselves to act and role-play, which requires extra cognitive effort. Fifth, liars have to suppress the truth while they are lying and this is also cognitively demanding. Finally, whereas activating the truth often happens automatically, activating a lie is more intentional and deliberate, and thus requires mental effort.

The core of the imposing cognitive load technique is to exploit this difference in cognitive load that truth tellers and liars sometimes experience by making the interview setting more difficult. This should affect liars more than truth tellers because they have fewer cognitive resources left over to deal with this request. One way to impose cognitive load on interviewees is by asking them to tell their stories in reverse order. This increases cognitive load because (a) it runs counter to the natural forward-order coding of sequentially occurring events (Gilbert & Fisher, 2006) and (b) it disrupts the reconstructing of events from a schema (Geiselman & Callot, 1990). In one experiment, half of the liars and truth tellers were requested to recall what they did last Saturday night in reverse order, whereas no instruction was given to the other half of participants (Evans, Michael, Meissner, & Brandon, 2013). Truthful stories were detected at a similar level of accuracy in the control condition (55%) and reverse order condition (59%), but lies were detected with much higher accuracy in the reverse order condition (75%) than in the control condition (18%). A similar beneficial effect of the reverse order technique was found by Vrij et al. (2008b).

Encouraging Interviewees to Say More

The second technique to elicit differences between truth tellers and liars is encouraging truth tellers to provide more information. If truth tellers provide much information they are more likely to be believed, because the richer an account is perceived to be in detail, the more likely it is to be believed (Johnson, 2006). Moreover, the additional information truth tellers provide could provide leads for investigators to check. Liars may find it cognitively too difficult to add as many details as truth tellers. Alternatively, if liars do add a sufficient amount of detail, the additional information may be of lesser quality or may sound less plausible. In addition, liars may be reluctant to add more information out of fear that it will provide leads to investigators and, consequently, give their lies away. Due to these constraints liars have, the result will be that methods to encourage interviewees to say more will have a stronger effect on truth tellers than liars, resulting in differences between them.

Research has successfully demonstrated several ways to encourage truth tellers in particular to say more. One of them is being supportive as an interviewer. Being supportive during an interview facilitates talking and encourages cooperative witnesses (e.g. truth tellers) to provide more information (Bull, 2010; Fisher, 2010). In Mann et al. (2013) a second interviewer, who remained silent throughout the interview, was supportive throughout (e.g. nodding his head and smiling), suspicious throughout (e.g. frowning) or just neutral. Indeed, truth tellers provided the most detail in the supportive condition and only in that condition did they provide significantly more detail than liars.

A second way of increasing the amount of detail truth tellers generate is by providing interviewees with a model example. Interviewees have inadequate expectations about how much detail is expected from them (Fisher, 2010) and interviewees say less when they do not know the interviewer well (Fisher, 2010; Fisher, Milne & Bull, 2011). Investigators can alter the participants' expectations about how much detail is required by providing them with a model answer, as research has demonstrated (Leal, Vrij, Warmelink, Vernham, & Fisher, 2015). In the experiment, half of the participants listened to an audiotape in which someone gave a detailed account of an event unrelated to the event under investigation and were told that the audiotape should give them an idea of what a detailed account actually entails. In the control condition of the experiment no differences emerged between truth tellers and liars, but in the model statement condition truth tellers' statements sounded more plausible than liars' statements.

The use of drawings is a third way to encourage truth tellers to provide more information. Drawing has been introduced successfully to elicit differences between truth tellers and liars in sketching the layout of a room. The request to sketch the layout of a room implies that the interviewee has to convey spatial information (e.g. a bin needs to be positioned at an exact location in the room, such as at the left-hand side of the table), whereas such exact locations of an object are not a necessary requirement for a verbal description ('e.g. there was a table, there was a bin…'). Therefore when liars verbally describe a room and the objects in the room, they may be less specific about the location of the objects, but being vague is not an option when they sketch the room and its objects. Rather than sketching the objects in the wrong position, liars may prefer not to sketch the objects at all. In an occupation experiment truth tellers discussed their real occupation whereas liars discussed an occupation they pretended to have (Vrij, Mann, Leal, & Fisher, 2012). When asked to describe the layout of their office *verbally*, truth tellers' and liars' answers were equally detailed, but when asked to *sketch* the layout of their office, truth tellers' drawings were more detailed than liars' drawings.

Asking Unexpected Questions

A consistent finding in the deception literature is that liars prepare themselves for anticipated interviews. They do so by preparing possible answers to questions they expect to be asked (e.g. Hartwig, Granhag & Strömwall, 2007). This strategy of preparing answers for possible questions is successful, as planned lies typically contain fewer cues to deceit than spontaneous lies (DePaulo et al., 2003). However, preparing for answers has a limitation. It will be fruitful only if liars correctly anticipate which questions will be asked. Investigators can exploit this limitation by asking questions that liars do not anticipate. Though liars can refuse to answer unexpected questions by saying 'I don't know' or 'I can't remember', such responses will create suspicion if these questions are about central aspects of the target event. A liar, therefore, has little option other than to fabricate a plausible answer on the spot, which is cognitively demanding. One way proven to be successful in using the unexpected questions approach is by asking interviewees first expected questions followed by unexpected questions. Liars are likely to have prepared answers to the expected questions and may therefore be able to answer them in considerable detail. Liars will not have prepared answers for the unexpected questions and may therefore struggle to generate detailed answers to them. For truth tellers the unexpected questions will be equally unexpected. However, they should not find it more difficult to answer the unexpected questions. Indeed, in two experiments, where a mixture of expected and unexpected questions were asked, liars showed a larger decline in detail between anticipated and unanticipated questions than truth tellers (Lancaster, Vrij, Hope, & Waller, 2012; Warmelink, Vrij, Mann, Jundi, & Granhag, 2012).

The Strategic Use of Evidence

Liars (guilty suspects) and truth tellers (innocent suspects) generally enter interviews with different counterinterrogation strategies (Granhag & Hartwig, 2008). Research suggests that liars are inclined to use avoidance strategies (e.g. avoiding mentioning where they were at a certain time) or denial strategies (e.g. denying having been at a certain place at a certain time when asked directly). In contrast, truth tellers are generally more forthcoming and 'tell the truth like it happened' (Hartwig et al., 2007).

When investigators possess critical and possibly incriminating background information (evidence), they can exploit these differential truth tellers' and liars' strategies by introducing the available evidence during the interview in a strategic manner (the Strategic Use of Evidence technique, SUE). When questions about the evidence are asked, guilty suspects tend to use more avoidance strategies, whereas innocent suspects use more forthcoming strategies (Granhag & Hartwig, 2008); hence, innocent suspects' accounts will be more consistent with the available evidence than guilty suspects' accounts.

In one of the first SUE studies police trainees were taught to use some basic elements of the SUE technique. Results showed that participants who received training clearly outperformed their untrained colleagues: 85% versus 56% deception detection performance (Hartwig, Granhag, Strömwall, & Kronkvist, 2006). The SUE technique has been found to be successful in eliciting cues to deception for lying adults and lying children, for lying single suspects and lying multiple suspects, and for suspects lying about their past actions and lying about their intentions (Vrij & Granhag, 2012).

Lying in Witness Statements: Identifying Linguistic Strategies for Deception

Witness statements are a unique and valuable data in the study of the language of lying. They are products of highly stressful real-life situations where liars are motivated to succeed with their deception in order to avoid the serious consequences of the truth being known. Consequently, witness statements may therefore contain stronger and more pronounced verbal cues to deception compared to experimental situations when participants are given permission to lie (DePaulo et al., 2003; Mann, Vrij & Bull, 2002). However, the temporal and narrative nature of witness statements has implications for the identification of deception, which we explore in this part of the chapter.

Witness Statements in Context

A witness statement is defined as a written narrative relating to an event that the writer (victim, suspect or witness) allegedly has experienced. Such statements are either written by the witness him/ herself or by an attending investigator together with the witness as part of the information-gathering process of an investigation. In the

United Kingdom, it is normal procedure that the investigator writes the statement for the witness, where possible, using the witness' own words (Rock, 2001). These statements are never verbatim accounts and investigators make decisions what to include and what to leave out. As a result, the statements are very much a joint effort, a product of both witness' and investigator's input (Rock, 2001). However, there are certain situations (such as corporate internal fraud investigations) and some jurisdictions in the United States where witnesses are told to write their statements themselves in their own words, with little prompting from investigators other than to instruct 'write what happened' (Adams & Jarvis, 2006).

Witness statements fall under the Labovian definition of a narrative, being 'a report of a sequence of events that have entered into the biography of the speaker by a sequence of clauses that correspond to the original events' (Labov, 1997). However, witness statements are not simple reflections of events. Narrators re-interpret events in the light of their own social and emotional involvement, linguistically reconstructing reality according to their own personal perspective. Narrators select (and omit) incidents and re-order the narrative structure to create a chain of events that expresses their theory of causality. This sequentiality is a key characteristic of narratives as it is the sequence of its clauses rather than the truth or falsity of any single clause that gives meaning to characters and incidents in the plot (Bruner, 1990). For example, the meaning in the sentence *The man continued to swing his belt, and when we didn't back down, he swung the belt at Joe* would change if the sequence of clauses were reversed *He swung the belt at Joe, and when we didn't back down, the man continued to swing his belt*, giving a false impression of causality even though the information contained in the clauses is correct.

Verbal Cues to Deception

Approaches to linguistic deception detection work on the premise that people behave and communicate differently when they lie compared to when they are telling the truth and that behaviours triggered by emotions and cognitive pressures associated with high stakes lying 'leak' out into their language. However, to date, no single verbal cue or combination of verbal cues has emerged as consistently indicative of linguistic deception. In fact, the extensive verbal deception literature shows how unreliable cues are.

It has been argued that verbal cues are influenced by properties of the experiment. Factors such as type of stimuli (e.g. viewing videotapes versus web-based decision-making tasks) (Bond & Lee, 2005; Colwell, Hiscock-Anismas, Memon, Rachel, & Colwell, 2007; Zhou, Burgoon,

Nunamaker, & Twitchell, 2004), the choice of topic (highly emotional versus mundane) (Hancock, Curry, Goorha, & Woodworth, 2005; Newman, Pennebaker, Berry, & Richards, 2003), weak incentives to lie (Sporer, 1997; Zhou et al., 2004) and the experiment population (college students versus offenders) (Kassin, Meissner & Norwick, 2005; Porter & ten Brinke, 2010) may be responsible for contradictory results. For example, cues change according to differences in media (such as when lying in speech or in writing and when communicating through different types of computer-mediated technology) because they present different opportunities for planning and speed of response (real-time as in face-to-face and Instant Messaging or asynchronous as in emails and letters) (Burgoon, Blair, Qin, & Nunamaker, 2003; Woodworth, Hancock & Goorha, 2005; Zhou, Burgoon & Twitchell, 2003).

Verbal cues may also change along the span of the communication as deception is not a single act but a continuous process (Zhou, Burgoon & Twitchell, 2003), a progression of acts that happens over time (White & Burgoon, 2001). Zhou et al. found in their longitudinal analysis of language behaviour in emails that deceivers varied the number and type of verbal cues they used across different phases of their deception. This may have implications for the analysis of witness statements given the temporal nature of narratives.

Deception as a Narrative Progression

Anolli, Balconi and Ciceri (2002) argued that both truth tellers and liars use the same cognitive mechanisms and processes to plan their messages and both use a variety of linguistic strategies to communicate them. This involves managing expressions of information (beliefs, emotions, thoughts, etc.) using language patterns best suited to the contextual conditions and which communicators deliberately adopt in order to achieve specific effects on their addressees (Sperber & Wilson, 1986). The successive changes to language arising from information management and strategy selection identify the message's *internal gradient*, the linguistic route taken by the author in the construction of the communication package. During deception, the author's goal – to present false information as if it were true and remain undetected – and the context in which it is delivered exert a strong influence on the message's construction, encouraging the production of specific linguistic styles in the course of the communication (Anolli, Balconi & Ciceri, 2002). In seeking to lie by omitting, hiding or blurring the information, liars resort to a number of linguistic strategies, which differ from truth tellers and may be identified in witness statements through analysing narrative structure.

Studies into oral-type narratives (which include witness statements) found that authors manage information flow and facilitate their readers'

understanding of events by alerting them to discontinuity in the narrative, such as changes in thematic direction or gaps in the timeline
(Bestgen & Vonk, 2000; Prideaux, 2000). This is done through the use of
marked sentence structures, which signpost the change and mark the
start of a new discourse unit (*episode*). In English, sentences containing
a subordinate adverbial clause or phrase may be coded in two ways:
(1) in its normal (*unmarked*) form, where the *main clause* precedes the
subordinate adverbial clause (as in 1 below) and (2) in its rarer (*marked*)
form, where the *subordinate adverbial clause* precedes the *main clause*
(as in 2 below) (McEwen & Prideaux, 1997; Prideaux, 1989).

1. (a) We met with a larger group of friends after we got to the train
       station.
   (b) I got hit on the head with the belt at one point.
2. (a) After we got to the train station, we met with a larger group of
       friends.
   (b) At one point, I got hit on the head with the belt.

Using marked sentence structures to identify the start of a new
episode (and consequently the end of the previous episode) allows the
subdivision of narratives into its constituent discourse units, each of
which may be analysed for the presence (or absence) of verbal cues.
Analysing a narrative as a sequence of profiled units allows its internal
gradient to be mapped, and in turn facilitates identification of the
linguistic strategy adopted by the narrator.

Linguistic Styles of Deceptive Witness Statements

According to Picornell (2012a), two main linguistic strategies are associated with deception in witness statements: (i) *Prolix and Personal*
and (ii) *Impersonal*. These strategies are identified by analysing the
use of the following verbal cues: First Person Singular Pronouns (*I, me,
my, mine, myself*); Third Person Pronouns (*she, her(self), he, him(self),
it(self), they, them(selves), their(s)*); Negation (*no, not, never, none, nothing, no-one, nobody, nowhere*); Cognitive Verbs (describing a cognitive
function, e.g. *think, seem, appear, decide, hope, figure out*); Indefinite
Pronouns (e.g. *somebody, anyone, everything*) and Verb Strings (two
or more verbs functioning as a single verb, e.g. *tried to call, started
running, needed to see*). The pronouns *I, me* and *my* are also analysed
individually as self-references convey different relational information
and are not all equally weighted psychologically in their use (Pennebaker,
Mehl & Niederhoffer, 2003). While First Person Singular and Third
Person Pronouns identify an author's general focus of attention (*self* or
other), *I, me* and *my* identify more subtle perspectives of immediacy
and distancing. Negation, Cognitive Verbs, Indefinite Pronouns and Verb

Strings serve as ambiguity cues, allowing deceivers to be non-committal by generating evasive negation (saying what they did not know of did not do), non-specific language and subjective information.

The first strategy associated with deception is the *Prolix and Personal* approach. This style is verbose and immediate, defined by very high use of First Person Singular Pronouns in at least half of the clauses in a statement, of which at least 10% contain use of *my*. However, the impression of immediacy is an illusion. Although self-references are used extensively throughout the statement, the information associated with them is subjective or difficult to confirm, made unclear by use of ambiguity cues (in at least a quarter of the clauses). Liars compensate by providing much detail of their possessions and parts of their own body, resorting to frequent use of *my* (e.g. *my hair, my head, my forehead*).

In this strategy, liars are cooperatively vague, appearing helpful by providing plenty of information about the situation in which they maintain a presence but which is rendered safe through irrelevancy and ambiguity.

---

*at that time **I noticed** the passenger getting out of the car and walking towards us. He **wasn't** running at **me** or **anything** but kinda like coming out to check out what was going on with his buddy or **something** like that.*

*the driver pushed **me** and hit **me**. **I** hit him back and then we were just kind grabbing arms and wrestling around. Then **I** felt **something** hit **me** and **I** saw stars.*

*Next thing **I remember** it the driver on top of **me** punching **me** around **my** chest and **I trying to grab** arms. **I** held his right arm but he was still moving it like a punching motion. He was hitting around **my** left side and **I** felt **something** cold. He **went to hit me** again and **something** cut the palm of **my** left hand and it scared the hell out **me** so **I** grabbed my side curled up and **started yelling** and screaming. **I think** they kicked **me** a little (but **I'm not** sure) but he got off **me** and left **me** alone for a second.*

*Then **someone** grabbed **my** wallet (right back pocket) and they **started to leave**. **I didn't** move or make a noise and **one** came back grabbed **my** hair lifted **my** head and cut **my** forehead and said 'little bitch'.*

This verbose but non-committal strategy has been described in earlier literature (Buller & Burgoon, 1994; Hancock et al., 2005; Knapp, Hart & Dennis, 1974). Anolli et al. (2002) suggested that this combination of verbosity and vagueness in interpersonal deception is the likely strategy adopted by liars facing unresponsive or gullible addressees. In the monologue context of written witness statements, it may be that the absence of an addressee produces the same effect.

The second deceptive strategy is an *Impersonal* approach. This presents a strong *Other* focus characterized by overall a very high use of Third Person Pronouns (in at least half the clauses). As the narrative progresses, the author become increasingly represented by *my* and/ or *me*, whose overall combined use comes close to equalling or even surpassing that of *I*.

> At 13.45 *I* left to go back to work. A man ran out of the alley and fell down. *I* thought maybe *I* hit *him* but *I* didn't hit *him*. *I* started to check on him and *he* pushed *me* in *my* car and
>   then made *me* drive
>   then *he* told *me* to stop crying. *He* told *me* to stop the car. *He* took tape out and put *it* on *my* hands and then *he* cut *my* lips with *his* knife and then put tape on *my* face. *He* cut *my* dress. *He* was mad cuz *he* said *his* damn knife was dull. *He* wanted a souvenir and *he* couldn't get but *he* cut *my* hair. *He* started driving and called someone and said to meet *him* at that place. *He* locked *my* keys in *my* car and then a white van came and got *him*. *I* waited for a while and
>   then *I* started to walk.
>   *I* tried to kick *him* and *he* grabbed *my* leg and *my* hose tore. *He* said stop that.

In this strategy, clauses tend to be short and the language direct. Liars have no need to hide behind ambiguity as their purpose is to direct readers' focus towards a third party and to reduce their own presence to a minimum. This strategy has also previously been identified in an interpersonal communication context and referred to as *depersonalization* (Anolli et al., 2002; Buller & Burgoon, 1994).

There is converging evidence to suggest that these strategies may be used to identify deceivers. Changes in the use of first person pronouns, particularly decreasing use but also sometimes increasing use (e.g. Ebesu & Miller, 1994), has been shown for statements by suspects (Jensen, Bessarabova, Adame, Burgoon, & Slowik, 2011), witnesses (Newman et al., 2003), prisoners (Bond & Lee, 2005) and online daters (Toma & Hancock, 2010). It has also been shown to differentiate liars that occur outside of the criminal process, such as those who fake TripAdvisor reviews (Ott, Coi, Cardie, & Hancock, 2011) and insiders who deceive co-workers about their true intentions within an organization (Taylor et al., 2013). Similarly, evidence supports the language correlates proposed for the verbose but non-committal strategy and the impersonal strategy. For example, Miller (2008) found that witnesses coming forward with person-of-interest reporting tended to use more generalized terms than truth tellers. Similarly, several researchers have shown that increased third person pronoun use is associated with deception (Newman et al., 2003; ten Brinke, MacDonald, Porter, & O'Conner, 2012).

Recently, Picornell (2012b) examined the value of these strategies within the narrative framework, using statements supplied by an American police force that routinely required witnesses to write their own statements. The statements all related to serious crime (e.g. arson, rape, robbery, child abuse) and were selected on the basis of case resolution (through law enforcement investigation, evidence of other witnesses, forensic evidence and court decisions on the basis of witness and/or forensic evidence), which determined their truth or falsity. The findings revealed that, although no single verbal cue was specifically related to deception, multiple cues became diagnostic if the way language unfolds in a narrative was taken into account. Picornell (2012b) concluded that, in the context of written witness statements, deception may be identified not so much by which verbal cues are used but how they are used.

INTERPERSONAL PROCESSES AND DECEPTION

So far, the focus of this chapter has been on the changes in language shown by an individual liar. However, researchers are increasingly interested in the interpersonal aspect of communication and its impact on when and how liars give themselves away. Early evidence for the importance of interpersonal dynamics comes from research testing Interpersonal Deception Theory (Buller & Burgoon, 1996), which argues that cues to deception will result principally from changes in the dynamic of the conversation rather than from changes in a liar's internal state. For example, Burgoon, Buller, Guerrero, Afifi, and Feldman (1996) demonstrated that others perceive deceptive responders as less conversationally complete in their presentation style compared to truth tellers. Conversational completeness was defined by and (absence) of language features that are the 'role obligations' of parties engaging in dialogue (e.g. backfeeds). Similarly, Burgoon, Buller, White, Afifi, and Buslig (1999) demonstrated that deceivers manipulate the degree of expressivity the provider influences, particularly when they have the social skill to do so and particularly when the interviewer shows detachment that leads them to question their believability. A liar's behaviour is a direct function of their questioner's behaviour.

The importance of interpersonal dynamics to the relationship between language and deception has since been demonstrated at several levels. At a strategic level, it is evidenced by the influence that questioning style (Snook, Luther, Quinlan, & Milne, 2012) and use of interpersonal tactics (Beune, Giebels & Taylor, 2010) have on a suspect's willingness to provide information and confess. For example, Granhag, Montecinos and Oleszkiewicz (in press) demonstrated that interviewers who adopt a friendly, confident, conversational style to their questioning were able to elicit information from liars without them realizing. Similar evidence is beginning to emerge for the importance of including rapport-building communication during early stages of an interview (Abbe & Brandon, 2014).

Perhaps more important, however, is evidence that suggests the association between veracity and language plays out at the level of basic conversational processes. One important process is communication accommodation (Coupland and Giles, 1988), which occurs when speakers increase or decrease the social distance between themselves and another by adjusting the content and timing of their speech (Cappella & Panalp, 1981). In the Cognitive Interview framework, such accommodation is referred to as the 'principle of synchrony' and is believed to promote cooperation (Walsh & Bull, 2012). Consistent with this idea, Richardson, Taylor, Snook, Conchie, and Bennell (2014) have shown that, over time, suspects who confess tend to accommodate to the language style of their interviewer to a greater extent than those who do not confess. Barker et al. (2008) have demonstrated the relationship between high accommodation and citizen's trust in, and willingness to cooperate with, the police. Finally, Dunbar et al. (2011) have shown that liars show significantly lower accommodation ('verbal synchrony' in the researchers' coding) than truth tellers during periods of accusatory questioning, but not during periods of background questioning or suspicious questioning. This finding suggests that there is a direct association between accommodation and the amount of pressure placed on the suspect by the interviewer.

The basis for the association between language accommodation and veracity has recently been explored by Taylor et al. (2013), who examined the way in which insiders trying to steal sensitive information change their communication with co-workers. Taylor et al. argued that the act of conducting an insider attack is characterized by cognitive and social challenges that may affect the insider's self-focus, clarity of thought and sociability in ways that may leak into the insider's language choices. To test this idea, they ran a series of one-day work simulations in which three teams of four employees worked together in four one-hour sessions in which they were required to assimilate information and problem solve. After the first session, which served as a control, one person in each team was offered a financial reward in return for information. Once they had agreed to act, the insiders showed a reduction in the extent to which they matched the language style of co-workers. Moreover, their matching became significantly lower than the average matching found among non-malicious co-workers. This reduction, which suggests an inadvertent social distancing by the insiders, increased over time, such that by the end of session four, it was possible to use this metric in a statistical model to identify 92.6% of insiders.

As well as revealing deceit, some evidence emerged suggesting that communication accommodation can impact suspects' use of language in a way that might lead to different judgements of veracity. It has long been known that accommodation is not simply a process of choice and that the lexical, syntactic and semantic choices of one person can influence the choices of their interlocutor (Pickering & Ferreira, 2008; Santesteban, Pickering & Mclean, 2010). Recently, Richardson and Taylor (2013) examined the extent to which such priming effects can influence the degree to which suspects present verbal cues traditionally associated with deception. By having interviewers vary their question construction in such a way that they emphasized either personal pronouns, affective language, perceptual language (i.e. contextual embedding) or negations, Richardson and Taylor were able to shape the way in which truth tellers and liars communicated their experience (or fabricated experience). The nature of interviewers' questions shaped the content of interviewees' responses to a degree that impacted subsequent judgements of veracity based on a Criteria Based Content Analysis, suggesting that priming can have a significant practical impact on judgements of veracity.

Cultural Differences in Verbal Deception

Basic conversational processes such as those described in the previous section are shaped by interpersonal norms and expectations. Within the deception literature, one set of norms that have been shown to have a dramatic impact on language use originates from the speaker's culture. Such norms include differences in turn-taking etiquette (Gumperz, 1982), differences in expressions of emotions and memories (Scherer, Banse & Wallbott, 2001) and differences in beliefs about how to interact with authority figures (Rosenquist & Megargee, 1970). In everyday conversations, these norms make the complex of interaction possible by simplifying the task of anticipating and making sense of one's interlocutor. In cross-cultural interaction, however, the inferences that are made on the basis of norms are often inappropriate and lead to misunderstandings and suspicion (Black & Mendenhall, 1990).

In their review of cross-cultural deception detection, Taylor, Larner, Conchie, and Van der Zee (2014) highlight eight common communicative errors that stem from these differences in language expectations. They are differences in: (i) the expectation for small talk; (ii) role expectations; (iii) expectation for dialogue that fits a story-telling framework; (iv) the giving and feedback of empathy; (v) the use of rationale persuasion; (vi) the use of ultimatums; (vii) the use of resistance; and (iv) issues of face. Each of these factors are responsible for misunderstandings in cross-cultural communication and can lead honest communicators to be perceived as liars. For example, many cultures are accustomed to recalling memories in a narrative style, which feature lengthy descriptions of background, deviations into other stories and the expectation of participation (e.g. questioning) from the listener. To a Western interviewer, who seeks to ascertain a linear account of what occurred during the period of the crime, such story-telling can be frustrating and may appear evasive (Cook-Gumperz & Gumperz, 2002). Similarly, while identifying inconsistencies, debating relative values and pointing out the absence of evidence are characteristic of an interview approach that is successful in cultures where communication focuses on message content (e.g. North American), it is an approach that is far less successful amongst cultures who resolve conflicts in ways that are less direct (e.g. East Asia; Beune, Giebels & Taylor, 2010; Giebels & Taylor, 2009). This can appear avoidant and suspicious to somebody who expects debate to be central to the interaction (Moston & Engelberg, 1993).

Given the differences identified by Taylor et al. (2014), which span differences in self-construal, episodic memory and social dynamics, it is not surprising that researchers have observed cross-cultural differences in deceivers' behaviour. For example, while the primary concern within individualistic cultures is the self, there is far greater focus on the social group than with collectivist cultures (Oyserman, 2002). Similarly, research suggests that individualistic cultures base their memories around objects and perceptual stimuli, while collectivist cultures focus far more on relationships and social hierarchies (Markus & Kitayama, 1991). These differences have important implications for practices that associate self-references (e.g. use of first person pronouns) and contextual embedding (e.g. inclusion of perceptual details) with genuine accounts (e.g. criteria based content analysis; Vrij, 2005).

In an early examination of cultural differences, Taylor et al. (2014) collected 60 true and 60 false accounts of an experience from four cultural groups (Arabian, Pakistani, North African and White British) and compared those statements on categories of language affect, the extent of negations and the provision of spatial information (as a proxy for contextual embedding). The extent of positive affect shown by participants was predictive of deception across all cultures, with an elevated positive affect occurring more in deceptive than genuine accounts. However, critically, the degree of spatial information shown by participants was culturally dependent, with White British and (to a lesser extent) Arabian participants decreasing the amount of spatial information included in their lie, but Pakistani and (to a lesser extent) North African participants increasing the amount included in their lie. This occurs, they argue, because Pakistani and North African participants give less relational information in their lie (which they would include if drawing on a genuine memory) and this brings perceptual detail to the fore.

A final impact of culture and language relates to how people judge suspects speaking in their first or second language. Cheng and Broadhurst (2005) had Cantonese and English postgraduate students make judgements about the veracity of statements when giving an opinion on capital punishment. Compared to statements given in their native language, a statement given by a speaker in their second language was more likely to be identified as a lie. The effect of this bias in judgements of second language accounts was to remove the 'truth bias' that is typically observed in deception judgements. That is, when assessing somebody speaking in their second language, judges increase their capacity to correctly identify liars, but they also make more false accusations of truth tellers. Da Silva and Leach (2013) have shown a similar result when comparing native-language speakers to second-language speakers. Their participants were more likely to exhibit a truth bias when observing native-language speakers, whereas they were more likely to exhibit a lie bias when viewing second-language speakers. As these examples illustrate, the cues present in language are being interpreted using a cultural lens that is inappropriate to the judgement being made.

CONCLUSION

This chapter presented a wealth of approaches to examine speech in relation to deception. We discussed existing verbal veracity tools, interview styles aimed at eliciting verbal cues to deceit, an analysis of deceptive linguistic strategies and the interpersonal aspect of communication and its impact on when and how liars give themselves away. We started this chapter by saying that practitioners tend to pay more attention to non-verbal behaviour than to speech when they attempt to detect deceit. We hope that this chapter will encourage them to take speech content into account.

REFERENCES

Abbe, A., & Brandon, S. (2014). Building and maintaining rapport in investigative interviews. *Police Practice and Research: An International Journal, 15*, 207–220.

Adams, S. H., & Jarvis, J. P. (2006). Indicators of veracity and deception: an analysis of written statements made to police. *International Journal of Speech, Language and the Law, 13*, 1–22.

Aguinis, H., Pierce, C. A., & Quigley, B. M. (2006). Conditions under which a bogus pipeline procedure enhances the validity of self-reported cigarette smoking: A meta-analysis review. *Journal of Applied Social Psychology, 23*, 352–373.

Anolli, L., Balconi, M., & Ciceri, R. (2002). Deceptive Miscommunication Theory (DeMiT): A new model for the analysis of deceptive communication. In L. Anolli, R. Ciceri, & G. Riva (Eds.), *Say not to say: New perspectives in miscommunication* (pp. 73–100). Amsterdam, The Netherlands: IOS Press.

Barker, V., Giles, H., Hajek, C., Ota, H., Noels, K., Lim, T.-S., & Somera, L. (2008). Police–civilian interaction, compliance, accommodation, and trust in an intergroup context: International data. *Journal of International and Intercultural Communication, 1*, 93–112. doi: 10.1080/175-1-305-080189-1986

Bestgen, Y., & Vonk, W. (2000). Temporal adverbials as segmentation markers in discourse comprehension. *Journal of Memory and Language, 42*, 74–87.

Beune, K., Giebels, E., & Taylor, P. J. (2010). Patterns of interaction in police interviews: The role of cultural dependency. *Criminal Justice and Behavior, 37*, 904–925.

Black, J. S., & Mendenhall, M. (1990). Cross-cultural training effectiveness: A review and a theoretical framework for future research. *Academy of Management Review, 15*, 113–136.

Bond, G. D., & Lee, A. Y. (2005). Language of lies in prison: Linguistic classification of prisoners' truthful and deceptive natural language. *Applied Cognitive Psychology, 19*, 313–329.

Bruner, J. (1990). *Acts of Meaning*. Cambridge, MA: Harvard University Press.

Bull, R. (2010). The investigative interviewing of children and other vulnerable witnesses: Psychological research and working/professional practice. *Legal and Criminological Psychology, 15*, 5–24.

Buller, D. B., & Burgoon, J. K. (1994). Deception: Strategic and nonstrategic communications. In J. A. Daly & J. M. Wieman (Eds.), *Strategic interpersonal communication* (pp. 191–223). Hillsdale, NJ: Erlbaum.

Buller, D. B., & Burgoon, J. K. (1996). Interpersonal deception theory. *Communication Theory, 6*, 203–242.

Burgoon, J. K., Blair, J. P., Qin, T., & Nunamaker Jr, J. F. (2003). Detecting deception through linguistic analysis. In *Proceedings of the symposium on intelligence and security informatics*. New York: Springer-Verlag.

Burgoon, J. K., Buller, D. B., Guerrero, L. K., Afifi, W., & Feldman, C. (1996). Interpersonal deception: XII. Information management dimensions underlying deceptive and truthful messages. *Communication Monographs, 63*, 50–69.

Burgoon, J. K., Buller, D. B., White, C. H., Afifi, W., & Buslig, A. L. S. (1999). The role of conversational involvement in deceptive interpersonal interactions. *Personality and Social Psychology Bulletin, 25*, 669–686. doi: 10.1177/0146167299025006003

Cappella, J. N., & Panalp, S. (1981). Talk and silence in sequences in informal conversations: Interspeaker influence. *Human Communication Research, 7,* 117–132.

Cohen, J. (1988). *Statistical power analysis for the behavioral sciences* (2nd ed.). Hillsdale, NJ: Erlbaum.

Colwell, K., Hiscock-Anismas, C., Memon, A., Rachel, A., & Colwell, L. (2007). Vividness and spontaneity of statement detail characteristics as predictors of witness credibility. *American Journal of Forensic Psychology, 25,* 5–30.

Cook-Gumperz, J., & Gumperz, J. (2002). Narrative accounts in gatekeeping interviews: Intercultural differences or common misunderstandings? *Language and Intercultural Communication, 2,* 25–36.

Coupland, N., & Giles, N. (1998). Introduction: The communicative contexts of accommodation. *Language and Communication, 8,* 175–182.

Da Silva, C. S., & Leach, A. M. (2011). Detecting deception in second-language speakers. *Legal and Criminological Psychology, 18,* 115–127.

DePaulo, B. M., & Kirkendol, S. E. (1989). The motivational impairment effect in the communication of deception. In J. C. Yuille (Ed.), *Credibility assessment* (pp. 51–70). Dordrecht, The Netherlands: Kluwer.

DePaulo, B. M., Lindsay, J. L., Malone, B. E., Muhlenbruck, L., Charlton, K., & Cooper, H. (2003). Cues to deception. *Psychological Bulletin, 129,* 74–118.

Driscoll, L. N. (1994). A validity assessment of written statements from suspects in criminal investigations using the SCAN technique. *Police Studies, 17,* 77–88.

Dunbar, N. E., Jensen, M. L., Burgoon, J. E., Bradley, Adame, K. J., Roberston, K. M., & Kelley, L. H. (2011). A dyadic approach to the detection of deception. In *Proceedings of the credibility assessment and information quality in government and business symposium,* Koloa, HI.

Ebesu, A. S., & Miller, M. D. (1994). Verbal and nonverbal behaviors as a function of deception type. *Journal of Language and Social Psychology, 13,* 418–442. doi: 10.1177/0261927X94134004

Evans, J. R., Michael, S. W., Meissner, C. A., & Brandon, S. E. (2013). Validating a new assessment method for deception detection: Introducing a psychologically based credibility assessment tool. *Journal of Applied Research in Memory and Cognition, 2,* 33–41. doi: 10.1016/j.jarmac.2013.02.002

Fisher, R. P. (2010). Interviewing cooperative witnesses. *Legal and Criminological Psychology, 15,* 25–38.

Fisher, R., Milne, R., & Bull, R. (2011). Interviewing cooperative witnesses. *Current Directions in Psychological Science, 20,* 16–19.

Geiselman, R. E., & Callot, R. (1990). Reverse and forward order recall of script based text. *Applied Cognitive Psychology, 4,* 141–144.

Giebels, E., & Taylor, P. J. (2009). Interaction patterns in crisis negotiations: Persuasive arguments and cultural differences. *Journal of Applied Psychology, 94,* 5–19.

Gilbert, J. A. E., & Fisher, R. P. (2006). The effects of varied retrieval cues on reminiscence in eyewitness memory. *Applied Cognitive Psychology, 20,* 723–739.

Granhag, P. A., & Hartwig, M. (2008). A new theoretical perspective on deception detection: On the psychology of instrumental mind-reading. *Psychology, Crime and Law, 14,* 189–200.

Granhag, P. A., Montecions, S. C., & Oleszkiewicz, S. (in press). Eliciting intelligence from sources: The first scientific test of the Scharff technique. *Legal and Criminological Psychology.* doi:10.1111/lcrp.12015

Gumperz, J. (1982). *Discourse strategies*. Cambridge, UK: Cambridge University Press.

Hancock, J. T., Curry, L., Goorha, S., & Woodworth, M. (2005). Automated linguistic analysis of deceptive and truthful synchronous computer-mediated communication. In *38th Hawaii international conference on systems sciences*, pp. 22c.

Hartwig, M., Granhag, P. A., & Strömwall, L. (2007). Guilty and innocent suspects' strategies during interrogations. *Psychology, Crime and Law, 13*, 213–227.

Hartwig, M., Granhag, P. A., Strömwall, L., & Kronkvist, O. (2006). Strategic use of evidence during police interrogations: When training to detect deception works. *Law and Human Behavior, 30*, 603–619.

Inbau, F. E., Reid, J. E., Buckley, J. P., & Jayne, B. C. (2013). *Criminal interrogation and confessions* (5th ed.). Burlington, MA: Jones & Bartlett Learning.

Jensen, M. L., Bessarabova, E., Adame, B., Burgoon, J. K., & Slowik, S. M. (2011). Deceptive language by innocent and guilty criminal suspects: The influence of dominance, question, and guilt on interview responses. *Journal of Language and Social Psychology, 30*, 357–375.

Johnson, M. K. (2006). Memory and reality. *American Psychologist, 61*, 760–771. doi: 10.1037/0003-066X.61.8.760

Johnson, M. K., & Raye, C. L. (1981). Reality monitoring. *Psychological Review, 88*, 67–85.

Johnson, M. K., & Raye, C. L. (1998). False memories and confabulation. *Trends in Cognitive Sciences, 2*, 137–146.

Kassin, S. M., Meissner, C. A., & Norwick, R. J. (2005). 'I'd know a false confession if I saw one': A comparative study of college students and police investigators. *Law and Human Behavior, 29*, 211–227.

Knapp, M. L., Hart, R. P., & Dennis, H. S. (1974). An exploration of deception as a communication construct, *Human Communication Research, 1*, 15–29.

Köhnken, G. (1996). Social psychology and the law. In G. R. Semin & K. Fiedler (Eds.), *Applied social psychology* (pp. 257–282). London, UK: Sage Publications.

Köhnken, G. (2004). Statement validity analysis and the 'detection of the truth'. In P. A. Granhag & L. A. Strömwall (Eds.), *Deception detection in forensic contexts* (pp. 41–63). Cambridge, UK: Cambridge University Press.

Köhnken, G., & Steller, M. (1988). The evaluation of the credibility of child witness statements in the German procedural system. *Issues in Criminological and Legal Psychology, 13*, 37–45.

Labov, W. (1997). Some further steps in narrative analysis. *The Journal of Narrative and Life History, 7*, 395–415.

Lancaster, G. L. J., Vrij, A., Hope, L., & Waller, B. (2012). Sorting the liars from the truth tellers: The benefits of asking unanticipated questions. *Applied Cognitive Psychology, 27*, 107–114. doi: 10.1002/acp.2879

Leal, S., Vrij, A., Warmelink, L., Vernham, Z., & Fisher, R. P. (2015). You can't hide your telephone lies: Providing a model statement as an aid to detect deception in insurance telephone calls. *Legal and Criminological Psychology, 20*, 129–146.

Mann, S., Vrij, A., & Bull, R. (2002). Suspects, lies, and videotape: An analysis of authentic high-stakes liars. *Law and Human Behaviour, 26*, 365–376.

Mann, S., Vrij, A., Shaw, D., Leal, S., Ewens, S., Hillman, J., Granhag, P. A., & Fisher, R. P. (2013). Two heads are better than one? How to effectively use two interviewers to elicit cues to deception. *Legal and Criminological Psychology, 18*, 324–340. doi: 10.1111/j.2044-8333.2012.02055.x

Markus, H., & Kitayama, S. (1991). Culture and the self: Implications for cognition, emotion, and motivation. *Psychological Review, 98*, 224–253.

Masip, J., & Ces, C. (2011). Guilty and innocent suspects' self-reported strategies during an imagined police interview. Paper presented at *The 4th international congress on psychology and law*, Miami, FL.

Masip, J., Sporer, S. L., Garrido, E., & Herrero, C. (2005). The detection of deception with the reality monitoring approach: A review of the empirical evidence. *Psychology, Crime and Law, 11*, 99–122. doi:10.1080/10683160410 001726356

McEwen, S., & Prideaux, G. D. (1997). The development of marked structures to code episode boundaries. *Journal of the Canadian Association of Applied Linguistics, 19*, 49–59.

Mehrabian, A. (1971). *Silent messages* (1st ed.). Belmont, CA: Wadsworrth.

Miller, C. M. (2008). *High-stakes, real-world deception: An examination of the process of deception and deception detection using linguistic-based cues* (Unpublished PhD thesis), Oklahoma State University, Stillwater, OK.

Moston, S., & Engelberg, T. (1993). Police questioning techniques in tape recorded interviews with criminal suspects. *Policing and Society, 6*, 61–75.

Nahari, G., Leal, S., Vrij, A., Warmelink, L., & Vernham, Z. (2014). Did somebody see it? Applying the verifiability approach to insurance claims interviews. *Journal of Investigative Psychology and Offender Profiling, 11*, 237–243. doi:10.1002/jip.1417

Nahari, G., & Vrij, A. (2014). Can I borrow your alibi? The applicability of the verifiability approach to the case of an alibi witness. *Journal of Applied Research in Memory and Cognition, 3*, 89–94. doi:org /10.1016/J/ Jarmac.2014.04.005

Nahari, G., Vrij, A., & Fisher, R. P. (2012). Does the truth come out in the writing? Scan as a lie detection tool. *Law and Human Behavior, 36*, 68–76. doi:10.1037/h0093965

Nahari, G., Vrij, A., & Fisher, R. (2014a). Exploiting liars' verbal strategies by examining unverifiable details. *Legal and Criminological Psychology, 19*, 227–239. doi:10.1111/j.2044-8333.2012.02069.x

Nahari, G., Vrij, A., & Fisher, R. P. (2014b). The verifiability approach: Countermeasures facilitate its ability to discriminate between truths and lies. *Applied Cognitive Psychology, 28*, 122–128. doi:10.1002/acp.2974

Navarro, J. (2008). *What every BODY is saying*. New York: Harper-Collins Publishers.

Newman, M. L., Pennebaker, J. W., Berry, D. S., & Richards, J. M. (2003). Lying words: Predicting deception from linguistic styles. *Personality and Social Psychology Bulletin, 29*, 547–675.

Ott, M., Coi, Y., Cardie, C., & Hancock, J. T. (2011). Finding deceptive opinion spam by any stretch of the imagination. *Proceedings of ACL 2011: HTL*, pp. 309–319. eprint: arXiv:1107.4557.

Oyserman, D. (2002). Rethinking individualism and collectivism. *Psychological Bulletin, 128*, 3–72.

Pennebaker, J. W., Mehl, M. R., & Niederhoffer, K. G. (2003). Psychological aspects of natural language use: our words our selves. *Annual Review of Psychology, 54*, 547–577.

Pickering, M. J., & Ferreira, V. S. (2008). Structural priming: A critical review. *Psychological Bulletin, 134*, 427–459.

Picornell, I. (2012a). The rake's progress: Linguistic strategies for deception. In *Proceedings of the IAFL 10th Biennial conference* (pp. 153–168), Centre for Forensic Linguistics, Aston University, Birmingham, UK.

Picornell, I. C. (2012b). *Cues to deception in a textual narrative context* (Unpublished thesis), Aston University, Birmingham, UK. Available for download from British Library EThOS.

Porter, S., & ten Brinke, L. (2010). The truth about lies: What works in detecting high-stakes deception? *Legal and Criminological Psychology, 15*, 57–75.

Prideaux, G. D. (1989). Text data as evidence for language processing principles: The grammar of ordered events. *Language Sciences, 11*, 27–42.

Prideaux, G. D. (2000). Discourse analysis and psycholinguistics: Breaking down barriers. *LACUS Forum, 26*, 1–16.

Richardson, B., & Taylor, P. J. (2013). The effect of linguistic priming on cues to deception. Presentation to be given at the European Association of Psychology and Law Conference, Coventry, UK.

Richardson, B., Taylor, P. J., Snook, B., Conchie, S. M., & Bennell, C. (2014). Language style matching and confessions in police interrogation outcome. *Law and Human Behavior, 38*, 357–366. doi: 10.1037/lhb0000077

Rock, F. (2001). The genesis of a witness statement. *International Journal of Speech, Language and the Law, 8*, 44–72.

Rosenquist, C. M., & Megargee, E. I. (1970). *Delinquency in three cultures.* Austin, TX: University of Texas Press.

Ruby, C. L., & Brigham, J. C. (1998). Can criteria-based content analysis distinguish between true and false statements of African-American speakers? *Law and Human Behavior, 22*, 369–388.

Santesteban, M., Pickering, M. J., & Mclean, J. F. (2010). Lexical and phonological effects on syntactic processing: Evidence from syntactic priming. *Journal of Memory and Language, 63*, 347–366.

Sapir, A. (1987/2000). *The LSI course on Scientific Content Analysis (SCAN).* Phoenix, AZ: Laboratory for Scientific Interrogation.

Scherer, K. R., Banse, R., & Wallbott, H. G. (2001). Emotion inferences from vocal expression correlates across languages and cultures. *Journal of Cross-Cultural Psychology, 32*, 76–92.

Snook, B., Luther, K., Quinlan, H., & Milne, R. (2012). Let 'em talk! A field study of police questioning practices of suspects and accused persons. *Criminal Justice and Behavior, 39*, 1328–1339.

Sperber, D., & Wilson, D. (1986). *Relevance: Communication and cognition.* Oxford, UK: Oxford University Press.

Sporer, S. L. (1997). The less travelled road to truth: Verbal cues in deception detection in accounts of fabricated and self-experienced events. *Applied Cognitive Psychology, 11*, 373–397.

Steller, M., & Köhnken, G. (1989). Criteria-based content analysis. In D. C. Raskin (Ed.), *Psychological methods in criminal investigation and evidence* (pp. 217–245). New York: Springer-Verlag.

Taylor, P. J., Dando, C. J., Ormerod, T. C., Ball, L. J., Jenkins, M. C., Sandham, A., & Menacere, T. (2013). Detecting insiders threats through language change. *Law and Human Behavior, 37*, 267–275. doi:10.1037/lhb0000032

Taylor, P. J., Larner, S., Conchie, S. M., & Van der Zee, S. (2014). Cross-cultural deception detection. In P. A. Granhag, A. Vrij and B. J. Verschuere (Eds.), *Detecting deception: Current challenges and cognitive approaches.* Chichester, UK: Wiley Blackwell.

ten Brinke, L., MacDonald, S., Porter, S., & O'Conner, S. (2012). Crocodile tears: Facial, verbal and body language behaviors associated with genuine and fabricated remorse. *Law and Human Behavior, 36*, 51–59. doi:10.1007/s10979-011-9265-5

Toma, C., & Hancock, J. (2010). Reading between the lines: Linguistic cues to deception in online dating profiles. In *CSCW proceedings of the ACM conference on computer-supported cooperative work* (pp. 5–8), New York.

Trankell, A. (1963). *Vittnespsykologins Arbetsmetoder*. Stockholm, Sweden: Liber.

Undeutsch, U. (1967). Beurteilung der Glaubhaftigkeit von Aussagen. In U. Undeutsch (Ed.), *Handbuch der Psychologie Vol. 11: Forensische Psychologie* (pp. 26–181). Göttingen, Germany: Hogrefe.

Vrij, A. (2005). Criteria-based content analysis: A qualitative review of the first 37 studies. *Psychology, Public Policy and Law, 11*, 3–41.

Vrij, A. (2008a). *Detecting lies and deceit: Pitfalls and opportunities* (2nd ed.). Chichester, UK: John Wiley & Sons, Ltd.

Vrij, A. (2008b). Nonverbal dominance versus verbal accuracy in lie detection: A plea to change police practice. *Criminal Justice and Behavior, 35*, 1323–1336.

Vrij, A. (2014). Myths and opportunities in verbal and nonverbal lie detection. In M. St-Yves (Ed.), *Investigative interviewing: The essential*. Toronto, ON, Canada: Thomson Reuters.

Vrij, A. (2015a). A cognitive approach to lie detection. In P. A. Granhag, A. Vrij, & B. J. Verschuere (Eds.), *Detection deception: Current challenges and cognitive approaches* (pp. 205–229). Chichester, UK: John Wiley & Sons, Ltd.

Vrij, A. (2015b). Verbal lie detection tools: Statement validity analysis, reality monitoring and scientific content analysis. In P. A. Granhag, A. Vrij, & B. J. Verschuere (Eds.), *Detection deception: Current challenges and cognitive approaches* (pp. 3–36). Chichester, UK: John Wiley & Sons, Ltd.

Vrij, A., & Granhag, P. A. (2012). Eliciting cues to deception and truth: What matters are the questions asked. *Journal of Applied Research in Memory and Cognition, 1*, 110–117.

Vrij, A., Fisher, R., Mann, S., & Leal, S. (2008a). A cognitive load approach to lie detection. *Journal of Investigative Psychology and Offender Profiling, 5*, 39–43.

Vrij, A., Mann, S., Fisher, R., Leal, S., Milne, B., & Bull, R. (2008b). Increasing cognitive load to facilitate lie detection: The benefit of recalling an event in reverse order. *Law and Human Behavior, 32*, 253–265.

Vrij, A., Mann, S., Leal, S., & Fisher, R. (2012). Is anyone out there? Drawings as a tool to detect deception in occupations interviews. *Psychology, Crime and Law, 18*, 377–388.

Walsh, D., & Bull, R. (2012). How do interviewers attempt to overcome suspects' denials. *Psychiatry, Psychology and Law, 19*, 151–168. doi:10.1080/13218719.2010.543756

Warmelink, L., Vrij, A., Mann, S., Jundi, S., & Granhag, P. A. (2012). Have you been there before? The effect of experience and question expectedness on lying about intentions. *Acta Psychologica, 141*, 178–183.

White, C. H., & Burgoon, J. K. (2001). Adaptation and communicative design: Patterns of interaction in truthful and deceptive conversation. *Human Communication Research, 27*, 9–37.

Woodworth, M., Hancock, J., & Goorha, S. (2005). The motivational enhancement effect: Implications for our chosen modes of communication in the 21st century. In *38th Hawaii international conference on systems sciences* (pp. 22a).

Zhou, L., Burgoon, J. K., & Twitchell, D. P. (2003). A longitudinal analysis of language behaviour of deception in email. *Intelligence and Security Informatics, 2665*, 102–110.

Zhou, L., Burgoon, J. K., Nunamaker Jr, J. F., & Twitchell, D. (2004). Automating linguistic based cues for deception detection in text based asynchronous computer mediated communication. *Group Decisions and Negotiation, 13*, 81–106.

Zhou, L., Twitchell, D. P., Qin, T., Burgoon, J. K., & Nunamaker Jr, J. F. (2003). An exploratory study into deception detection in text-based computer-mediated communication. In *36th Hawaii International Conference on Systems Sciences* (pp. 44b).

13

Vulnerable Individuals, Intermediaries and Justice

Brendan M. O'Mahony[1], Ruth Marchant[2] and Lorna Fadden[3]
[1] Private Practice, UK
[2] Triangle, UK
[3] Simon Fraser University, Burnaby, BC, Canada

VULNERABLE INDIVIDUALS AND THE USE OF INTERMEDIARIES

It is well known that the provision of accurate and complete information is essential for justice to prevail. Unfortunately, there are some instances where witnesses and defendants are, because of a particular vulnerability, unable to manage the communication demands (e.g. being able to interpret complex questions) that are sometimes inherent in police interviews and/or cross-examination at court. A direct consequence of being unable to convey experiences effectively is that the evidence required to make informed decisions (e.g. lay charge, render verdicts) is unheard, or is heard partially or inaccurately. One response to the improvement of communication with vulnerable individuals is the provision of skilled intermediary assistance. Witnesses can be vulnerable during questioning for a number of reasons, such as psychological,

Communication in Investigative and Legal Contexts: Integrated Approaches from Forensic Psychology, Linguistics and Law Enforcement, First Edition. Edited by Gavin Oxburgh, Trond Myklebust, Tim Grant and Rebecca Milne.
© 2016 John Wiley & Sons, Ltd. Published 2016 by John Wiley & Sons, Ltd.

environmental and cultural. We will provide examples of the breadth of vulnerabilities that can cause miscommunication by examining communication in a global context. Although intermediaries are used with vulnerable witnesses in England and Wales, especially children and adults with intellectual disabilities, the provision of such assistance for vulnerable suspects and defendants appears to be more limited and less well received by some in the legal system.

In the current chapter, we describe the development of intermediary practices in England and Wales. An example of a case where an intermediary proved valuable with a witness case is then presented. We then discuss the use of intermediaries with suspects and defendants and provide a second case study. The function of intermediaries in a cross-cultural context is then discussed using examples from Australia and Canada. This raises a series of questions about the boundaries and clarity of the intermediary function so that the legislation pertaining to intermediaries is more inclusive. We conclude with a discussion of the need to expand the use of intermediaries across the breadth of interviews and across the globe to help prevent miscarriages of justice.

THE INTERMEDIARY: A DEVELOPMENTAL HISTORY IN THE UK

Within England and Wales, statutory provision for intermediaries was enacted as a Special Measure within the Youth Justice and Criminal Evidence Act 1999 (YJCEA). This act emerged because of a growing body of research that demonstrated that children and vulnerable adults had difficulties communicating their evidence to the police and at court (Dent & Flin, 1992; Flin, Stevenson & Davies, 1989; Kebbell, Hatton & Johnson, 2004).

In England and Wales the role of an intermediary, put very simply, is to facilitate communication between a witness or defendant and others in the justice process (Ministry of Justice, 2012). Specifically, intermediaries are responsible for facilitating the two-way communication between a witness (e.g. a prosecution witness or a defence witness or the defendant as a witness or a defendant throughout the trial) and other criminal justice workers (e.g. police officers, legal teams, witness service and/or the court) (Ministry of Justice, 2012). A primary goal of an intermediary's function is to ensure that the communication process is as complete, coherent and accurate as possible. Although the role of the intermediary varies across jurisdictions, it usually involves providing guidance on communication issues such as recommending ground rules (these will be discussed later in the chapter) for questioning, monitoring and rephrasing of questions, interpreting and passing on answers through and taking over questioning in its entirety. Critically, the intermediary must assume an impartial role because they are officers of the court; they are not advocates for the police, prosecution or the defence. Further, in England and Wales the Registered Intermediary is not a witness supporter, an Appropriate Adult, an interpreter or an expert witness whilst undertaking the specific duties as an intermediary (Ministry of Justice, 2011, p. 10).

In England, Wales and Northern Ireland, Registered Intermediaries are trained professionals with backgrounds such as psychology, speech and language therapy, social work, occupational therapy, nursing and teaching (O'Mahony, 2010). They are recruited on the basis of their competence to facilitate communication; they then attend a short training course of 6 days duration arranged by the Ministry of Justice, where they receive instruction about the adversarial criminal justice system. Currently, there are just over 100 active Registered Intermediaries operating in England and Wales (Personal communication, National Crime Agency (NCA) Matching Service, 2014).

Many of these intermediaries hold full-time employment positions within the National Health Service (NHS) and therefore are routinely unavailable to take on cases at short notice. They rely on their employer to grant them the time off to engage in intermediary practices. Others may be independent practitioners mixing the intermediary function with other professional roles; some intermediaries may engage in the role full-time.

More than 12,000 intermediary referrals have been made in England and Wales since the inception of the intermediary scheme in 2004. Referrals to the Witness Intermediary Scheme can be made at different stages of the investigation or trial process. The investigating officer can make a referral prior to conducting an investigative interview or sometimes after an initial attempt at an interview has revealed communication issues. The Crown Prosecution Service (CPS) can also make a referral pre-trial, even if no intermediary was involved at interview.

Having identified the witness as being a vulnerable witness, the police officer or CPS worker makes contact with the NCA Matching Service, where the skills and location of intermediaries are matched with the referral (O'Mahony, 2010). Ideally the intermediary completes a full communication assessment of the witness prior to the investigative interview or trial and has the opportunity to liaise with external professionals such as social workers, psychologists and school teachers so that a comprehensive report of the witness's communication needs is completed should the witness need to attend court.

At court the intermediary will accompany the vulnerable witness in the witness box or in the separate live link room. The intermediary will facilitate communication between counsel and the witness and must intervene when necessary if complex questions are asked or if the agreed 'ground rules' are not adhered to. Intermediaries must only accept a referral to assess a vulnerable person who has needs within their particular skill set.

Following completion of a two-year pilot in six 'pathfinder areas' (Merseyside, West Midlands, Thames Valley, South Wales, Norfolk and Devon and Cornwall), the intermediary package was rolled out nationwide in 2007 (Plotnikoff & Woolfson, 2007). The findings from the pilot evaluation showed that there were a number of reported benefits to the scheme, including increasing access to justice for vulnerable witnesses and informing the police and the courts of appropriate questioning styles (Plotnikoff & Woolfson, 2007). The Special Measures introduced through the YJCE Act 1999 were intended solely for use with vulnerable witnesses and intentionally excluded vulnerable defendants.

In the last two decades, witness intermediary schemes have been implemented in a number of other countries including South Africa, Norway, Austria, Northern Ireland and Zimbabwe. In most cases, these schemes have been implemented exclusively for child witnesses and have not included other groups of vulnerable persons such as those with mental disorders or physical communication disorders. The implementation of intermediary schemes is also being considered in several other jurisdictions, such as Namibia, Ethiopia, Scotland, Australia and New Zealand (Caruso & Cross, 2012; Jackson, 2003; Matthias & Zaal, 2011). Later in this chapter we will examine how the term intermediary has been used in Australia to facilitate communication in a cross-cultural context and we will use a case study that highlights that complex sentence structure is also an issue in cross-cultural cases.

THE VULNERABLE WITNESS: AN EXAMPLE

This example is based on a combination of different cases in England and Wales in order to protect the anonymity of the vulnerable persons. The three-year-old child was taken to hospital with injuries compatible with oral and vaginal rape; the child had been sleeping upstairs at an adult party. She was distressed and withdrawn, and would not answer any questions about what had happened during the evening. An initial intermediary communication assessment was arranged by the investigating officer for the following morning. The intermediary spoke with the child's parents and nursery teacher to gather information about her favourite activities, along with her development and communication needs. The child was given a letter containing a photographic image of the intermediary, which explained the process (coming to do talking and playing) and introduced the setting (photographs of the room, play materials and the intermediary).

The next morning, 45 minutes were spent in activities designed to quickly assess the child's communication, vocabulary and attention abilites; her ability to understand language and question forms; her ability to use language to describe events, clarify issues, shift her perspective and refute inaccurate suggestions. This included supporting the child to talk about a recent fun event, in order to assess her ability to give a narrative account and to respond to different question types. The time was also used to assess the child's ability to concentrate, to attend and to manage her own arousal levels, to try out approaches for keeping her calm and engaged, and to introduce 'talking rules'. Time was given during the assessment to enable the child to separate from her parents; which she managed to do without difficulty once she was familiar with the assessor and the environment. At the end of the assessment the child helped set up the interview room with appropriate furniture, communication aids and calming play materials.

The child then took a complete break for play and lunch, and the intermediary provided feedback to the interviewing officer and assisted with an interview plan. The interview went ahead after lunch, with the intermediary providing communication support to the child. Specifically, the intermediary worked to ensure that the child remained calm and engaged, and to maintain effective communication, for instance, by reframing questions in the past tense and simplifying language. Although the child had difficulty sequencing events and needed to use her own human figure drawings to clarify body parts and positions, she ultimately provided a detailed account. The Crown Prosecution Service made a charging decision and the case was fast tracked at the intermediary's recommendation; nevertheless, the case still took five months to reach court. The child was four years and one month old at trial.

The intermediary recommended the use of a number of special measures, all of which were put in place. The intermediary was involved in making sure the pre-trial court familiarization visit and explanations were developmentally appropriate for the child. The visit included a practice session on a video-link with questions unrelated to the child's evidence. This practice run was used to help the child to understand that the court could see and hear her, and to ensure that she continued to use her face and hands to support her communication. It was agreed that the child would, with appropriate support, refresh her memory of her testimony in advance of the trial by viewing her video-recorded evidence-in-chief.

In addition, the intermediary attended a 'Ground Rules Hearing' with the prosecutor, defence counsel and trial judge. The Ground Rules Hearing is the opportunity for the trial judge and advocates to plan any adaptations to questioning that may be necessary to facilitate the evidence of a vulnerable person, for example to avoid the use of double negatives in a question (Judicial College, 2013, p. 58). The hearing was held four weeks ahead of the trial so that the child could be prepared according to the agreed-upon ground rules. The allotted time also gave the defence counsel enough time to prepare questions. As part of the discussions at the Ground Rules Hearing the intermediary requested the following three additional measures given the child's needs:

- In-room brief breaks where the court is not adjourned.
- Screening the defendant's view of the television screen in the courtroom and confirmation of silence in court (other than the judge and questioners).
- It was agreed that the intermediary would provide play materials for calming the child and helping her maintain her attention to the questioner; these were chosen to be quiet and non-symbolic: stress balls, tangle toys, colouring and squeezy toys.

It is worth noting that intermediaries can also assist in recommending appropriate communication aids. Courts have permitted a wide range (e.g. pen and paper, models, picture cards, signal boards, visual timetables, human figure drawings and technology) to augment or replace oral testimony. Aids have helped improve the quality of evidence and given access to justice to some witnesses previously excluded (Judicial College, 2013, p. 58). The following communication aids were agreed for the four-year-old witness at trial:

- Visual representations of rules
- Cards depicting that a break was required
- Plain A4 card
- Colouring pens
- The child's own drawings produced at interview
- Human figure drawings.

It was also agreed that the intermediary would monitor the child's anxiety levels and assist with directing her attention and provide assistance to calm her if required, for example by attending gently to her behaviour, giving a non-directive commentary and setting boundaries and limits when needed. The intermediary would support brief breaks from questioning in the live-link room when needed. Rather than adjourn the court, it was agreed that the court would wait for up to three minutes. Simple 'Stop–Pause–Go' cards and an egg timer were used to help the child predict and pace breaks, as illustrated by the symbols in Figure 13.1.

Figure 13.1   Stop–Pause–Go cards used during the child's court testimony.

Table 13.1 sets out the strategies for counsel that were outlined by the intermediary and agreed by all parties during the ground rules hearing.

The intermediary sat with the child in the video live-link room throughout the cross-examination and re-examination. The child was questioned for a total of 45 minutes, spread across two hours with in-room and out-of-room breaks. Some interventions were made on the basis of the above ground rules. The judge took over a number of interventions as questioning progressed, particularly about question length and structure. Of note, intermediaries can assist the judiciary to monitor the questioning of vulnerable witnesses and defendants; the responsibility to control questioning, however, remains with the judge or magistrates (Judicial College, 2013, p. 55).

Interestingly, some needed interventions were not predicted. For example, the defence counsel asked 'Do you remember the day you went to hospital?' and the child replied with 'no'. The intermediary intervened at this point and advised the court that the child may have meant she did not know the day of the week and suggested this be rephrased to 'Do you remember what happened the day you went to hospital?' The child then answered 'yes'. According to the Judicial College,

> It can also be difficult to keep in mind all aspects of questioning that may be problematic for the individual witness. An intermediary who has already assessed the witness's communication is able to alert the court to any problems or loss of concentration.
>
> (Judicial College, 2013, p. 56)

Other intermediary interventions at cross-examination included a request for the pacing to speed up; to have questions without a preamble; to have a double question broken into two parts; to remind the child that no one was allowed to shout at her in court and to add a third option to a forced-choice alternative question (this or this or something else). Good practice indicates that the intermediary duty extends to enabling a witness to understand the outcome of the trial process. The intermediary met one more time with the child and her parents to help explain this and to close her involvement. There was a

Table 13.1 Communication strategies used during the child's court testimony and accompanying examples and rationales for each strategy

Strategy	Example	Rationale
Use short simple sentences and age-appropriate vocabulary	Replace 'I want to take you back to the day of the incident' with 'I want to ask about the day you went to hospital'	Most children this age will not understand multipart, embedded sentences, complex vocabulary or non-literal language
Limit questions to four concepts and 'scaffold' additional concepts (e.g. with a visual aid)	Use the child's drawings to enable clarity if longer questions are needed	The child's auditory working memory is limited and it is important that she processes the whole question
Use your hands, face and intonation to strengthen your spoken communication	Ask questions in a questioning tone; use a puzzled facial expression if challenging her account; use a 'don't know' hand gesture to prompt further detail	This child is very sensitive to non-verbal communication; she also is more likely to communicate non-verbally herself if the questioner does so, which will make her own communication clearer
Give the child time to respond to questions; do not rephrase unless requested to do so	Count silently to three before repeating	This child needs time to process language; repeating too quickly or rephrasing can disrupt this
Ask suggestive questions with caution and always in a questioning tone	Replace 'It was raining wasn't it?' with 'Was it raining?'	This child is only just processing statement questions and tag questions and is very vulnerable to suggestion. Therefore her answers to such questions may be unreliable
Ask open questions or simple directives (who, what, where, how)	'Tell me what happened, then what happened, who, what, where, how'	This child can process these question types
Be careful with 'when' and 'how many' questions	Instead of 'how many' try 'once or more than once', using hand gestures	This child's grasp of time concepts is at an early stage; she is learning to count and knows that a 'how many' question seeks a number in response so is likely to guess
Avoid 'why' questions	Instead of 'why' try 'what made…?'	This child is still reversing 'why' and 'because' which may create confusion

unanimous guilty verdict and an 11-year custodial sentence was awarded to the defendant.

The above case has focused on vulnerability in the context of witnesses but communication difficulties also can occur with vulnerable defendants. In the next section we will examine the support that is available to vulnerable suspects whilst in police detention. We will then look at how their communication needs can be supported if they are subsequently charged and required to attend a criminal court.

THE VULNERABLE SUSPECT DURING POLICE INTERVIEWS

Prior to being charged with a criminal offence a person is known as a *suspect* in England and Wales. If the suspect is subsequently charged with a criminal offence and required to attend court, they are then referred to as a *defendant*. Following the successful implementation of the intermediary scheme to vulnerable witnesses and victims in England and Wales, academics and practitioners started to examine the extent to which the comparable support should be afforded to vulnerable suspects. Although the Police and Criminal Evidence Act – PACE (1984) provides vulnerable suspects (e.g. children) with the safeguard of having an Appropriate Adult in attendance during the interview (Home Office, 2005), research on the effectiveness of Appropriate Adults suggests that this seemingly useful protective feature may be ineffectual (Medford, Gudjonsson & Pearse, 2003). One reason for this is that Appropriate Adults do not often actively facilitate communication with a vulnerable suspect in the same way that an intermediary does with a vulnerable witness. Indeed, professional training and qualifications are not required to act as an Appropriate Adult (O'Mahony, Smith & Milne, 2011).

The first problem emerges at the police station when trying to identify those persons who are vulnerable (Jacobson, 2008). A body of research began to emerge about the needs of police suspects with learning disabilities (Jacobson, 2008). As a result, in many cases Appropriate Adults were not being requested and thus PACE was not being complied with. Failure to identify vulnerable suspects was also in part due to the lack of screening mechanisms (Jacobson, 2008, p. 28). When identified Jacobson (2008, p. 36) concluded that some of the Special Measures that are available to vulnerable witnesses should be made available to vulnerable suspects as well, such as the provision of intermediaries to facilitate communication and guidance on interviewing. However, the function of the intermediary role within the police suspect interview could clash with the provision of the Appropriate Adult as outlined in PACE 1984, and this role associated with support for the vulnerable suspect during the police interview requires incisive discussion (O'Mahony, 2010).

Police officers in England and Wales are issued with some advice for when they have cause to interview vulnerable suspects. For instance, interviewing officers are made aware of the following:

> Although juveniles or people who are mentally disordered or otherwise mentally vulnerable are often capable of providing reliable evidence, they may, without knowing or wishing to do so, be particularly prone in certain circumstances to provide information that may be unreliable, misleading or self-incriminating. Special care should always be taken when questioning such a person (Code 'C' Notes for Guidance 11C; Home Office, 2005).

However, investigative interviewers are not provided with guidance on *how* to actually carry out interviews with vulnerable suspects (O'Mahony, Milne & Grant, 2012). This concern is illustrated with the following simulated interviewer–suspect exchange where some inconsistencies in the suspect's account need to be challenged:

OFFICER: You said earlier that you had been in the post office at about 10 am. We have a witness statement that states you left the post office at 9.40 am so it can't be true, can it, that you were there at 10 am?

SUSPECT: No (meaning *no, it can't be true that you have witness evidence*)

OFFICER: So, you have either made a mistake or lied to us when you said you were in the post office at 10 am. You were actually in the High Street at 10 am, weren't you?

SUSPECT: Yes (meaning *I must have made a mistake; it must have been 9.30 am when I was in the post office; I am no good at times*)

OFFICER: So, you agree you were in the High Street at 10 am?

SUSPECT: No.

The police officer's challenge in this account is very complex in terms of communicating with a person with an intellectual disability. In fact, it would likely cause a great deal of confusion for someone without a cognitive disability. The challenge is likely to lead to confusion because it includes tag questions (see, for example, Blankenship & Craig, 2007; Harres, 1998), which are known to be highly complex for children and adults with an intellectual disability. Moreover, coercive tag questions such as 'you hit her, didn't you?' can force the interviewee to agree with the interviewer (Harres, 1998), which may certainly in some cases lead to acquiescence by the vulnerable person and therefore answering a question in the affirmative, believing that this is the response wanted by the person in authority. Alternatively it may lead to compliance, whereby the vulnerable person complies with a request in order to leave the police station as soon as possible (Gudjonsson, 2003). In the fictitious example provided above, the question, 'you were actually in the High Street at 10 am, weren't you?' is a tag question. Rephrasing the challenge is not an easy task to do without lengthening the challenge, which in turn may cause difficulties if the vulnerable person has impaired working memory (O'Mahony et al., 2012).

Beyond the aforementioned example, there is a wealth of research showing that the questioning practices by investigative interviewers tend to be subpar, which exposes vulnerable individuals to providing incomplete and inaccurate accounts (see, for example, Baldwin, 1993; Clarke & Milne, 2001).

Intermediary assistance would be of much value in police interviews where the suspect is vulnerable to the nature of inappropriate questioning habits. It seems that there are two possible solutions to ensuring that vulnerable suspects can communicate effectively during a police interview. Either the Appropriate Adult Scheme employs qualified communication specialists to undertake the role or the Registered Intermediary Scheme is extended to include suspect interviews. In Northern Ireland a pilot scheme commenced in May 2013 where, in addition to vulnerable witnesses, vulnerable suspects and vulnerable defendants giving oral testimony at court are given access to a Registered Intermediary. During the course of the 18 month pilot a total of 260 requests were made for intermediaries in Northern Ireland: of these 32 requests were made for police suspect interviews and 12 requests for defendants. The review of the pilot scheme documents that suspects were enabled to participate effectively in police interviews (Department of Justice, 2015). None of the defendants who were assessed by an intermediary went on to give oral testimony in court with the support of an intermediary. The reasons for this vary. In one case the defendant was assessed as not requiring an intermediary at court, charges were withdrawn against another and one was found unfit to plead. Five of the 12 defendant cases assessed by an intermediary resulted in a guilty plea on the original charge or a lesser charge at court. A further phase of the pilot study is proposed to commence for 12 months from April 2015 due to the limited experience to date of RI utilization in the court room for both witnesses and defendants (Department of Justice, 2015).

THE VULNERABLE DEFENDANT AT COURT

Some courts in England and Wales have used their 'inherent jurisdiction' in common law and requested an intermediary to be present when a vulnerable defendant is on trial at court (Cooper & Wurtzel, 2013;

OMahony et al., 2011). Such a practice was visible prior to the introduction of Section 104 of the Coroners and Justice Act (CJA) 2009 – yet
to be implemented in England and Wales – which makes provision for
an intermediary to be present when the defendant gives oral evidence
at court (O'Mahony et al., 2011). Under these circumstances, the intermediary would conduct an assessment of the vulnerable defendant and
write a report for the court – similar to the process that is followed with
vulnerable witnesses.

However, the Ministry of Justice intermediary training programme,
policies and procedures are only valid for Registered Intermediaries
working with vulnerable *witnesses* and do not apply to intermediaries
working with vulnerable *defendants*. In other words, persons accepting
intermediary cases with vulnerable defendants are not on any national
register and it is down to the discretion of the court as to whether a
proposed intermediary has the requisite training and credibility to fulfil
the role. In practice it would seem that some courts such as the Central
Criminal Court (CCC; more often known as the Old Bailey) may have a
preference for Registered (Witness) Intermediaries to undertake
defendant cases, although the increasing demands for defendant intermediaries mean that the courts have to adopt a more flexible approach.
The CCC only provides details of a small number of Registered
Intermediaries to any solicitor who requests information about making
contact with an intermediary (Personal communication, August 2014).
Ultimately, it is for the judge to decide whether a person has the necessary qualifications and skills to act as a defendant intermediary in each
individual case. There are a number of Registered Intermediaries who
accept defendant referrals either as sole traders or as directors of private companies specializing in this area. Regardless of their background
and training, intermediaries accepting defendant cases are not permitted to use their Ministry of Justice (MOJ) identification or the MOJ
paperwork when undertaking defendant cases. They receive no additional training by the MOJ and are not accountable to the MOJ or the
National Crime Agency for their work on defendant cases.

Whilst the impending introduction of S104 of the Criminal and
Justice Act 2009 has been helpful in many ways, it has also been criticized for its limitations (Hoyano, 2010). Hoyano has argued, for
instance, that if a defendant is assessed as requiring an intermediary
whilst providing testimony, then it seems natural that the defendant
would also require support in the dock throughout the criminal trial in
order to make sense of proceedings. This extended support is not always
requested or indeed available in reality. An example illustrating the
need for support in the dock was a trial where the defendant was tasked
with listening to a transcript of the police suspect interview being read
aloud at court. The defendant could not follow the interview being read

in this way and it appeared that having a (different) police officer and a lawyer read the parts of the suspect interview was confusing to the defendant who struggled with the altered perspective. The defendant could not concentrate on the interview dialogue and remarked 'They were not at my police interview. They are supposed to be reading *my* interview' (Personal experience, O'Mahony).

In a transcript made at a trial where a vulnerable defendant had access to an intermediary at court (O'Mahony, 2012) the defendant, a young adult, had been charged with murder. The court had agreed that an intermediary should be made available throughout the trial to help the vulnerable defendant understand the witnesses' testimonies and to facilitate communication during meetings with lawyers. The judge, understandably, has the job of keeping the trial on track. However, the following example illustrates that the judge did not appreciate the complexities that a person with impaired cognitive functioning might be presented with during cross-examination:

PROSECUTION COUNSEL (TO THE DEFENDANT):	If you do not understand a word I use please can you indicate it?
DEFENDANT:	Yes.
PROSECUTION COUNSEL:	If you don't indicate it I am going to assume you understood the word; do you follow?
DEFENDANT:	Yeah.
INTERMEDIARY INTERVENTION:	Your honour, (the defendant) may not even understand the word 'indicate', so if you could just check that.
JUDGE:	Hang on, let's keep a balance here. (To the defendant) if you don't understand (counsel's) questions, you say so. That is simple. If you don't say that you don't understand we are entitled to assume that you do understand.
DEFENDANT:	Okay, yeah.
JUDGE:	That's pretty simple with the problems you have. Either you can tell us you understand or you don't. I don't see a problem with that.
PROSECUTION COUNSEL (TO THE DEFENDANT):	Do you understand the word 'indicate'?
DEFENDANT:	No.
PROSECUTION COUNSEL:	You don't, I see, you were thrown by that.

Note that this intervention by the intermediary was perhaps not as succinct as it may have been but it illustrates the small window of opportunity that an intermediary has to recognize that an intervention is required and to quickly make the intervention.

The above transcript excerpt illustrates that it is not enough to appear to be providing equity of service to the vulnerable defendant by providing an intermediary. Equity of service must actually happen in practice through a proper check of comprehension. A second example of this issue became apparent in a different trial. When the intermediary – who was appointed to the trial for a vulnerable defendant – requested shorter periods of cross-examination (15 minute periods) in the afternoon, the judge was displeased and rejected the request. The defendant became cognitively fatigued very quickly and the intermediary advised the court that the defendant appeared to be acquiescing to every question. It was further stated that the defendant could not answer any further questions that afternoon. The judge made it known that this was unacceptable as the court had to continue until 4 pm. The judge failed to appreciate the defendant's vulnerability and the concern that the defendant might acquiesce to questions and thus, unintentionally, mislead the court. The above cases provide some examples of the practicalities of the intermediary role but they do not offer an insight into the affect and cognitions of the intermediary. The following section addresses this lack of knowledge by examining how intermediaries have experienced their role undertaking defendant cases.

The Defendant Intermediaries' Perspective

Registered Intermediaries who had undertaken the defendant intermediary role before the Ministry of Justice ceased allocating Registered Intermediaries to defendant cases were interviewed about their

Table 13.2 Summary of issues identified by each participant that relate to the 'Professional Identities" theme

Participant number	Issue identified
1	Making sense of 'me' Role, confidence and impartiality
2	Appearance, isolation at court, role, impartiality and self-esteem
3	Self-esteem, rejection, vulnerability, anxiety, boundaries, role conflict, reconciling conflict, competing agendas
4	Assertiveness, weakened by position within the court, feeling exposed, inferiority, anxiety about how others perceive me, impartiality
5	Empowerment and disempowerment, neutrality, resilience
6	Objectivity and affiliation, role conflict, influence of previous experiences in the CJS, different facades, resilience

experiences (O'Mahony, 2013; O'Mahony, Creaton, Smith & Milne, in press). *Professional Identities* was a theme that emanated from this research.

As outlined in Table 13.2, it seems that defendant intermediaries are finding it to be an uncomfortable experience asserting their role within the court and this in turn is making them feel isolated. When a defendant intermediary enters the court building, they are likely to find themselves reflecting on their positioning within the hierarchy of the court. In the following example it is evident that some initial categorizations made by the intermediary about other professionals in the court may have led to the use of the word 'brutal' when there is no evidence that brutality is apparent; rather the dock officers in question were probably constrained by their own professional guidelines:

P2:	Well, he (defendant) wasn't allowed anything (in court cells). And he tended to be either climbing the walls and hyped up by the time we got to court or else, um, he'd, he'd switched off completely with the boredom of it all (line 7)
INTERVIEWER:	Right
P2:	...would have worked a lot better if he'd had a couple of slices of toast and a magazine...
INTERVIEWER:	Okay
P2:	and I found it quite hard. I found that hard because I thought this is a lad who is actually at that particular point innocent. He hadn't been proved guilty (line 19)
P2:	Well they were harsh, the custody...it was brutal.

At this point in the court proceedings the intermediary may have internalized the dock officers as being brutal. This perception could have consequences for their professional relationship, even if subconsciously, later in the trial. In the second example, the same intermediary provides us with an insight into how having pre-conceived ideas about court security staff could lead to seeking information to confirm the differences between the intermediary's identity and the perceived identity of the dock officers:

P2:	I shouldn't have been because they should have had a ...I insisted...they wanted to put an, um, a dock officer between me and the defendant I was working with but I did scotch that one right from the beginning and I really stood my ground on that and I said no way, I'm going to sit next to them and...Oh I was fine because I'd know him by then and I ...I mean I thought there's no way I'm going to...I had to go to the court clerk and the solicitor and we had a bit of a kafuffle over that one, but I did stand my ground. The dock officer was not a happy bunny because they had been overruled, which they didn't like. They were used to absolute control (line 189).

This social categorization (Grant & Hogg, 2012) may also be evident in the intermediary's relationships with other court staff such as barristers. This concern is illustrated in the following example, where the intermediary is making a comparison between their perception of how they act in court and the behaviour displayed by barristers in the courtroom:

> P4(2): ...the defendant goes down for an adjournment and the jury go out...and the rest of us are left there and defence and prosecution start chatting together, you know, about life and going out and what restaurant they went to, or about the case as well. And then they go into their roles for the other stuff. But, um, they were talking quite openly about what they felt the case... how it should...the outcome of the case...and of course, you know, as an impartial intermediary, I was quite shocked by this, to see them having those...that type of chat and thinking 'oh, that's very unprofessional', making sure I kept myself zipped... I just hung around there and if they were talking about something not to do with the case, I'd try and join in and be part of it, you know. Er, not to be too much like a lemon or a gooseberry (line 40).

One of the strongest voices emerging from all six participants interviewed is the potential conflict in roles between that of a professional from a health or caring background and that required when undertaking the impartial role of a defendant intermediary. The following selected excerpts from participant interviews illustrate this point:

> P2: There was nobody else really apart from me there who was interested in his well-being. I mean it wasn't entirely my role but I did feel that he would communicate a lot better and understand a lot better if he was sort of looked after a little bit (line 119).
> P4: But you actually just want that person to be functioning as well as they can, given the horrible situation. And you have some part to play in that directly and the other part is just as a fellow human being, you know, sitting beside someone...And of course you can't in either respect (witness or defendant case) put your arm around them and comfort them, but with the witness, they've got support people... But of course with this...with the defendant, you can't do anything, they are just grabbed and taken downstairs again (line 89).

When an individual embarks on a role in a new environment, they encounter an uncertain place where they have to learn the rules of how they and others behave in that context (Grant & Hogg, 2012, p. 538). It is therefore essential that intermediaries are supported in understanding their developing identity as they embark on working as an intermediary. If they do not understand the nature of changing identities there may be consequences in terms of perceived person–environment fit. For instance, a failure to understand changing identities may lead to frustration and a reluctance to engage in the role (Furnham & Walsh, 2001, p. 187). Certain preferences in cognitive styles can also impact on how the individual perceives their fit, or misfit, with their work environment. For example, some people prefer structured, well-defined environments and others are more comfortable in dynamic environments (Cools, Van den Broeck & Bouckenooghe, 2009, p. 170). Intermediaries are a relatively recent introduction to the criminal justice system and therefore will be attending the courtroom, where they are obliged to interact with other professional groups, for example barristers, who are well established in that environment. This research has identified that intermediaries have reflected on the relationships that they have with these other professionals in the court room and this reflection empowers them to become agents of change rather than victims of change (Hotho, 2008, pp. 721–722). The focus of this chapter so far has been on the communication difficulties that may be experienced by vulnerable persons as defined by the Special Measures legislation in England and Wales. However, communication difficulties can also arise in cross-cultural settings and this issue is examined in the next section in the context of Canadian and Australian settings.

Vulnerability in Cross-Cultural Interactions

Miscommunication in investigative and judicial settings can arise during cross-cultural interaction, particularly when members of minority groups are questioned by investigators or legal counsel belonging to the dominant culture. The vulnerability of witnesses in this context stems not from the types of communicative deficit discussed thus far, i.e. youth or cognitive limitation, but rather a mismatch in conversational behaviour, distinctly disadvantaging the minority witness or defendant.

Even in regions where everyone speaks the same language, different varieties of that language exist, and those spoken by members of racially, socially or culturally bound minority groups differ from the 'standard' although they are often mutually intelligible. Interactional sociolinguist Gumperz (1982) influenced much of the work on cross-cultural interaction, bringing to light the difficulties associated with speakers of different varieties, essentially failing to communicate owing to the cultural norms upon which their respective communicative styles are built. When one speaker's norms differ from another's, there is a tendency for one or both to find the other odd or uncooperative at best, or incompetent or deceptive at worst, and as this section will show, in legal settings that breakdown can have horrendous consequences.

To discuss the need for, and the implementation of, intermediaries assisting in cases where a vulnerable witness or defendant brings his or her non-standard variety to the legal context, we turn to Australia. Much like other former British colonies, the Australian justice system convicts and incarcerates a significantly disproportionate number of Aboriginal people, with Aboriginal adults being 14 times more likely to be incarcerated than white adults and Aboriginal youth being 22 times more likely to be in detention than their white counterparts (SCRGSP, 2011). While social and socioeconomic factors contribute to this over-representation, it has also been found that cross-cultural interaction between aboriginal witnesses speaking Australian Aboriginal English (AAE) and white investigators and legal counsel speaking Standard Australian English (SAE) is fraught with systematic and persistent miscommunication (Cooke, 1995; Eades, 1994, 2000, 2006, 2012; Mildren, 1999).

In a detailed and critical account of a police misconduct case, Eades (2008) thoroughly describes Australian Aboriginal English and shows how its use in the courtroom leaves witnesses vulnerable to misinterpretation. AAE speakers, she shows, are not given to direct questioning when seeking information, rather questioning in AAE is carried out indirectly, with information being offered by the asker in order to invite a sharing of information from the respondent. Long, silent pauses are well tolerated and expected, indicating that either the respondent is giving due attention to the matter at hand, as opposed to a marker of non-cooperation or deception, or, as Kearins (1991) notes, silence is used when the speaker does not feel he or she has the authority to speak about the matter at hand. Lengthy eye contact is considered rude or threatening in Aboriginal English speech communities (Kearins, 1991; Mildren, 1999) and unfortunately in the interview room or on the stand, a lack of eye contact often signals untrustworthiness. Most notably, and as it turns out most problematic in legal contexts, is the AAE discourse strategy of gratuitous concurrence, which involves agreement with asserted information regardless of truth value, for the purpose of putting on a socially agreeable, obliging face (see especially Eades, 1995, 2008). It is not difficult to imagine how gratuitous concurrence, noted as far back as Strehlow (1936, p. 334), can lead to wrongful presentations of evidence, and even false confessions when 'The White man putting the questions will usually receive answers which are calculated to avoid trouble or to excite his pleasure: he will be given the information which he desires to get.'

Before examining some excerpts to illustrate the discord that can arise in cross-cultural questioning, a short account of how Australia came to address linguistic variation in the justice system is warranted. The first state-backed move to remedy language variation-based problems came after *R v. Anunga* 1976 in the Supreme Court of Northern Territory. Anunga, a woman wrongfully convicted of murder, had been poorly represented by her own counsel who found her uncooperative before trial and on the stand. Her vulnerability in this case stemmed from her being a speaker of Australian Aboriginal English, as unaccustomed to white discourse practice as her white counsel was unaccustomed to hers. A set of guidelines spelled out in Justice Forster's ruling would come to be known as the Anunga Rules, and were intended for use by investigators and lawyers as a means of addressing the miscommunication problems that plagued her case. Besides calling for an interpreter unless a suspect 'is as fluent in English as the average white man of English descent', Justice Forster also recommended using question types that do not elicit simple yes or no responses, responses that often turn out to be unreliable. He also recommended that the police caution be explained line by line and that investigators pause often to enquire whether the witness understood.

In the early 1990s, the legal community of Queensland recognized the need to be more proactive than the Anunga Rules prescribed, to better understand and accommodate AAE speakers in legal contexts. To this end, sociolinguist Diana Eades supplied a thorough grammatical and pragmatic account of AAE for legal professionals, along with her recommendations to carry out questioning and understand responses in ways to minimize miscommunication. In *Aboriginal English and the Law: Communicating with Aboriginal English Speaking Clients: A Handbook for Legal Practitioners*, Eades (1992) makes a number of recommendations, including the use of more open-ended questions, that invite the witness' account in his or her own words to avoid gratuitous concurrence; to understand that the AAE speaker is not being intentionally vague about details of space and time, but rather he or she recounts special and temporal matters in relative terms, not explicit terms; and not to assume that the words spoken by an AAE speaker carry the same meaning as they do in SAE.

A short excerpt from the Pinkenba Case in Eades (2008) featuring long silences and gratuitous concurrence illustrates the degree to which an aboriginal witness in a hearing on police misconduct can be overpowered through language when an intermediary is not involved. In this case, 'DC1' is the defence counsel for the police, 'Albert' is one of three young men who were unlawfully detained by police, driven out of town and abandoned, and 'Mag' is the magistrate. Words in small caps indicate emphasis.

1 DC1:	Now LISTEN to me – that didn't happen at all – did it? (2.0) that you were grabbed – it DIDN'T HAPPEN – did it?
2 ALBERT:	No.
3 DC1:	Beg your pardon?
4 MAG:	He said no.
5 DC1:	Well WHY did you say that it did? (27.1) well – WHY? (12.2) I'll suggest this answer to you – that you were TRYING TO MAKE THINGS LOOK WORSE FOR THE POLICE – is that the correct answer? (27.8) is that the correct answer?
6 ALBERT:	(1.4) No.
7 DC1:	Beg your pardon?
8 ALBERT:	No.
9 DC1:	Well, WHAT IS the answer? (2.4) why did you lie about it? (33.4) WHY did you LIE?
10 PROS:	With respect – inconsistent answers don't necessarily imply lies and the witness hasn't yet accepted that either of them is a lie – I'd ask my friend to uh=
11 DC1:	=All right – well – I can take half an hour trying to get an answer from him (2.7) I think you told me that that didn't HAPPEN – what you claim there – [to solicitor] didn't he say that didn't happen – so if it didn't HAPPEN – is it a LIE THAT YOU'VE TOLD THERE?
12 ALBERT:	Yes.
13 DC1:	All right – well now why did you lie?
14 ALBERT:	I don't know.
15 DC1:	YOU LIED TO MAKE THINGS LOOK BAD FOR THE POLICE – DIDN'T YOU? (1.2) DIDN'T YOU?
16 ALBERT:	(3.5) Yes.

(Eades, 2008, pp. 103–104)

The long pauses within DC1's turns, recorded in seconds in parentheses, are points at which the interviewer expects a response to his question. However, Albert does not take the floor, typical of how speakers of AAE tolerate long silences quite comfortably, as opposed to speakers of SAE who hasten to fill silences. The questioner then expresses frustration with the perceived uncooperative behaviour on the part of Albert in line 11. Albert, while initially disagreeing with DC1's assertions in lines 1 and 5, then agrees with him, although the agreement is likely to be gratuitous owing to an AAE conversational strategy used to reduce discord between speakers when it arises. Furthermore, it is not stretching credulity to suggest that the power imbalance inherent in institutional settings causes the witness to simply comply with the demands made of him at the time, in effect giving the questioner what he wants. This issue was examined earlier in this chapter using the terms compliance and acquiescence to explain the behaviour.

Lexical differences, like discourse strategy, can also lead to miscommunication. Cooke (1995) recounts a case in which a witness, bilingual in AAE and Djambarrpuyngu, was asked of the victim's violent nature in an incident that took place prior to his murder. In the excerpt below, confusion arises because the lawyer is asking about a spear, but the incident actually involved 'a light length of wood', a stick, from which a spear would be made.

COUNSEL:	You knew that he'd thrown a spear at [his brother], didn't you?
WITNESS:	It wasn't a real spear, it was blunt in the nose.
COUNSEL:	It was what?
WITNESS:	It wasn't a real spear with a sharp edge on it.
COUNSEL:	When I asked you whether you know about these things...?
WITNESS:	I've heard it, yes. I've heard about that.
COUNSEL:	Please tell me that you have.
WITNESS:	Yes.
COUNSEL:	You'd heard about him throwing a spear at [his brother], hadn't you?
WITNESS:	Yes.

(Cooke, 1995, p. 104)

In the witness' first language, the same noun is used for *spear* and the light length of wood from which a spear is made. The victim had not thrown a spear at his brother, rather he threw a stick. With this confusion on the table, the witness resorts to gratuitous concurrence after he appears to recognize that his distinction between the two objects is not shared by counsel. Had it been possible for the intermediary to assist, the referential double duty of the single word 'spear' would not have gone unexplained, and the defendant's having thrown a piece of wood would not have been represented as his having thrown a spear. Linguistic intervention was left to the discretion of the coroner presiding over the hearing to determine points at which the intermediary (Cooke himself) was permitted to facilitate, and this was not one of those instances.

In the same case, where the intermediary was permitted to facilitate communication, he did, and confusion is remedied. Below, counsel is shown asserting a negative argument with a tag question. The confirming response in SAE would be 'no', but in AAE the confirming answer is 'yes'. The intermediary clarifies:

COUNSEL:	But the old man didn't go in the boat, did he?
WITNESS:	Yes.
COUNSEL:	I beg your pardon.
WITNESS:	Yes.
INTERMEDIARY:	Yes, he's affirming [that] he didn't go in the boat.
CORONER:	The old man didn't go in the boat.
SECOND COUNSEL:	He's answering you exactly on point.
CORONER:	You ask these questions that way and that's what you get.

(Cooke, 1995, p. 109)

Interestingly, the coroner conducting the hearing reminds counsel that he had asked his question in a manner not prescribed by the recommendations and in a way that gives rise to confusion. This type of 'tag' question was examined earlier in the chapter.

The Australian justice system's use of intermediaries is by no means a perfect solution because intermediary involvement is still at the discretion of the court, and an AAE speaker might convincingly present as a competent SAE speaker. Furthermore, as Eades sadly notes, the handbook has been used by some lawyers to linguistically manipulate AAE speaking witnesses, in effect using their discourse strategies against them (Eades, 2004, p. 501). This point demonstrates the need for linguistic assessment of a witness' competence in one or both dialects and a review of counsels' conduct, so that a linguistically vulnerable witness can be accommodated and participate fully.

In no other part of the English speaking world have intermediaries been formally engaged by investigators or the courts to facilitate understanding where cross-cultural language issues alone, such as those described in this section, threaten to derail clear communication, although there have been occasions when intervention would be appropriate. In Canada, noted differences between aboriginal varieties of English have led to miscommunication in institutional settings (Ball, Bernhardt & Derby, 2006; Fadden, 2007; Scollon & Scollon, 1981), most notably in schools where dialect differences are misdiagnosed as speech impediments and police interviews where discourse strategies of white questioners and aboriginal respondents do not align.

While the grammatical properties of the standard and aboriginal varieties in Canada are not as disparate as they are in Australia, there is enough of a difference that Aboriginal witnesses appear uncooperative and unreliable. In Western Canada, Aboriginal English speakers contribute significantly little to investigative interviews, deny allegations with a simple no, rather than dispute them with alternative accounts, and otherwise tend to mount little defence for themselves (Fadden, 2007). While the assistance of an intermediary might not be warranted in the case of Canadian Aboriginal English speakers, investigators, lawyers, judges and jury members should all be informed that the discourse features comprising this variety of English are not markers of deception, non-cooperation or untrustworthiness but are language differences. Little ground has been gained thus far in that regard and disabusing the legal profession and the public of these linguistic prejudices and preconceptions is yet to happen.

In the United States, despite a decade-long movement by linguists, educators and activists to recast African American English, or Black English (BE), as a legitimate dialect, governed by a grammar as descriptively robust as any other, linguistic prejudice and miscommunication endure both in the justice system and society at large (see Baugh, 2000, an overview of African American English varieties and their place among other varieties of American English). In 2013, the trial of George Zimmerman, the white night watchman who shot and killed a young black, Trayvon Martin, was carried out in a Florida court (*State of Florida v. G. Zimmerman*). This well-televised case highlighted the need for linguistic intervention for at least one African American English speaker called to testify for the prosecution. Rachel Jeantel, Martin's close friend, took the stand for several hours recounting the phone call between her and Martin in the moments before he was shot to death. Jeantel was chastized in the courtroom and maligned viciously in the media for her use of Black English. In much of the American reporting on her testimony, and to the prejudiced ear, she sounded rude, uneducated and spoke in 'ungrammatical' sentences. While a competent speaker of BE, she was a vulnerable witness in this environment whose testimony was not taken as credibly as one whose variety provokes no negative judgement.

If we accept that speakers of minority dialects are disadvantaged in the interrogation room and in the courtroom, and they are deemed vulnerable witnesses by virtue of the fact that their testimony is compromised, then linguists and practising intermediaries have considerable work ahead to facilitate communication as the Australians have begun to do and also to dispel linguistic prejudice so that access to justice is not denied.

CONCLUDING REMARKS

Vulnerability has been referred to throughout this chapter and we have demonstrated that the term can have different meanings within different jurisdictions. In England and Wales vulnerability is defined in terms of age, mental disorder, intellectual disability or a physical disorder that may impact on communication. Whilst vulnerability may be defined differently in other jurisdictions, with the focus being on cross-cultural communication, the excerpts used in this chapter have highlighted that other issues such as the use of tag questions can also lead to a vulnerable person acquiescing or being compliant towards a person in authority. Racial prejudice is an additional layer to compound the problem.

The provision of information to lawyers and members of the jury should assist in enabling justice to be done, as well as making the vulnerable person's journey through the criminal justice system less discriminatory and less of an ordeal. Realistically, though, we cannot expect lawyers and jurors to become experts in communication assessments, cross-cultural linguistics and appropriate interventions and therefore intermediaries ought to be considered, whatever their specific role, in each jurisdiction. The intermediary will have little intervention to make at court if the lawyers understand the rationale behind the communication strategy and are able to adopt their questioning accordingly. In England and Wales we are hearing anecdotal comments that some courts are accepting the intermediary report and stating that the intermediary is not required at trial as the lawyers are quite capable of implementing the proposed communication strategies. However, we would strongly argue that the presence of a suitably qualified and skilled intermediary is essential when the witness is cross-examined as the intermediary is trained to respond to unanticipated communication issues that may occur during cross-examination.

Intermediaries are instrumental in bringing good practice issues to the attention of the court. For instance, the intermediary can make a recommendation to the court that the vulnerable witness views their video-recorded interview for the purposes of memory-refreshing at a time prior to attending court for cross-examination. Vulnerable witnesses can become fatigued very easily and in many cases it is just not acceptable that they should be made to watch their interview at the same time as the jury. Additionally, intermediaries have been instrumental in advising police officers responsible for holding video identification procedures about the best way to adapt communication so that the vulnerable witness can understand the identification procedure (Plotnikoff & Woolfson, 2011).

It is essential that the criminal justice system does not engage the use of intermediaries in defendant cases merely to 'be seen to be doing good' whilst at the same time attempting to reduce the number of interventions made by the intermediary at court, as demonstrated in the illustrated defendant case in this chapter. The intermediary must remain a reflective practitioner and ensure that interventions are made as appropriate regardless of whether the prosecutor or defence counsel has asked a question in an inappropriate form. It is the duty of the intermediary to assist all parties within the courtroom and not just the party that initially requested the communication assessment. Intermediaries need to be resilient as they carry out their duties in the courtroom, sometimes without the support of lawyers and the judiciary.

Whilst this chapter has used a child case to illustrate the use of a witness intermediary and an adult with intellectual disabilities to illustrate the defendant case within the England and Wales context, we must stress that persons can be vulnerable through many communication difficulties arising from organic or traumatic brain injury and intermediaries are used in cases for vulnerable persons who have had strokes, Parkinson's disease, ADHD, dementia, mental illness and many other types of communication need.

Finally, we have noted a dearth of academic research about the function of the intermediary in witness and defendant cases and we urge readers to consider the opportunities available to create an evidence base for the progress and development of worldwide intermediary schemes. To date, whilst anecdotal evidence from the police and the courts has been generally positive, empirical research has not been conducted to inform us of how effective the intermediary presence is at the police interview stage and at court. Significantly, there has been no research to find out what impact, if any, the intermediary has on juror decision-making. Nevertheless, the vast amount of communication research suggests that improving communication should improve justice outcomes.

REFERENCES

Baldwin, J. (1993). Police interview techniques. Establishing truth or proof? *British Journal of Criminology, 33*, 325–352.

Ball, J., Bernhardt, B., & Derby, J. (2006). *Exploring First Nations English dialects and implications for policy and practice.* Project Proceedings, School of Audiology and Speech Sciences, University of British Columbia and School of Child and Youth Care, University of Victoria.

Baugh, J. (2000). *Beyond Ebonics: Racial pride and linguistic prejudice.* London, UK: Oxford University Press.

Blankenship, K. L., & Craig, T. Y. (2007). Language and persuasion: Tag questions as powerless speech or as interpreted in context. *Journal of Experimental Social Psychology, 43*, 112–118.

Caruso, D., & Cross, T. (2012). The case in Australia for further reform to the cross-examination and court management of child witnesses. *The International Journal of Evidence and Proof, 16*, 364–397.

Clarke, C., & Milne, R. (2001). *National evaluation of the PEACE investigative interviewing course.* London, UK: Home Office.

Cooke, M. (1995). Interpreting in a cross-cultural cross-examination: An Aboriginal case study. *International Journal of the Sociology of Language, 113*, 99–111.

Cools, E., Van den Broeck, H., & Bouckenooghe, D. (2009). Cognitive styles and person-environment fit: Investigating the consequences of cognitive (mis)fit. *European Journal of Work and Organizational Psychology, 18* (2), 167–198.

Cooper, P., & Wurtzel, D. (2013). A day late and a dollar short: In search of an intermediary scheme for vulnerable defendants in England and Wales. *Criminal Law Review,* (1), 4–22.

Dent, H., & Flin, R. (1992). *Children as witnesses*. Chichester, UK: John Wiley & Sons, Ltd.

Department of Justice. (2015). *Northern Ireland registered intermediaries schemes pilot project: Post-project review*. Northern Ireland: Author. Retrieved from http://www.dojni.gov.uk/index/publications/publication-categories/pubs-criminal-justice/ri-post-project-reviewfeb15.pdf

Eades, D. (1992). *Aboriginal English and the law: Communicating with Aboriginal English speaking clients: A handbook for legal practitioners*. Brisbane, Australia: Queensland Law Society.

Eades, D. (1994). A case of communicative clash: Aboriginal English and the legal system. In J. Gibbons (Ed.), *Language and the law* (pp. 234–264). London, UK: Longman.

Eades, D. (1995). Cross-examination of Aboriginal children: The Pinkenba case. *Aboriginal Law Bulletin, 3*(75), 10–11.

Eades, D. (2000). 'I don't think it's an answer to the question': Silencing Aboriginal witnesses in court. *Language and Society, 29*(2), 161–196.

Eades, D. (2004). Understanding Aboriginal English in the legal system: A critical sociolinguistics approach. *Applied Linguistics, 25*, 491–512.

Eades, D. (2006). Lexical struggle in court: *Aboriginal Australians v. The State. Journal of Sociolinguistics, 10*(2), 153–181.

Eades, D. (2008). *Courtroom talk and neocolonial control*. Berlin, Germany: Mouton de Gruyter.

Eades, D. (2012). The social consequences of language ideologies in courtroom cross-examination. *Language in Society, 41*, 471–497.

Fadden, L. (2007). Quantitative and qualitative analyses of police interviews with Canadian Aboriginal and non Aboriginal suspects. In K. Kredens & S. Gozdz-Roszkowski (Eds.), *Language and the law: International outlooks*. Frankfurt am Main, Germany: Peter Lang GmbH.

Flin, R. H., Stevenson, Y., and Davies, G. M. (1989). Children's knowledge of court proceedings. *British Journal of Psychology, 80*, 285–297.

Furnham, A., & Walsh, J. (2001). Consequences of person–environment incongruence: Absenteeism, frustration, and stress. *The Journal of Social Psychology, 131*(2), 187–204.

Grant, F., & Hogg, M. A. (2012). Self-uncertainty, social identity prominence and group identification. *Journal of Experimental Social Psychology, 48*, 538–542.

Gudjonsson, G. H. (2003). *The psychology of interrogations and confessions: A handbook*. Chichester, UK: John Wiley & Sons, Ltd.

Gumperz, J. (1982). *Discourse strategies*. Cambridge, UK: Cambridge University Press.

Harres, A. (1998). 'But basically you're feeling well, are you?': Tag questions in medical consultations. *Health Communication, 10*(2), 111–123.

Home Office. (2005). *Police and Criminal Evidence Act 1984: Codes of Practice A-G*. London, UK: TSO.

Hotho, S. (2008). Professional identity – product of structure, product of choice. Linking changing professional identity and changing professions. *Journal of Organizational Change Management, 21* (6), 721–742.

Hoyano, L. C. H. (2010). Coroners and Justice Act 2009: Special measures directions take two: Entrenching unequal access to justice? *Criminal Law Review,* 345–367.

Jackson, H. (2003). *Child witnesses in the Western Australian criminal courts*. Paper presented at the Child Sexual Abuse: Justice Response or Alternative Resolution Conference convened by the Australian Institute of Criminology, Adelaide.

Jacobson, J. (2008). *No one knows: Police responses to suspects with learning disabilities and learning difficulties: A review of policy and practice*. London, UK: Prison Reform Trust.

Judicial College. (2013). *Equal treatment bench book*. London, UK: Author.

Kearins, J. (1991). Factors affecting Aboriginal testimony. *Legal Service Bulletin, 16*(1), 3–6.

Kebbell, M. R., Hatton, C., & Johnson, S. D. (2004). Witnesses with intellectual disabilities in court: What questions are asked and what influence do they have? *Legal and Criminological Psychology, 9*, 23–35.

Matthias, C. R., & Zaal, F. N. (2011). Intermediaries for child witnesses: Old problems, new solutions and judicial differences in South Africa. *International Journal of Children's Rights, 19*, 251–269.

Medford, S., Gudjonsson, G., & Pearse, J. (2003). The efficacy of the appropriate adult safeguard during police interviewing. *Legal and Criminological Psychology, 8*, 253–266.

Mildren, D. (1999). Redressing the imbalance: Aboriginal people in the criminal justice system. *Forensic Linguistics, 6*(1), 137–160.

Ministry of Justice. (2011). *The registered intermediary procedural guidance manual*.

Ministry of Justice. (2012). *The registered intermediary procedural guidance manual*. Victims and Witnesses Unit.

O'Mahony, B. M. (2010). The emerging role of the Registered Intermediary with the vulnerable witness and offender: Facilitating communication with the police and members of the judiciary. *British Journal of Learning Disabilities, 38*, 232–237.

O'Mahony, B. M. (2012). Accused of murder: Supporting the communication needs of a vulnerable defendant at court and at the police station. *Journal of Learning Disabilities and Offending Behaviour, 3*(2), 77–84.

O'Mahony, B. M. (2013). *How do intermediaries experience their role in facilitating communication for vulnerable defendants?* (Professional Doctorate in Criminal Justice DCrimJ). University of Portsmouth, Portsmouth, UK.

O'Mahony, B. M., Creaton, J., Smith, K., & Milne, R. (in press). Developing a professional identity in a new work environment: The views of defendant intermediaries working in the criminal courts. *The Journal of Forensic Practice*.

O'Mahony, B. M., Milne, B., & Grant, T. (2012). To challenge or not to challenge? Best practice when interviewing vulnerable suspects. *Policing: A Journal of Policy and Practice, 6*(3), 301–313.

O'Mahony, B. M., Smith, K., & Milne, R. (2011). The early identification of vulnerable witnesses prior to an investigative interview. *The British Journal of Forensic Practice, 13*(2), 114–123.

Plotnikoff, J., & Woolfson, R. (2007). *The 'go-between': Evaluation of intermediary pathfinder projects*. London, UK: Ministry of Justice.

Plotnikoff, J., & Woolfson, R. (2011). *Registered intermediaries in action: Messages for the CJS from the Witness Intermediary Scheme Smartsite*. London, UK: Lexicon Limited.

Scollon, R., & Scollon, S. (1981). *Narrative, literacy and face in interethnic communication*. Norwood, NJ: Ablex.

SCRGSP. (2011). *Overcoming indigenous disadvantage: Key indicators 2011*. Melbourne, Australia: Productivity Commission.

Strehlow, T. G. (1936). Notes on native evidence and its value. *Oceania, 6*(3), 323–335.

14

The Interpreter-Mediated Police Interview

Yvonne Fowler[1], Martin Vaughan[2] and Jacqueline Wheatcroft[3]
[1] Aston University, Birmingham, UK
[2] University of Portsmouth, UK
[3] University of Liverpool, UK

> Not all texts are created equal. Some occupy special positions within a culture and become the focus of multiple realisations ... others fade away.
>
> (Silverstein and Urban, 1996, p.12)

INTRODUCTION

Interview evidence is a fundamental and integral part of criminal justice in jurisdictions around the world (Wheatcroft, Caruso & Krumrey-Quinn, 2014). It is of the utmost importance in the legal process as witness reports may outweigh other evidence and be one of the most powerful factors in the determination of acquittal or conviction (Kebbell & Giles, 2000). Interview evidence has particular relevance when an individual requires interpreting assistance. This chapter will focus on the interpreter-mediated interview from two perspectives, that of the police

Communication in Investigative and Legal Contexts: Integrated Approaches from Forensic Psychology, Linguistics and Law Enforcement, First Edition. Edited by Gavin Oxburgh, Trond Myklebust, Tim Grant and Rebecca Milne.

officer and that of the interpreter, and will consider how these differing perspectives can be brought together to forge an effective professional working relationship. It will also integrate psychological literature that informs our understandings and perceptions of interaction in interview settings. The chapter will firstly explore the use of interpreters in a suspect interview setting and will discuss commonly held beliefs among police officers about the nature of language and how interpreters operate. There will follow an exploration of the cognitive witness interview as a case in point to demonstrate in greater detail the impact of the interpreter and the unusual and challenging complexity of a triadic witness interview setting. It will also highlight the urgent need for the training of police officers to enable them to work collaboratively with interpreters so that suspects and witnesses who do not speak English can be on a level footing with those who do. This chapter draws largely upon the legal jurisdiction of England and Wales unless otherwise stated.

As a point of definition it is important to distinguish between *interpreting* and *translating*, two terms that may be commonly seen as interchangeable. Within the field of interpreting, these terms have a more precise definition: *interpreting* means the act of transferring a *spoken* utterance from one language to another while *translation*, on the other hand, is taken to mean the act of transferring the *written* word from one language to another language. In the former procedure, the end result is spoken. In the latter, the end result is written. Lay people and the press often use these terms interchangeably. Confusingly, academics have long appropriated the term 'translation' to mean the process of transferring a concept from one language to another, whether spoken or written (House, 1997; Pöchhacker, 2004; Rabin, 1958; Wadensjö, 1998). Interpreters are usually concerned with the spoken language but in the case of witness statements they are often required to *translate* written witness statements into another language. In the case of written witness statements, for example, interpreters both *interpret* spoken material during the oral phase and *translate* written material during the writing phase. In addition, interpreters may also need sight or oral translation skills, a procedure involving the transfer of written text in one language to spoken text in the other. Conversely, translators may not be qualified to interpret and should not be asked to do so. In some areas there can be very few competent, properly trained, qualified and experienced public service interpreters, and additional competence to translate cannot be assumed by officers when deploying them. Further to these task and competence issues, most interpreters in the United Kingdom are now hired through agencies and thus operate under commercial pressures, which can constrain their professional interest in the service they provide.

INTERPRETING AS TRIADIC COMMUNICATION

Triadic communication is different from dyadic communication and interpreting is a special case in this regard Hale (2007). As Wadensjö argues, 'meanings conveyed by language use are conceptualised and co-constructed between speakers and hearers *in interaction*' (Wadensjö, 1998, p. 41). Thus when an officer interviews a witness in their native language, for example, their turn will trigger some sort of verbal response or non-verbal reaction from the hearer. The hearer then responds according to the meaning they think was intended by that prior turn. In interpreter-mediated interaction, the third party is present, so questions, answers and meanings are being jointly constructed *in the course of the interaction* by *three* different people, two of whom are entirely dependent on the renditions of the interpreter. Different interpreters will render turns differently, using different grammar, vocabulary and cultural meanings according to their own understanding, experience, education, background, culture and extent of training (Hale, 2007). This crucial concept is generally not understood by those communicating through interpreters including police officers. One accepted lay view of interpreters is that they are 'transmission belts' or 'machines' and that texts fed in at one end are transposed in a machine-like manner only to emerge in the target language at the other as if by magic (Wells, 1991). In triadic communication the two participants who cannot speak each other's language are responding to the interpreter's turns, not to each other's. Moreover, judicial contexts have their own specialized vocabularies and cultures, and an interpreter is an outsider to this culture. Interpreters untrained in pragmatics and other aspects of judicial language will find themselves unable to, as Hale (2007, p. 13) puts it, 'reduce the differences between the original and interpreted versions by matching...the illocutionary...force and producing a similar perlocutionary act (the reaction of the hearer)'. In plain terms, an interpreter should be able to render someone's speech in such a way as to evoke the same or similar effect in the hearer as if the speaker were able to communicate directly with that hearer. This can be a challenge even for a highly trained professional interpreter.

A POLICE PERSPECTIVE OF THE INTERPRETED INTERVIEW

Across many jurisdictions, police officers are well aware that professional and competent interpreting services are of pivotal importance in preventing possible miscarriages of justice, and also that the quality of interpreting services has a direct bearing on the outcome level of justice. Within UK jurisdictions police guidance stipulates that interviewers and interpreters must work together throughout the interview, that the professionalism of interpreters should be acknowledged, and that every effort must be made to fully engage with them at all stages throughout the interview process. Given this guidance it is perhaps surprising that there is still little meaningful or explicit advice for officers about how such collaboration can be achieved.

Theoretically at least, there is guidance available to police officers in the UK regarding the deployment of interpreters. Police officers in England and Wales are trained under a variety of legal and professional frameworks, which include working with interpreters. There is mention in:

(a) The framework of the Human Rights Act 2000, which incorporates the European Convention on Human Rights into English and Welsh Law.

(b) The Police and Criminal Evidence Act 1984 (PACE).

(c) The Codes of Practice that accompany the PACE, the PEACE model of interviewing (discussed elsewhere in this volume), training material used by all police forces in England and Wales for specialist interviews with suspects, produced initially by the National Policing Improvement Agency (NPIA) (Association of Chief Police Officers, 2004). It is important to note that the NPIA's functions have since (in 2013) been incorporated into the Home Office, the National Crime Agency (NCA) and the College of Policing. Nevertheless, information is drawn upon for the purposes of this chapter.

From a broader European perspective there is also Article 6 of a recent European Directive (Commission Directive, 2010/64/EU), which stipulates that member states are responsible for providing appropriate training of judges, prosecutors, police and judicial staff involved in interpreter-mediated criminal proceedings with respect to the Directives. The Directive was incorporated into PACE Code C 13.1A, highlighting the legal requirement to comply with the EU Directive. Again, detailed training has yet to materialize.

Whilst all of these frameworks acknowledge the need for interpreters, they lack any kind of useful detail. An examination of the most recent training material for UK investigative interviewing as provided by the NPIA has the following three elements in Unit 2H6:

2H6.1   Plan and prepare specialist interviews with suspects.

2H6.2   Conduct specialist interviews with suspects.

2H6.3   Evaluate specialist interviews with suspects and carry out post- interview processes

Contained within each of these elements are references to interactions with interpreters; for example, 2H6.1 performance criteria 7, states *'Consult with relevant others (including interpreters) to establish an interview strategy'*, but does not explain what such a consultation would entail nor how the interpreter would impact upon the interview strategy. The units also contain a range of 'Knowledge and Understanding' factors that are to be demonstrated throughout the interview process. These include a section on *'How to deal with suspects and relevant others (including interpreters) in an ethical manner'*, but does not explain what form ethical behaviour might take in an interpreter-mediated setting. Moreover, the NPIA nationally agreed timetable for the course does not provide any training regarding the use of interpreters in the interview process.

The NPIA training unit addressing Managing, Advising and Co-ordinating interviews for complex or major investigations, Unit 2H7, focuses on the work of the Interview Adviser, whose role is to assist the Senior Investigating Officer by managing the interview process. This Unit itself has four elements:

2H7.1   Provide strategic advice on interview processes.

2H7.2   Co-ordinate interview processes.

2H7.3   Monitor interview processes.

2H7.4   Evaluate interview processes.

Again, contained within each element are references to interactions with interpreters, for example 2H7.2, performance criteria 9, states *'Ensure the appropriate attendance of any relevant others (includes interpreters) in order to expedite the interview process.'* However, no explanation is given regarding what is meant by 'appropriate attendance' of interpreters or how to ensure that interpreters who are engaged are appropriate. Police interviewers and interview advisors are thus left with rather vague instructions but without currently the systematic training or necessary skills required for conducting interpreter-mediated interviews with witnesses or with suspects. This deficit may be partly because of the lack of knowledge of the research base in this area and a lack of consultation with experts in interpreting.

One principal assumption commonly held by non-experts, including police officers, when considering interpretation is the notion of 'the language barrier' and this in itself is likely to make the working relationship between police and interpreter more problematic. It can be common for police officers to cite 'the language barrier' as a negative factor in police interviews. They tend to see communicating with a person who does not speak the mainstream language as problematic in itself, in contrast with communication with native speakers. There is perhaps a perception that communication between native speakers is a transparent process free from too much difficulty. As far as the role of the interpreter is concerned, police can worry that such features as 'nuance' and 'emphasis' may be lost in the interpreting process and conceive of 'accuracy" as the verbatim transfer of meanings and words from one language to another. The notion of the interpreter as mediator, co-constructing the text with police officers and witnesses and suspects, is one that, in their view, is highly contentious and risks distortion of meaning. (The concept of the interpreter as mediator will be more fully explored later in this chapter.) There is sometimes little belief and trust that an interpreter can interpret between the two languages in such a way that 'effective communication' can take place and there is little thought about the nature of effective communication from a linguistic or accuracy point of view. There are a number of key points during the investigation of an offence where lack of training for both officers and interpreters can disadvantage the suspect or witness and may hinder the course of an enquiry. We turn to these next.

One significant initial issue can be the selection of the interpreter. In the UK, police officers are recommended, in the provided guidance that does exist, to ensure that the interpreter is 'appropriate' for the case in question in terms of culture, language, age, education and religion, but, in reality, these elements are often taken on trust. There can be a perception that it will be more appropriate to use a female rather than a male interpreter in certain sensitive cases such as rape or domestic violence, and indeed this may be a vulnerable witness' preference. A properly trained and qualified interpreter, however, can be expected to act in a detached manner in most contexts within a strictly defined code of practice (National Register of Public Service Interpreters Code of Practice, 2011) and will be used to dealing with a variety of sensitive situations such as medical consultations. Expecting police officers to assess the competence and suitability of interpreters in terms of language and qualifications is inappropriate, but systems of accreditation and lists of approved interpreters are under attack. This issue is exacerbated for rarer second languages in any particular geographic area.

The next issue that might occur is at the start of the interview process with the administration and explanation of the caution. In the UK context this explanation of the detainee's rights takes place on arrest, again when a suspect first arrives at the police station and also at intervals during the interview itself. The formal caution reads as follows:

> *You do not have to say anything, but it may harm your defence if you do not mention when questioned something which you later rely on in court. Anything you do say may be given in evidence.*
>
> (PACE 1984: Code C paragraph 10)

Even for the native speaker the reading aloud of the written caution is problematic and Cotterill (2000), amongst others, highlighted some of these issues. For the interpreter-mediated interview this problem is compounded. As Nakane's research (2007) demonstrates, rendering a written legal text in face-to-face spoken mode is a challenging task for interpreters, and this is perhaps unsurprising. Cotterill in her work showed that English-to-English re-phrasing and paraphrasing of the caution can be challenging tasks for police officers. She stated that 'asking linguistically untrained officers to provide paraphrases which are graded for both language and comprehensibility is unreasonable' (Cotterill, 2000, p. 1). Russell's (2001) analysis of interpreter-mediated interviews focused on the cautioning process and found that there were more interpreter problems with its administration and explanation than in the body of the interview itself.

There may be a divide in the delivery of the interpreted caution between well-trained well-prepared interpreters who frequently attend police interviews and less experienced interpreters for whom a police interview is a rarer assignment. One issue may be that those interpreters, who may rarely be involved in interviews, may have as much difficulty as the general public in fully understanding the implications of the caution. Russell (2001) recommends that all interview interpreters should work to standard versions of the caution to promote consistency of practice. Such standard translations of the caution have long been available to police officers to show to arrested persons who do not speak English but may still be underused by inexperienced interpreters. On the other hand, police officers may understandably be unaware that an experienced, trained and well-qualified interpreter can be expected to have undertaken considerable prior analysis of the caution during training and that those competent, professional interpreters will carry with them a previously translated written caution to which they will refer at the appropriate moment (UK Home Office, 2014).

A further difficulty might be in the assessment of a suspect's understanding of the caution. It is well documented that simply asking suspects whether they have understood the implications of the caution can be problematic (e.g. Gibbons, 2001; Liberman, 1980; Shuy, 1997). In the interpreted interview this can be compounded where officers may demonstrate their misunderstanding of the role of interpreters by asking the interpreter whether the suspect understands the caution. The interviewer of course should be asking the suspects themselves to explain the caution and its implications in their own words; the interpreter's role is to mediate this interaction.

In the Anglo-Welsh legal system suspects under arrest are entitled to consult a legal adviser either in person or by telephone prior to any interview. The implications for interpreters are considerable, in that they have a double duty of confidentiality. First, they must not divulge details of the case in general and, second, they must not reveal to the police any instructions the suspect may give to the legal adviser during the consultation. There can be confusion amongst police officers about how this should be handled. Should there be one interpreter for the legal consultation and another for the police interview? Officers often express concern that information discussed during the legal consultation may 'leak' into the suspect interview proper, but the Code of Practice for interpreters is clear in principle about the ethics of this, stating that:

> Practitioners shall respect confidentiality at all times and shall not seek to take advantage of information acquired during or as a result of their work. The duty of confidentiality shall not terminate on the completion of a commission of work and shall persist, where appropriate, beyond the cessation of registration as in 2.1.
>
> (National Register of Public Service Interpreters
> Code of Practice, 2011, 3.13)

A well-trained and well-qualified interpreter will be aware of their professional obligations and aware of the potential for leakage between a legal discussion and the interview. This awareness means that there should be no professional, ethical or linguistic reason why the same trained and qualified interpreter should not interpret in both situations without compromising confidentiality or impartiality.

INTERVIEW TECHNIQUES USED WITH WITNESSES: THEORY AND PRACTICE

There are different techniques applied to witness and suspect interviews as described and critiqued throughout this volume. In conversation management interview techniques 'the interviewee is asked first to say what happened and the officer then subdivides the account into a number of individual parts which are enquired about in turn for further details' (McGurk, Carr & McGurk, 1993, p. 8). In the cognitive approach to interviewing 'the interviewee is asked to think back and mentally relive the event, initially with minimal interference from the interviewing officer. The officer does not interrupt, makes effective use of pauses and avoids leading questions. The officer will then identify evidential topics that will be explored further via a range of questioning techniques. In this complex interaction it is particularly important that the correct form and type of question is used so as to not confuse the witness' (see Wheatcroft, Caruso and Krumrey-Quinn, 2014, for a debate on questioning in legal contexts). In the conversation management approach the locus of control is said to rest with the police officer; in the cognitive approach it is said to rest with the witness. Most witness statements are taken at police stations, but some are taken at the home of the witness. On occasions, and rather disturbingly, there are anecdotal reports that some police officers have failed to understand the role of interpreters and find it difficult to understand the need for a police officer to be present at such an interview at all. Thus interpreters report occasions where officers put pressure upon interpreters to conduct the witness interview by themselves at a witness's home or in a separate room at the police station (Fowler, 2003). Compliant interpreters to such practices may then be employed in preference to those who insist upon adhering to their code of conduct (to which the UK police are also signatories; see the National Agreement, 1997).

ORAL AND WRITTEN PHASES OF STATEMENT-TAKING

In England and Wales, most witness statement-taking procedures generally begin with an oral phase and end with a written phase and they are not normally recorded. Some witness statements are video recorded and subsequently transcribed and translated but this usually only applies to vulnerable witnesses and serious offences such as rape. In general, witness statement procedures are time-consuming, a process that is necessarily prolonged when there is an interpreter required. Elsewhere in this volume doubt has been cast on several aspects of written statement-taking, not only in terms of reliability and efficacy when compared to audio- and video-recorded text but also in terms of inhibiting the free flow of information from the witness as well as over-emphasizing the taking of the written statement at the expense of the witness's account. However, with few exceptions, this is still the most common outcome of a witness interview in the Anglo-Welsh system and it is one we shall examine in some detail.

COGNITIVE INTERVIEWS AND INTERPRETERS

When it comes to the questioning and interviewing of suspects, police officers may be better used to using conversation management techniques to elicit information from suspects or witnesses when using interpreters. An officer poses a question, the interpreter listens and interprets that question to the suspect or witness who answers in his/her language and the interpreter interprets that answer to the officer. Suspect, as opposed to witness, interviews in England and Wales are mandatorily audio-recorded (and sometimes video-recorded). Audio-recordings preclude overlapping speech, for the sake of the clarity of the recording. The key characteristic of a cognitive interview, however, is that officers are supposed to allow the witness to freely recall what they remember with the minimum of interruption; this technique is said to elicit the greatest number of remembered facts without inducing a greater number of errors (see Wagstaff & Wheatcroft, 2012). This gives rise to the following concern. If an interview between a witness and a police officer is to be mediated by an interpreter, is it possible to maintain the original objective of a cognitive interview format, which is to elicit a free narrative flow with the minimum of interruptions, bearing in mind the need for the interpreter to hold material in her short-term memory before rendering it into the appropriate language? Interpreters certainly vary in terms of their short-term memory capacity and the more deficient they are in this respect, the greater the impact they will have upon the interview. This deficiency will necessarily manifest itself in a greater number of interpreter interventions (requests for repetition, requests for shorter turns), and this will undoubtedly interfere with the officer's intended method of communication using the cognitive approach.

Research shows that a shortened procedure is viable. For example, some time ago Davis, McMahon and Greenwood (2004) demonstrated that a shortened version of the enhanced cognitive interview was as effective as the traditional version. As the original versions of the cognitive interview have been found wanting in some regards the process has become recognized for being too time-consuming in both administration and training. Moreover, police officers have been found not to adhere to the procedure (Dando, Wilcock & Milne, 2009) or adopt selected components they believe are useful (see Wheatcroft, Wagstaff & Russell, 2014). More recently a 'toolbox' approach to obtaining information has surfaced (see Wheatcroft & Wagstaff, 2014) and, given this, it is conceivable that a different model or technique for the 'toolbox' could be adopted for the context described in this chapter. So where does this leave the interpreter, the police officer, the foreign language-speaking witness and cognitive techniques? Must officers resign themselves to using an interview technique that is known to be less effective simply to accommodate the interpreter?

CHUCHOTAGE AND 'LONG CONSECUTIVE' TECHNIQUES

A simple solution to this dilemma is for the interpreter to sit close beside the interviewing police officer facing the witness and to use the simultaneous interpreting technique, known in the public service context as *chuchotage*. The interpreter listens to the witness and delivers a whispered (*sotto voce*) rendition of what the witness is saying, at the same time as the witness is speaking. No interpreting equipment is used. *Chuchotage* is said to minimize interpreter interventions or avoid them altogether (Colin & Morris, 1996, p. 48). Another solution is for the interpreter to use so-called the *long consecutive* technique (Hale, 2007). This requires the interpreter to take extensive notes whilst listening to the witness speaking. The interpreter then asks the witness to stop after about five minutes or so whilst the interpreter renders the whole of that segment to the police officer, with the aid of notes. This continues, with the interpreter delivering the witness's speech in segments throughout the interview. Whilst the witness has less control over how much she delivers in one go in order to accommodate the interpreter, long consecutive (as compared to short consecutive) also tends to minimize interpreter interventions. Whilst these two techniques are available and appropriate for cognitive witness interviews that are not audio-recorded, there are some disadvantages. First, there are very few interpreters who have the necessary training or skills to deliver these techniques and, second, police officers often find it difficult to adapt themselves to receiving information through *chuchotage* or long consecutive and require training in order to enable them to do so. For obvious reasons, the use of a simultaneous technique is not amenable to audio or video recording, whereas long consecutive is. Therefore, long consecutive is preferable to short consecutive, but unfortunately both methods will include damaging interruptions that interfere with witness memorial processes. In any case the use of these techniques also requires prior discussion between the interpreter, officer and witness so that interactants are fully prepared and know what to expect. Alternatively, the long consecutive technique could be applied in the following way. First, the witness recalls the incident freely without interruption with the interpreter taking simultaneous notes, thus maintaining free recall and maximizing useful information. Only then does the interpreter relay the interpreted information to the officer who constructs the statement. Of course, this may add a little time compared to *chuchotage* but ensures (a) maximal efficacy is maintained by the process of free recall, (b) careful clarifications may be sought and (c) questions devised to explore identified topic areas are based on accepted forensic practice. Such recommendations should form part of a package of rigorous training and best practice guidelines for interpreters and police officers alike.

IMPACT UPON WRITTEN STATEMENT-TAKING PROCEDURES WITH AN INTERPRETER

As we have seen, the impact of the interpreter upon the actual method of interviewing (such as the cognitive approach) can be considerable. However, the impact upon the written phase of the procedure is particularly problematic. Experimental work by Fowler (2003) involved four non-English-speaking 'witnesses' who were shown a short film clip, the details of which they were subsequently asked to recall using conversation management through two experienced, trained and qualified interpreters and two police officers who were experienced trainers of interview technique at a local police training college. In the oral phase of questioning using the conversation management technique, few problems were noted. It was during the written phase that many practical issues presented themselves. Who should actually write the statement? Should it be the police officer or should it be the interpreter? In which language should the statement be taken down first, the language of the witness or in English? Many officers make an unquestioning assumption that witness statements ought to be taken down first 'in the language of the witness', but is this, in fact, the best way to proceed? What are the advantages and disadvantages of both procedures? Fowler's (2003) conclusions about the best method were based not only on her own observations but upon the comments made by police officers themselves as they took statements. In her design, each of the two officers was asked to take a written statement after the oral questioning phase had been completed, first by asking the interpreter to compile the written statement in the witness's language and in the second condition by compiling the written statement themselves in English. Each statement was subsequently translated. The results support writing the first written statement in English. Reasons for this may be that interpreters are not trained to *take* witness statements; this is the task of a police officer who knows which evidential points are important. If a police officer asks an interpreter to take the written statement down in the language of the witness, this will necessarily exclude the officer from the interaction between the witness and the interpreter, who will be required to *compose* the statement herself by communicating directly with the witness. The police officer will, in effect, have nothing to do. However, interpreters transfer spoken utterances from one language to the other; they are not composers of text. Any resulting statement will lack the formal institutional structure and internal consistency required in a witness statement and will be the result of the interaction between the witness and interpreter, rather than the result of triadic interaction between the witness, interpreter and police officer. Sometimes officers try to circumvent the problem of 'leaving the interpreter to get on with it' by dictating the statement, sentence by sentence, to the interpreter, who then listens and translates each English sentence into the foreign language before proceeding with the next. In terms of coherence, this could create difficulties, as the interpreter-turned-translator does not know what the speakers are going to say next and may be tempted to adhere inappropriately to the grammar and structure of the source language. In theory, a police officer could hold an interpreter responsible for mistakes and inaccuracies not of his or her making, since the final dictated foreign language statement produced by the interpreter is a translation of words uttered by the police officer, and the words uttered by the police officer are the result of the interpreted version of the witness's own words; these added layers of complexity are likely to distort the original intentions of the witness. Fowler found that officers themselves preferred the English-statement-first method because they had more control and could tailor follow-up questions to elicit information relevant to the case. In addition, the procedural advantage for officers was the possession of the written statement in English. Legal advisers present at the police station would then be able to read through the statement prior to any suspect interview in the case and, even more importantly, the officer is in possession of evidence required to continue the investigation. Interestingly, officers also noticed that writing the statement in English first meant that they were able to check facts *in the act of* composing the statement, writing and speaking at the same time. It is much more difficult for interpreters to compose a statement and interpret at the same time. From a legal point of view the officers pointed out that interpreters could provide verification that the statement had been sight translated to the witness by means of a caption to that effect. However, as with any procedure, there are always disadvantages, the main one being that the witness cannot read the statement until it has been translated, and this would require the witness to come back to sign it. Tables 14.1 and 14.2 provide a brief summary of the advantages and disadvantages of the two possible procedures.

One exception is statements taken through Sign Language (SL) interpreters, which would be written in the mainstream language only, as SL is a visual language (the same will apply to any language that does not have a written script). Not all foreign language speaking or

Table 14.1   Summary of advantages and disadvantages of writing the statement in the mainstream language first

Advantages	Disadvantages
Officers retain control over what goes into the written statement by being involved in the interaction	Witnesses cannot read and sign the statement immediately after production because it is written in English
Officers know evidential points to prove and can tailor questions to elicit relevant information at the writing stage	Witness has to come back to the police station to read and sign the statement in the foreign language
Officer has possession of the statement to continue investigation	
Suspect's legal adviser is able to read the statement before any suspect	
Interpreter can produce a more competent piece of work when not under pressure to produce an instant English translation	

Table 14.2   Summary of advantages and disadvantages of writing the statement in the foreign language first

Advantages	Disadvantages
Provided the witness can read, she/he can read over the statement immediately and verify its contents	Officer has little control over what goes into the statement
	Interpreter decides what goes into the statement
	Officer cannot participate in interaction between the interpreter and witness at the writing stage
	Interpreter's translation is a translation of her own version of the written statement
	Interpreter goes beyond her prescribed role by compiling the statement

deaf witnesses can read, so the interpreter's ability to sight-translate the document prior to the witness signing is crucial. Considering the advantages and disadvantages of each method, a written statement produced in the mainstream language first will result in a document that is more faithful to the witness's intentions than one that is produced in the foreign language first. It puts the police officer in control of its production rather than the interpreter and it assigns to the interpreter her proper role of transferring meanings from one language to another. In any case, as other authors (Westera, Powell and Fowler in Chapter 15 in this volume) have maintained, it is probably time to abandon traditional written statement-taking procedures in favour of audio- or video-recorded statements, which will present fewer problems in interpreter-mediated interviews. What is urgently required is pre- and in-service training for all police officers and interpreters in conducting interpreter-mediated interviews of any kind, as well as proper national training infrastructures and meaningful registration systems for interpreters. Until these are in place, the competence of interpreters cannot be guaranteed and foreign language speaking witnesses will continue to be ill served in the judicial system. Lack of training means that neither officers nor interpreters are equipped to understand the very different dynamics of triadic interaction. The resultant gap between theory and practice in interpreter-mediated statement taking will inevitably impact adversely on the witness and in the perceptions drawn of the witness in the wider legal process.

INTERPRETED WITNESS EVIDENCE – FROM INTERVIEW TO COURTROOM

It is well attested in this volume and elsewhere (e.g. Wheatcroft & Wagstaff, 2014) that there are widely differing operational contexts and witness types encountered by police officers in the course of their investigative work. Such work also points out the dangers of relying on a single interview format (the cognitive interview) in the eliciting of information destined to be used in witness statements. A further complication is that police interview training tends to be predicated upon the assumption that witnesses are either native speakers of the language of the country they are in or that they speak that language well enough to communicate on some level or other. Research shows that the presence of an interpreter impacts significantly on the dynamics of the interaction. The characteristics of dyadic interaction (between two people) are qualitatively different to that found in triadic interaction (three people) (Wadensjö, 1998). Moreover, in terms of training, the multilingual nature of most urban policing settings often goes unacknowledged. Cotterill (2004) points out that the crucial importance of witness statement-taking procedures in the judicial system should not be underestimated. Of witness testimony she says, 'the accounts presented [in the courtroom] form part of a chain of forensic narratives extending back to the original police interviews and forwards to potential future appeal proceedings (Cotterill, 2004, p.149).

The role of an interpreter in courtroom proceedings is to mediate between individuals of different language communities in order to facilitate communicative interaction by providing linguistic and cultural equivalents such that the original message is conveyed in the interpreted utterance (Berk Seligson, 2002; Hale, 2002; Laster & Taylor, 1994; Lee, 2009). Previous work also suggests that the perception of the witness can be affected by the interpreter's translation style (Angermeyer, 2009; Berk Seligson, 2002; O'Barr, 1982). Further, psychology has long known the effects of dual-tasking, which takes the view that human processing resources are limited and shareable (Kahneman, 1973; Navon & Gopher, 1979). In this sense, juror perceptions of the interaction are critical.

In this courtroom context it is important that task guidelines have clarity of purpose and that one can rely on the efficacy of the process. For example, jurors may attend to the witness when they reply to the question put via the interpreter. The juror may, without clearly understanding what is said, form his/her impression of the witness from the interpreter's style rather than the witness' spoken evidential manner. The common practice applied by interpreters is to maintain the content of the speech without conveying the style, which increases the likelihood for the witness of being judged by the interpreter's style rather than his or her own. Taking into account the intrusive role of an interpreter it is worth asking whether the presence of an interpreter affects perceptions formed about the witness. This may be particularly important in, for example, cross-examination, where complex linguistic techniques are routinely employed by barristers. Experimental work conducted by Wheatcroft and Kieres (2014) explored juror perceptions of witnesses who had provided evidence via an 'interpreter' during cross-examination and found two main findings: jurors' perception of witness intelligence and the promptness of the witness response was greater with the use of an interpreter. However, ratings of witness accuracy and clarity remained unaffected by interpreter use. The findings are thus mixed. On the one hand, they support Berk Seligson (2002), who suggests that an interpreter is an intrusive element in proceedings that can impact on the trial whilst, on the other hand, some important assessments remained stable when the interpreter communicated the witness response. Nevertheless, one is uncertain as to whether jurors are using the information appropriately and thereby further research in this area is clearly warranted. Regardless, the presence of an interpreter in any witness interview appears to disturb the forensic narrative chain and interpretative assessments; as such, this forces us to reassess the effectiveness of current statement-taking procedures.

REFERENCES

Angermeyer, P. S. (2009). Translation style and participant roles in court interpreting. *Journal of Sociolinguistics, 13*(1), 3–28.
Association of Chief Police Officers (ACPO). (2004). *National occupational standards*. London, UK: Skills for Justice.
Berk Seligson, S. (2002). *The bilingual courtroom, court interpreters in the judicial process*. Chicago, IL: The University of Chicago Press.
Colin, J., & Morris, R. (1996). *Interpreters and the legal process*. Winchester, UK: Waterside Press.
Cotterill, J. (2000). Reading the rights: A cautionary tale of comprehension and comprehensibility. *Forensic Linguistics, 7*, 4–25.
Cotterill, J. (2004). 'Just one more time....' Aspects of intertextuality in the trial of O.J. Simpson. In J. Cotterill (Ed.), *Language in the Legal Process*. Basingstoke, UK: Palgrave Macmillan.
Dando, C., Wilcock, R., & Milne, R. (2009). The cognitive interview: Novice police officers' witness/victim interviewing practices. *Psychology, Crime and Law, 15*, 679–696.
Davis, M. R., McMahon, M., & Greenwood, K. M. (2004). The efficacy of mnemonic components of the cognitive interview: Towards a shortened variant for time-critical investigations. *Applied Cognitive Psychology, 19*(1), 75–93.
Fowler, Y. (2003). Taking an interpreted witness statement at the police station: What did the witness actually say? In L. Brunette, G. Bastin, I. Hemlin, & H. Clarke (Eds.), *The critical link 3*. Amsterdam, The Netherlands: John Benjamins Translation Library.
Gibbons, J. (2001). Revising the language of New South Wales police procedures: Applied linguistics in action. *Applied Linguistics, 11*, 229–237.
Hale, S. B. (2002). How faithful do court interpreters render the style of non-English speaking witnesses' testimonies? A data-based study of Spanish–English bilingual proceedings. *Discourse Studies, 4*, 25–47.
Hale, S. B. (2007). *Community interpreting*. Basingstoke, UK: Palgrave Macmillan.
House, J. (1977). *A model for translation quality assessment*. Tubingen, Germany: Gunter Narr Verlag.
Kahneman, D. (1973). *Attention and effort*. Englewood Cliffs, NJ: Prentice-Hall.
Kebbell, M. R., and Giles, D. C. (2000). Lawyers' questions and witness confidence: Some experimental influences of complicated lawyers' questions on witness confidence and accuracy. *The Journal of Psychology, 134*, 129–139.
Laster, K., & Taylor, V. (1994). *Interpreters and the legal system*. Sydney, Australia: Federation Press.
Lee, J. (2009). Conflicting views on court interpreting examined through surveys of legal professionals and court interpreters. *Interpreting, 11*(1), 35–56.
Liberman, K. (1980). Ambiguity and gratuitous concurrence in intercultural communication. *Human Studies, 3*, 65–85.

McGurk, B. J., Carr, M. J., & McGurk, D. (1993). *Investigative interviewing courses for police officers: An evaluation* (Police Research Series Paper No. 4). London, UK: Home Office.

Nakane, I. (2007). Problems in communicating the suspect's rights in interpreted police interviews. *Applied Linguistics, 28*, 87–112.

Navon, D., & Gopher, D. (1979). On the economy of the human-processing system. *Psychological Review, 86*, 214–255.

O'Barr, W. M. (1982). *Linguistic evidence: Language, power, and strategy in the courtroom*. New York: Academic Press.

Pöchhacker, F. (2004). *Introducing interpreting studies*. London, UK: Routledge.

Rabin, C. (1958). *The linguistics of translation*. London, UK: Secker and Warburg.

Russell, S. (2001). 'Let me put it simply...': The case for a standard translation of the police caution and its explanation. *Forensic Linguistics, Special Issue on Comprehensibility, 7*, 26–48.

Silverstein, M., & Urban, G. (1996). *Natural histories of discourse*. Chicago, IL: University of Chicago Press.

Shuy, R. W. (1997). Ten unanswered language questions about Miranda. *International Journal of Speech Language and the Law, 4*(2), 175–196.

Wadensjö, C. (1998). *Interpreting as interaction*. London, UK: Longman.

Wagstaff, G. F., & Wheatcroft, J. M. (2012). *The Liverpool Interview Protocol: Manual*. Liverpool, UK: University of Liverpool.

Wells, W. A. N. (1991). *An introduction to the law of evidence* (4th ed.). Adelaide, Australia: Government Printer.

Wheatcroft, J. M., Caruso, D., & Krumrey-Quinn, J. (2014). Rethinking leading: The directive, non-directive divide. *Criminal Law Review, 5*, 340–346.

Wheatcroft, J. M., & Kieres, K. (2014). The influence of an interpreter during bilingual cross-examination: Juror perceptions of witness attributes (Unpublished masters dissertation manuscript). University of Liverpool, Liverpool.

Wheatcroft, J. M., & Wagstaff, G. F. (2014). An example of a solution-focused academic-practitioner co-operation: How the iIIRG facilitated the development of the Liverpool Interview Protocol. *Investigative Interviewing: Research and Practice (II-RP), 6*(1), 42–50.

Wheatcroft, J. M., Wagstaff, G. F., & Russell, K. (2014). Specialist police interviewer perceptions of the enhanced cognitive interview: Usefulness, confidence and witness reliability. *Police Practice and Research, 15*(6), 505–518.

ACTS OF PARLIAMENT, CODES AND DIRECTIVES

Commission Directive. (2010/64/EU). Directive 2010/64/EU of the European Parliament and of the Council of 20 October 2010 on the right to interpretation and translation in criminal proceedings.

Human Rights Act. (2000). Retrieved from http://www.legislation.gov.uk/ukpga/1998/42/contents, http://www.legislation.gov.uk/ukpga/1998/42

National Agreement on arrangements for the use of interpreters, translators and language service professionals in investigations and proceedings within the criminal justice system. (1997). Retrieved from http://www.cps.gov.uk/legal/h_to_k/interpreters/

Police and Criminal Evidence Act. (1984). Retrieved from http://www.legislation. gov.uk/ukpga/1984/60/contents

Police and Criminal Evidence Act. (1984). Codes of practice. Retrieved from https://www.gov.uk/police-and-criminal-evidence-act-1984-pace-codes-of-practice

UK Home Office. (2014). Notice of rights and entitlements: A person's rights in police detention. Retrieved from https://www.gov.uk/notice-of-rights-and-entitlements-a-persons-rights-in-police-detention

Section VI

Conclusions and Future

15

Improving Communicative Practice: Beyond the Cognitive Interview for Adult Eyewitnesses

Nina J. Westera[1] and Martine Powell[2]

[1] Griffith University, Mt Gravatt, Queensland, Australia
[2] Deakin University, Melbourne, Victoria, Australia

INTRODUCTION

Communicating for investigative purposes is complex. However, as a result of the fields of psychology and linguistics we now understand the fundamentals of effective communication between an investigator and an interviewee (e.g. Fisher & Geiselman, 1992; Milne & Bull, 1999; Oxburgh, Myklebust & Grant, 2010; Powell, Fisher & Wright, 2005; Rock 2001). For example, 10 years ago Powell, Fisher and Wright (2005) were able to describe four features common to most empirically based interviewing protocols: developing rapport between the interviewer and interviewee, the interviewer establishing a clear outline of investigative needs, using open-ended questions and exploring alterative hypotheses. Despite the longevity of this strong empirical research base, a general trend around the world remains – there is a chasm between what empirical research suggests is best

Communication in Investigative and Legal Contexts: Integrated Approaches from Forensic Psychology, Linguistics and Law Enforcement, First Edition. Edited by Gavin Oxburgh, Trond Myklebust, Tim Grant and Rebecca Milne.
© 2016 John Wiley & Sons, Ltd. Published 2016 by John Wiley & Sons, Ltd.

practice in investigative interviewing and actual practice (e.g. Clarke & Milne, 2001; Griffiths & Milne, 2006; Schollum, 2005; Snook, Luther, Quinlan & Milne, 2012). In this chapter, we address this problem by suggesting that for communicative practice to improve, scholars need to refine and develop methods that take into account the range of scenarios police commonly face in their everyday work.

We argue that to improve investigative communications we need to better understand the context of these communications. For an investigative interview, the purpose of the communication is to establish what, if any, offending has occurred and the identity of the alleged offenders (Kebbell & Wagstaff, 1997). However, in the police operating environment, no two investigative communications are the same. Each communication is a dynamic interaction between an interviewer and an interviewee to elicit information that meets the particular needs of that criminal investigation (Fisher & Geiselman, 1992). In a perfect world, all interviewers would be capable and highly trained, and spend as long as it takes with every witness for every type of crime, but in reality, how an interview is conducted is affected by an interviewer's objectives, skill level and access to resources, by an interviewee's characteristics (e.g. intellectual ability, communication skills, psychological well-being and motivations) and by the type of information needed for the investigation (e.g. information that identifies an offender, clear descriptions of a few incidents from a series of many assaults).

The complexity of the investigative context prohibits us from exploring all varieties of interview purposes and interviewees in this chapter. Instead, we focus on the most common type of interviews conducted by police (Schollum, 2006), which are also considered the most important source of information for investigations (Kebbell & Milne, 1998) – interviews of witnesses. We limit the discussion to adults, to avoid the further complicating factors associated with interviewing child witnesses, and to the cognitive interview (CI), which is the most tested method used by police with adult witnesses (Memon, Meissner & Fraser, 2010). Although the focus of this chapter is on adult witnesses, we suspect that the broad framework proposed will also apply to other types of interviews (e.g. suspects (adult or child) and child witnesses).

In sum, this chapter explores the varied contexts the CI is used with adult witnesses and raises questions about applicability of this protocol across these contexts. We examine what we know from the research and what we still need to discover in relation to the varying contexts of the interviewer, the witness and the type of crime. First, we describe how the CI is working in practice.

THE COGNITIVE INTERVIEW IN PRACTICE

The CI has placed scientific practice in interviewing adult eyewitnesses on the police agenda. Developed 30 years ago by Fisher and Geiselman, the CI is an interviewing protocol that investigators can use to help an eyewitness remember more about a crime (Fisher & Geiselman, 1992). The CI combines memory aides (mnemonics) with communication skills and has been shown to increase the completeness of eyewitness recall and reporting (Fisher & Geiselman, 1992; Fisher, Milne & Bull, 2011; Geiselman et al., 1984; Köhnken, Milne, Memon & Bull, 1999; Memon, et al., 2010). The scientific merit of the CI has been demonstrated in a study space analysis and meta-analytic review, where Memon et al., (2010) reviewed 65 experiments and found that the CI elicits substantially more correct details than control groups with only a small increase of errors.

Field testing of the CI suggested it could improve the amount of information in cases where the offender was unknown to the witness (Fisher, Geiselman & Amador, 1989). As a result Fisher and Geiselman produced a book, *Memory Enhancing Techniques for Investigative Interviewing* (1992), describing the CI to practitioners. In this book they explained: 'Although the Cognitive Interview is an effective investigative instrument, its utility will vary from one situation to another' (p. 6). They also stated how the CI will take more time to use and is primarily useful for motivated witnesses with good communication skills whose testimony is central to the investigation (e.g. robbery, battery). Regardless of these caveats, the robust empirical findings supporting the usefulness of the CI led England and Wales to adopt the CI as the primary method used for all police officers as part of the national implementation of 'PEACE' interview training in 1993 (Clarke & Milne, 2001). The CI, and modifications of it, are now used by many countries as the standard method for interviewing adult witnesses to all types of crime (e.g. Australia, New Zealand; Clarke & Milne, 2001; Schollum, 2005).

Despite the broad-scale adoption of the CI, its success in practice has been limited. In a small-scale study examining the utlity of the methods for police in England, Clifford and George (1996) found that the field interviews of seven experienced police officers contained more information after officers received a two-day CI training that included instruction, practice and expert feedback. These officers used context reinstatement, imagery and concentrate hard instructions, and were more proficient at using open questions when compared to control groups, but they seldom used change order, change perspectives and report everything. Another group of seven officers received suspect interview training immediately after CI training and showed no improvement in the amount of information gathered, use of CI mnemonics or open questioning. Later in a national evaluation of PEACE, Clarke and Milne (2001) reviewed 48 audio-recorded eyewitness interviews conducted by CI trained officers in the field and found 'the overall standard of these interviews was poor with no evidence of the techniques for enhancing witness recall being used' (p. ii). Together the findings of these and other field studies suggest a variable use of CI methods in practice: establish rapport, free recall are commonly used; context reinstatement, report everything, witness compatible questioning, concentrate hard, transfer control and imagery are sometimes used; change order and change perspectives are rarely used (Clarke & Milne, 2001; Clifford & George, 1996; Dando, Wilcock & Milne, 2009; Memon, Bull & Smith, 1995).

There are many reasons the methods are often not used in practice. Part of the difficulty are inadequate programmes for learning interviewing skills; studies examining officers' use of CI skills in a mock interview immediately post-training have found no change in the amount of information obtained (Memon, Holley, Milne, Kohnken & Bull, 1994); and many CI methods were not used (Dando, Wilcock & Milne, 2009; Memon et al., 1994). Many training regimes do not incorporate some of the essential components to learning skills (Ericsson, Krampe & Tesch-Römer, 1993; Schollum, 2006; Shepherd & Milne, 2006) – key principles that underpin practice, clear instruction about the application of practice, effective on-going practice, expert feedback and regular evaluation of practice (Powell, 2008; Powell et al., 2005). In addition, field studies suggest that officers find the skills complex and difficult to use (Clifford & George, 1996; Dando, Wilcock & Milne, 2009; Memon et al., 1995). Officers also see some of the methods – reflecting those seldom used in practice – as unuseful (Dando, Wilcock & Milne, 2008; Kebbell, Milne & Wagstaff, 1999; Wheatcroft, Wagstaff & Russell, 2013). A survey of 96 English officers trained in the CI suggests that officers perceive using the CI as time consuming and officers are often pressured for time to conduct interviews (Kebbell et al., 1999; also see Dando et al., 2008).

WHERE TO FROM HERE?

The research is clear – the CI can substantially increase the amount of detail an eyewitness remembers, but uptake into practice by officers is poor. Part of the difficulty may lie in the mismatch between what the

CI was designed for and the police operational environment. The CI was designed for circumstances such as an armed robbery where the offender is unknown, the crime is serious and the witness is a cooperative bystander who is capable of undertaking complex cognitive tasks (Fisher & Geiselman, 1992). In these types of serious crimes, the interviewer is likely to spend whatever time it takes to obtain details that might lead to solving an otherwise unsolvable crime. Indeed, Fisher and colleague's (1989) original field-testing of the CI deliberately only examined crimes where the offender was unknown and where appropriate resources were likely to be available.

The CI is based on principles of memory retrieval that should (mostly) generalize to other eyewitnesses. However, not all witnesses have the same cognitive abilities or want to speak to police, not all types of crime require the same level or type of detailed information and not all interviewers receive the same training, have the same objectives or have access to the same resources. We suggest the challenge for scholars is to build on the strong foundation provided by 30 years of research into the CI, and to test, develop and refine methods that are fit for purpose in the police operating environment. To improve the uptake of methods in practice, this testing must go beyond the laboratory and into the field to test how learnable and usable the methods are for officers in practice (Memon et al., 2010). In some contexts the CI is likely to be the most appropriate method; in others it may need refining or new methods will need to be developed.

These types of adaptations are already happening. For example, in the evaluation of 'PEACE' Clark and Milne (2001) recommended 'a more holistic and flexible approach to interviewing' (p. 114) and Dando, Wilcock, Behnkle and Milne (2011) modified the CI to make it easier for frontline police interviewers to use (we will explore these and other innovations later). Common to these approaches is the tailoring of methods to meet the specific operational needs of the interviewer. Scholars cannot, of course, map out and test every context police are likely to come across. Nor do the practical realities of policing mean that practitioners can only use methods supported by a strong empirical base. There are, however, three main variables that affect every interview – the interviewer, the witness and the type of crime. These variables can provide a framework to test the utility of the CI to the varying contexts of practice.

First and foremost, interviewers will only use interviewing methods if they have the requisite knowledge and skills and their motivation to use the skills outweighs competing operational pressures not to use them. Different interviewers have different roles within a policing organization that have different priorities, which directly determine access to learning support and operational priorities.

Table 15.1 Witness interview contexts

	Frontline	Criminal investigation
Description	Methods that are simple, easy to learn and time efficient	Methods that produce the highest quality of information depending on investigative and/or evidential needs
Resourcing	Minimal learning Limited time Statement or smart devices	Moderate to intensive learning Less time-dependent Video recording, statement, smart devices
Crime type	Minor	Serious: • Offender known versus unknown • Complex mental elements • Long, repeated and historic events
Witness	Suitable for all	Tailored to interviewees' needs: • Vulnerable (intellectually impaired, mental disorder, alcohol and drug addiction) • Non-native language speaker • Reticent • Possible suspect
Purpose	Investigation only	Multipurpose: • Investigation • Evidence • Complainant satisfaction

These priorities are likely to influence whether an officer will spend the time and choose to use the methods (if he or she has the skills to) and his or her access to resources (e.g. time, recording equipment) that can limit the use of the methods. Taking into account these different organizational roles when developing interview methods is likely to improve the user-friendliness of the methods.

As displayed in Table 15.1, a useful starting point is the common division between frontline and criminal investigation divisions in many police services in Western countries. Officers in these roles investigate different types of crime and have different priorities and hence different interviewing capacity and capability.[1] A frontline interviewer, who is under pressure to respond to the next emergency and call for help is likely to have different priorities and adopt a different approach to a detective, who is specially trained and given time to investigate a serious crime.

Another way to maximize the utility of the methods is to ensure that the methods meet the challenges interviewers commonly face in practice. First, witnesses have different characteristics and capabilities. Interviewing a witness who is a high school graduate with no mental health problems may require a different approach to interviewing a witness who is an alcoholic and suffering from depression. Second, interviews are conducted as one of many means of gaining information for an investigation. The type of crime influences what information is important to that investigation and therefore the interview purpose. An interviewer may require a different approach with a witness to a non-fatal car crash to a victim of repeated assaults by an intimate partner. Next, we describe how the needs of frontline and then more serious crime interviewers vary according to the type of witness and crime.

FRONTLINE INTERVIEWS

A majority of witness interviews are for minor offences and conducted by generalist uniformed frontline police officers (e.g. thefts, minor assaults, burglaries, missing persons). These officers usually operate in a time-pressured operational environment where they are required to rapidly respond from one incident to the next. Like all investigations, quality of information from a witness is important, but so too is efficiency. Just like a frontline officer is unlikely to spend time and resources to call in a specialist to examine the scene for a shop theft, they are unlikely to spend hours interviewing a witness to this type of offence. Instead, they are likely to do the job as efficiently as possible so they are free for the next emergency call for assistance. These officers are expected to interview most witnesses they come into contact with, regardless of vulnerability, but are likely to have little interview training. Sometimes they are first to attend a more serious crime, where their role is to have initial contact with a witness and obtain sufficient information to establish what type of offending has occurred and arrange any immediate actions to prevent the loss of life or destruction of evidence. Currently, most frontline staff only have the resources to record witness interviews on a written statement.

Given this context, a large number of officers need skills that are as easy to learn as possible (see Table 15.1). Frontline officers need methods that enable them to obtain the most relevant and reliable information in the least amount of time. Ideally, these methods will work with most types of witnesses and limit the risk of memory contamination when a substantial interview is later needed. Some of these interviewers will go on to become detectives, so ideally the methods learnt would form the basis for more advanced interviewing skills. A number of recent innovations have targeted the need to simplify the methods, making them easier to learn and more time efficient.

INNOVATIONS

At the end of the 1990s, officers' concerns about the time taken to conduct the full CI resulted in calls for a time-efficient version of the CI (Kebbell & Wagstaff, 1996). In their evaluation of PEACE, Clarke and Milne (2001) noted: 'It is clear that not every interview with a witness or victims requires a full CI but interviewees do need to be allowed to provide an uninterrupted account, which can then be examined to provide more detail' (p. 113). They recommended a tiered approach to interviewing, where frontline officers (then Tier 1; now Professionalizing Investigations Programme Level 1 (of a four tier programme)) would learn a 'cut down' version of the CI. This approach was adopted by police in England and Wales, but has not been evaluated. Davies, McMahon and Greenwood (2005) have tested the efficacy of the CI without the change of order and change in perspectives mnemonics seldom used in practice and found that the interviews took 77% of the time while still eliciting 87% of the information. Dando, Wilcock and Milne (2009) examined the interviewing practices of 48 frontline (Tier 1 trained with change of order, change of perspectives and imagery removed) interviewers and found that post-training officers did not use many of the CI skills taught. These findings suggest the skills are too complex for frontline officers (Dando, Wilcock & Milne, 2009) and more research on what methods are most effective for frontline officers is required.

Dando, Wilcock, Milne and Henry (2009) responded to this need by attempting to make the CI easier to use by replacing context reinstatement with asking the witness to draw sketch plans and talk about what they were drawing. They found the sketch plan resulted in as much additional information as the use of mental reinstatement of context and reduced interview times. Dando et al. (2011) also found that when a sketch plan is used, interviewers use less questions and the witness produces less confabulations, which was attributed to a witness generating his or her own retrieval cues rather than relying on the external cues provided by the interviewer. Studies have also found that sketch plans are effective with older adults and children suffering from autism (Dando, 2013; Mattison, Dando & Omerod, 2015). These results suggest that sketch plans may provide scaffolding that aids these and other vulnerable witnesses to recall and, importantly for frontline officers, could be an effective method for a variety of witnesses.

Eye-closure during recall is another easy to use method that can increase visual and auditory recall (Perfect et al., 2008; Wagstaff et al., 2004) through reduced environmental distractions or by aiding concentration (Perfect et al., 2008). Vredeveldt and Penrod (2013) found that eye-closure increased free recall only in indoor settings but increased cued recall in both indoor and outdoor settings, suggesting that it may be useful in the field (although physical context may have confounded these results). Susceptibility to misinformation (integrating incorrect information received after the event into memory) may also be reduced with eye-closure, but only when accompanied with the less practical method of focused meditation (involving 1.5 minutes of slow breathing; Wagstaff, Wheatcroft, Burt, et al., 2011; Wagstaff, Wheatcroft, Caddick, Kirby & Lamont, 2011). More research is required to compare the effectiveness of eye-closure to and with other CI techniques; indeed Fisher and Geiselman (1992) orginally suggested using eye-closure with context reinstatement (Perfect et al., 2008). Whether witnesses and police officers in more realistic settings are comfortable enough to benefit from this method needs to be further explored.

Another potential variation of the CI that frontline officers could use is the self-administered interview (SAI). This method aims to reduce forgetting and misinformation effects by providing an opportunity for the witness to provide a detailed account early in the investigation (Gabbert, Hope & Fisher, 2009). The SAI was designed for when police do not have the time to interview the witness immediately, such as when there are large numbers of witnesses to a crime. It comes in the form of a booklet where the witnesses write down their recall aided by instructions developed from many of the CI methods. Testing of the SAI has found it can generate more accurate details than free recall, improve recollection at subsequent interviews and reduce susceptibility to misinformation (Gabbert et al., 2009; Gabbert, Hope, Fisher & Jamieson, 2012; Gawrylowicz, Memon & Scoboria, 2014). Although the method is not designed to replace face-to-face interviewing (Hope, Gabbert & Fisher, 2011), it is possible that in some circumstances this method could be more effective than a minimally trained interviewer, especially when compared to the unreliable method of taking a written statement. What still needs to be examined is the effectiveness of the SAI with factors common to police interviews (e.g. people with low literacy, suffering from trauma or unmotivated; Hope et al., 2011). The increased use by police of 'smart electronic devices' with the capability to audio- and video-record interviews provides the possibility of an audio rather than a written version of the SAI, which may overcome some of these limitations. If field testing of the SAI suggests it is suitable for more extensive use, the broader implications for practice need to be examined. How does the SAI affect the witness's experience of the interview? Are some witnesses more comfortable using this method? How does using the SAI influence an officer's ability to develop interviewing skills? Is the SAI time efficient (given that many frontline officers will have to remain with the witness until it is complete)?

Finally, another avenue for research is to respond to innovations in practice – most notably, the introduction of smart electronic devices and body cameras that make audio and video recording interviews instead of the unreliable statement-taking process more feasible. Officers report that the need to reproduce what the witness said at interview into a written document reduces their ability to encourage free-flowing information (Westera, Kebbell & Milne, 2011). Clarke and Milne (2001) described the practices of frontline interviewers as follows: 'The volume crime interviews were in fact statement taking exercises and not interviews at all' (p. ii). In a linguistic analysis, Rock (2001) examined how the statement-taking process transforms the information given by a witness and jeopardizes the completeness and accuracy of the information. In itself, moving away from this process may help to improve interviewing practices and, because the officer does not need to write out the statement, will reduce interview times. Promisingly, the ability of scholars to scrutinize the more transparent audio or video record of the interview is likely to create a greater understanding of the needs of frontline officers. This technology may also increase the likelihood of interviews being conducted on the roadside, on a doorstep or at the scene of a crime. This raises research questions around how to effectively interview when there are more environmental distractions and the effects of interviewing the witness in the same environmental context where the crime occurred.

In sum, research into developing methods that are easier to use and more time efficient is well under way. Continuing these efforts, examining how to effectively learn the skills required and whether the methods can apply to various witnesses is vital to helping frontline officers effectively perform their role. Many of these promising advances are also likely to benefit interviews for serious crime.

INTERVIEWS BY CRIMINAL INVESTIGATORS

Serious crime interviews (e.g. robbery, serious violence, sexual assault, homicide) are normally conducted by detectives or specialist interviewers who receive more training than frontline officers in the investigation process (which may or may not include witness interviewing depending on the police service). Although detectives are often pressured for time, these interviews are less about efficiency and more about quality. Compared to frontline interviewers, these interviewers have greater access to resources and sometimes the ability to audio- or video-record the interview. However, the level of response still varies depending on the seriousness of the crime. The interview and how it was conducted may undergo intense scrutiny during the investigation and later in the courtroom. Given the context of these interviews, we suggest that research needs to explore how these interviews can be tailored to better meet the needs of each investigation depending on the type of offending, the characteristics of the interviewee and whether the video record of the interview is likely to later be used as the basis for the witnesses courtroom evidence, as is available in some countries (see Table 15.1). The interviewer may need to have multiple methods available and to adopt what is sometimes referred to as a 'tool belt' approach where different methods are used depending on the skills of the interviewer and the needs of the case (Milne & Bull, 2002).

TYPE OF OFFENDING

Each investigation is unique and requires different types of information to meet its objectives depending on the circumstances of the crime. The CI has primarily been tested on witnesses who are bystanders to a single (staged or video recorded) short emotionally neutral event (Memon et al., 2010), where the offender is unknown. Police often respond to crimes that are far more complex than these testing conditions; they may involve a known offender, crimes that occur over a long period of time, multiple crime events and witnesses who are actors in the event (e.g. victims). Research is required to explore how to effectively interview in these varieties of events.

In a survey of 159 police officers, Kebbell and Milne (1998) found that officers perceived that eyewitnesses usually or always remembered enough person description details only 24% of the time. This suggests that where the offender is unknown and every detail is important the CI – which was designed to maximize detail – is likely to be the best method. Nevertheless, officers also reported that witnesses usually or always remembered enough action details 73% of the time. Thus, in crimes where the offender's identity is not an issue, a generic increase in detail may not be the objective. Whether the CI is the most appropriate method for these types of crimes is unknown. Indeed, police may rarely use change of order and change in perspectives simply because these methods (which are typically used at the end of the interview) are often surplus to investigative requirements.

In many serious crimes (especially sexual and violent crimes), the primary witness (the victim) knows the offender (Phillips & Park, 2006). In these cases certain types of detail may be legally important. For example, in cases of interpartner repeated sexual assault and other serious violence, establishing the elements to some well-remembered offences may take priority over gathering large amounts of detail about one incident. Many serious crimes often have complicated *mens rea* (mental state of the alleged offender) legal proof elements. In rape, establishing that the complainant did not consent and the alleged offender knew she did not consent, may require information about what was said, thought and felt (Ellison, 2007; Kebbell & Westera, 2011). For a serious assault, establishing whether the alleged offender intended to cause death, serious bodily harm or no harm can make a significant difference to the charges laid. Relevant here is the fact that more research is required to understand what defines evidentially relevant information and how to obtain these types of details. People generally report from visual information, so the change of sensory modality mnemonic in the CI may help elicit details with auditory, thought and touch details that are particulalry relevant in some cases (e.g. establishing a lack of consent in rape), but there is limited empirical testing of these methods. How to overcome social factors that affect reporting, such as the embarrassment of having to disclose highly personal information (e.g. about sexual acts), also needs exploring.

Extending testing of the CI beyond a single recent (video or staged) event where the witness is a bystander to events that simulate more complex crimes is also required (Memon et al., 2010). Many witnesses are not just observers but are physically involved in the event (e.g. a victim of an assault). This involvement may create additional retrieval cues that may make the CI mnemonics more or less effective. The CI has mainly been tested on scenarios less than 10 minutes long (Memon et al., 2010), whereas investigators need to interview for incidents that range from a short one-off interaction to a prolonged assault that happened over days or an abusive relationship that happened over years. It is impossible to say how long each crime takes, but in 2009 a video recorded serious crime interviews in Wellington, New Zealand, that took on average 116 minutes (personal communication with Detective Deborah Braun from the New Zealand Police), far beyond the time taken when conducting interviews in the laboratory. This long time period may affect the methods used, especially if recalling information is stressful and tiring for the witness and certain types of information need to be prioritized.

A crime may not be reported until months and years after the alleged event. However, only two studies examine a delay of more than two weeks between the to-be-remembered event and the interview and no studies examine a delay of longer than 6 months – more research is also needed in this area (Memon et al., 2010). Finally, many interviews require witnesses to recall repeated offences (e.g. interpartner violence, repeated sexual abuse). Testing is limited on how recalling repeated events affects adult memory and no strategies that we are aware of have been tested that interviewers can use as techniques to help witnesses overcome this complex memory task. Hope, Mullis and Gabbert (2013) developed a timeline method for multiple offender incidents to help witnesses establish who did what when and was shown to increase the amount of correct detail reported. This method may assist witnesses to organize their memory for repeat events, but again this has not been tested.

CHARACTERISTICS OF THE INTERVIEWEE

Few studies have gone beyond testing the CI on student participants (Memon et al., 2010), yet vulnerable people (e.g. people with a mental illness or communication impairment) have a high risk of becoming victims when compared to other types of witnesses (see Bull, 2010). Limits to the cognitive ability and social skills of these witnesses mean that these interviews are likely to be challenging to conduct (Bull, 2010; Memon et al., 2010). When tested on children, older adults and those with an intellectual disability, the CI (and modified versions of it) has been shown to increase the amount of correct detail recalled (e.g. Milne & Bull, 2002; Milne, Clare & Bull, 1999; Wright & Holliday, 2007). Extending this type of research to the variety of witnesses police come across would be useful for practice – people who are suffering from mental disorder (anxiety, depression), drug and alcohol addiction, dementia and head injury. These characteristics may affect the cognitive ability of the witness to understand instructions and recall information, and the social dynamics of the interview. For example, some interviewees may find narrative reporting too cognitively demanding. As mentioned earlier, recent work by Dando and colleagues shows promise in this area by finding that the use of sketch plans may help to enhance the reports of elderly witnesses and children suffering from autism (Dando, 2013; Mattison, Dando & Omerod, 2015).

Many witnesses will find experiencing a crime stressful, but there is little research into the use of the CI with recall for emotionally charged events (for a discussion see Memon et al., 2010). Fisher and Geiselman (1992) provide advice on how to help a witness to control anxiety (likely borrowed from other disciplines such as psychotherapy, e.g. reassurance that fear is a natural feeling), but these methods have not been empirically tested. How the CI methods influence anxiety is another question for research. For example, how does mental reinstatement of context affect the ability to recall highly emotional events? Does it increase the stress levels of an already traumatized interviewee? The ethical difficulties with conducting this type of research means that innovative methods are required to examine these and other relevant issues to practice.

Another area of research that requires attention is the multilingual nature of many interviews with adult witnesses. Research into the effectiveness of the CI has not taken the non-English-speaking witness into consideration, mostly because there appears to be little disciplinary/academic overlap between psychology, linguistics and interpreting studies. The work on the use of interpreters in police interviews tends to overlook the impact of police procedure and interview methods on having an interpreter present (e.g. Gallai, 2013; Krouglov, 1999; Russell, 2000). Some of the key features of interviewing witnesses, such as encouraging narrative responses, complicate the already complex interpretation process. The interpreter-mediated interview itself is considered in greater detail elsewhere in this volume.

Another difficult to test but important issue for practice is how to deal with witnesses who are reluctant to talk to police – a failure to report rather than a failure to recall. The CI was designed for cooperative adults (Fisher & Geisleman, 1992) and has mainly been tested on student witnesses who are likely to be motivated to talk (Memon et al., 2010). In practice, interviewers often need to obtain information from witnesses who have reasons not to talk to police – they do not like police, have allegiances to the alleged offender, are afraid or intimidated, or simply have no belief in the criminal justice system. Can research help interviewers develop strategies to overcome these obstacles? One approach is to use methods from motivational interviewing or suspect interviewing like conversation management (Miller & Rollnick, 1991; Shepherd, 2007). However, these methods have not been examined with eyewitnesses.

The complexity of the police operating environment means that it may be helpful to adopt an interdisciplinary approach to broadening the research base for interviewing adult witnesses. For example, examining how to interview witnesses who are suffering from depression may require cognitive and clinical psychologists to work together. Some issues may be beyond testing, where theory informs 'best practice' (based on the best evidence currently available; Malpass et al., 2008). A balance is needed between scholars retaining integrity in deciding what they can and cannot advise on and practitioners wanting all the help they can get. Regardless of the constraints, there is still a significant contribution research can make in both testing what methods are effective and who are the best people to interview these witnesses and how interviewers can best learn these skills.

Multipurpose Interviews

Another area of research highly relevant to practice in many countries is how best to interview when the video record of the interview may be used as the basis for an adult witness's evidence-in-chief (e.g. in England & Wales, New Zealand; see Criminal Justice System, 2007; Mahoney, McDonald, Optican & Tinsley, 2007). In this mode of evidence the video is played followed by any supplementary questions from the prosecutor and cross-examination by the defence counsel. The freshness of the account, the use of narrative-encouraging interview methods and the more relaxed interview environment are likely to make video-evidence superior to live evidence in the quality and quantity of information about legal elements of the alleged offence (Deffenbacher, Bornstein, Penrod & McGorty, 2004; Powell et al., 2005; Read & Connolly, 2007; Westera, Kebbell & Milne, 2013). In countries where video-evidence is available for adults (e.g. England and Wales, New Zealand), the CI is the primary method of interview used, but its effectiveness as the basis for evidence-in-chief has not been extensively examined.

Using one interview for multiple purposes can create a conflict of needs. One main difference between an investigative and evidential interview is the desire for coherent evidence (Davis, Hoyano, Keenan, Maitland & Morgan, 1999; Powell & Wright, 2009; Westera et al., 2013). Legal professionals are concerned that the long narrative responses in the interview are less persuasive to a jury than the short responses encouraged by lawyers (Criminal Justice Joint Inspection, 2009; Stern, 2010; Westera et al., 2013). The one study that examined this question, by Fisher, Mello and McCauley (1999), found no differences in credibility judgements of students when the CI was compared to a standard interview. The mnemonics themselves (without changes to the information elicited) have been found to have no effect on credibility judgements (Kebbell, Wagstaff & Preece, 1998; Westera et al., 2011).

More empirical testing is required. Research by Powell and colleagues, exploring prosecutor's perceptions about what is effective evidence, provides a useful approach to examining how to improve the likelihood that interviews meet courtroom needs (e.g. Burrows & Powell, 2013; Powell, Wright & Hughes-Scholes, 2010).

Finally, the justice system is moving towards alternative resolutions beyond prosecution (Daly & Bouhours, 2010; Innes & Brookman, 2013). Some victims, for example victims of sexual assault, may not want prosecution but would prefer just to report the crime to police, be listened to and be believed (Herman, 2005; Jordan, 2001). The free narrative approach of the CI may enable such an outcome. For example, McMillan and Thomas (2009) interviewed eight rape victims in England and found that they viewed giving an uninterrupted account as a positive process, but that giving high levels of detail was onerous (also see Patterson, 2011). No research that we are aware of examines witnesses' experiences of different interview methods. This area of research also may have implications for the quality of information the witness provides.

CONCLUSION

This chapter has used the example of adult witness interviewing to explore how scholars can refine and develop interviewing methods to make these methods more useful to police practice. The framework proposed – exploring the varying contexts of the interviewer, the interviewee and the type of information required – are likely to also apply to other types of police communications (e.g. interviewing suspects). The challenge now is for scholars to build on the strong foundation of interviewing research and incorporate the diverse and challenging environment police operate in when setting research agenda. This outcome can only be achieved if scholars work closely with police (and vice versa) to ensure that interviewing methods developed are fit for purpose and future proof.

NOTE

1. We acknowledge that these roles may change and other people in police conduct interviews (e.g. crime scene attendants, personnel on crime reporting lines).

REFERENCES

Bull, R. (2010). The investigative interviewing of children and other vulnerable witnesses: Psychological research and working/professional practice. *Legal and Criminological Psychology, 15*(1), 5–23.

Burrows, K. S., & Powell, M. (2013). Prosecutors' recommendations for improving child witness statements about sexual abuse. *Policing and Society*, iFirst, 1–19. doi:10.1080/10439463.2013.784305

Clarke, C., & Milne, R. (2001). National evaluation of the PEACE investigative interviewing course (Police Research Award Scheme: Report No. PRAS/149). Portsmouth, UK: University of Portsmouth, Institute of Criminal Justice Studies.

Clifford, B. R., & George, R. (1996). A field evaluation of training in three methods of witness/victim investigative interviewing. *Psychology, Crime and Law, 2*, 231–248.

Criminal Justice Joint Inspection. (2009). *Report of a joint thematic review of victim and witness experiences in the criminal justice system*. London, UK: Home Office.

Criminal Justice System. (2007). *Achieving best evidence in criminal proceedings: Guidance in interviewing victims and witnesses, and using special measures*. London, UK: Home Office.

Daly, K., & Bouhours, B. (2010). Rape and attrition in the legal process: A comparative analysis of five countries. *Crime and Justice: An Annual Review of Research, 39*(1), 565–650.

Dando, C. (2013). Drawing to remember: External support of older adults' eyewitness performance. *PloS One, 8*(7), e69937.

Dando, C., Wilcock, R., Behnkle, C., & Milne, R. (2011). Modifying the cognitive interview: Countenancing forensic application by enhancing practicability. *Psychology, Crime and Law, 17*(6), 491–511.

Dando, C., Wilcock, R., & Milne, R. (2008). The cognitive interview: Inexperienced police officers' perceptions of their witness/victim interviewing practices. *Legal and Criminological Psychology, 13*, 59–70.

Dando, C., Wilcock, R., & Milne, R. (2009). The cognitive interview: Novice police officers' witness/victim interviewing practices. *Psychology, Crime and Law, 15*, 679–696.

Dando, C., Wilcock, R., Milne, R., & Henry, L. (2009). A modified cognitive interview procedure for frontline police investigators. *Applied Cognitive Psychology, 23*, 698–716.

Davies, M. R., McMahon, M., & Greenwood, K. M. (2005). The efficacy of mnemonic components of the cognitive interview: Towards a shortened variant for time-critical investigations. *Applied Cognitive Psychology, 19*, 75–93.

Davis, G., Hoyano, L., Keenan, C., Maitland, L., & Morgan, R. (1999). *An assessment of the admissibility and sufficiency of evidence in child abuse prosecutions: A research report from the Home Office*. London, UK: Home Office.

Deffenbacher, K. A., Bornstein, B. H., Penrod, S. D., & McGorty, E. K. (2004). A meta-analytic review of the effects of high stress on eyewitness memory. *Law and Human Behavior, 28*, 687–706.

Ellison, L. (2007). Promoting effective case-building in rape cases: A comparative perspective. *Criminal Law Review, 9*, 691–708.

Ericsson, K. A., Krampe, R. T., & Tesch-Römer, C. (1993). The role of deliberate practice in the acquisition of expert performance. *Psychological Review, 100*(3), 363–406.

Fisher, R. P., & Geiselman, R. E. (1992). *Memory enhancing techniques for investigative interviewing: The cognitive interview.* Springfield, IL: Thomas.

Fisher, R. P., Geiselman, R. E., & Amador, M. (1989). Field test of the cognitive interview: Enhancing the recollection of actual victims and witnesses of crime. *Journal of Applied Psychology, 74,* 722–727.

Fisher, R. P., Mello, E. W., & McCauley, M. R. (1999). Are jurors' perceptions of eyewitness credibility affected by the cognitive interview? *Psychology, Crime and Law, 5,* 167–176.

Fisher, R. P., Milne, R., & Bull, R. (2011). Interviewing cooperative witnesses. *Current Directions in Psychological Science, 20*(1), 16–19.

Gabbert, F., Hope, L., & Fisher, R. P. (2009). Protecting eyewitness evidence. *Law and Human Behavior, 33*(4), 298–307.

Gabbert, F., Hope, L., Fisher, R. P., & Jamieson, K. (2012). Protecting against misleading postevent information with a Self-Administered Interview. *Applied Cognitive Psychology, 26*(4), 568–575.

Gallai, F. (2013). 'I'll just intervene whenever he finds it a bit difficult to answer': Exploding the myth of literalism in interpreter-mediated police interviews. *Investigative Interviewing Research and Practice, 5,* 57–78.

Gawrylowicz, J., Memon, A., & Scoboria, A. (2014). Equipping witnesses with transferable skills: The Self-Administered Interview©. *Psychology, Crime and Law, 20*(4), 315–325.

Geiselman, R. E., Fisher, R. P., Firstenberg, I., Hutton, L. A., Sullivan, S. J., Avetissian, I. V., & Prosk, A. L. (1984). Enhancement of eyewitness memory: An empirical evaluation of the cognitive interview. *Journal of Police Science and Administration, 12,* 74–80.

Griffiths, A., & Milne, R. (2006). Will it all end in tiers? Police interviews with suspects in Britain. In T. A. Williamson (Ed.), *Investigative interviewing: Rights, research, regulation* (pp. 167–189). Cullompton, UK: Willan.

Herman, J. L. (2005). Justice from the victim's perspective. *Violence Against Women, 11,* 571–602.

Hope, L., Gabbert, F., & Fisher, R. P. (2011). From laboratory to the street: Capturing witness memory using the Self-Administered Interview. *Legal and Criminological Psychology, 16*(2), 211–226.

Hope, L., Mullis, R., & Gabbert, F. (2013). Who? what? when? using a timeline technique to facilitate recall of a complex event. *Journal of Applied Research in Memory and Cognition, 2*(1), 14–19.

Innes, M., & Brookman, F. (2013). Helping police with their enquiries: International perspectives on homicide investigation. *Policing and Society,* 1–7. doi:10.1080/10439463.2013.771542

Jordan, J. (2001). Worlds apart? Women, rape and the police reporting process. *British Journal of Criminology, 41,* 679–706.

Kebbell, M. R., & Milne, R. (1998). Police officers' perceptions of eyewitness performance in forensic investigations. *Journal of Social Psychology, 138,* 323–339.

Kebbell, M. R., Milne, R., & Wagstaff, G. F. (1999). The cognitive interview: A survey of its forensic effectiveness. *Psychology, Crime and Law, 5,* 101–115.

Kebbell, M. R., & Wagstaff, G. F. (1996). Enhancing the practicality of the cognitive interview in forensic situations. *Psycoloquy, 7.* Retrieved from http://psychprints.ecs.soton.ac.uk/archive/00000508/

Kebbell, M. R., & Wagstaff, G. F. (1997). Why do the police interview eyewitnesses? Interview objectives and the evaluation of eyewitness performance. *The Journal of Psychology, 131,* 595–601.

Kebbell, M. R., Wagstaff, G. F., & Preece, D. (1998). The effect of belief that testimony was elicited with a cognitive interview on jurors' judgments of guilt. *Psychology, Crime and Law, 4*, 17–25.

Kebbell, M. R., & Westera, N. J. (2011). Promoting pre-recorded complainant evidence in rape trials: Psychological and practice perspectives. *Criminal Law Journal, 35*, 376–385.

Köhnken, G., Milne, R., Memon, A., & Bull, R. (1999). The cognitive interview: A meta-analysis. *Psychology, Crime and Law, 5*(1), 3–27.

Krouglov, A. (1999). Police interpreting: Politeness and sociocultural context. *The Translator, 5*(2), 285–302.

Mahoney, R., McDonald, E., Optican, S., & Tinsley, Y. (2007). *The Evidence Act 2006: Act and analysis*. Wellington, New Zealand: Brookers.

Malpass, R. S., Tredoux, C. G., Compo, N. S., McQuiston-Surrett, D., Maclin, O. H., Zimmerman, L. A., & Topp, L. D. (2008). Study space analysis for policy development. *Applied Cognitive Psychology, 22*(6), 789–801.

Mattison, M. L., Dando, C. J., & Ormerod, T. C. (2015). Sketching to remember: Episodic free recall task support for child witnesses and victims with autism spectrum disorder. *Journal of Autism and Developmental Disorders, 45*, 1751–1765.

McMillan, L., & Thomas, M. (2009). Police interviews of rape victims: Tensions and contradictions. In M. Horvath & J. Brown (Eds.), *Rape: Challenging contemporary thinking* (pp. 255–280). Cullompton, UK: Willan.

Memon, A., Bull, R., & Smith, M. (1995). Improving the quality of police interviews: Can training in the use of the cogntive interview techniques help? *Policing and Society, 5*, 53–68.

Memon, A., Holley, A., Milne, R., Kohnken, G., & Bull, R. (1994). Towards understanding of the effects of the interviewer training in evaluating the cognitive interview. *Applied Cognitive Psychology, 8*, 641–659.

Memon, A., Meissner, C. A., & Fraser, J. (2010). The cognitive interview: A meta-analytic review and study space analysis of the past 25 years. *Psychology, Public Policy and Law, 16*(4), 340–372.

Miller, W. R., & Rollnick, S. (1991). *Motivational interviewing: Preparing people for change*. New York: Guilford Press.

Milne, R., & Bull, R. (1999). *Investigative interviewing: Psychology and practice*. Chichester, UK: John Wiley & Sons, Ltd.

Milne, R., & Bull, R. (2002). Back to basics: A componential analysis of the original cognitive interview mnemonics with three age groups. *Applied Cognitive Psychology, 16*, 743–753.

Milne, R., Clare, I. C., & Bull, R. (1999). Using the cognitive interview with adults with mild learning disabilities. *Psychology, Crime and Law, 5*, 81–99.

Oxburgh, G. E., Myklebust, T., & Grant, T. (2010). The question of question types in police interviews: A review of the literature from a psychological and linguistic perspective. *International Journal of Speech – Language Pathology, 17*, 46–66.

Patterson, D. (2011). The impact of detectives' manner of questioning on rape victims' disclosure. *Violence Against Women, 17*(11), 1349–1373.

Perfect, T. J., Wagstaff, G. F., Moore, D., Andrews, B., Cleveland, V., Newcombe, S., & Brown, L. (2008). How can we help witnesses to remember more? It's an (eyes) open and shut case. *Law and Human Behavior, 32*(4), 314–324.

Phillips, J., & Park, M. (2006). Measuring domestic violence and sexual assault against women. Canberra, Australia: Parliament of Australia. Retrieved from http://www.aph.gov.au/About_Parliament/Parliamentary_Departments/Parliamentary_Library/Publications_Archive/archive/ViolenceAgainstWomen.

Powell, M. B. (2008). Designing effective training programs for investigative interviews of children. *Current Issues in Criminal Justice, 20*(2), 189.

Powell, M. B., Fisher, R. P., & Wright, R. (2005). Investigative interviewing. In N. Brewer & K. Williams (Eds.), *Psychology and law: An empirical perspective* (pp. 11–42). New York: Guilford.

Powell, M. B., & Wright, R. (2009). Professionals' perceptions of electronically recorded interviews with vulnerable witnesses. *Journal of the Institute of Criminology, 21*, 205–218.

Powell, M. B., Wright, R., & Hughes-Scholes, C. H. (2010). Contrasting perceptions of child testimony experts, prosecutors and police officers regarding individual child abuse interviews. *Psychiatry, Psychology and Law*, iFirst, 1–11.

Read, J. D., & Connolly, A. (2007). The effects of delay on long-term memory for witnessed events. In: M. P. Toglia, J. D. Read, D. R. Ross, & R. C. L. Lindsay (Eds.), *Handbook of eyewitness psychology, volume I: Memory for events* (pp. 117–155). New York: Lawrence Erlbaum Associates.

Rock, F. (2001). The genesis of a witness statement. *Forensic Linguistics, 8*, 44–72.

Russell, S. (2000). 'Let me put it simply...': The case for a standard translation of the caution and its explanation. *International Journal of Speech, Language and the Law, 7*(1), 26–48.

Schollum, M. (2005). *Investigative interviewing: The literature.* Wellington, New Zealand: New Zealand Police.

Schollum, M. (2006). *Investigative interviewing: The current situation.* Wellington, New Zealand: New Zealand Police.

Shepherd, E. (2007). *Investigative interviewing: The conversation management approach.* Oxford, UK: Oxford University Press.

Shepherd, E., & Milne, R. (2006). 'Have you told management about this?' Bringing witness interviewing into the twenty-first century. In A. Heaton-Strong, E. Shepherd, G. H. Gudjonsson, & D. Wolchover (Eds.), *Witness testimony: Psychological, investigative and evidential perspectives* (pp. 131–152). Oxford, UK: Oxford University Press.

Snook, B., Luther, K., Quinlan, H., & Milne, R. (2012). Let'em talk! A field study of police questioning practices of suspects and accused persons. *Criminal Justice and Behavior, 39*(10), 1328–1339.

Stern, V. (2010). *The stern review.* London, UK: Home Office.

Vredeveldt, A., & Penrod, S. D. (2013). Eye-closure improves memory for a witnessed event under naturalistic conditions. *Psychology, Crime and Law, 19*, 893–905.

Wagstaff, G. F., Brunas-Wagstaff, J., Cole, J., Knapton, L., Winterbottom, J., Crean, V., & Wheatcroft, J. (2004). Facilitating memory with hypnosis, focused meditation, and eye closure. *International Journal of Clinical and Experimental Hypnosis, 52*(4), 434–455. doi:10.1080/00207140490889062

Wagstaff, G. F., Wheatcroft, J. M., Burt, C. L., Pilkington, H. J., Wilkinson, K., & Hoyle, J. D. (2011). Enhancing witness memory with focused meditation and eye-closure: Assessing the effects of misinformation. *Journal of Police and Criminal Psychology, 26*(2), 152–161.

Wagstaff, G. F., Wheatcroft, J. M., Caddick, A. M., Kirby, L. J., & Lamont, E. (2011). Enhancing witness memory with techniques derived from hypnotic investigative interviewing: Focused meditation, eye-closure, and context reinstatement. *International Journal of Clinical and Experimental Hypnosis, 59*(2), 146–164.

Westera, N., Kebbell, M. R., & Milne, R. (2011). Interviewing rape complainants: Police officers' perceptions of interview format and quality of evidence. *Applied Cognitive Psychology, 25*(6), 917–926.

Westera, N., Kebbell, M., & Milne, B. (2013). It is better, but does it look better? Prosecutor perceptions of using rape complainant investigative interviews as evidence. *Psychology, Crime and Law, 19*, 595–610.

Wheatcroft, J. M., Wagstaff, G. F., & Russell, K. (2013). Specialist police interviewer perceptions of the enhanced cognitive interview: Usefulness, confidence and witness reliability. *Police Practice and Research, 15*, 505–518.

Wright, A. M., & Holliday, R. E. (2007). Enhancing recall of young, young–old and old–old adults with the cognitive interview and a modified version of the cognitive interview. *Applied Cognitive Psychology, 71*, 19–43.

16

Communication in Forensic Contexts: Future Directions and Conclusions

Trond Myklebust[1], Gavin Oxburgh[2], Tim Grant[3] and Rebecca Milne[4]
[1] Norwegian Police University College, Oslo, Norway
[2] Newcastle University, UK
[3] Aston University, Birmingham, UK
[4] University of Portsmouth, UK

INTRODUCTION

The chapters in this volume have provided an up-to-date knowledge base of developments in the ever-changing complex area of communication in forensic contexts. Interviews with all types of interviewee have been examined and across the criminal justice spectrum, from the police interview room to discourse in the courtroom. Through the discussions of theoretical and methodological issues, we have attempted to bridge the gap between the fields of psychology, linguistics and law enforcement. This is an important blend of dialogue across the disciplines for us to move forward and fully understand the underpinning issues with regards to investigative interviewing.

The chapters have demonstrated that rigorous and collaborative scientific endeavours can help both academics and practitioners understand the dynamic between the interviewer and interviewee. It is this interchange that directly impacts upon the output, providing

Communication in Investigative and Legal Contexts: Integrated Approaches from Forensic Psychology, Linguistics and Law Enforcement, First Edition. Edited by Gavin Oxburgh, Trond Myklebust, Tim Grant and Rebecca Milne.
© 2016 John Wiley & Sons, Ltd. Published 2016 by John Wiley & Sons, Ltd.

valid and reliable information that can be used in subsequent legal processes. As argued by the editors and contributing authors, it is vitally important to identify the limitations (as well as the strengths) of the investigative interview in relation to the interviewer and the interviewee, but also in relation to the context where the interview takes place – this is of particular note in the light of recent theoretical advances in our understanding of human memory, linguistics and forensic practice.

Regarding future research, we will attempt to address some of the areas we think are important and of interest to both researchers and practitioners for communication in legal and investigative contexts.

FUTURE RESEARCH

General Areas

It is clear that the contributions from all the authors in this volume demonstrate that investigative practice and the focus on communication in legal and investigative contexts has changed considerably over the last few decades. Such change has included the development of structured interview models such as the Cognitive Interview (CI) in the late 1980s, the PEACE model of interviewing and the Conversation Management (CM) approach in the early 1990s and the National Institute of Child Health and Human Development (NICHD) protocol in 2000. The knowledge surrounding the basic principles on how to conduct an effective investigative interview using structured models seems to be well versed. However, there is still somewhat of a gap between the knowledge and its implementation into practice; this is the challenge for the forthcoming years for both academics and practitioners.

To make the research more practice-based for practitioners, one important area for research will be to streamline procedures so that practitioners can use them more efficiently in their day-to-day situations. An example of this has been the development of the CI into a more user-friendly and front-line version – the Self-Administered Interview (SAI) (Hope, Gabbert & Fisher, 2011). The SAI is a structured interview protocol, drawing on the core principles of the CI, used to elicit comprehensive initial statements from witnesses, quickly and efficiently. It takes the form of a standardized protocol of clear instructions and questions that enable witnesses to provide their own statement, and is therefore ideal for practitioners to use when the circumstances and restricted resources mean that a 'traditional' interview is not possible. Dando and her colleagues also examined how to adapt the CI for use in more time-constrained situations, representing a new way for both practitioners and academics to tailor structured interview models to specific tasks (see Dando & Ormerod, 2009; Dando, Wilcock, Behnkle & Milne, 2011; Dando, Wilcock & Milne, 2009).

As investigative interviewing models spread internationally, the focus and transparency with respect to the process of structured communication models will draw the attention of others working in the public and private sector (e.g. interviews for vetting and national security purposes, negotiations, crisis management, banking and insurance). Additional research is needed to examine effective interviewing in the wider investigative context, including persons of high value (e.g. terrorists). We are confident that considerable progress will continue to be made along each of these lines to widen the knowledge and examine implementation into practice, both for researchers and practitioners of communication.

Technological developments are also important factors to consider. The video-recording of investigative interviews has become more the rule than the exception for many practitioners, implementing new routines for how to evaluate interviews. The development of computer software will increase the use of video-link and online activities in decision-making procedures for investigators and courts. Today's video-link interviews from the court of suspects in custody, or children from specially designed interview suites, is just the start. The potential for training/academic institutions is in its relative infancy, from the basic streamed auditorium presentations to the more specialized simulations of sexual abuse interviews using computer-generated child avatars (Pompedda, Zappalà & Santtila, 2015). For the short and long term, the potential and impact of using video-links and other audio-visual equipment are important research areas for further development.

Whilst there are many other important areas for future research, many of which have been outlined in the chapters, we believe that there are three broad areas of vitally important research that is urgently needed: (i) vulnerability, (ii) the use of intermediaries and interpreters in the interview room, and (iii) questioning techniques. It is to these topics that we now turn.

Specific Areas

Vulnerability

Psychological and linguistic research over the last decades has learnt an enormous amount about cognitive strengths and limitations within different groups of interviewees, especially those who are referred to as 'vulnerable'. Vulnerability can be defined as 'psychological characteristics or mental state which render an [individual] prone, in certain circumstances, to providing information which is inaccurate, unreliable or misleading' (Gudjonsson, 2006, p. 68). One of the vulnerable groups that has generated a concentrated body of work over the years is the investigative interviewing of children. Indeed, many aspects of our current approach to interviewing children that are now considered *conventional wisdom* were once bitterly contested, challenged and debated. Strategies to minimize error in interviews of children and other vulnerable interviewees include:

1. Making the topic of information that is requested clear.
2. Using the interviewees terminology.
3. Simplifying the language.
4. Watching carefully for signs of fatigue and poor concentration.
5. Using meaningful labels for concepts related to investigation relevant information (IRI). IRI refers to items of information obtained during the interview that may be of relevance to the ongoing investigation and can be broken down into the following categories: Person information, Action information, Location information, Item information, and Temporal information. It is argued the amount of IRI obtained in interviews is more important to consider, as opposed to the elicitation of confessions, given that the primary function of any investigative interview is to ascertain what happened, how it happened, in addition to who did what, when, and where (Fisher & Geiselman, 1992; Oxburgh & Ost, 2011; Stern, 1903/1904; Walker, 2013).

There is strong international consensus of the importance of using structured and forensically validated interview protocols for eliciting extensive, accurate accounts from such interviewees. However, protocols for investigative interviews of children tend to only focus on interviews of those who are victims and/or witnesses. There are situations where the child (or another vulnerable person) is a suspect. Unfortunately, there is a dearth of literature regarding how best to interview such vulnerable suspects. It should also be borne in mind that: (i) committing a crime does not suddenly make the child an adult and (ii) children bring the same vulnerabilities to the interview room (cognitive, social, linguistic, etc.) irrespective of whether the child is a witness, victim or suspect.

The documented experiences and studies of vulnerable interviewees illustrate how theoretical advances in the broad field of experimental psychology can provide valuable directions for applied research, highlighting many of the methodological difficulties with which applied researchers are confronted, and show how carefully controlled experimental research can be used to make meaningful contributions to the solutions of everyday problems. An example of the latter is the practice and use of those who facilitate communication in the interview room – the intermediary and interpreter.

Intermediaries and Interpreters

Realistically, we cannot expect investigators, prosecutors, lawyers, judges and jurors to be experts in communication assessments, cross-cultural linguistics and appropriate interventions with all groups of people. As such, an intermediary's role is primarily one that should assist an individual with their communication needs to provide the best evidence they can during the criminal justice process and should be utilized throughout. Indeed, in some countries (e.g. England and Wales) there is a professional and accredited Registered Intermediary training course delivered by the Witness Intermediary Scheme as part of the Ministry of Justice (see O'Mahony, 2010, for further details). Persons can be vulnerable for a number of reasons, which may impact on their receptive and expressive communication abilities. In general terms, intermediaries can be used for any young person (generally under the age of 18 years), or whose quality of evidence may be affected by mental disorder, or impairment of intelligence and social functioning, or physical disability. The intermediary must remain a reflective and independent practitioner and ensure that all interventions made are appropriate.

Unfortunately, however, the level of empirical research in this area is very limited (but see O'Mahony, Smith & Milne, 2011). Important questions that require examination and research include: (i) the specific training an intermediary should have, (ii) what the vulnerable person's thoughts and experiences are of using an intermediary, (iii) how effective the presence of an intermediary is at both the interview stage and at court and (iv) the impact of the involvement of an intermediary on judges and juror decision-making. We conclude that further research into these areas is required.

Cross-cultural communication is an emerging area of work, which may also affect communication in forensic contexts. Consequently, and in line with the preceding discussion on intermediaries, the same questions arise regarding the use of interpreters in legal and investigative contexts. Global economic migration has increased the number of interviews being conducted through language and cultural interpreters, and thus the need to understand and improve this procedure is of paramount importance. There is now a wealth of research from linguists on interpreter-mediated communication and indeed on specific issues that arise with interpretation in forensic interactions. It is nevertheless true that this research has not yet had a sufficient impact on practitioners and trainers in investigative interviews or other forensic contexts. Furthermore, there can still be relatively low-level knowledge amongst the wider research community. For example, psychological studies on the monolingual investigative interview, and recommendations arising from these studies, need revaluating in the context of the research interpreter-mediated interview. Even in traditionally monolingual countries and regions, there are increasing populations for whom the official language may be a poor second language and consequently, in such jurisdictions, the numbers of interpreted interviews will continue to rise. We would urge practitioners, in cooperation with academic researchers, to consider the opportunities available to create an evidence-base for the progress and development of worldwide intermediary and interpreter schemes in investigative and legal settings.

Future Research: A Wider Focus

The principal focus of research within investigative and legal contexts has, to date, been mostly influenced by psychologists and the principal question addressed has been about how to maximize accurate and reliable recall from interviewees. This focus is fundamentally crucial and has been driven by the investigative/legal practitioners' very real needs. Alongside this principal issue, within this volume we have addressed subquestions including how to question different kinds of respondents – cooperative, uncooperative, adult, child, vulnerable adult, etc. – and also how to avoid eliciting poor, perhaps even incorrect information, through the contamination of memory. The focus on this set of questions has been equally crucial and, as this volume attests, over the last few decades it has borne fruit. Largely, we now know (ideally) how to question vulnerable and non-vulnerable populations to elicit accurate and reliable information, but in gaining this knowledge, we come to recognize the importance of further questions. Linguistic research encourages us to consider the wider context of the interaction – the forensic communication is not just any interaction with a questioner and answerer, but rather is a specific forensic interaction. As such, it has more than one purpose and more than one audience – the investigative interview does have to elicit accurate and reliable information for overall investigation, but also, as the interview product is taken to court, it has to serve its purpose as a persuasive forensic text. Thinking about the functions of any interaction helps consideration of the wider context. Haworth (2006) has written about how interviews are taken and used as evidence in court and how an investigators' knowledge of this function can give them a power advantage over the interviewee. At a lower level, we have seen in this volume that thinking about the function of questions elicits albeit useful, but qualitatively different, classification schemes.

Moving the focus from what words an interviewer uses in asking a question to how their question functions in the interaction gives rise to a more realistic and sophisticated understanding of what is happening in that interview and how it relates to the wider contexts and purposes of the interview. Future research on the understanding of all the functions of the investigation might focus on the needs of the investigative interview, the organization where it takes place, the court, and perhaps even other areas such as the therapeutic needs of the interviewees. All this will provide a rich terrain for the further improvement of forensic interviewing practice.

CONCLUSION

The purpose of this volume was to provide the reader with an in-depth coverage of the complex area of communication in forensic contexts. Through the theoretical and methodological issues presented, we have tried to bridge the gap between the fields of psychology, linguistics and law enforcement. In this concluding chapter, we have outlined what we and some of the contributing authors believe are the upcoming areas of research. It is only with evidence-based techniques that accurate and reliable accounts can be gained from interviewees. In turn, justice can only be done when decision-makers are armed with reliable communication techniques. Researchers and practitioners should therefore together keep striving for such goals.

REFERENCES

Dando, C., & Ormerod, T. C. (2009). Effects of change temporal order technique on eyewitness memory. In N. A. Taatgen & H. van Rijn (Eds.), *Proceedings of the 31st Annual Conference of the Cognitive Science Society*. Austin, TX: Cognitive Science Society.

Dando, C. J., Wilcock, R., Behnkle, C., & Milne, R. (2011). Modifying the cognitive interview: Countenancing forensic application by enhancing practicability. *Psychology, Crime and Law, 17*, 491–511.

Dando, C. J., Wilcock, R., & Milne, R. (2009). The cognitive interview: The efficacy of a modified mental reinstatement of context procedure for frontline police investigators. *Applied Cognitive Psychology, 23*, 138–147.

Fisher, R. P., & Geiselman, R. E. (1992). *Memory-enhancing techniques for investigative interviewing: The cognitive interview*. Springfield, IL: Charles C. Thomas.

Gudjonsson, G. (2006). The psychological vulnerabilities of witnesses and the risk of false accusations and false confessions. In A. Heaton-Armstrong, E. Shepherd, G. Gudjonsson, & D. Wokchover (Eds.), *Witness testimony: Psychological, investigative and evidential perspectives*, (pp. 61–75). Oxford, UK: Oxford University Press.

Haworth, K. (2006). The dynamics of power and resistance in police interview discourse. *Discourse and Society, 17*, 739–759.

Hope, L., Gabbert, F., & Fisher, R. P. (2011). From laboratory to the street: Capturing witness memory using the Self-Administered Interview. *Legal and Criminological Psychology, 16*, 211–226.

O'Mahony, B. (2010). The emerging role of the Registered Intermediary with the vulnerable witness and offender: Facilitating communication with the police and members of the judiciary. *British Journal of Learning Disabilities, 38*, 232–237.

O'Mahony, B., Smith, K., & Milne, R. (2011). The early identification of vulnerable witnesses prior to an investigative interview. *The British Journal of Forensic Practice, 13*, 114–123.

Oxburgh, G., & Ost, J. (2011). The use and efficacy of empathy in police interviews with suspects of sexual offences. *Journal of Investigative Psychology and Offender Profiling, 8*(2), 178–188.

Pompedda, F., Zappalà, A., & Santtila, P. (2015). Simulations of child sexual abuse interviews using avatars paired with feedback improves interview quality. *Psychology, Crime and Law, 21*, 28–52.

Stern, W. (1903/1904). *Beiträge zür Psychologie der Aussage*. Leipzig, Germany: Verlag von Johann Ambrosius Barth.

Walker, A. G. (2013). *Handbook on questioning children: A linguistic perspective* (3rd ed.). Washington, DC: American Bar Association, Center on Children and the Law.

Index

Page numbers in *italics* refer to Figures and **bold** refer to Tables

*Communication in Investigative and Legal Contexts: Integrated Approaches from Forensic
Psychology, Linguistics and Law Enforcement*, First Edition. Edited by Gavin Oxburgh,
Trond Myklebust, Tim Grant and Rebecca Milne.
© 2016 John Wiley & Sons, Ltd. Published 2016 by John Wiley & Sons, Ltd.